Ralph J. Bunche

Selected Speeches and Writings

Edited with an Introduction by
Charles P. Henry

Ann Arbor
THE UNIVERSITY OF MICHIGAN PRESS

Copyright © by the University of Michigan 1995
All rights reserved
Published in the United States of America by
The University of Michigan Press
Manufactured in the United States of America
⊗ Printed on acid-free paper

1998   1997   1996   1995   4   3   2   1

*A CIP catalog record for this book is available
from the British Library.*

Library of Congress Cataloging-in-Publication Data

Bunche, Ralph J. (Ralph Johnson), 1904–1971.
    [Selections. 1995]
    Ralph J. Bunche : selected speeches and writings / edited with an
introduction by Charles P. Henry.
        p.   cm.
    Includes bibliographical references and index.
    ISBN 0-472-10589-2 (alk. paper)
    1. Afro-Americans—Politics and government. 2. Afro-Americans—
Civil rights. 3. Africa—History—20th century. 4. United
Nations—Africa. I. Henry, Charles P., 1947–   . II. Title.
E748.B885A25   1995
973'.0496073—dc20   95-38748
                                                            CIP

For my children, Adia, Wes, and Laura, with love

Contents

Acknowledgments

Several people deserve special mention for their help in putting this volume together. Earl Lewis invited me to teach at the University of Michigan during the winter of 1993 and gave me the opportunity to present a graduate course on Ralph Bunche. The general unavailability of Bunche's work convinced me of the need for a collection of his work. Robert Chrisman introduced me to the people at the University of Michigan Press, and with the help of Malcolm Litchfield and LeAnn Fields, this work was made possible.

Half of the twenty-six articles in this collection are previously unpublished. Dr. Bunche's essays have been lightly edited to improve consistency and readability. Brian Urquhart has been most generous in making available his extensive research materials on Bunche and permitting me to publish "Upheavals in the Ghettos" and "The Black Revolution." The staff of the Special Collections Department in the University Research Library at the University of California at Los Angeles has given me much assistance over the years, and the remaining eleven unpublished pieces are drawn from the 120 linear feet of documents that constitute its Ralph Bunche Collection. The remaining articles were previously published by the *Journal of Negro History, Journal of Negro Education, Negro History Bulletin, Negro Digest, American Magazine,* Columbia University Press, and Kennikat Press. A special thanks to my friend and former research assistant Lea Redmond, who typed most of the manuscript.

As usual, my wife, Loretta, and my children, to whom this book is dedicated, bore my travels and long absences with their typical grace. I am forever in their debt.

Grateful acknowledgment is made to the following authors, publishers, and journals for permission to reprint previously published materials.

The Association for the Study of Afro-American Life and History for Ralph J. Bunche, "Africa and the Current World Conflict," *Negro History Bulletin,* 4, no. 4 (October 1940), copyright © 1940; Ralph J. Bunche, "The *Irua* Ceremony among the Kikuyu of Kiambu District, Kenya," *Journal of Negro History,* 26, no. 1 (January 1941): 46–65, copyright © 1941. Reprinted with permission from the Association for the Study of Afro-American Life and History.

The Bunche estate for "What Is Race?" in *A World View of Race* (1936; reprint, Port Washington, NY: Kennikat Press, 1968); "Nothing Is Impossible for the Negro," commencement address; "What America Means to Me," *American Magazine*, (February 1950); "Race and Alienation," paper presented at the Fifth East-West Philosophers Conference, 1969. Reprinted by permission of the Bunche estate.

Columbia University for "The UN Operation in the Congo" from *The Quest for Peace*, edited by Andrew Cordier (New York: Columbia University Press, 1964). Copyright © 1964 by Columbia University. Reprinted with permission of the publisher.

Journal of Negro Education for "A Critical Analysis of the Tactics and Programs of Minority Groups, Inc.," *Journal of Negro Education* 4, no. 3 (1935): 308–20; "A Critique of New Deal Social Planning As It Affects Negroes," *Journal of Negro Education* 5, no. 1 (1936): 59–65; "The Problems of Organizations Devoted to the Improvement of the Status of the American Negro," *Journal of Negro Education* 8, no. 3 (1939): 539–50; "The Negro in the Political Life of the U.S.," *Journal of Negro Education* 10, no. 3 (1941): 567–84; "French Educational Policy in Togoland and Dahomey," *Journal of Negro Education* 3, no. 1 (1934): 69–97; "The Role of the University in the Political Organization of Negro Youth," *Journal of Negro Education* 9, no. 4 (1940): 571–79.

Every effort has been made to trace the ownership of all copyrighted material in this book and to obtain permission for its use.

Introduction

In May 1927, just as he was about to graduate at the top of his class at the University of California at Los Angeles (UCLA), Ralph Bunche wrote to W. E. B. Du Bois, the foremost black scholar-activist of his time. Reminding Du Bois that they had met in Los Angeles, he asked for the older man's help in reaching his goal of service to "my group." Indeed, Du Bois could have found no protégé more equipped to carry on a legacy of socially responsible scholarship than Ralph Bunche. In his mid-twenties Bunche was already an accomplished scholar, athlete, and youth leader. Moreover, he was headed to Du Bois's alma mater, Harvard, to study political science, which had been an early interest of Du Bois's. Within a few years, however, the views of these two men would diverge dramatically, and in time, a serious rift would divide them personally.

Bunche's political views would move from the Left to the center over the years as he filled posts of increasing responsibility. He followed his racial "firsts" as valedictorian of his high school and college graduating classes with the first doctorate achieved in political science in the United States by a black American. In addition, his dissertation was awarded a prize as the best of the year in the Government Department at Harvard. Taking a position at Howard University in Washington, D.C., he established the Political Science Department, cofounded the National Negro Congress, and became the principal black social scientist on the influential Carnegie-Myrdal study. He left Howard, at first temporarily, to serve as the only black section head in the Office of Strategic Services during World War II. Bunche then moved to the State Department as the first black desk officer in the department and then the only black in the U.S. delegation to the meetings that established the United Nations. In 1950 he became the first black to win the Nobel Peace Prize, for his mediation of the Palestinian conflict. Bunche was the first African-American to serve as president of the American Political Science Association and retired as undersecretary-general of the United Nations—the highest ranking black in that body. Bunche declined a number of other potential firsts, including a position as assistant secretary of state and an offer to teach at Harvard.

Despite this legacy of firsts, Bunche is virtually forgotten today. Partly, he was the victim of his own success. The fame he achieved in the 1950s was used by reactionary forces to blunt the demands of the developing civil rights movement of the period. In short, Bunche's individual success was used to deny group grievances, which alienated Bunche from more militant members of the group. In addition, Bunche was such an effective "insider" that many of his accomplishments at the UN went unrecognized publicly. Finally, due to the enormous responsibilities placed on him right up to his death, Bunche neither found the time to record his recollections nor to publish any of the remarkable notes and memoranda he produced in the 1930s and 1940s.

This work is dedicated to both rescuing Bunche's intellectual work and reconstructing his political image. The introduction is structured along the major themes of the book in order to provide some historical context for each selection. Bunche's keen insight and the force of his words speak for themselves.

Born Ralph Johnson Bunch on August 7, 1903,[1] in Detroit, young Ralph had a supportive extended family headed by his maternal grandmother. Fred Bunch, Ralph's father, was a barber from Zanesville, Ohio, but the family was dominated by the maternal side—Ralph's grandmother, Lucy Johnson; her daughter and Ralph's mother, Olive; Olive's brothers, Tom and Charlie; and her sister, Ethel. Looking for work, the Bunch family left Detroit about 1907, moving successively to Cleveland, Ohio; Knoxville, Tennessee; and Toledo, Ohio. Ralph's sister Grace was born in 1909 in Toledo, but Olive's illness and lack of work drove them back to Detroit. Olive spent two years in a tuberculosis sanatorium while Lucy cared for the children.

By 1915 most of the family had migrated to Albuquerque, New Mexico, where the climate was better for Olive' and Charlie's (who had also developed TB) health. Despite the change in climate, Olive died in February 1917, and a despondent Charlie (Ralph's favorite uncle and surrogate father) blew his brains out three months later. Fred Bunch lost contact with the family after this double tragedy, and Lucy Johnson (called "Nana") moved the family—Tom, Ethel, Ralph, and Grace—to Los Angeles by 1918.

While a number of articles portrayed Ralph's early life as a rags to riches tale, he and especially his Aunt Ethel resisted this characterization. Ralph contended that the family seldom went hungry and that he had had a happy childhood of baseball, picnics, and family songfests. In fact, Ralph would state that he never really encountered discrimination until he reached Los Angeles. In Detroit Italians were the "outsiders" to him and his Austro-Hungarian friends, while in Albuquerque it had been Mexicans and Indians. Bunche had playmates from all of these groups, and this early experience no doubt contributed to his broad views on race and racism.

Much has been written on the Roaring Twenties. Those works that focus on African-Americans center around the Harlem Renaissance, with its Garveyite parades and integrated Communist protests. Little is recorded of the

Black experience in the West, where young Ralph Bunche confronted racism head-on as one of the few black students at Jefferson High School in south-central Los Angeles. Bunche was not invited to join the Ephebian Society, the citywide special honors society for high scholastic achievers. His response was to drop out of school and go to work full-time in a linotype shop and laying carpet, which were his after-school jobs. Ralph's grandmother, Nana, refused to let him drop out and instilled in him a desire to compete with whites and overcome their sense of superiority. Her admonition had been to "let them, especially white folks, know that you can do anything they can do."[2]

As a standout athlete and scholar in high school, Bunche won an athletic scholarship to UCLA. It was while playing football for UCLA that Ralph sustained a leg injury that would leave him with phlebitis permanently and cause constant problems throughout his life. The injury, however, only forced the young Bunche to switch from football to basketball; his team won three Southern Conference championships. Yet it was as a scholar and student leader that Bunche excelled. Bright, personable, and good-looking, he was liked and admired by students and faculty alike. The years at UCLA were not free of racial incidents, yet Bunche seemed to take them in stride and grow stronger from the experience. A good example is his speech "That Man May Dwell in Peace." Ralph had been denied admission into the official debating society on campus, leading him and his friends to set up their own interracial discussions as the Southern Branch Debating Society.[3] This early speech emphasizing the themes of international organization and the international mind, or will, reflect the influence of courses in international relations and philosophy on the young scholar. These influences would lead him away from the study of law and toward political science.

A year later Bunche took aim at a "For Colored Only" swimming pool in Los Angeles. His uncompromising views on discrimination, his racial pride, and his outstanding achievements at UCLA made Ralph a popular symbol of racial progress in Black Los Angeles. His reputation, further enhanced by winning class honors (valedictorian at commencement) and a scholarship to Harvard, led the Iroquois Friday Morning Civic and Social Club of Los Angeles (a black women's group) to raise over a thousand dollars to support his trip and study in the East.

When Bunche arrived at Harvard in the fall of 1927 he became the latest of a remarkable collection of black students then assembled in Cambridge. William Hastie, later the first black federal judge; Robert Weaver, later the first black to serve in the cabinet; and John P. Davis, later cofounder of the National Negro Congress (NNC), all became good friends. Weaver remarks that it was Bunche's optimism, combined with his capacity to produce stupendous amounts of work over long, sustained periods of application, that led to his spectacular career. Bunche's friends also tended toward socialist politics, which had an influence on his own views. Two papers the young political scientist produced at Harvard in 1928, "Negro Political Philosophy" and "Negro Political Laboratories" (his first published work), signal this radicalization. Labeling Negro political thought as generally "conservative," he calls for the overthrow of blind loyalty to the Republican Party in national politics and the establishment of a more pragmatic local politics open to socialist and even "Bolshevist" ideas.

Full radicalization would come with his move to Washington, D.C., to teach and organize the political science department at Howard University. Howard, in the late 1920s and 1930s, was home to an outstanding collection of black intellectuals, including Abram Harris, Sterling Brown, E. Franklin Frazier, Charles Thompson, Kelly Miller, Alain Locke, Charles Wesley, Ernest Just, and Percy Julian. Locke, Harris, and a young political scientist, Emmett Dorsey, had the most influence on the new "Harvard man." Harris, Dorsey, and later Frazier represented a new breed of black intellectual that regarded the old race-centered views of such scholars as Du Bois, Kelly Miller, and Carter Woodson as "ethnic chauvinism." This younger generation focused on race only to the extent that it was used as a tool to divide the working class. Bunche moved from overthrowing the Republican Party in his 1928 work to overthrowing the capitalist system in his 1929 paper on "Marxism and the 'Negro Question.'"

Howard president, Mordecai Johnson, who quickly moved to make Bunche his faculty assistant, was unusually tolerant of faculty diversity but less so of student protest. Bunche, however, remained supportive of student action on behalf of civil rights throughout his time on campus. One young student activist, Kenneth Clark, credits Bunche with saving him from expulsion.[4] Another student of Bunche's, Ruth Harris, from Montgomery, Alabama, married Ralph on June 23, 1930.

Even before their marriage the young couple was separated for extended periods when Ralph returned to Harvard to complete predoctoral courses. Doctoral work also caused him to miss his second and third anniversaries. This pattern of frequent extended absences from home would become a lifelong occurrence and was the source of considerable friction between Ruth and Ralph. Nonetheless, their first child, Joan, was born in June 1932, to be followed by Jane in May 1933.

A sign of Bunche's early prominence is his invitation to join 32 other black intellectuals at Amenia, the Hudson River estate of NAACP president Joel Spingarn in August of 1933. W. E. B. Du Bois had called the meeting to review and possibly revise the organization's traditional legal and political approach in light of the economic reality of the Great Depression. Harris, Frazier, and Bunche led the attack on the older "race men" such as Du Bois and

James Weldon Johnson, charging them with a racial provincialism that favored the black business elite and ignored the economic needs of the masses. The young radicals advocated black and white labor solidarity to force through the necessary reform legislation. Although they were appointed to a special investigative committee to follow up the Amenia conference with specific recommendations for the NAACP, their report was debated but ultimately rejected.

Undoubtedly, the failure of the NAACP to act on the recommendations of the Bunche group, along with the failure of the New Deal to address black concerns, led Bunche and his fellow Harvard graduate John P. Davis to organize a conference focusing on Roosevelt's policies and the Negro. The 1935 conference, with over 500 participants from all walks of Black life, became a vehicle for launching a new broad-based coalition called the National Negro Congress. The initial organizing meeting was held at Bunche's home and included the well-known black Communist leader James Ford—a fact that would come to haunt Bunche during the McCarthy era.

While Bunche and Davis agreed on asking labor leader A. Philip Randolph to lead the congress, Bunche lost in an effort to narrow the range of groups represented to a more labor-oriented focus. Consequently, Bunche was only minimally involved in the first congress meeting in 1936 and was out of the country in 1937 and 1938. By the time he returned to the 1940 meeting, over the objection of Davis, the organization had been taken over by the Communist Party USA (CPUSA).

While the NNC years represent the highpoint of Bunche's career as an activist, they also mark the period of his greatest scholarly output. Beginning with the completion of his prize-winning dissertation "French Administration in Togoland and Dahomey" in 1934 and ending with his 3,000-page contribution to the Carnegie-Myrdal study in 1940, the busy Howard scholar produced a remarkable stream of work. And, in the middle of it all, he accepted a two-year Social Science Research Council Fellowship to pursue postdoctoral studies in anthropology and colonial policy at the London School of Economics and at the University of Cape Town in South Africa and to conduct field research in South, East, and West Africa.

Bunche's attacks on the tactics and ideology of Negro organizations and his critique of the New Deal mix empirical data with political theory to produce convincing arguments for radical changes. Of particular note is his rejection of the legal strategy of the NAACP and of the "moral dilemma" approach to race relations. Bunche was accused of being an "armchair radical" by Roy Wilkens of the NAACP, yet, within five years, the rise of fascism and the influence of Gunnar Myrdal would cause him to moderate his views.

The Carnegie-Myrdal study, which would change the study of race relations for decades to come, employed a number of Bunche's friends and colleagues, including Sterling Brown, Franklin Frazier, Doxey Wilkerson, Alain

Locke, and Kenneth Clark. It was with Bunche, however, that Myrdal established a close personal and professional relationship cemented by a memorable extended field trip together in the South. An outspoken white man traveling with a less-than-servile black man led to many interesting adventures—some dangerous. Bunche saw that the New Deal had some positive impact on the lives of blacks, while Myrdal was struck by the allegiance of Southern whites to the American creed, despite their openly racist practices. *An American Dilemma* reflects Myrdal's belief that significant reform could be made within the existing system by moral appeals to the consciences of middle- and upper-class whites, rather than the calls for structural change through black and white labor solidarity that Bunche favored. Both the Swede and the American shared the view that African-American culture was derivative from white American culture and had no links with the African past. This negative cultural perspective, combined with their social engineering approach to race relations, led them to underestimate the capacity of blacks to shape their own destinies. The wealth of data Myrdal, Bunche, and their associates collected remains the most detailed and comprehensive examination of Southern politics in existence. Utilizing this data, Bunche wrote a prophetic report for the Republican National Committee, calling for racial quotas in federal labor contracts and national health care.[5]

Myrdal was fanatical about meeting deadlines and Bunche often complained that the time given to complete tasks was woefully unrealistic. Although Myrdal and others encouraged him to publish all or parts of his memoranda in book form, Bunche felt that they were hurried and incomplete. His shift to government service in 1941 prevented him from following up on the publication of his work with Myrdal, just as his joining the Carnegie-Myrdal study in 1939 prevented him from publishing the results of his fieldwork in Africa.[6]

Even with all of his other responsibilities at Howard, Bunche was able to work on American and African politics simultaneously. The year after the Howard conference that helped launch the NNC, he convened a Howard conference on "The Crisis of Modern Imperialism in Africa and the Far East." Urged by Alain Locke, Bunche produced a monograph entitled *A World View of Race* in 1936. Although Bunche would later claim that the work was an embarrassment, it accurately reflects his class-oriented views at that time. Based on his dissertation, the tone is much more polemical, as Bunche compares the manipulation of race in the domination of blacks in the United States to capitalist exploitation of Africa through such concepts as the "white man's burden" and "mission civilisatrice." Robert Edgar has suggested that Bunche chose not to publish his dissertation because it did not adequately voice African concerns about colonialism, especially its impact on culture. This factor, along with Bunche's desire to escape the burdensome teaching and administrative duties at Howard, led him to pursue postdoctoral study and research in Africa. Edgar points out that not only was Bunche the only African-American funded by a private foundation to go to Africa for research until the 1950s, but he was also surprised to be given two year's funding.[7]

Although Bunche would study with the three leading cultural anthropologists of the day—Melville Herskovits at Northwestern University, Bronislaw Malinowski at the London School of Economics, and Isaac Schapera at the University of Cape Town—and take extensive field notes and film footage over a two-year period, he found little time to publish his work. His brilliant essay "The Irua Ceremony among the Kikuyu of Kiambu District, Kenya" is a model of interdisciplinary research combining anthropological fieldwork with political and economic analysis and leaves one wishing he had had more time to complete his planned book on South Africa. Bunche's fascinating experiences as one of the few African-Americans to visit Africa at the time were matched by the contacts he made while staying in London. Among his new friends were Jomo Kenyatta and Peter Koinange from Kenya; Addo Kessie, Afurata, and deGraaf Johnson from the Gold Coast; Myanza and Akiki Nyabongo from Uganda; George Padmore and Eric Williams, whom Bunche had taught at Howard; Essie and Paul Robeson, Max Yergan, Arthur Davis, Ras Makonnen, C. L. R. James and I. T. A. Wallace.[8] Although Bunche mixed easily with many of these prominent Pan Africanists, he remained convinced that it was another form of racial chauvinism that romanticized the precolonial past and ignored the basic issue that was changing the imperialist nations themselves. When Bunche found himself frequently giving impromptu talks in South Africa, however, he often sounded like a Pan Africanist. By 1940 the Howard radical was viewing British and French imperialism as a more benevolent, more hopeful system of rule than the emerging German and Italian fascism.

Two months before Pearl Harbor, Conyers Read phoned Bunche to offer him the position of senior social science analyst in the Library of Congress. Greatly in need of an African expert, the institution that would later become the Office of Strategic Services (OSS) and still later the Central Intelligence Agency (CIA) asked Harvard for recommendations. Several faculty put forth Bunche's name as "the best graduate student of his race at Harvard" and the only one "able to compete for fellowships on equal terms with the better white students."[9] Bunche left college teaching, fully intending to return once his wartime government service was complete.

Responsible for work on the British Empire in Africa, the Howard professor found few resources on Africa other than encyclopedias in the Library of Congress collection. One of his first tasks was to write a manual for every GI sent to North Africa or West Africa. Bunche sought out firsthand sources of information and expressed a particular concern for the place of African-Americans in the U.S. military. Most important, perhaps, as the only black professional dealing with colonial affairs in the United States government, Bunche became an important contact for African and Caribbean leaders.

So outstanding was Bunche's work that he was one of the few OSS staff invited to participate in the Institute of Pacific Relations Conference at Mont Tremblant, Quebec, in December 1942. This conference, which Bunche believed was the best he ever attended, laid the basis for chapters 11, 12, and 13 of the United Nations Charter.[10] Meeting with colonial officials and experts concerned about postwar planning gave Bunche his first taste of international politics and also provided a showcase for his talents. His major goal was to see that the provisions of the 1941 Atlantic Charter applied to the peoples in colonial territories as well as the victims in Europe.

As the tide of the war turned toward the Allies, Bunche became convinced that there was little expertise or interest in colonial matters in the United States and that, once the Axis threat was removed, European colonialism would reassert itself. His desire to play a role in shaping colonial policy in the postwar era led him to accept a reassignment to the Department of State to work under Leo Pasvolsky on planning for the United Nations. Despite great resistance from OSS, which was reluctant to let him go, Bunche transferred at the beginning of 1944.

As an expert on colonial policy, Bunche served as an advisor at the Dumbarton Oaks and San Francisco conferences on the United Nations. At these conferences and at the subsequent Preparatory Commission and first General Assembly meeting in London in 1946, Bunche lobbied for a progressive American position that would ensure colonial peoples the right of self-determination. The key was getting all dependent territories included in a trusteeship system with international accountability. Through his expertise and work with other delegations, Bunche was instrumental in shaping the chapters of the UN Charter dealing with colonial administration. Recognizing his talent, the UN secretariat requested Bunche's service for six weeks to set up the agenda for the Trusteeship Council. Bunche agreed to go to New York; he never returned.

The move to New York was a watershed event for the Bunche family. It marked a move away from the strict segregation that limited the movements of family members in the nation's capital. In fact, when President Harry Truman dispatched Dean Rusk to New York in 1948 to talk Bunche into accepting the post of assistant secretary of state, Bunche cited his personal experience with discrimination including segregated pet cemeteries, among other indignities, in refusing to return to Washington. Undoubtedly, Bunche would have soon outgrown this mid-level post and been frustrated in efforts to move beyond it due to his race.

Ironically, it was not his race but, rather, his nationality that would limit Bunche to a number two role at the UN. However, race was also a factor in many situations in New York. United Nations housing was segregated, as was as the private Quaker girl's school he wanted to enroll his daughters in. In addition, the fast-paced life of a UN official meant the Bunche family spent even less time together. Ralph Jr. had been born in 1943, and Ruth was now faced with raising three children virtually alone.

In December 1946 Bunche became permanent director of the Trusteeship Division. Once the exciting work of decolonization was under way, the professor intended to return to Howard or accept one of the attractive offers being made by other universities. Fate, however, or what Bunche called "Bunche luck," would intervene to place him on a world stage.

In 1947, the British government had decided to dump the question of Palestine on the United Nations, and Bunche was assigned to the United Nations Special Committee on Palestine as special assistant to Dr. Victor Hoo, the secretary-general's representative. In an early display of the objectivity that would eventually win him plaudits, Bunche drafted both the majority and minority reports on Palestine partition.

When the Security Council named Count Folke Bernadotte of Sweden as mediator of the Arab-Israeli War in 1948, Bunche was chosen by Secretary-General Trygve Lie as his chief representative in the negotiations. Then Bunche luck struck. Through a series of mix-ups Bunche was late to a meeting with Bernadotte in Jerusalem. Bernadotte left without him, taking Colonel Andre Serot, head of the UN military observers, in his place on a trip to Government House. On the return trip both were assassinated by Israeli terrorists.

Immediately, Bunche was named as acting mediator. With no precedent to guide him, Bunche chaired a series of intense meetings between Egypt and Israel on the Isle of Rhodes that, over a period of 81 days, led to four armistice agreements that ended the fighting in 1949. His life would never be the same.

It is difficult to imagine what Bunche's diplomatic success meant in terms of race relations in the United States. Certainly, Jackie Robinson and Joe Louis were famous as black athletes, just as a number of black entertainers were known to most Americans. After all, the wildly popular "Amos and Andy" radio program would make the change to television in a few years. "Militant" black leaders such as Paul Robeson and W. E. B. Du Bois were far outside the mainstream, and the major NAACP court victory in Brown was still five years away. Young African leaders were fighting in national struggles for liberation that was years away. No African-American, save perhaps George Washington Carver,[11] was acclaimed for accomplishments outside the fields of race relations, sports, and entertainment.

The NAACP started it off by awarding Bunche the Spingarn Medal at the Hollywood Bowl in his adopted hometown of Los Angeles. Apparently, earlier criticisms were forgotten, as Bunche was named a lifetime director of the NAACP. Next Harvard University awarded their Alumnus an Honorary Doctor of Laws—to be followed by 68 additional honorary degrees over the years. Then, the coup de grace, Bunche beat out Harry Truman and Winston Churchill for the 1950 Nobel Peace Prize. He was now the most honored black person in the world.

The Nobel award provided a much needed boost for the UN as well, and Bunche would use his newfound status as a bully pulpit for the organization. His 1950 speech "Man, Democracy, and Peace" is a longer version of his Nobel lecture, in which he links the themes of equality of man, democracy, and peace. Of particular note is Bunche's conception of human rights, which gives equal weight to political and economic rights and calls for the positive uses of state authority—a position historically counter to the U.S. emphasis on negative rights and political rights alone. In the literally hundreds of speeches Bunche would give in the following years, these themes would almost always emerge in one form or another. His 1951 speech on Israeli-Arab relations to the National War College is one of his most detailed accounts of the negotiations that made him a household word.

Palestine was the beginning, not the end, of Bunche's diplomatic career.[12] For the next two decades Bunche would be the key United Nations figure in such crises as Cyprus, Sinai, Yemen, the Congo, and Bahrain. He was considered indispensable by the first three secretaries-general—Trygve Lie, Dag Hammarskjöld, and U Thant. Hammarskjöld appointed Bunche undersecretary-general (without portfolio) in 1954. During the mid-1950s Bunche was the chief UN figure involved in the peaceful uses of atomic energy. He helped organize and then direct the UN peacekeeping operations in the Middle East after the 1956 Suez Crisis and in 1957 became undersecretary-general for Special Political Affairs with prime responsibility for peacekeeping. In his most dangerous and controversial mission Bunche directed the initial UN operations in the Congo in 1960. It was ironic that this lifelong opponent of colonialism would almost be killed by Congolese troops, who mistook him for a Belgian, while the Soviets accused him of favoring American neocolonialism. Bunche explains the situation in "The UN Operation in the Congo."

Ralph Bunche and race existed in a kind of dialectical relationship. He used the presumed inferiority of blacks as a spur to his own achievement, and his work centered on the effects of racism in the United States and colonialism abroad. At the same time, Bunche refused to accept the validity of race as a rational or scientific concept and therefore doubted its permanence. His 1936 work, *A World View of Race,* clearly points out the inherent limitations Bunche finds in racial thinking. As a modern social scientist familiar with the latest anthropological and sociological research, he emphasized the role of environment and culture in creating "racial traits." As a radical, he emphasized the role class plays in explaining the economic status of blacks.

Two forces drove Bunche's views toward the political center. The primary force was the rise of European fascism. Bunche feared not only a Nazi victory but also the rise of fascistic forces in the United States. Consequently, he spoke early and often about the necessity of supporting an imperfect American democracy against totalitarianism. This included, said Bunche, an active and committed university faculty and administration giving students a preference for democracy, as outlined in his essay "The Role of the University in the Political Orientation of Negro Youth."

A second moderating influence was the New Deal. Working with Myrdal in the South had given Bunche a new appreciation for the impact of Roosevelt's administration. Moreover, Myrdal's emphasis on the "moral dilemma" of individuals, combined with the excesses of Stalin, eventually moved Bunche to focus more on the psychological aspects of racism. By the time he became an international figure, Bunche was optimistic that education along with constant agitation would resolve the race question.

Bunche's move toward the center of American politics during the 1940s coincided with a new optimism in race relations following World War II. The Democratic Party included human rights in its 1948 platform for the first time, and President Truman integrated the armed services. Professional sports were opening up to African-Americans, who were becoming a largely urban and increasingly Northern population. With the federal government firmly on their side for the first time, blacks had access to better-paying industrial jobs, better education, including GI Bill support for higher education, and voting power. They were quickly leaving behind the "peasant mentality" that the Howard scholars had written about in the 1930s.

In his 1951 NAACP Convention address and his 1952 Gandhian Seminar speech, Bunche called for full integration not only of the North and South in the United States but also of the "Eastern" and "Western" minds. He wanted a greatly accelerated campaign for full equality that would rely primarily on spiritual and moral power. It is easy to see why Bunche could embrace the nonviolent, direct action campaigns of Atlanta native Martin Luther King Jr., just as King had embraced Bunche as a role model.[13] Still, his postwar homage to Gandhi represents a shift from Bunche's earlier criticism of Gandhian methods as inappropriate for the United States.

Certainly, Bunche's own success must have contributed to his optimism about race relations. In 1953 he became the first African-American to head the leading professional organization in his field, the American Political Science Association (APSA), in its fifty-year existence. But, beyond professional accomplishments, Bunche became an icon of racial progress. John D. Rockefeller dined at his home. Movie stars sent him fan letters. Schools were named after him. He was the houseguest of admirals and celebrities when he traveled. Both political parties asked him to run for office. Job offers poured in from Harvard, Chicago, the University of California at Berkeley, and other prestigious universities. The Brooklyn Dodgers sent season tickets, and Broadway shows vied to have him attend their openings. When the Westside Tennis Club refused to admit his son as a member, there was a national outcry that forced the club to change its mind. Throughout the 1950s, honors, invitations, requests for jobs, and fan mail (as well as hate mail) continued to pour into his office. Bunche always maintained his modesty and constantly reminded his black audiences that he was not free as long as they were not free, yet in many ways he had risen above race.

While continually refusing to accept the label "Negro leader," Bunche consciously sought to use his fame to promote those values and attitudes he thought essential to racial progress. In "Nothing Is Impossible for the Negro" and "What America Means to Me" as well as in a national television dramatization of his early life and in countless other articles and speeches, Bunche sought to redefine the term *American*. Throughout U.S. history the term *American* had been reserved for whites—usually males. From the legal system to popular culture, from Jefferson and Tocqueville to Faulkner and Twain, blacks were designated as the "other." In fact, several observers had commented that the first thing immigrants learned that made them American was the term *nigger*. By embracing the American creed as a natural part of his upbringing, socialization, and success, Bunche sought to destroy the notion of black "otherness."

It was no accident that the properly dressed and well-spoken young leaders of the civil rights movement often looked and sounded like Ralph Bunche. But Bunche could not control the uses of his success by others. During the McCarthy era,[14] as the United States battled the Soviet Union and China for influence in the "third world," the prominence of Ralph Bunche would become a major weapon in defense of the "American way of life." How could the United States be such a bad place for minorities if it could produce a Ralph Bunche? Consequently, by the mid-1960s Stokeley Carmichael would announce "You can't have Bunche for lunch!"[15]

Nothing could have prepared Bunche for the criticism he received from the black community. All of a sudden his attempt to embrace and even personify "Americanism" made him an "Uncle Tom" and a "sellout" to his people. Malcolm X and Adam Clayton Powell launched full-scale attacks and even Martin Luther King Jr., suggested that Bunche's success had been used to retard black progress. At first Bunche lashed out, challenging black hate groups and calling members of the Nation of Islam escapists. His old Garveyite critiques were polished up and applied to the Black Power advocates. The relationship probably reached a low when Bunche issued a public statement apologizing for the lawlessness and violence in Watts in August 1965.

But, unlike many of his contemporaries in the NAACP and Urban League, Bunche changed. In 1967 and 1968, with his health failing, Bunche wrote two remarkable pieces analyzing the violence in the ghettos and the response to it. While refusing to endorse the violence, Bunche shared both the bitterness that caused it and the grievances of inner-city residents. He rejected the official response that "outsiders" are the cause. Although he believed that most Black Power advocates deliver more rhetoric than substance, he endorsed the new black pride in their identity, labeling it "Blackism." Reverting to "lyrical history," he even went so far as to identify the new Black Power movement with the National Negro Congress of the 1930s.

The acceptance of Blackism by Bunche was accompanied by a decline in his optimism about race relations. This was reflected both at the personal level, as in a *Psychology Today* interview in 1969 in which he indicated that he had been the token at too many parties and stated, "I'm not worth a damn as an example,"[16] and at the international level, when he linked the war in Vietnam to race in his speech before the Fifth East-West Philosophers' Conference in 1969.

As his life drew to a close in 1971, Bunche realized that he had been a role model few could follow. Although he attributed his success to his grandmother, it was his own extraordinary talent and hard work that led him to heights no African-American had seen. His efforts to more broadly define *Americanism* would lead to his rejection by a younger generation of blacks whose members could have benefited greatly from his internationalism and critical insight. In the post–Black Power era there is no better guide to the kind of world most people want than the work of Ralph Johnson Bunche.

Part 1
The Early Years

CHAPTER 1

That Man May Dwell in Peace
1926

*This 1926 speech, delivered while Bunche was a student at UCLA, is notable
for three features—the setting, the international theme, and the emphasis on
spirituality. The setting is the Southern Branch Debating Society, an interracial
group that Bunche and some friends set up after the official debating society
did not accept him. This action is typical of Bunche's refusal to allow racism to
hinder his development. The speech opens with Bunche's favorite quotation,
from Isaiah, which stresses the theme of peace. The young Bunche warns,
however, of another major war unless nations overcome the sentiments of
nationality and race pride to develop an effective international organization.
Finally, Bunche argues that to be effective an international organization must
be constructed in a new spirit of international citizenry demanding peace and
willing to sacrifice for its realization. This human dimension of spirituality is
stressed again later in Bunche's valedictory address at UCLA. Bunche believes, with modern psychology, that human nature is infinitely modifiable and
can be shaped by social education. The three features of this speech remain
constant in Bunche's thinking throughout his life, with the brief exception of the
1930s, during which he thought class factors played a more important role in
individual success than psychology.*

> They shall beat their swords into ploughshares; and their spears into pruning
> hooks; nation shall not lift up sword against nation—neither shall they learn war
> anymore.
>
> —Isaiah 2:4

Would that the nations of the world today might witness the fulfillment of this
prophecy of Isaiah! What vast, undreamed of achievement might await man
would he but devote his entire interest to promoting the common weal of a
universal human brotherhood! (May the prayer he offered that weapons be cast
aside, and emerge coordinated, to the end that a greater, nobler civilization be
evolved, never more to be disrupted by the roar of cannon.)

But twelve years since, the ominous rumble of drums summoned forth the
pick of the world's manhood to be offered in unholy sacrifice to a bestial war-

god. During four interminable years the revolting carnage progressed, while a suffering world looked on in silent, helpless terror.

And why this slaughter?

—"To make the world safe for democracy?"—Can it be said you say that the world of 1926 is actually "safe for democracy"?

—"To effect disarmament?"—At this very moment every nation of the world is working feverishly to perfect the most *fiendish* devices for human destruction!

—"To protect the rights of minorities?"—Consider the Tyrol, Poland, Romania!

—"To end imperialism, provincialism, aggression?"—In the daily papers we may read of military depredations upon Syria, Morocco, China!

No! That ruthless butchery of 23 million innocent humans offers but a single, an ominous *warning,* emblazoned in the crimson blood of its myriad victims . . . [unreadable]. World leagues? World courts? By world conferences, pacts, treaties?

The proposal which I would present as an antidote for world "war-poisoning" is centered about *two basic principles,* essential, I believe, to any rational peace plan. These are *International Organization,* involving *every* nation of the world; and the *full development* of the *"International Mind, or Will."*

It is manifest that no longer can the nations of the world be permitted the exercise of unabridged liberty—each framing its own laws of conduct or none at all; anymore than we as individual members of a social and political group are exempt from the dictates of law. Just imagine, if you can, that each and every one of us were to recognize no restraining law except that of his own volition! (What a frightful debacle our existing society would soon become!) Yet that is just what nations of the world have been doing for centuries past, and with horrifying consequences.

Undeniably, the people of the world are today inextricably bound together by bonds of common interest which make imperative an effective, active international organization. Indeed, the League of Nations and its World Court are quite indispensable as initial steps in the inevitable banding together of all national entities into an international body-politic, whose interests shall hold precedence over and above those of the individual national groups. Certainly, the League of Nations and the World Court, though faulty in many respects, are inspiring harbingers of future world harmony—of the peace to come.

As such, they merit universal endorsement—and the United States, as a nation which, in the scant 150 years of its national existence, has fought five wars with foreign powers and the bloodiest civil strife in history, should lead rather than retard such approbation.

But in the development of this Parliament of Man, what is to become of the great virtue of patriotism—of the sentiment of nationality? Is love of country incompatible with the welfare of mankind? Must we altogether condemn nationalism and race pride? No, I think not. Patriotism is noble; patriotism is great, but, as Nurse Cavell protested in the throes of death, "*Patriotism is not enough!*"

But why may not this nationalistic sentiment be harnessed in the interests of world peace? Allow me to draw a simple analogy. Right here on our own threshold we have developed a form of government organization which may well be adaptable to the needs of international difficulties.

Our original Thirteen Colonies were rent by social and economic rivalries, dislikes, distrusts, and sectional jealousies, comparable in many respects to those prevalent among the nations of the world today. Nevertheless, common bonds of human interest drew them into a single political union in which their differences were dissolved and from which there emerged our present great commonwealth.

May there not be a similiar evolution from the League of Nations (or an international organization under any other title, if that may prove more palatable to some)—may there not be evolved a *universal political society,* in which each nation would retain its individuality, its nationality, if you please; extensive freedom of action and autonomy within its own domain; yet maintaining, withal, an abiding consciousness of membership in the more significant international society? Essentially, the welfare of the world body must take precedence over nationalistic interests in periods of crisis.

But international organization of itself *is not enough!* The bare framework of a world league and court constitutes no guarantee of perpetual or even immediate peace! The soul of international organization must be determined in the *spirit* evinced by the peoples of the world—all peoples and nations must *think* of themselves as component parts of a great whole.

World Courts, world leagues, world pacts of *all sorts,* are *futile* unless *solidly* backed by an international citizenry resolutely *demanding* peace and willing to *sacrifice* for its realization.

We may speak of treaties without end—of pacts and agreements of every kind. But the texts of pacts and treaties and agreements have no *inherent* remedial powers. Treaties are, when signed, only what the nations and the signatory governments make of them. They may for the moment close the gates of conflict, but at any time the devastating war-flood may again be unloosed!

The world must, then, look to the cultivation of a universal *desire* for peace—a universal *cooperation* among *all peoples* that a *lasting peace* may be attained.

It will be immediately urged that such a foundation cannot be laid without a rather comprehensive *change* in human nature.

I believe that, before a permanent peace can *ever* be achieved by this strife-ridden world, such a "change" is *absolutely* essential. The league and the court are assuredly commendable steps in the proper direction, but the physical framework without the *soul*—without *universal goodwill*—is impotent.

We must *cultivate a spirit of World brotherhood!* But many will insist that such a process is quite outside the realm of practicability and at best but idealistic.

However, psychology informs us that human nature is plastic indefinitely, yes, infinitely modifiable. Sociology further reveals that man is by nature a *social product.* Individually, we are but human vessels into which society pours the ingredients which make of us character-possessing, rational individuals.

Why, then, is it not possible to accomplish with human beings what the late Luther Burbank has done with horticultural specimens? Why can we not, by means of *social education* centering about a new concept of the human self as a member of a *world society,* turn thorny, unproductive, shirking, exploiting, cross-grained human natures into cooperating members of a *great united human brotherhood?*

I do not maintain that anything magical is to occur—but gradually, by means of *social education,* we must strive to *supplant* mutual fears and hatreds among the world's citizenry with mutual *coordination of wills* toward world peace.

Hatreds are superficial—based upon fear, ignorance, blind prejudice, or a desire to dominate for selfish ends. They are simply mental attacks upon others, perchance calling for a physical attack or war in self-defense and retaliation.

If people can, by *educational processes,* mutually arrive at greater understanding and sympathy, these hatreds will in large measure be dissipated. For *understanding* eschews dislikes, vitiates fear, and gives rise to faith and trust, in which lies the spirit of cooperation.

Being then but *mental* faults, why cannot hatreds, distrusts, fears, be wholly eradicated by concentrated effort on the part of the *educational agencies* of the world? Why cannot the full remedial powers of the school, the press, the cinema, the platform, and the pulpit be brought to focus upon this human ailment?

Let us here in America assume the lead and begin to sow propaganda for *world peace just as intensely* as we *sowed vicious, destructive, hatred-instilling propaganda* during the World War. Let us call a halt to all *ethnocentric chauvinism*—to that type of *dangerous "nationalism"* which teaches school children that, right or wrong, their nation is always *right!* Let us begin *immediately* the development of a *universal, rational-minded citizenry,* converted to world peace, conscious of membership in a world fraternity of nations and peoples, and willing to make both individual and national sacrifices to the end that *world-tranquility may be eternally preserved!*

CHAPTER 2

Across the Generation Gap
1926–27

It was not until his family moved to Los Angeles that Bunche fully experienced racism directed toward blacks. In demonstrating his activism against swimming pool segregation, he also manifests an intense racial pride. While calling on Negroes to break the binds that blindly tie them to the Republican Party, Bunche argues that the "New Negro" has to move beyond Republican and Democrat to judge candidates on what they are likely to do to benefit the "Race." This talk of racial pride is paradoxically used in a speech that includes a story about an "old Southern darkey." The speech concludes with an appeal for more education as the "panacea" for the Negroes' ills.

It is with a feeling of mingled pride and trepidation that I have brought myself to accept this quite flattering invitation to speak here this evening, which has been accorded me by your honorable president, Mr. Duncan.

Pride, in that one young in years and experience should be felt worthy of addressing this audience.

And *trepidation,* in the knowledge that the audience before me is a highly intellectual and critical one—seasoned with the experience which comes only with years.

But I took courage, and acceded—and so here I am.

Really, I've been in quite a predicament to know about just what to speak upon.

I might have chosen one of the many vital problems confronting the race and, with my meager knowledge, attempt to analyze and solve it.

But I must know that there are many here who could do such more thoroughly and authoritatively than I.

I might have loaded myself down with statistics or facts, or pro and con arguments, and come here to try to convince you of the truth or falsity of some profound proposition.

But I was pretty clever, and I anticipated that there would be a *woman* or two in the audience, and so I knew it would be utterly futile to try to convince them of anything.

(Never try to convince a woman
—merely try to *persuade her.*)

That's one truth I've learned even at my tender age.

And so I have chosen a topic more to my liking and, I hope, one which may prove more to yours.

I have decided merely to attempt to portray briefly for you the thoughts of one of the "younger fry" upon some of our modern problems—to illustrate, perhaps, that the younger Negro is really alive to his and his Race's needs—and that he is, perhaps, doing a bit of *constructive, progressive thinking.*

It occurs to me that the older and the younger generations of our race are quite estranged.—They live, so to speak, in worlds apart.—They lead different lives, think differently upon differing issues, and are far too often arraigned against one another. But the good of our kind demands *universal unity.*

I sincerely hope that the *general* opinion of the younger Negro as held by the older folk isn't that generally expressed in the customary barbershop ballyhooing.

I rarely ever step into my barbershop but what I hear some "old-timer" ranting and raving about the evils of the modern-day society.

He invariably disparages the young Negro.—Calls him wild—criminal—evil—everything but good. And without fail he ends up by the sinister prophecy that the young Negro of today is dancing and "motoring" his way straight to hell. You all know the type—and the future of the race is indeed a dark and ominous one, if we are to accept his rantings as gospel. But I'm not so inclined.

And so it is, perhaps, a good thing that we may be permitted to exchange ideas—true, the exchange may be an unequal one—for your ideas are the children of a far more fertile experience than ours—but there really is, you know, much that is truthful in that well-known saying *"Out of the mouths of babes."*

In taking up some of our more immediate problems, it is no doubt appropriate to dwell briefly upon one which is most timely at present—namely, *politics.*

Politics have played quite an important role in the history of our people.—It was politics intermingled with economic motives which led to our enslavement.—And it was certainly politics plus the same economic motives, and a certain degree of philanthropic decent-mindedness in the North, which led to our liberation.

I don't wish to detract from the glory of that most glorious of men—Abe Lincoln—no man ever stood for the right more staunchly than he. But had it not been for this great game of *politics* and its attendant virtues or vices, however we may regard them, Abe Lincoln could never have convinced the North and held them to his course.

Due to the very nature of the circumstances surrounding its emancipation, the Negro Race became almost solidly Republican in its party affiliation. And this position it has, and largely continues to maintain, to the present day. Whenever a block of Negro votes is to be found, there is a block of Republican votes. And this irrespective of the merits or demerits of the party candidate.

If he is a Republican—he is *good*—if he is anything else, he is unworthy of consideration.

Such an attitude has had its advantages in the past—likewise its disadvantages. But I believe such a policy has fulfilled its mission and is no longer called for today.

I think that I can truthfully sound a warning to you that the New Negro isn't thinking in terms of *Republican* or *Democrat* any longer—he is thinking in terms of *men* and *merits!*

The young Negro will no longer support a candidate merely because he signs his name—*John So and So—Republican.* We don't intend to follow in the rut of single-track Republicanism or anything elsism. We are interested not so much in knowing the candidate's party affiliation as in knowing what he *has* done—and what he is *likely to do*—and more important—what are the probabilities of his benefiting the Race?

The young Negro voter is becoming emancipated from the chains of traditional blind party allegiance just as surely as our forebears were freed of the more obvious but no more restricting bonds of physical servitude.

The young voting Negro today might well be likened to the Texas colored man who had been in a virtual state of slavery to his Southern white "boss." But by dint of careful saving he was able to take a short trip to Los Angeles and partake of the freedom and grandeur of the Southland and, more particularly, the pure, liberty-inspiring atmosphere of our own Central Avenue.

Needless to relate, the Texas colored man returned home truant and rebellious. He didn't try to regain his old job—oh no.—But his Southern master finally came to him and said:

—"Sam, you'd better come back on the job.—We've just killed the batch of hogs, and I've got some mighty fine hog-jowls for you."

But Sam just shook his kinky head wisely and, with a superior air, told the white man:

—"Uh uh boss—You ain't talkin' to me—no suh—I've been to Los Angeles, and I don' want yo' old hog-jowls, cuz I'm eatin' *highoh up* on de hog now!"

And so it is with the rising voter—he's kicking off the shackles—and voting for men—not parties or traditions—he's looking a *"little higher"* than mere party ties.

Then to dwell a bit upon an ever-vital question among our group—that of racial discrimination and segregation.

Whatever may be the attitude of you older people toward this dastardly practice of insolently slapping the Race in the face, I can tell, in all sincerity, that there is a violently smoldering fire of indignation among those of us who are younger in years and who have not yet become inured to such insults.

And I sincerely offer the prayer that we never shall become so.

I hope that the future generations of our Race rise as one to combat this vicious habit at every opportunity until it is completely broken down.

I want to tell you that when I think of such outrageous atrocities as this latest swimming pool incident, which has been perpetuated upon Los Angeles Negroes, my blood boils.

And when I see my people so foolhardy as to patronize such a place, and thus give it their sanction, my disgust is trebled.

Any Los Angeles Negro who would go bathing in that dirty hole with that sign "For Colored Only," gawking down at him in insolent mockery of his Race, is either a fool or a traitor to his kind.

It is true we have made a rather feeble protest against it. But why stop with that—because of a slight setback? Must we go on passively like lambs in the fold and accept such conditions, which can only be the forerunner of greater discriminations in the future?

Or should we not rise in a body to fight such an absurd action in a state which guarantees freedom and equality to all alike?

If we have a segregated swimming pool—segregated in the ultimate sense of the word, too—for that pool is for colored and colored only—no white people are admitted—tho there are white residents in the neighborhood who desire to make use of this so-called public utility.

If we accept this, can't you see that we will only too soon have separate, inferior schools, parks, and who knows, perhaps even *jim-crow cars* forced upon us?

I think I speak sanely when I say that, if it costs the Negroes of Los Angeles a cold million dollars to overcome this menace, the money should be willingly contributed, for it would certainly be well spent.

If we don't combat such segregation to the bitter end, we can draw only one conclusion—that the Los Angeles Negro is *cowed*—that he lacks *racial pride* and racial consciousness.

My ideal type of Negro is that type personified in the story of the old Southern darkey who owned a small bit of land on which he planted sugarcane.

It happened that, soon after the great Teddy Roosevelt had returned from his famous big-game hunting trip, he and a small party were making a short trip thru the South by motor. The party, by chance, stopped momentarily close by the old darkey's abbreviated plantation.

Roosevelt was fond of sugarcane and, spying the choice stalks growing upon the old Negro's land, with characteristic impetuosity, strode over and broke off several stalks.

The old man had been watching every move and, seeing the president's actions, ran over and began to demonstrate excitedly with him about the theft.

A member of the president's party immediately interceded, explaining to the old Negro in awe-inspiring tones that the accused was "the great Teddy Roosevelt."

The old Negro looked upon the interceder with a look of scornful disdain and replied:

—"Huh! White man—I don't care if he's *Booker T. Washington,* he can't steal my sugarcane."

To that old man, Booker T. Washington, his fellow Race-man, personified the greatest of all men.

I only wish that the great men of our race, and there are a goodly number of them, were better known by our people.

If they were, I am sure that racial pride and integrity would be at a much higher ebb.

And this leads to the final topic to be discussed, which, perhaps, is to our Race the most vital of all at the present time.

Whatever progress we may make in the future, whatever forward steps may be taken toward the breaking down of this infernal inferiority complex which besets so many of our kind; whatever success we may have in convincing the other races of our absolute equality in every line of endeavor, must come thru the medium of ever-increasing *education.*

Education, to the Negro, is the keynote for his advancement. Education is the panacea for his ills.

Young Negroes must attain higher education in increasingly larger numbers. Else we need not hope to successfully compete with other peoples.

We must meet their standards or be left in the rut. And heaven knows we've been in the rut long enough already.

And it's up to all of you older folks to lend encouragement and help to the coming generations in their struggle for education. Other races do it, so why not ours?

Our youngsters have a terribly difficult task in their efforts to obtain an education as it is, and we can hope to educate the Race universally only by an extensive, spontaneous spirit of helpfulness on the part of the older folks.

There is much that our Negro businessmen can do in aiding aspiring Race students along such lines as part-time employment, scholarship awards, etc. Our local business agencies and our many clubs as well have wonderful opportunities of aiding the educational movement.

But it's no secret that much that could and should be done *isn't being done.*

You know it's often said of our Race that we are *"kings of the alibi."* We can have more good intentions and do less than any other people on earth, but when we are brought to task for our failure to do *"so and so"* we can always immediately produce a ready alibi.

But you know Hell is paved with good intentions!

Say what we will, this matter of increased educational advantages is a very serious one.

Before we can build up successful business organizations which can meet our white rivals on an equal footing, we must have *educated, trained* men to run them.

We can't run a ship without seamen, and we can't run our businesses successfully without trained experts.

The best and wisest investment our Race can make today is along increased educational opportunities for our coming generations.

I'm sure that the returns will far exceed our fondest hopes. All we younger folks ask of you is to give us a little cooperative encouragement—just a little better than a fighting chance, and we'll guarantee you achievements which will compel the other races to afford the Negro that respect which is his due birthright!

We have *youth*—we have *racial pride*—we have *indomitable will* and boundless optimism for the future.—So we can't help but come out on top of the heap!

True, we have certain modern ways and mannerisms which some of you can't quite reconcile with what you term "decency." But times change, you know. Short skirts, bobbed hair, dancing the Charleston, etc. All find accord in the conventions of today.

So don't disparage us too much for our modernism. We are merely the children of our age just as you were in your youth.

All we ask is for you to lend us a helping hand—jump on the band-wagon with us, and we'll assure you that by the time we've had the advantage of a few more years experience, we'll make you all *proud* of the young Negro.

He'll make his mark in the world today, just as you have made yours; and then he'll go you one better!

CHAPTER 3

Negro Political Philosophy
1928

Written while attending graduate school at Harvard, a companion essay entitled "Negro Political Laboratories" became Bunche's first published work, this essay suggests a transition to a more pragmatic and more radical scholar than his 1926 UCLA speech. In it Bunche focuses on the domestic political philosophy of American Negroes, labeling it conservative. The conservatism, he says, may be attributed to the peasant background of most blacks, along with their ties to the long-dead Republicanism of Lincoln. Bunche advocates a shift away from national elections to an emphasis on local elections, in which their vote is more likely to be "the balance of power."* The young scholar argues that blacks must become more opportunistic and less idealistic than in the past. Negroes must open their minds to liberal political philosophies and even to socialism and Bolshevism.

Behind the 12,000,000 Negro citizens and the 2 to 3 million Negro voters who constitute one-tenth of America's population and electorate, there will be found actuating motives which determine the nature and course of the political activity of this minority group. In these motives must be sought a definition of the political philosophy of the Negro.

Perhaps the most immediately striking of all the characteristics of Negro thought in politics is its extreme *conservatism*. What is conservatism in political philosophy? There are, generally speaking, two types of political philosophy—(1) conservatism and (2) criticalism.

Conservatism marries the status quo—it is the creed of those who have no plaints to make, who preach a gospel of "let well enough alone." Criticalism, on the other hand, is the philosophy of the dissatisfied and disgruntled—it is the philosophy of those who, having grievances to air, desire that changes be made. Criticalism is the natural philosophy of the American Negro, but he has so far failed to grasp it or its significance to any appreciable extent. Negro

---

*In 1948 Henry Lee Moon of the NAACP published a book entitled *Balance of Power* in which he argued that the urban black vote in Northern states could be decisive in presidential elections.

philosophy, by every means of reckoning, should be *critical* philosophy—he has every reason to advocate *change*—change in social, change in political structure.

Contrariwise, however, he has seemingly developed a hostility to anything suggesting change—to liberalism, progressivism, and radicalism. Most Negroes regard these philosophies rather in the light of contraband. The inevitable conclusion submits itself that the Negro masses must be *content* with inequality, injustice, discrimination, and this inexplicable docility is found in astounding degree even among the upper strata of the group—among the "intelligentsia." What a contrast is this attitude with that of the Jew, himself oppressed but an active leader in liberal thought. Certainly it is that no group can soar higher than its hope nor sink lower than its despair.

Where are we to seek the reasons for this conservatism of the Negro philosophy? At the outset it is apparent that a conservative attitude is the Negro's natural heritage. He is of a peasant class—he is of the soil; urbanization of the Negro is strictly a contemporaneous phenomenon. The mental shackles of peasantry have not yet been discharged. Peasant peoples have ever allied with conservatism. The radical movements of history have been led by artisans—by the hand and brain workers of the cities—the proletarians. In the French Revolution the peasant-folk had gone far enough when the proletarians were but starting. It is the proletarian who first comes to appreciate what political liberty, equality, and fraternity really mean. This fact is well illustrated by Dr. Wesley in his volume on "Negro Labor in the U.S." The leaders were ex-slaves who had escaped to the cities and joined the artisan class.

The security of sustenance in slavery tended also to develop a complacent, conservative temperament in the Negro. Too much security is dangerous to any people—we become under its influence too much like domestic animals—we hope and look for "bones" from masters. This attitude is too often found in our philosophy. We still have with us the old "Uncle Tom," hat-in-hand Negro—inviting condescension and solicitousness from the other race—always looking for the white man to "do something" for him, because he has a moral obligation toward all black men. The sooner we get rid of such philosophy the better off we'll all be. The other race owes us nothing—absolutely nothing—what it has it has gotten thru industry and using the head for purposes other than adornment. As a race we must follow suit.

Ignorance affords a further explanation of Negro conservatism. The conservative fears to look beyond his nose lest he find something there to upset him. That something is as often as not a theory which he cannot understand, or which his narrowness and bigotry prevent him from accepting. The ignorant, the illiterate, sees in the untried experiment the mysterious, the dangerous, and the undesirable. What he cannot understand he rejects. Where in this country do we find greater ignorance, and where greater bigoted conservatism, than in our South?

Most of the liberated Negro population was illiterate; a large percent of our southern Negro population is still illiterate, and this density is a chief obstacle to the dissemination of even moderately liberal political philosophy among the masses. Ignorance breeds suspicion; suspicion rejects change.

Still a further influence toward conservatism in Negro philosophy is what might be called the "Lincolnian Legend." The Negro's postslavery alliance with the party of liberation has been the most outstanding feature of his political history. Following emancipation the Negro sought a haven of refuge in the Republican Party—for protection against his enemies and as a token of gratitude for his deliverance. It must be this latter, sentimental reason which keeps us aligned with the Republican Party today.

Lincoln has been dead a long time. Whatever the motives of Lincoln and the Republican Party might have been in 1861–64—and I question that they were more philanthropic than selfish, more political than economic—whatever the motives of Lincoln and Republicanism of those years, many decades have elapsed since then, and many changes have been made in party principles, organization, and composition.

The Republican Party today, along with its weak shadow posing as rival—the Democratic Party—stands avowedly for that system of economic organization which dooms the Negro along with millions of others of the petit bourgeois and the proletarian classes to that dire economic slavery which is indeed a poor substitute for former physical servitude. Both Republican and Democratic parties sentence these lower-class peoples to abject subjection. Under the existing system, all that the Negro businessman can hope to do, except in very rare instances, is to mimic on a miniature scale the activity and methods of his white prototype. The money which the Negro businessman, be he butcher, baker, or candlestick maker, must depend upon for the continued success of his enterprise is the "small change" of the proletarian Negro workman—a few pennies a week earned by sweat of his brow from hard-fisted, hard-shelled capitalist-exploiter belonging to the other group.

The Negro bourgeois, rare specimen that he is, for it takes more than bourgeois psychology and tastes to make a middle-classman, along with his sole means of support—the Negro workman, is practically entirely subject to the whim and caprice of capitalist "Simon Legrees." He has merely exchanged iron for economic shackles. He is the vassal in an economic feudalism, and the Negro workman is the serf.

Our existing national parties then are parties of reaction, and the Negro casts most, if not all, his votes in that direction.

A second attribute of Negro political philosophy is what may be referred to as pseudo-nationalism. Perhaps the greatest fallacy in the political philosophy of the Negro is the tendency to place what to me appears to be a decided overemphasis upon national elections. The entire race suddenly becomes intensely "political" every four years with the presidential elections. Our so-called political leaders and "bosses," often self-appointed and always self-seeking, suddenly emerge as from a deep slumber, emblazon their names across the front pages of the black press, and exhort indifferent and often illiterate Negro masses to support this or that party—usually "this"—"this" being Republican. The ballyhoo, bought and paid for by white dollars, consists of eulogies of "*the* party," the intense interest "*the* party has always evidenced in the welfare of the poor Negro race, that a vote for the *other* party will surely bring on the immediate lynching of the whole race—and so, on and on—a great mass of asinine propaganda and empty promises—"flapdoodle," pure and unadulterated.

But the masses pour forth on election day, misguided, bewildered by breath-taking oratory, and cast a vote for the party's candidate for president, not expecting much of anything to come from it, but at least secure in the conviction that they have voted "right."

Yet they know and desire to know nothing about party platforms or national issues. The presidential candidate's proposed foreign policy, his tariff views, his proposals for flood control and farm relief, mean little or nothing to them. The fact that a candidate may make the deeply significant statement that governmental ownership of Boulder Dam is "state socialism" and therefore inimical, or intimate that efficiency and law enforcement, whatever the law, are more important to our government than democracy and the will of the people, is shed off their craniums like water off the mallard's back. Still they are voting a "national" ticket, supporting a "national" candidate.

But what does the race minority get for all this verbosity, for all this energetic "politicianing" in presidential elections? A few, several, if we are fortunate, crumbs of the great patronage loaf which is cut and distributed to hungry politicians every four years. An assistant-to-the-assistant of the Atty. General, maybe—an office or two in the customs bureau, several clerkships with dignified names, a flock of minor post office jobs, and a whole lot of notoriety with *no* representation. Then we go back into our political shells, take up our menial tasks, and wait until the next election.

Isn't it all so ridiculous? Don't we know that Harding, Coolidge, Hoover, could and would have been elected had there never been a black man in the country? Just what can we expect to get out of it all except a small crust of the patronage pie? Must we not sooner or later recognize that we are merely a minority group—a rather scattered, disinterested, and often divided minority group at that? In fact we are not a *national* minority group at all in a strict sense—we are a congeries of several minority groups defined by the nation's geographical and sectional divisions. Our potential political power is at its lowest ebb in national elections.

But our weakness in national elections is our strength in local, city and state, elections. Wherever we have congregated in large numbers we invariably constitute a political minority which may hold the balance of power in the event of keen rivalry between the dominant party groups. The minority group thus, unconsciously, becomes the strategic force in local politics.

Segregation, voluntary, or enforced by law, contract, gentlemen's agreements, or intimidation is the basis of this political phenomenon. The rapid urbanization of the race—the startling Negro migrations of the past two decades—from farm to city and from South to North—whose main foci are in the large cities of the East and Midwest, have speeded up the process.

Thus, two forces, the natural gregariousness of the Negro and the severe exclusion policy of white groups, have tended to create powerful Negro minorities in the great centers—independent of and separated from the surrounding white residents. With the separation and consequent self-dependence of the group, there develop a racial self-confidence and an expanded sense of pride and unity. Thus presenting a solid front, Negroes are able to exert a political and moral force which they have but recently discovered will command a consideration not previously attainable, as, for example, better police protection, new political recognition, housing reform, sanitary measures, economic equality, and Negro representatives in positions of responsibility. Such considerations, commonplace enough to the average city group, are not unpleasant revelations to the Negro.

Let us turn briefly to our two largest municipalities and see this newly discovered power in operation.

Although 250,000 of any group is not many people in New York City, this number of Negroes has political significance to Tammany because of the compactness of the group. The great preponderance of these people live in the small crowded area known as Harlem. It is quite widely recognized that, were it not for a lack of cohesion due largely to dissensions between American and "foreign" Negroes, this race would hold a clear balance of power in three districts and dominate two others. Tammany has regularly made overtures to them, and New York Democratic leaders as far back as Croker have proselyted among them. The "Wigwam" applies the same methods to the Harlem voters as to the New York immigrant groups—Irish, German, Jew, and Italian; that is, patronage and favor are exchanged for ballots. There have been 2 Negro Tammany aldermen, 1 member of the municipal civil service commission, a fire lieutenant, 54 policemen, an assistant district attorney, over 100 schoolteachers, and a host of minor appointments. The list is growing rapidly.

Chicago affords another interesting illusion of the profitable exercise of the franchise by Negro citizens. There the Thompson forces have consistently courted the Negro vote, and it is largely through the enthusiastic response of the "south side" of Negro wards that the Thompson administration has remained so long in the ascendancy in Chicago politics. It is conceded that the

Negro vote won the mayoralty for Thompson in 1927 in Chicago's most exciting campaign. Big Bill was victorious over the incumbent, Dever, by a plurality of 82,938 votes, of which 59,215 were rolled up in the Negro strongholds.

Because of its potency in municipal affairs, the Chicago Negro population enjoys a greater degree of political participation and representation than any Negro group in the nation. A Negro serves as member of the civil service commission of three—a cabinet office; another holds position as legal advisor to the city in matters pertaining to state legislation of vital interest to Chicago. Six of the best trained young lawyers of the group hold appointments as assistant corporation counsels. An assistant city attorney sits in the city attorney's office. In the office of the city prosecutor are five more as assistant city prosecutors. Two Negro representatives are also found as assistant attorneys for the board of local improvements; another, an appointee as member of the library board with no salary, having jurisdiction over approximately 3,000 employees. These men are all entrusted with responsible positions. Additional appointments in the many city departments as teacher, clerks, police, etc., total hundreds.

But, as in New York, all representation is not only by appointment. In the two strong Negro wards the majority group has elected two of its members aldermen. A municipal court judge, with a salary of $10,000, has been elected. The natural outcome of such local political activity has increased Negro influence in state affairs. Four Negroes have been elected to the lower house of the state legislature and one to the state Senate. A Negro serves as the governor's appointee on the powerful Illinois industrial board and another as state commerce commissioner. And, of course, Oscar De Priest will take his oath of office as representative from the first Congressional District of Illinois to the 71st National Congress on Monday.

The situation in New York and Chicago finds duplication in most other large municipalities of the East and Midwest. In local elections the Negro vote receives far higher dividends than it can ever hope for in any national balloting. Let us make our heaviest investments where returns are highest!

Despite general impression to the contrary, I do not feel that Negro political philosophy is sufficiently pragmatic. We are living in a materialistic age. Negro political philosophy must perforce be pragmatic. Idealism is commendable, but it is for the few well-to-do—for those who can afford it—not for the petit bourgeois or the proletarian. The latter's philosophy must be one of stern reality—it must be composed in terms of bread and butter, dollars and cents. Even God cannot appear before the poor except in the shape of food.

There must be still more of opportunism in Negro political thought and action. By this I do not imply more of the selfishly individualistic opportunism of which we have already become nauseated, but opportunism of the group.

Sentimentalism and tradition, no matter how sacred, must be cast overboard, and the Negro must ever be on the alert to make the best of any and every opportunity which presents itself to send a Negro representative or a friendly white one to city, state, or national legislative chambers.

Opportunism can be developed only with the development of keen wisdom. We must learn to make the best of those practices and institutions which at first glance seem impossibly noxious. Take the matter of residential segregation, for example. Whatever else we may say or think, segregation *is*—it is an actuality, cold and unrelenting. We may do one of several things with it—accept it placidly, spend all of our time and money crying aloud and protesting about the injustice of it, or we can fight it strategically by removing its objectionable features.

If we refrain from abstract moralization over absolute rights, absolute equality, and absolute liberty, we must note that the fundamental practical basis of protest against segregation is in the fact that it has, as its correlative, *inferiority*—inferior public service, inferior paving, lighting, sewage, schools, police and fire protection. The segregated community wears the badge of inferiority only for this reason. But is it not true that perhaps the remedy is to be found in the circumstance? By the very fact of his segregation the Negro becomes a potentially powerful minority group. As such, if he has skillful political leaders, he will be able to win for himself by the ballot the same type of public service that is afforded any other section of the city—perhaps even better, in those instances where he has become a controlling factor in municipal elections, as in Chicago.

I have seen Negro residential districts, though segregated, both for voluntary and compulsory reasons, as beautiful, as clean and well served publicly, as any section of the city. When that goal is attained the outstanding objection to segregation is removed. Then perhaps, the path will be opened to the complete elimination of residential as of all other forms of segregation.

There ought to be more liberalism too in Negro political philosophy. The Negro should at least begin to listen with an open mind to those liberal political philosophies whose aim is the amelioration of the obvious social evils of a capitalist regime. Radicalism is an extreme view; liberalism is the moderate view of the rational individual, who, knowing that all things cannot be right, proposes to remedy those that are wrong.

The mere mention of socialism or Bolshevism or anything related thereto in my classes will occasion an obvious ripple and a lifting of the eyebrows. To defend a tenet of socialism is something akin to heresy or sacrilege. Such rank conservatism even on the part of our youth is absurd. There is much in socialist thought which would be more than helpful to the Negro, and the world will undoubtedly place a new evaluation upon the Soviet experiment in Russia within the next few years.

Socialism is no longer a term upon the mention of which eyes and mouth are to be tightly closed and hands clapped over the ears. Socialism, in many of its aspects, is already with us in fact as it has long been in theory. Can we not at least intelligently investigate what it has to offer us for our sufferings?

We, as a race, have been altogether too inhospitable to new and progressive ideas. The man or the race whose opinions are never altered is like standing water, and breeds reptiles of the mind.

Finally, why should we not be strictly opportunistic in relation to political parties? What does either of our two dominant parties promise to do for us today? The Democrats have traditionally scorned us, and now the Republican party attempts to steal its rival's thunder, "out-Democrating" the Democrats not only by scorning but by repudiating us.

How else can my respected fellow Californian's recent statement be interpreted when it begins in this vein:

"It has been the aspiration of Republican presidents over many years to build up a sound organization in the southern states of such character as would commend itself to the citizens of those states"?

Is it not the clear intent of the president's language that the Republican Party now purposes [*sic*] to be lily-white in the states where the colored man has no vote and to deprive the Negro of his constitutional rights within the party councils? Perhaps the president is justified by the facts, but it is equally clear that the raison d'être of the new position is this: Hoover and the Republican Party are making a serious effort to hold the Republican gains made in the south at the last election.

We as a race have had enough evidence that embracing Republicanism does not cleanse the hearts of prejudiced southerners of their maliciousness. But, if we still doubt it, more evidence was contributed just last week when the Hooverized Republican representative from North Carolina refused to occupy an office next to that of Congressman-elect De Priest!

When the South permeates the Republican Party the Negro's final political refuge is lost. That will be, I think, a !arge step forward in his political emancipation. American political parties are for majorities—let the Negro bargain with them, use them, by coalition with their rivals, defeat them, and then *forget* them!

CHAPTER 4

Marxism and the "Negro Question"
1929

This essay, written only three years after "That Man May Dwell in Peace" reveals a sharp rise in Bunche's radicalism. No doubt influenced by his reading and his friends at Harvard and Howard, Bunche replaces the call for peace through social education with "the overthrow of capitalist democracy thru the concentration of political power in the hands of the proletariat." Bunche, the young race leader in Los Angeles, now regards the destruction of any "racial unity" among all classes of blacks as a "profoundly progressive and revolutionary phenomena." "Marxism and the 'Negro Question'" foreshadows several central themes that the radical Bunche would put forward in his writings in the 1930s. First, although Bunche uses the then-fashionable language of the Communist movement, he demonstrates his independence by rejecting the Sixth World Congress's "national minority" theory. Throughout his life he would argue against black nationalism, contending that the Negro had none of the characteristics necessary for the formation of a nation. Thus, he applauds the demise of Garveyism and derides black economic cooperatives. According to Bunche, a truly Marxist theory of the "Negro question" and even a truly Marxist analysis of its main features still remains for the future. Yet in this essay he proceeds to supply some of the core elements for such a theory—an emphasis on the caste status of blacks and the superexploitation of black labor, the hegemony of bourgeois ideology through the incorporation of race prejudice, and the organization of Negro society along the lines of an internal colony.

The Fundamental Features of the Status of the Negro in American Society, of the Struggle for Negro Emancipation, and of Its Relation to the Proletarian Struggle

Introduction

1. Of all questions facing the American working class and the American Communist movement, the "Negro Question" is the most specifically Ameri-

can of all questions, with only secondary analogies to conditions elsewhere. It is a question of first-rate importance to the American proletariat. And yet of all questions it is the one to which the least serious attention on the part of the Marxist theoreticians has been devoted; there has, in fact, not yet been made in America any serious analysis of the Negro Question from the Marxist viewpoint. The general backwardness and sterility of socialist theory in America and the traditional American Socialist "nihilism" on the Negro Question as an indirect expression of the "white supremacy" ideology ("There is no Negro question!"—"There is only an economic question of workers against bosses") are partly responsible for this condition. And, altho the Communist movement rapidly broke with the shameless white chauvinism of large sections of the prewar Socialist movement, the theoretical reorientation has been much slower. Until very recently the Communist movement remained content with vague and platitudinous phrases and, when recently a new theoretical departure was attempted under the stimulus of the Communist International, it went astray as a result of a fundamentally false orientation ("national minority" theory). A truly Marxist theory of the Negro question and even truly Marxist analysis of its main features still remains for the future.

2. At the same time distinct signs are not absent pointing to a definite revival of the independent social activity of the Negro masses in the North and in the South, in the urban and in the rural centers, under the stimulus of the economic crisis, the great growth in unemployment, and the incredible chaos in the cotton economy of the South. In this situation the unsatisfactory state of current Communist theory on the Negro question (especially in this country) is very serious and even dangerous.

The Status of the American Negro

3. The status of the Negro in the United States is in a very real sense specific to this country; only in the most general sense does it bear any relation to the status of colored peoples in other parts of the world, in the West Indies, in Africa, in South America, etc. Only against the background of the special course of American historical development, only in connection with the concrete relation of social forces in this country, can the status of the American Negro be understood and the problems deriving therefrom appreciated.

4. The Negro people in the United States do not constitute a colonial people under the heel of American imperialism. All of the essential characteristics of a colony (geographical separation from metropolis, the distinctness of the national economy of the colony and its specific relation to the imperialist economy of the metropolis, etc.) [sic]. But just as little do the Negro people constitute a national minority in the real sense of the term. For the formation of a nation there is necessary a community (and distinctness) of language, of territory, of economic life (a national economy), of psychic structure (culture)

and tradition. Not a single one of these conditions is characteristic of the Negroes in the United States. The attempt to supply the necessary community of territory by the creation of a fictitious "Negro-land" (the "Black Belt") runs contrary to every fact of American history and to every conception of contemporary tendencies and movements among the Negro people. The fundamental falsity of the "national minority" orientation comes to erase expression in the obvious inappropriateness of the slogan of "self-determination" (the proper slogan for a people suffering from national oppression) to the condition of the Negroes in America. The slogan of self-determination, in a situation where every force of bourgeois law, custom, and public opinion constantly operated to maintain and widen the breach between the races, is an objective support to jim-crowism. The point of view of the Negro people as a national minority is false in conception and dangerous in concrete application.

5. The Negro people in the United States constitute, in the words of Lenin, *a subject caste on a racial basis.* The Negro people form an integral element of the American nation and of the American national economy; their culture, territory, language, are all characteristically American. In the American social edifice they, as a race, occupy a peculiar and depressed status, a caste status. A close analogy would be the position of the "depressed classes," the "untouchables," in Hindu society in India.

6. The depressed caste status of the American Negroes is expressed primarily in the semi-servile condition of the Negro farmer in Southern agriculture and the inferior position of the Negro worker in industrial life. The underprivileged state of the Negro socially (jim-crow, segregating, lynch law), and politically, follow directly. Fundamentally, the Negro in the United States forms a well-defined subject caste, with a distinctly inferior economic, social, and political status.

The Historical Roots of the Caste Status of the Negro

Caste status is, as Lenin has pointed out more than once, essentially a precapitalist institution, a phase or a *remnant* of a non-capitalist social (and economic) order. How to account for the existence of this "remnant of feudalism" in the highly developed capitalist system of this country is the first problem of a Marxist approach to the Negro question.

8. The roots of the present subject status of the Negro in America must be traced back to the days of slavery, nearly three-quarters of a century ago. Under slavery there was an immediate and obvious basis for the social subjection of the black man as such—their economically enslaved condition as a race. Had the American Civil War really effected the complete emancipation of the Negro slave, there would indeed have been no ground for the continued existence of the Negro as an inferior caste. But the victorious industrial bourgeois of the North adopted a course of action that led to quite other results. It rejected

the "Radical" plan for reconstruction, a plan that envisaged the complete destruction of the economic and political power of the slaveocracy and the real emancipation of the Negro slaves, i. e., their transformation into free peasant-proprietors and into free proletarians. On the contrary, the Northern bourgeois, after considerable hesitation and vacillation, threw its support to the "Conservative" plan of Reconstruction, which aimed at conciliating the old slave owners by abolishing chattel slavery in name but retaining it in somewhat modified form in fact. The bourgeois democratic revolution—the essence of the Civil War—was thereby stifled and distorted; the emancipation of the Negro was rendered incomplete, even from a consistent bourgeois standpoint. Thus, the present economic status of the Negro was rendered incomplete, even from a consistent economic bourgeois standpoint. Thus, the present status of the Negro farmer is essentially a survival of slavery. And when, in the course of time, the Negro farmer comes to enter industry, he naturally brings with him his caste status. The specially depressed economic position of the Negro farmer is essentially a survival of slavery. The specially depressed economic position of the Negro is the basis upon which the whole system of social, political, and cultural subjection is reared.

The caste status of the American Negro is essentially a pre-capitalist survival, a "relic of feudalism." But such pre-capitalist survivals find a welcome place in the decaying structure of capitalism in its final, imperialist-monopolistic epoch. The bourgeois is no longer, as it was in the great days of its youth, the ruthless destroyer of the obsolete and the reactionary. In its senility, "the decaying bourgeois . . . supports everything that is backward, dying and medieval . . ." (Lenin). The specially depressed economic status of the Negro peasant and proletarian serves as a valuable source of super-profit for monopoly-capital—in a strictly analogous manner to colonial exploitation. At the same time it serves as a point of support for the class domination of the bourgeois "Divide and rule"! For this reason the race oppression of the Negro has become an integral element of the bourgeois-imperialist stystem in this country.

10. [*sic*] It is in the specific caste status of the American Negro, and the integration of this status into the American imperialism, that race prejudice ("white chauvinism") has its roots. Class interests are directly transmuted into class ideology; this is a fundamental social mechanism. The caste status of the American Negro—so advantageous to the ruling class from the viewpoint of economic profit and class power—is transformed into the corresponding class ideology—"the theory of the inherent racial inferiority" of the Negro, race prejudice, etc. But "the ruling ideas of any age are the ideas of the ruling class" (Marx). Race prejudice thus develops into an element of the currently accepted social thought (bourgeois ideology) and is absorbed by the other classes of society to the degree that they are under the ideological influence of the ruling

class. It is because the white American workers and farmers are so "backward," i.e., so much under the spiritual influence of the bourgeois, that they are so afflicted with anti-Negro race prejudice. A secondary factor in the same direction is the role that the feeling of racial superiority plays as a form of psychic compensation to the backward masses of the white toilers for the incredible miseries of their everyday existence. Nor can the deliberate activities of the white ruling class in stirring up race hatred be minimized.

The Structure of American Negro Society

11. The great Negro migrations during the last two decades, in the course of which scores of thousands of Negro farmers swarmed to the great Northern industrial centers and to the basic industries of the land, really introduced a new stage in the history of the American Negro. They effected a profound social fermentation and a basic realignment of class forces. They faced the Negro masses with a whole series of new problems arising out of the new urban and industrial environment. They really created the modern Negro preletariat. They greatly stimulated the development of the Negro bourgeois and petty bourgeois and seriously transformed the relations between these classes. They had a profound effect upon the Negro peasantry in the South, sunk in the mire of peonage and semi-reform. They also greatly influenced the relations between the two races in the North as well as in the South. All of these phenomena soon made themselves evident in their effect upon the changed structure of American Negro society.

12. The social organization of the Negro people in this country, altho, of course, closely related to and in fact integrated into American society as such, bears a characteristic aspect, especially in the relation of classes and the specific gravity of each in the whole. The organization of Negro society bears, in certain important aspects, a significant resemblance to the organization of society in a colony or a subject nation.

13. The Negro bourgeois is rather weak numerically, absolutely and relatively, and even weaker economically. It has no hold upon or contract with basic industry; it is almost exclusively confined to certain very unimportant branches, usually organized on a small scale, or to commercial and related occupations that emerge in the large Negro sections of the big cities, South as well as North. But through the Negro bourgeois, through the more pliant elements of the petty bourgeois, and through the conservative sections of the professional "race leaders," the white American bourgeois exerts tremendous influence over the masses of the Negro people and it operates with borrowed power. The fundamental standpoint of the Negro bourgeois was theoretically formulated by Booker T. Washington in the famous "Atlanta Compromise": The Negro is to be content with his place in the bourgeois American scheme of

things. He is to bend his energies toward becoming an efficient servant of the white master. Any present aspiration for social and political rights—not to speak of social equality—is a vain and dangerous delusion. In the South the Negroes are to acquiesce in their complete political disfrachisement; in the North they are to serve as blind voting cattle for the Republican Party. Lastly, an infamous flirtation with the Democratic Party (in North and South) has been initiated (the De Priest "nonpartisan" conference). Within the last year the crusade against Communism has become an important part of the services rendered by the Negro bourgeois to their white masters. The political activities of the race leaders of this class are marked by clique squabbles, gross corruption, and shameless patronage—all at the expense of the Negro masses. Of the emancipation of their people they know nothing and care less.

14. Thru the sham social power of prestige, lent it by the white ruling class, the Negro bourgeois and its professional race leaders have been able hitherto to dominate the social and political ideas of the backward Negro masses. In this work the wide-spread network of Negro social and fraternal societies (especially the churches) have played a very important role.

15. The Negro petty bourgeois and professionals (most of the professionals belong to the petty bourgeois) are more numerous altho proportionately also smaller among the Negroes than among the whites (only in the proportion clergy to the population do the Negroes show precedence) and of considerable consequence. Like the bourgeois, this class found a firm basis of existence (especially in the North) only with the great Negro migrations and the creation of the huge Negro cities in the relatively free atmosphere of the North. In the post-war "renascence," a relatively free atmosphere of the period of deep-going fermentation and real achievement, the Negro intellectual played a brilliant role, especially in literature and fine arts.

16. As a consequence of the characteristic caste status of the Negro people in American society, the Negro petty bourgeoisie is destined to play a far more significant and progressive social role in the struggle of the Negro people for emancipation and in the general social struggle than is the white bourgeoisie in the analogous situation. As a significant factor in the life and development of the Negro race, petty bourgeoisie is second only to the Negro proletartiat.

17. A large part of the Negro petty bourgeoisie is bound up, economically, organizationally, and ideologically, with the Negro bourgeoisie, which it aids in carrying out its specific role as the agency of white capitalism among Negroes. Considerable sections, however, have already gone a long way in freeing themselves, more or less, from the spiritual domination of the bourgeoisie, or at least from the greatest bourgeoisie prejudices. The social outlook of these sections of the petty bourgeoisie has hitherto been marked, quite inevitably considering their class position, by its lack of persistency and resolu-

tion, by its extravagant oscillations from one extreme to the other, by its fantastic utopianism combined with an equally fantastic "practicalism," but all within the framework of the basic bourgeoisie preconceptions. Especially characteristic is its strange faith in the belief that the Negro question can be solved within the framework of capitalism, perhaps with the benevolent aid of the white capitalist themselves. At one time, Garveyism, an essentially reactionary philosophy based on an inverted form of the "white supremacy" gospel of the white charlatanism, had considerable hold over the lower middle class elements of the large Negro cities. Now Garveyism is happily dead. Today the Negro intellectuals and professionals are lost in the absurd utopia of creating a self-contained Negro economy through utilizing the "organized buying power" of the race or through some equally efficacious means. The capricious and ever changing vagaries that dominate the Negro petty bourgeoisie are a certain indication of the gulf that exists between it and the masses of the Negro people, the peasants and workers, whose interests are poles apart from the unreal fantasies of the small man or professional, I to [*sic*] enstrangement from its own people with the consequent lack of political and social stability, is unquestionably the greatest inner weakness of the Negro petty bourgeoisie.

17. [*sic*] Nevertheless, from the general historical viewpoint, the Negro petty bourgeoisie still has progressive potentialities in view of the essentially democratic character of the struggle against the caste oppression of the Negro. Some sections of the Negro intellectuals are already marching leftwards, primarily as a result of the profound impression made upon them by the example of the Soviet Union. But the actual realization of its historical potentialities implies an end to reactionary and futile utopian dreaming, an organic approach to the masses, a participation in their interests and aspirations, a close alliance with the advanced sections of the proletariat, white and black.

18. As has already been pointed out the Negro farmer in the South (where the bulk of the Negro people are to be found) are not "free" farmers in the capitalist sense of the term. They occupy an intermediate position between free farmers and slaves—a semi-serf-position that is the basic element of the caste status of the Negro people in this country. There are practically no Negro agricultural capitalists and almost as few wealthy farmers. The vast majority of the Negro farmers—whether tenants (the proportion of tenancy is very high) or nomimal "owners"—find themselves in the category of the rest of the poor, exploited in pre-capitalist and semi-feudal forms of exploitation (peonage, sharecropping, etc. [*sic*], in many cases even forced labor. The Negro agricultural worker is not a free laborer in the bourgeois sense; he also toils under semi-slave relations of exploitation. On this basis, a superstructure of caste oppression has been raised of incredible viciousness. The most elementary form of economic organization is prohibited under penalty of death (the cases of the Phillips County, Arkansas, and the Camp Hill, Alabama sharecropping unions).

19. Yet even here the wave of Negro migrations and the experiences of the World War have had an immense effect. The bleak seclusion, the dreary isolation of decades, the helpless desolation, was broken.

A vigorous breath of fresh air swept through the poisonous atmosphere of the Old South. The vision of the Negro peasant was suddenly and immensely enlarged; intimate contacts were established with migrated friends and relatives in the North; an understanding began to dawn that things must not be always—and are not everywhere—the same. The Negro peasant as a vital factor in the movement for freedom.

20. The Negro proletarian is primarily to be found in unskilled and semi-skilled capacities in large-scale basic industry. Altho he has become a proletarian he has brought his caste status with him; he occupies a position of distinct inferiority in the scheme of things in industry. He has no access to the more desirable situation; he is hindered in his approach to skilled or semi-skilled jobs; he is forced into the least paid and most menial occupations; he is discriminated against in wages and working conditions. His recent peasant background and his lack of collective experience in the labor movement are expressed in his backwardness in class consciousness and in his indifferent or even negative attitude on many of the basic questions of class struggle. (This attitude is, of course, helped by the antagonistic attitude of the white workers and labor leaders. The white employing class has not been slow in utilizing this backwardness of the Negro workers and the antagonism between the Negro and white workers in their attacks on the labor movement and on the working class as a whole.

21. Yet in spite of all temporary circumstances, the Negro proletariat constitutes historically the natural leadership of the Negro people in its social struggle in American society. The leading role of the proletariat within the Negro people is made inevitably by the inner processes of capitalist production, which thrust the proletariat to the fore of modern society, organizes it, stimulate its class consciousness, widen its political horizon, and give it that collective self-confidence, solidarity, and consciousness of aim which are the necessary attributes of class leadership. The emergence of the Negro proletariat as the leader of the Negro people still remains for the future but the creation of the modern Negro proletariat, thru the migrations, is certainly the most significant event in the history of the Negro since the days of Reconstruction.

The Negro Worker and American Labor

22. The sudden influx of tens of thousands of black workers into Northern industry inevitably aggravated the anti-Negro prejudice of the backward. At the same time the narrow and exclusive craft structure and the opportunist [sic]

philosophy of American trade unionism served from the very beginning as a most serious obstacle in the way of the black workers in industry. The conservative trade unions, in spite of occasional fine phrases, have practically closed their doors to the Negro workers and have all but invited them to throw in their lot with the white capitalists as scabs and strike-breakers—a course incessantly urged by the conservative Negro leaders as well. The darkest page in history of the American organized labor movement is its shameful record of antipathy and discrimination against the black worker.

23. But the progress of the class struggle promises to heal even this ominous breach in the ranks of the American proletariat. The white heat of the class struggle will burn out the corruption of race prejudice. The fraternization of white and colored workers in the South during the recent strikes, however hesitating, uncertain, and unstable, is a straw in the wind. The slow but inevitable deepening of the class consciousness of the white proletariat, i.e., its growing ideological liberation from the bourgeoisie, will certainly deliver the white workers from the thoroly [*sic*] bourgeois curse of race prejudice.

24. The submergence of national and racial differences within the proletariat in the firm ties of class solidarity is an indispensable requisite for the triumph of the revolutionary struggle against capitalism. The struggle against race prejudice of the white workers is the fundamental task of all revolutionary forces in the labor movement. In the Communist movement, in which all inner-class distinctions vanish, any open or disguised manifestations of race prejudice, which come as a result of the pressure of bourgeois ideology of the class, must be deliberately and consciously eliminated.

Negro Emancipation and the Proletarian Revolution

25. The whole burden of the analysis of the status of the Negro people in this country goes to prove that the deliverance of the Negro people from their caste existence is in its content essentially a democratic task—the only form of an uncompleted bourgeois revolution in the United States today. In that respect it is similar to the liberation of subject nations of colonies. Only the elimination of the underlying economic conditions upon which the subjection of the American Negro is predicated can make possible any real emancipation. The radical eradication of the semi-feudal forms of exploitation, of peonage, tenancy, sharecropping, furnishing, the shattering of the power of the Southern landlords thru the nationalization of the land and its distribution among the cultivators, the elimination of all elements of inferiority of the Negro's status in industry—these are the basic conditions upon which the social and political liberation of the colored people is conditioned. These measures represent merely the demands of consistent democracy: they are in all respects akin to the classical ideals of the bourgeois-democratic revolution, the Great French

Revolution, for example. Not a single one is a specifically socialist demand—not one necessarily implies the socialization of all the means of production, etc.

26. But the democratic character of the task of the Negro liberation from caste status by no means implies that the Negro question today can be solved within the framework of the capitalist democracy. So anti-democratic has the bourgeois become in its period of decay, so organically bound up with every-thing that is outlived, reactionary, and decadent, that the realization of the basic democratic demands is possible only thru the overflow of capitalist "democracy" thru the concentration of political power in the hands of the proletariat. In such directional contradiction does history move that only the dictatorship of the proletariat can guarantee democracy to the masses and bring real democracy, for the first time, to the Negro people. A whole historical period has passed since the Civil War; a bourgeois revolution in the USA today is a historical impossibility—today only a proletarian revolution can accom-plish what the American bourgeois revolution that was the Civil War failed to do.

27. From this viewpoint, the class differentiation, now rapidly taking place among the Negro people and destroying any possible "racial unity" of all classes, is to be regarded as a profoundly progressive and revolutionary phe-nomenon. The Negro bourgeoisie can only be a reactionary force in the strug-gle for the emancipation of its own race, so firm and numerous are the bands that tie it to white capital. The more completely and more rapidly that takes place the class separation of the popular masses of the Negro people from the Negro bourgeoisie, the better. At the opposite end of the pole stands the Negro proletariat, whose tremendous historical role as the chosen vanguard of the Negro people is only emphasized by the close organic link between the democratic emancipation on the Negro people and the socialist revolution of the proletariat in this country. Under the hegemony of and close alliance with the proletariat, the Negro peasantry and the broad sections of the Negro petty bourgeoisie can play a profoundly revolutionary role. The process of class differentiation among the Negro people lays the basis for the liberation of the Negro masses from the influence of the white bourgeoisie (transmitted through the Negro bourgeoisie) and for the achievement of the hegemony of the pro-letariat in the struggle for Negro emancipation.

28. It is clear that the racial, that is, caste, emancipation of the Negro cannot come as the result of any "purely racial" movement of [sic] any move-ment deliberately aiming to subordinate, in the name of an unreal racial unity the masses of the Negro people to the narrow interests of the Negro bourgeoisie (who work hand in glove with their white paymasters), of any movement conscientiously striving to divorce the liberation struggle of the Negro people from the chief social movement of our times, the class war of labor against capital. The racial emancipation of the American Negro, in the present histor-

ical situation, is possible only as an integral aspect and as inevitable consequence of the revolutionary overthrow of the capitalist system, of the victory of the proletariat.

The Immediate Struggle and the General Perspective

29. It is clear that this far-reaching perspective can today assume vitality and general significance only if it can be shown in life itself to emerge as a natural development of a program of immediate action immediately associated with every phase of Negro life under the caste oppression of American society. The Communist must defend and represent the basic interests of the Negro workers, of the Negro peasants, and of the Negro petty bourgeoisie, to the degree that the latter constitutes a progressive historical force. The Communists must try to weld together the masses of the Negro people (workers, peasants, city petty bourgeoisie) under the leadership of the Negro proletariat and against the white ruling class and its Negro agents (the Negro bourgeoisie). The Communists throw all energies into breaking down all barriers between the Negro and the white workers and into strengthening the bonds between the white workers and the Negro people. The Communist program must champion the abolition of peonage and the serf conditions of the Negro farmers in the South, the organization of leagues of sharecroppers and tenants and unions of farm-laborers. The Communists must stand for the complete equality of the Negro in industry, the smashing of the barriers against the Negro workers in the trade unions, the organization of the unorganized and the unskilled colored workers. The Communists must take up the struggle against lynching, jim-crowism, and discrimination. The Communists demand the complete social and political equality of the Negro race. The Communists strive to break the hold of the capitalist political parties over the Negro masses and to win these masses to the cause of labor, which is their cause as well, and to labor class political action (the labor party as the champion of the oppressed Negroes). Thru the participation of the Negro masses in these struggles (and of Negroes and whites side by side), thru the development of these struggles to ever higher and higher levels, the road will be opened for the realization of the far-reaching perspective of the final emancipation of the Negro people from their submerged caste position as a phase of the general emancipation of the toiling masses from the yoke of capitalism.

Part 2
American Politics

CHAPTER 5

A Critical Analysis of the Tactics and Programs of Minority Groups
1935

Bunche's radicalism peaks in his work in the mid-1930s. In this essay the earlier attacks on black nationalism, economic separatism, black Republicanism, and middle-class black leadership are all reiterated. More important, new critiques of "economic passive resistance" and civil libertarianism that would flower in his work on the Myrdal project are first presented here. Yet, unlike the Myrdal memoranda, in which Bunche criticizes the NAACP and Urban League strategies, here he rejects the entire framework of the "moral dilemma" thesis as likely to lead to "genteel programs of interracial conciliation."

J. S. Mill in his fine treatise *Representative Government* expressed the belief that it is virtually impossible to build up a democracy out of the intermingling of racially differentiated groups of men. It may be that historical experience has indicated the error of Mill's thesis insofar as different "racial" groups among the white peoples of the world are concerned, but there is apparently much evidence to substantiate it when related to the intermixture of white and black populations in the same society. Throughout the world today, wherever whites and blacks are presented in any significant numbers in the same community, democracy becomes the tool of the dominant elements in the white population in their ruthless determination to keep the blacks suppressed. This is true whether the blacks constitute the overwhelming majority of the population, as in South Africa and Algeria, or the minority, as in the United States.

The responsibility, however, rests not with the institution of democracy, per se, nor in the readily accepted belief that black and white simply cannot mix amicably on a common political and economic basis. Recent world history points out too clearly that modern democracy, conceived in the womb of middle-class revolutions, was early put out to work in support of those ruling middle-class interests of capitalist society which fathered it. It has remained their loyal child and has rendered profitable service for them. But when in modern European countries it came to be vigorously wooed by those mass interests of society whose lot under modern industrialism has been that of cruel oppression, democracy was quickly discredited and disowned, and fascism became the favored child of big business–controlled governments. The significant fact is that democracy, while never offered in any large measure to the black populations of the world, has been extended to the great masses of the working-class population only so long as it was employed by them as a harmless device involving no real threat to the increasing control of the society by the ruling classes.

Minority populations, and particularly racial minorities, striving to exist in any theoretically democratic modern society, are compelled to struggle strenuously for even a moderate participation in the democratic game. Minority groups are always with us. They may be national minorities, i.e., distinct ethnic groups with an individual national and cultural character living within a state which is dominated by some other nationality, as in German and Polish Upper Silesia, or they may come under the looser definition of minorities employed by the League of Nations, including any people in any state differing from the majority population in either race, language, or religion, such as the Negro in the United States. But whatever the nature of the minority group, its special problems may always be translated in terms of political, economic, and social disadvantages. Group antagonisms develop, which are fed by mythical beliefs and attitudes of scorn, derision, hate, and discrimination. These serve as effective social barriers and fix the social, and hence the political and economic, status of the minority population. The mental images or verbal characterizations generally accepted as descriptive of the members of the particular racial group—the "pictures in our heads" so aptly discussed by Walter Lippmann—give greatest significance in race relations.[1] These race distinctions, along with similar class and caste distinctions, are so rooted in our social consciousness as to command serious attention in any consideration of programs whose objective is equitable treatment for minority racial groups.

Many are the non-scientific solutions for the problem of black-white race relations that have been pled for far and wide. But these solutions ignore the seemingly basic fact that whenever two groups of peoples in daily contact with each other, and having readily identifiable cultural or racial differentiations, are likewise forced into economic competition, group antagonisms must inevitably prevail.

The Negro as a Minority Group in the U.S.

The Negro group in the United States is characterized by the conditions of easy racial identification and severe economic competition with the dominant white population. In addition, the position of the Negro in this country is conditioned by the historical fact of his ancestral slavery. All of the present-day relations between the disadvantaged Negro group and the majority white group are

influenced by this master-slave heritage and the traditional competition between "poor-white" and Negro masses. The stamp of racial and social inferiority placed upon the Negro, the detached, condescending paternalism of
the "better elements" of the Southern white population, the "missionary" enterprise of Northern philanthropy, the bitter antipathies between black and white
laboring masses, "Uncle Tomism" in both its cruder and more polished modern
forms, and the inferiority complex of the Negro group itself may be directly
traced to these historical roots.

The factors of race and the slavery tradition do not fully explain the
perpetuation of the "race problem," however. Much of what is called prejudice
against the Negro can be explained in economic terms, and in the peculiar
culture of the Southern states, with their large poor-white populations. The
determination of the ruling class of the large land-holders in the South to
perpetuate in law and custom the doctrine of the racial inferiority of the Negro
was made possible only because this numerically preponderant poor-white
population feared the economic competition and the social and political power
of the large black population. The cultural, political, and economic degradation
of the Negro also gave the poor-whites their sole chance for "status."

Intelligent elements in the white Southern population have in recent years
begun to admit that other factors than mere "race" are involved in many of the
abusive practices employed to intimidate the Negro in the South. For example,
Mr. Arthur Raper, in his excellent study *The Tragedy of Lynching* explains that
the bases of the lynching of Negroes in the South reside in the determination of
the white South to exploit the Negro, culturally, politically, and economically.
Such "social pressures," as he calls them, are exemplified, for instance, when a
planter assures the outsider that the propertyless Negroes in his community are
wholly satisfied with their small pay, their one-teacher schools and plantation-
unit churches, and their chronic economic and political dependency. "The
query," writes Raper, "but are they really satisfied?" is answered quickly and
firmly: "Well, if they're not they'd better be!"[2] In other words the large white
land-holding and industrial groups in the South are determined to keep the
Negro in a servile condition and as a profitable and almost indispensable labor
supply. In so doing, black workers have been aligned against white, from
slavery days on, and bitter antagonisms have developed between these groups.
The resulting "racial" situation has not been in any sense disadvantageous to
the employing class, which is not insensitive to the merits of the policy of
divide et impera in labor-employer relationships.

In reality the Negro population in the United States is a minority group
only in the narrowly racial sense. In every other respect it is subject to the same
divisive influences impinging upon the life of every other group in the nation.
Economically, the Negro, in the vast majority, is identified with the peasant
and proletarian classes of the country, which are certainly not in the minority.

Politically, the Negro, until recent years under the spell of the "Lincolnian Legend," was almost completely identified with the Republican Party. He was aligned, therefore, with what constituted with monotonous regularity the majority political group. The Negro thus has been subjected to the same sectional, political, and economic forces which have influenced the white population, with admitted additional aggravation due solely to the race equation.

Negro leadership, however, has traditionally put its stress on the element of race; it has attributed the plight of the Negro to a peculiar racial condition. Leaders and organizations alike have had but one end in view—the elimination of "discrimination against the race." This attitude has been reflected in the tactics which they have employed to correct abuses suffered by their group. They have not realized that so long as this basic conflict in the economic interests of the white and black groups persists, and it is a perfectly natural phenomenon in a modern industrial society, neither prayer, nor logic, nor emotional or legal appeal can make headway against the stereotyped racial attitudes and beliefs of the masses of the dominant population. The significance of this to the programs of the corrective and reform organizations working on behalf of the group should be obvious. The most that such organizations can hope to do is to devote themselves to the correction of the more flagrant specific cases of abuse, which because of their extreme nature may exceed even a prejudiced popular approval; and to a campaign of public enlightenment concerning the merits of the group they represent and the necessity for the establishment of a general community of interest among all groups in the population.

Objectives Sought by Minority Groups

In general, the objectives which minority groups traditionally struggle for are those tenets of social justice embraced by eighteenth-century liberalism, with its democratic creed of liberty, equality, and fraternity. This liberalism purported to guarantee the individual's economic and political freedom. Economic freedom for the individual assumed his right to the protection of the state in the acquisition and use of his property for his private benefit and profit. In fact, however, democratic liberalism did little to create those conditions which would facilitate the acquisition of property by any great numbers of the society. To the contrary, its principles were applied in countries whose economic structures were so ordered that the great masses of the populations were presupposed to be non-property-holding workingmen, whose opportunities for obtaining property became progressively less easy, and whose economic status was increasingly less certain as a result of technological and financial developments within the economic structure—resulting in periodic unemployment, loss of income, and dissipation of meager savings. In the United States the presence of the frontier, with the free land it offered and its rich natural resources, vitalized the American Dream that every energetic and thrifty American could win economic independence. The American frontier, however, was never widely open to the Negro population, and this was one of the factors that forestalled the development of class stratification, and a consciousness of it, in the Negro population to the same degree as found in the white.

Political freedom for the individual assumed his right to equality before the law, the right to freedom of speech, press, religion, assemblage, and movement, and to democratic participation in the government through the unabridged use of the ballot.

Tactics of Minority Groups

On this assumption that members of minority groups, like those of the majority populations in democratic countries, possess certain inalienable rights—political, social, and economic—which they must struggle to preserve, leaders and organizations of minority groups map out programs and techniques of action designed to protect their people. Roughly, and rather arbitrarily, the tactics which such groups ordinarily employ in this struggle can be summarized as follows:

1. Violent
   a) Direct rebellion and secession by force.
   b) Cooperation with other dissentient elements toward immediate or ultimate revolution.
2. Non-Violent
   a) Zionism and Garveyism, involving migration to new and foreign soil.
   b) Economic, including passive resistance (the Gandhi movement) and economic separatism.
   c) Conciliation, including interracial organizations.
   d) Political, including a determined fight for the ballot and justice through laws, lobbying, picketing, mass demonstrations, and the courts.

While each of these methods has been employed at one time or another by some minority group, those listed under the non-violent heading have been the tactics most seriously advocated by American Negro leadership in efforts to free the group from political and economic inequality.

Violent Tactics

Numerically, the American Negro is so overwhelmed by the white population, and in addition the members of the group are so scattered throughout this vast country, that serious consideration need not be afforded the tactic of direct secession and rebellion by force. Likewise, the Negro masses are so lacking in radical class consciousness, they are so conservative and deeply imbued with a peasant psychology and the lingering illusion of the American Dream, that any possibility of large-scale identification of the Negro population with revolutionary groups can be projected only in the future. The Communist Party has seriously proselyted among the Negro group but with only indifferent success. The immediate task of such movements in this country is to develop radical class-consciousness among the working-class masses of both white and Negro populations, with a view to the ultimate recognition of an identity of interest and consequent black and white solidarity in a militant labor movement.

Non-violent Tactics

Racial Separatism. Because of the seeming hopelessness of the fight to win equal rights for many minority racial groups, some of the leadership of such groups has often espoused a "defeatist" philosophy, which takes the form of racial separatism. This defeatism in its most extreme form follows the general design of the Zionist movement. For the American Negro the Garvey program may be characterized as the black counterpart of the Zionist movement. Thousands of American Negroes came to believe that the racial barriers to equality in this country could never be surmounted, and they flocked to the support of the Garvey "back-to-Africa" movement, which flourished after the last war. Like all programs of this character, Garveyism offered the Negro an emotional escape from oppressive conditions. Also like other such programs, it was impractical, for attractive land for such venture was no longer available, due to the consuming greed and the inexorable demands of imperialist nations. The Garvey movement could offer only Liberia to the American Negro—one of the most backward and unhealthy territories of an altogether uninviting West Africa. Moreover, the Liberians themselves did not want the American Negroes.

    Economic Passive Resistance. There are many variations of the non-violent economic tactics, but the most significant are those which advocate economic separatism. Supporters of economic passive resistance usually look to Gandhi for their guidance. They see powerful weapons available to the oppressed group in the employment of the economic boycott and in fearless self-sacrifice. Through such tactics they propose to wring economic and political justice from the dominant group by striking at its most sensitive spot, its markets, and by shaming its Christian conscience. In the first place, the Gandhi movement has not succeeded in India, despite the fact that it was attempted in the one country offering it its greatest possibilities of success. The natives of India are overwhelmingly preponderant in the population and are capable of self-immolation on behalf of a cause to a degree unknown to Western peoples.

Moreover, their country is not industrialized, and their low standard of living is such that it cannot be materially affected by the inevitable reprisals of the controlling groups. Even so, however, the movement could not break down the military and financial buttresses of the relative handful of Englishmen allied with the native ruling interests which control the country.

In a highly industrialized country the possibilities from the employment of this method of resistance are much less. It means, of necessity, that the members of the group in the mass must be willing at the outset to accept an even lower standard of living than that which they already enjoy. But more important still is the fact that it is unlikely that any such movement could long withstand the unyielding and inevitable resistance which would be launched against it by the business rulers of the country. Presumably, in industrial societies this tactic would involve the organization of group cooperatives for the production of industrial and agricultural products. As soon as such a movement assumed threatening proportions, it would be obliged to withstand severe counter-boycotts, which would deprive the members of the group of many necessary commodities which they could not produce themselves. Moreover, they would be denied essential credit and capital. The legal and police forces of the state would inevitably be aligned against them, and, in addition, they would be subjected to the characteristic gangster attacks which have recently proved so helpful to employers in labor disputes.

A mild version of this form of economic passive resistance has been from time to time advocated by Negro leaders in this country as one means of obtaining economic justice under the existing system. Particularly during the Depression has this doctrine gained circulation in the guise of the "don't-buy-where-you-can't-work" movement. The fallacy of this method is obviously discovered in its assumption that it can offer any real relief to the great masses of Negroes. Its outlook is narrowly racial, and it fails to realize that it can create no new jobs but that it can only gain jobs for Negroes by displacement of whites. Since there is already a woefully inadequate number of jobs, whenever a Negro is thus forced into a job in a Negro community a white man is forced out and must seek employment elsewhere. And, since the Negro communities do not offer sufficient economic activity to absorb even the number of Negroes now employed, in white communities this can only mean that Negroes employed are endangered of losing their jobs in proportion to the success of the movement. At best, it could create only a vicious cycle of job displacement. Moreover, the proponents of the doctrine fail to grasp the fact that the Negro is not out of a job simply because he is a Negro but, rather, because the economic system finds itself incapable of affording an adequate number of jobs for all— in fact, its productive system is so organized that it must have a marginal labor supply. But the most serious defect in the rationalization of this tactic is in the fact that it widens still further the already deplorable gap between the white and black working classes of the nation, by boldly placing the competition for jobs on a strictly racial basis. If the doctrine were carried out to its logical conclusion, it would necessarily advocate that Negro workers be organized as a great strike-breaking group.

Economic Separatism. As a result of the highly segregated life which racial minority groups are often compelled to live, there is a strong tendency for the doctrine of economic separatism to take root as a promising palliative for both political and economic oppression. This has been a particularly virulent creed among American Negroes, chiefly due to the impetus given the movement by Booker T. Washington and his successor, Major Moton. Negro businesses are almost entirely the product of segregation and can be characterized as "defensive enterprises." The promise of this hope of constructing an independent and segregated black economy is excellently discussed by Spero and Harris in the following words:

> Yet how such an independent economy is to rise and function when the white world outside controls credit, basic industry, and the state is something which the sponsors of the movement prefer to ignore. If such an economy is to rise it will have to do so with the aid of white philanthropy and will have to live upon white sufferance. If the great white banks and insurance companies decide that they want Negro business it is hard to see how the little black institutions can compete successfully against them. The same holds for the chain stores and various retail establishments. They will be able to undersell their Negro competitors if they want to, and the Negro world will not continue indefinitely to pay higher prices for its goods merely out of pride of race. Basic industry will continue to remain in the hands of the white world, for even the most ardent supporters of an independent black economy will admit that there is no prospect of the Negro capitalists amassing enough wealth to establish steel mills, build railroads and pipe lines, and gain control of essential raw materials.[3]

Political Tactics: Civil Libertarianism. Perhaps the favorite method of struggle for rights employed by minority groups is the political. Through the use of the ballot and the courts strenuous efforts are put forth to gain social justice for the group. Extreme faith is placed in the ability of these instruments of democratic government to free the minority from social proscription and civic inequality. The inherent fallacy of this belief rests in the failure to appreciate the fact that the instruments of the state are merely the reflections of the political and economic ideology of the dominant group, that the political arm of the state cannot be divorced from its prevailing economic structure, whose servant it must inevitably be.

Leaders of the American Negro like Dr. Du Bois, and organizations such as the National Association for the Advancement of Colored People, which he helped to found in 1909, have conducted a militant fight under this illusory banner. They have demanded full equality for the Negro, involving the eradication of all social, legal, and political restrictions tending to draw a line of distinction between the black citizen and the white. The Negro, like the white American, is to quaff the full draught of eighteenth-century democratic liberalism. The Negro individual citizen must have every right boasted by the individual white citizen, including the franchise, freedom of economic opportunity (consisting chiefly of the right to employment without discrimination), the right to accommodations in public places and on common carriers, the right to voluntary choice of his place of residence without involuntary segregation, the right to jury service, and equal expenditures of public funds for education and other public services. In pursuing this struggle, the Negro has been seriously handicapped, because he has never yet been able to win any large measure of participation in the franchise. It is estimated that today at least 90 percent of the adult Negroes in the Southern states are excluded from the suffrage, and it is here that the great masses of the Negro population are concentrated. Consequently, the group leadership has had to lean heavily upon sympathetic white supporters, lobbying, picketing, written and verbal protests, and appeals, mass demonstrations, and the courts.

The confidence of the proponents of the political method of alleviation is based on the protection which they feel is offered all groups in the society by that sacred document the Constitution. Particularly do they swear by the Bill of Rights and its three supplements, the Thirteenth, Fourteenth, and Fifteenth amendments, as a special charter of the black man's liberties. The Constitution is thus detached from the political and economic realities of American life and becomes a sort of protective angel hovering above us and keeping a constant vigil over the rights of all America's children, black and white, rich and poor, employer and employee, and, like impartial justice, blinded to their differences. This view ignores the quite significant fact that the Constitution is a very flexible instrument and that, in the nature of things, it cannot be anything more than the controlling elements in the American society wish it to be. In other words, this charter of the black man's liberties can never be more than our legislatures and, in the final analysis, our courts wish it to be. And what these worthy institutions wish it to be can never be more than what American public opinion wishes it to be. Unfortunately, so much of American public opinion is seldom enlightened, sympathetic, tolerant, or humanitarian. Too often it resembles mob violence.

Interracial Conciliation. It follows, therefore, that the policy of civil libertarianism is circumscribed by the dominant mores of the society. Its success, in the final analysis, must depend upon its ability to create a sympathetic response to its appeals among influential elements in the controlling population. In the long run its militancy must be softened, and the inevitable tendency is for it to conform to the general pattern of the genteel programs of interracial conciliation, which attempt to cultivate the goodwill of the white upper classes. The churches, the young men's and young women's Christian associations, the interracial commissions, and social welfare agencies such as the Urban League, are the leading institutions among the Negro engaged in the dubiously valuable work of developing interracial fellow feeling.

It is not surprising, therefore, that assertedly militant civil-libertarian organizations like the NAACP should employ tactics which are progressively less militant. Such organizations, if they remain constant in their faith, are forced into a policy of conciliation with the enlightened, i.e., the ruling interests, in the dominant group. They must rely upon sympathetic understanding and fair play in their campaigns for social justice, and they can scarcely expect to find these noble traits in the victimized and unenlightened masses. Consequently, the more "liberal" the better elements of the white South become, the less militant these associations can afford to be. They can be militant, but only politely so; they can attack, but not too harshly; they must entreat, bargain, compromise, and capitulate in order to win even petty gains. They must politely play the game according to the rules even though they have no stakes. In other words, they play cricket.

The Courts. Such policies merely reflect the fact, established by the legal and political history of the group, that the Negro in the United States is a special ward of the Supreme Court. The Negro has had countless experiences which sufficiently establish the fact that he has rights only as this august tribunal allows them, and even these are, more often than not, illusory. It is only inadvertently that the courts, like the legislatures, fail to reflect the dominant mass opinion. It must be futile, then, to expect these agencies of government to afford the Negro protection for rights which are denied to him by the popular will. Moreover, even could we optimistically hope that the Supreme Court, in its theoretical legal detachment, would go counter to the proscriptions imposed on the Negro, as it appeared to do in the Scottsboro cases, the condition of the group could not be greatly changed. In the first place, American experience affords too many proofs that laws and decisions contrary to the will of the majority cannot be enforced. In the second place, the Supreme Court can effect no revolutionary changes in the economic order, and yet the status of the Negro, as that of other groups in the society, is fundamentally fixed by the functioning and the demands of that order. The very attitudes of the majority group which fix the Negro in his disadvantaged position are part and parcel of the American economic and political order.

The peculiar position of the Negro as a ward of the judiciary is readily explained by his political history. The Civil War amendments were designed to give him a rather nebulous freedom and to protect him in his fundamental rights. The Thirteenth Amendment guaranteed his physical freedom. The Fourteenth purported to protect his right of life, liberty, and property, i.e., to afford him the full privileges and immunities of citizenship, due process, and equal protection of the laws. The Fifteenth Amendment assured him that he would not be deprived of the suffrage because of his race, color, or previous servitude. These measures were realistic; they recognized that the newly emancipated Negro citizen would be crushed by the Southern states unless special protection were afforded him. They were applied directly as limitations upon the states. But the Negro has never been accepted as a participating, legal member of his Southern state. There is perhaps a measure of government for the Negro in the South, but never of or by him. The Southern states recognize no duty to ensure or extend his legal rights, and the Constitution imposes no such positive responsibility upon them. The state governments, being "democratic" governments, were keenly responsive to the popular will and seriously devoted themselves to the task of preserving the inferior status of the Negro population. The issue is thus clearly drawn for the Negro. Against the subversive laws of the state legislatures and decisions of the state courts he opposes his "Constitutional rights." The burden of proof is always upon him. For the interpretation and realization of these rights he is forced to appeal to the Supreme Court.

Thus the Negro has been compelled to substitute the complicated, arduous, and expensive processes of litigation for the ballot box. What other groups are able to do for themselves, the Negro hopes the judiciary to do for him. There is more than ample evidence in the decisions of the supreme tribunal of the land on questions involving the rights of the Negro to disprove the possibility of any general relief from this quarter.

The fight for the rights of the group before the courts directs itself to such impairments and deprivations of civil liberties as segregation, together with inferior accommodations and instruction in the public schools, unequal apportionment of school funds, segregation and inferior accommodations on common carriers, residential segregation, exclusion form jury service, disfranchisement, and peonage. These evils have all been attacked through litigation but with only indifferent success. In scores of decisions on these questions the highest courts of the land have amply demonstrated their willingness to acquiesce in the prevailing attitudes of the dominant population in respect to the Negro.

The legal theory behind such decisions is that race discrimination is contrary to the Constitution only when it involves inequality in rights or the possession by one race of rights which are denied to another solely because of its race. Race "distinctions," on the other hand, if based on substantial differences, do not constitute discrimination. Such permissible race distinctions in law are usually ascribed to one or more of the following motives: (1) the prevention of race conflicts; (2) the preservation of race purity by the prevention of intermarriage or illicit sex relations; (3) the existence of race peculiarities which demand recognition in special legislation. It is well settled that statutes may be framed to attain any of these objectives which will not be objectionable to the protective clauses of the Fourteenth Amendment.

Thus, since the Fourteenth Amendment is directed only against action by the states, a common carrier may, in the absence of federal legislation, provide for the separation of white and Negro passengers in interstate commerce.[4] Similarly, a restrictive covenant in a deed of conveyance of real estate, by which the grantee covenants that the property described shall never be used or occupied by, or sold, leased, or given to, any Negro, has been held not to contravene the Fourteenth Amendment.[5] Statutes requiring separate public schools for white and Negro children have long been sustained by the courts, as was a statute of the state prohibiting the teaching of the two races in the same private school.[6] Likewise, a state is upheld in requiring Chinese pupils to attend the schools provided for Negro pupils.[7] Pursuing its racial theories to extreme, the Court has admitted that fornication, when committed by persons of different races, may be punished more severely by the state than when committed by persons of the same race.[8]

The ability of the courts to hand down what appear to be legally sound opinions and still permit popular abuses of the Negro's rights to persist is largely due to the adroitness of the white legislators in the art of drawing up and administering their laws. These abuses generally occur under the protection of laws which are "fair in their face," and unless the court is disposed to look behind the face of the law to its administration the Negro can receive no relief. This is admirably illustrated by a comparison of the court's attitude in the case of *Yick Wo* v. *Hopkins*[9] and *Plessy* v. *Ferguson.*[10] In the Yick Wo case, involving the discriminatory administration of law to the disadvantage of Chinese, the court, in deciding the case in favor of the appellants, said:

> Though the law itself be fair on its face and impartial in appearance, yet, if it is applied and administered by public authority with an evil eye and an unequal hand, so as practically to make unjust and illegal discriminations between persons in similar circumstances, material to their rights, the denial of equal justice is still within the prohibition of the Constitution.

Ten years later, however, in *Plessy* v. *Ferguson,* involving an attack by a Negro on a "separate-but-equal-accommodations" provision for common carriers in the law of the State of Louisiana, the court accepted the act at its face value and refused to admit the contention of violation of constitutional rights advanced by the plaintiff. The court, in fact, endorsed the provision, saying,

> . . . the case reduces itself to the question of whether the statute of Louisiana is a reasonable regulation, and with respect to this there must neces-

sarily be a large discretion on the part of the legislature. In determining the question of reasonableness it is at liberty to act with reference to the established usages, customs and traditions of the people, and with a view to the promotion of their comfort, and the preservation of the public peace and good order.

Perhaps no better example of the tendency of the Supreme Court to detach itself from political reality when questions involving Negro rights are concerned and to resort to legal fictions can be afforded than the opinion of Justice Roberts in the recent Texas primary case.[11] It is seemingly of no concern to the court in this unanimous decision that a party performs a vital political function, that the Democratic primary in Texas is in fact the only significant election, and that exclusion from the primary robs the Negro of his franchise. The Court could only see that the prohibitions of the Constitution are prohibitions against the actions of the state and that a political party is a private, voluntary association, presumable something akin to the Elks. It is significant to note that Chief Justice Hughes, in handing down an opinion in one of the celebrated Gold Clause cases, *Perry* v. *U.S.,*[12] while solemnly discussing the obligation of the government to keep faith with its contracts, said: ". . . the contractual obligation still exists and, despite infirmities of procedure, remains binding upon the *conscience of the sovereign.*"[13] But Justice Roberts, in meeting the argument that if Negroes are refused admission to the Democratic primary in Texas they are in fact altogether deprived of the suffrage, this sacred right of democratic government, failed to recognize that the sovereign had any conscience at all and sought refuge in the dialectical stratosphere by admonishing that:

So to say is to confuse the privilege of membership in a party with the right to vote for one who is to hold a public office. With the former the state need have no concern, with the latter it is bound to concern itself, for the general election is a function of the state government and discrimination by a state as respects participation by Negroes on account of their race or color is prohibited by the federal constitution.

Thus, although the Democratic primary actually takes the place of the general election in Texas (as in most other states below the Mason and Dixon Line), Mr. Roberts assures us that justice is served, since the Negro may still go through the useless exercise of casting a shadow vote at the general election. The decision is especially ironical in view of the fact that the court invoked the Fourteenth Amendment—the most important section of the Negro's charter of liberty—as the sanction for thus denying him the franchise.

The recent discouraging decision of the Supreme Court in the Herndon case gives eloquent testimony to the ability of the Court to avoid delicate issues by hiding behind legal technicalities.

Such economic political tactics, while winning a minor and too often illusory victory now and then, are essentially inefficacious in the long run. They lead up blind alleys and are chiefly programs of escape. No minority group should relent in the most determined fight for its rights, but its leadership should recognize the limitations of opportunistic and socially blind policies. The only realistic program for any minority group in modern America is one which is based upon an intelligent analysis of the problems of the group in terms of the broad social forces which determine its condition. Certainly no program of opportunism and no amount of idealism can overcome or control these forces. The only hope for the improvement in the condition of the masses of any American minority group is the hope that can be held out for the betterment of the masses of the dominant group. Their basic interests are identical and so must be their programs and tactics.

CHAPTER 6

A Critique of New Deal Social Planning as It Affects Negroes
1936

This attack on the early New Deal is one of the best critical analyses of the negative impact of New Deal programs on blacks. Its seamless blending of political theory and economic reality highlights the fundamental predicament of the New Deal: How do you introduce intelligent and scientific social planning in a capitalist state? Bunche's response is that a form of American state capitalism is created that follows the classic pattern of middle-class planning by compromise with big business—a policy fatal to the interests of labor. In addition, he argues that it is also fatal to the interests of blacks, who represent both surplus workers and surplus farmers.

New Deal "Equilibrium"

The New Deal, at its inception, confronting an economy of chaos, proclaimed its major purpose to be the application of planning to our entire social structure. In pursuance of this objective a whole series of complicated and contradictory mechanisms have been invented and set up with the purpose of effecting a regulated orderliness in the economic life of the nation. But after two years of frantic trial and error, the New Deal, and most of its elaborate machinery, remains suspended in mid-air, bewildered, and innocuous. Relief expenditures have continued to rise, and unemployment was greater at the end of the year 1934 than it was in December 1933. Even the staunchest supporters of the New Deal, though still weakly professing optimism, are often compelled to admit that its ideology is illogical, inconsistent, vague, and confused; that its program is composed of a mass of self-contradictory experimentation, and that, in its unblushing role of political coquette, it turns now to the left, now to the right.

The explanations of the New Deal and of its apparent failure are not far to seek. The New Deal merely represents our domestic phase of the almost universal attempt in capitalistic countries to establish a new equilibrium in the social structure, an attempt made necessary by the fact that the collapse of the economic structures under the world-wide Depression brought out, in bold relief, the sharp class antagonisms which the developing capitalistic economies had nurtured. The history of the operation of social forces in the Western world since the World War is sharply outlined in at least two particulars: (1) capitalists, i.e., Big Owners, have clearly indicated their inability and unwillingness to afford any leadership in the society which would promise even a meager measure of social justice to the masses of population, though the productive and organizational genius of capitalism is unchallenged; (2) on the other hand, the working classes of the countries of Western Europe, Russia excepted, though winning their way to a position of real power in the state, completely failed to take over the controls of the state, either through political channels or by force. The result has been a significant upsurge of the middle classes of the Western world, whose claim to national leadership is predicated on their assumed ability to reconcile these conflicting class interests in the society through the establishment of a new equilibrium—a new society, in fact, in which conflicting group interests and inequalities will be merged in a higher national purpose.

Unwittingly or not, President Roosevelt was responsive to these social forces when he sounded the key note of the New Deal in his radio address of May 7, 1933.

> It is wholly wrong to call the measures that we have taken government control of farming, control of industry, and control of transportation. It is rather a partnership in profits, for profits would still go the citizens, but rather a partnership to see that the plans are carried out.

The New Deal which was then visited upon us embraced no significant shift of ideas, traditions, or loyalties. In large degree it represented merely an effort to refurbish the old individualistic-capitalistic system and to entrust it again with the economic destinies and welfare of the American people. It recognized, of course, that the American economy had slowed down, and particularly that the forces within it were no longer in equilibrium—a rude awakening for our traditional class-consciousless society. The intellectual pilots of the New Deal would remedy this condition, though certainly not by revolution, nor even by fascist counter revolution (not immediately, at any rate); but in the words of one author: "abhorring the thought of violence and having no conscious class interests of their own, [they] have refused to agree that the mechanism has run down. They will wind it up again and, having done that, will suspend in balance and for all time the existing class relations in American society."[1]

The Tenets of the New Deal

Certain postulates have been laid down as fundamental in the New Deal program. The private ownership of the means of production is to continue, but, on the one hand, capitalism must be stopped from exploiting the producers of its raw materials and, on the other, its labor supply. Agriculture, despite its over-capitalized plant and its reluctant but almost complete restriction to the domestic market, is to be permitted a large enough return to allow for the meeting of fixed charges and the purchase of capital and consumers goods. Wage-earners, although it is admitted that in a machine economy there are too many of them in the white-collar and laboring categories, are to be assured employment and at least the means of subsistence, with a large hope thrown in for incomes conducive to a decent standard of living.

Our own rather short experience with middle-class planning, not to mention the clearer and even more disastrous experiences of Italy, Germany, and Austria with similar schemes, permits us to raise a serious question concerning the ability of the middle classes to construct a new equilibrium which will afford a proper consideration of the masses of the population. The weakness of the middle classes is precisely that they are "in the middle," i.e., they hold an intermediate position between the working masses and the finance capitalists. Included in their ranks are many whose economic status is continually precarious and who are weak, uncourageous, and unskilled. In the U.S. today they are largely petty bourgeois. There are many who would incline sympathetically toward the cause of the proletariat, but there are many others whose aspirations ally them ideologically with big business, thus adding greater confusion to the American scene.

Yet this rather ambiguous middle class—opportunistic and ambitious, lacking class cohesion and ideology—whose members have been completely captivated by the lure of the American Dream, has but two alternatives in the present situation. The middle class itself must take over and operate industry, or it must allow private industry to retain its tenacious grip on the economic structure of the nation. But the middle-class leadership is well aware of the violent nature of the struggle that would be necessary in any attempt to wrest industry out of the hands of big ownership. Consequently, the tendency is to take the easier path and to employ the power of the state to keep the masses in check while handling the industrialists with velvet gloves. That is merely another way of saying that the working masses become ever more dependent upon the intervention of the state in their struggle to obtain social justice from the owners and directors of industry. But, coincidentally, the alliance between the middle-class political power and the economic power of big business becomes more unholy. Italy and Nazi Germany afford classic illustrations of the sort of "balance" the working masses can expect from such a process.

The dilemma of the New Deal, then, merely reflects the basic dilemma of capitalism. Either capitalism must surrender itself to intelligent and scientific social planning (and this it cannot do, for such planning involves a single ownership of the means of production for use rather than for profit), or else it must blunder on, repeating the errors and perpetuating the rigidities which inevitably lead a poorly planned industrial society into periodic depression.

The measures of intervention employed by the New Deal have really been measures of state capitalism which have already been employed by social democratic and fascist governments in Europe, and which obviously have not restored prosperity there, nor settled any of the fundamental conflicts within the modern capitalistic state.

Class lines are more sharply drawn, but state capitalism attempts to balance these class interests within the limits of middle-class democracy. The NRA [National Recovery Administration], for example, began with sympathetic gestures toward labor, if section 7a can be so considered. But it soon became a means of preventing and settling strikes, usually to the disadvantage of labor, as witnessed by the defeat of labor in the settlements of the automobile, San Francisco, textile, and other strikes.

American state capitalism has no choice but this, for it proposes to salvage the old order. It retains formal democracy and may make minor concessions to labor. The government intervenes to aid industry, to limit input. But this is not the planned economy of socialism, where all phases of economic activity are placed under planful regulation and control, because here class interests remain in bitter conflict and big ownership retains its economic power. It is not without great significance to the subject of middle-class planning under capitalism that Secretary Wallace, in his book *New Frontiers,* readily acknowledges, with amazing frankness for one in his position, the enormous influence wielded over the New Deal administration and legislation by the paid lobbies of powerful industrial interests. He clearly suggests that several of the important features of the New Deal represent, not the mature wishes and policies of the Roosevelt administration, but the demands of self-seeking pressure groups, whose demands were too insistent and vigorous to be withstood. The NRA and its codes, he confesses, were not the brain-children of the brain-trusters, but were the products of a swarm of hard-headed businessmen intent on group price-fixing, who swooped down on Washington and its New Dealers. In America, then, the New Deal follows the classical pattern of middle-class planning by compromise with Big Business—a policy fatal to the interests of labor.

The New Deal and the Negro

For the Negro population, the New Deal means the same thing, but more of it. Striking at no fundamental social conditions, the New Deal at best can only fix the disadvantages, the differentials, the discriminations, under which the Negro population has labored all along. The traditional racial stereotypes—which have been inherited from the master-slave tradition and which have been employed by the ruling class of large land-holders in the South and industrialists in the North to give effective expression to their determination to keep the Negro in a servile condition and as a profitable labor supply—remain, and are indeed, often heightened by the New Deal.

Intelligent analysis and the dictates of a purely selfish policy of promoting the profit motive should have made clear the NRA that the competitive exploitation of any significant part of the population, such as the Negro, would frustrate its efforts toward recovery. The poverty of the Negro is an ever-present obstacle to the prosperity of the dominant population. Therefore the first efforts of the NRA should have been directed toward assuring Negro workers that real wage which would make possible for them a decent standard of living.

Negro Wage Earners

To the contrary, however, from the beginning, relatively few Negro workers were even theoretically affected by the labor provisions of NRA. The evils of part-time work, irregular work, and occupational and wage differentials, suffered especially by the great mass of Negro workers in the South, were perpetuated under NRA. Through the codes, occupational and geographical differentials were early used as a means of excluding Negro workers from the benefits of minimum wage and hour provisions. Subsequently, the continuation of the inferior economic status of the Negro was assured by the NRA through code provisions basing wage rates on the habitual wage differential existing between Negro and white workers. Such measures failing to keep Negro wages at the desired low level, there was still the device of securing a specific exemption from the code of the Negro wage-earners in any given plant. In the power laundry code approved by the president, in an industry employing nearly 30,000 Negro women, a 14 cent per hour minimum wage was established, and even this miserable level was not enforced. Dr. Peck,[2] executive director of the Labor Advisory Board, who has maintained staunchly that the NRA has benefited Negro workers, in that the "rates in codes have greatly narrowed the differentials which existed before codes," admits, however, that in the service industries in which so many Negroes are employed, "habit, standard of living, cost of living and the level of income of the local population may have a long-time result in a continuance of differential wages." To make still more illusory the theoretical benefits of the NRA to Negro wage-earners, the compliance machinery has been so constructed and operated as virtually to deny any just treatment to the Negro workman, especially in the South.

The FERA [Federal Emergency Relief Administration] relief figures portray graphically enough the effect of NRA upon the Negro. In October 1933, approximately 2,117,000 Negroes were in families registered on relief rolls, or about 18 percent of the total Negro population in 1930. In January 1935, about 3,500,000 Negroes in families on relief were reported, approximately 29 percent of the 1930 population. Most significantly, too, the proportion of Negroes on relief in relation to total population was greater in rural than in urban centers. In addition, it is reliably estimated that there are now some 1,000,000 male Negroes unemployed, exclusive of agricultural pursuits.

The dilemma of American agriculture is the dilemma of the American economy. There are too many farmers and too much land in cultivation, just as there are too many industrial workers and too much industrial production. These surpluses exist because American agriculture and industry have developed too much efficiency for our profit-motivated economic system. The welfare of the Negro farmer is bound up in the government's solution to the basic dilemma of capitalism—the necessity of providing a decent standard of living, based on a much higher consumption level, for all of the surplus workers and farmers, while retaining an economic order which is founded on profit and not on use. The New Deal, in its agricultural program expressed through the AAA, grabbed vigorously at one horn of the dilemma, and the Negro farmer and farm-worker have been left dangling precariously from the other. It goes without saying that the Negro tenant farmer has borne more than his share of this burden. The AAA bears the responsibility for other methods of fixing the Negro population as a poverty-stricken group. It has winked at widespread violations of the rights of tenant farmers under the crop-reduction contracts; though the acreage reductions under the government rental agreements dispensed with the need of a great number of the tenants, the government contract theoretically proscribed the reduction of tenants by the land owner. The AAA has blandly permitted the white owner to employ the traditional methods of intimidation of the Negro to deprive him of his benefits from the crop-reduction program in payment of parity checks.

The apparent failure of the government's pay-as-you-not-grow agricultural program, the growing conviction that the European market for our agricultural products is gone for good, together with the ever-present worry of too many farmers and too much land—we could probably get along with about one-half the number of the land now used through the application of efficiency and technical advances to the industry. It is these conditions which have compelled the administration in desperation to flirt with the essentially fantastic "planning" scheme of subsistence homesteads. This scheme proposed to move the inefficient farmers, who thereby are doomed, out of their present economic graveyards and transplant them to semi-rural villages, where they will establish "model" communities. Living on plots ranging from 5 to 40 acres, they will continue to till the soil, but only for family consumption, and are supposed to undergo a sort of economic atavism by reviving the fine old peasant pastimes of pottery making, woodwork, spinning, weaving, etc. To keep life from becoming too monotonous, as it most certainly would under such positive economic security, the government will provide some "factory" seeds for them to plant in the early spring. After the transplanted farmers get through fiddling around their garden plots, and have indulged in a bit of handicraft, they will thus have the chance to pick up a bit of pin money for automobiles, radios, and electric refrigerators, by working in the factories. In this way the submarginal farmer is to be kept on the land and so prevented from swelling the steadily mounting ranks of the industrial unemployed, and likewise kept out of competitive production. In other words the subsistence homesteader will be lifted out of the mainstream of our economic life and laid up on an economic shelf to dry (rot).

The real catch to the scheme is of course in the fact that the bill for the construction, the equipment, repair, taxation, and provision of social services for these communities of "official" peasants will be footed chiefly by the employed industrial wage-earners and the producing commercial farmers, not to mention the serious consequences for a capitalism which thrives on markets and profits, resulting from the consequential contraction of its domestic market for both consumer's and capital goods. This policy Mr. Webster Powell and Mr. Harold M. Ware aptly call "planning for permanent poverty."

Insofar as the program has applied to Negroes it has followed the traditional patterns of racial discrimination and segregation, two Jim Crow projects for Negroes having been recently established.

Primarily, the New Deal is a great relief program which guarantees at level best only a precarious livelihood of the most meager essentials for the millions of distressed workers and farmers who are on the outside of our economic life looking in. Middle-class New Deal planning has adequately demonstrated an utter inability to attain its necessary objectives of lower prices, greater output, and elimination of unemployment in industry. The New Deal policy of planning by separate private industries inevitably tends to raise prices and restrict output—that is to say, it tends to perpetuate an economy of scarcity. Whether consciously or not, it has placed agricultural scarcity in competition with industrial scarcity, and the resultant increases in the prices of both agricultural and manufactured products have deepened the economic depression in which both agriculture and industry had sunk. It has shown only confusion when faced with the problem of administering prices and production in the interest of the whole population.

In the nature of the case it could at best do but little for the Negro within the existing social structure. The Negro does not even boast a significant middle class which, at least, might share some of the gains made for that class by the New Deal. For the Negro middle class exists, in the main, only psychologically, and can be briefly defined as "a hope, a wish and caricature." In fact, the New Deal planning only serves to crystallize those abuses and oppressions which the exploited Negro citizenry of America have long suffered under laissez-faire capitalism, and for the same reasons as in the past.

CHAPTER 7

The Problems of Organizations Devoted to the Improvement of the Status of the American Negro 1939

By late 1938 Bunche was working with Gunnar Myrdal on the study that would become An American Dilemma. *As one of the six top staff and the principal black staff member, Bunche contributed over 3,000 pages of manuscript to the study. This article published in the* Journal of Negro Education *summarizes approximately 800 pages of the memorandum Bunche wrote for Myrdal. Starting with a critique of the Booker T. Washington-W. E. B. Du Bois debate at the turn-of-the-century, in which he says both were never very far apart in that they confined their thinking "within the periphery of race," Bunche analyzes all of the major organizations active in the black community during the first third of the century. Negro business advocates, the Negro church, and the NAACP receive some of the harshest criticism (Bunche later served on the NAACP Board of Directors). Of particular note is his examination of the National Negro Congress (NNC), an organization he helped found with John P. Davis in 1935. He suggests that the Congress would be more effective with greater labor representation and less participation from preachers and Negro business. The article concludes with a 13-step guide to more progressive policies for Negro organizations and leadership.*

Minority groups, such as the American Negro, inevitably tend to become introverted in their social thinking. Attention of the group is so firmly riveted on the struggle to attain release from suppression that its social perspective becomes warped. The group discovers early that the barriers between it and the status of the dominant majority are sturdy and formidable. Progress is insufferably slow, and the necessity for constant battering against the solid walls of majority prejudice and domination—a social heritage of each succeeding minority generation—gives rise to a psychological fixation in the minority population.

The problems of the group come to be analyzed in progressively narrow terms. Thinking, feeling, life itself, revolve about the narrow axis of "minority status." All agitation and protest, all programs and tactics, operate within this circumscribed framework.

If the assumed basis of minority group status is race rather than culture, as in the case of the American Negro, race ineluctably tends to become the overwhelmingly dominant factor in the social equation devised by the group to interpret its problem. Thus, with the Negro, racial interpretations are generally considered the only "realistic" ones. Events that cannot be explained on the color chart are relegated to categories of inconsequence to the Negro. The Negro is an American citizen, but his thinking is often more Negro than American. The white American may look with subjective interest upon Munich, but the American Negro regards the latest lynching as infinitely more important to him. The white American may recoil with horror at the German barbarisms against the Jew. But the American Negro cries, "Hitler be damned, and the Jew too; what about the Jim Crow here?" The Negro may evidence some momentary excitation about Italy's rape of Ethiopia, but the dismemberment of Czecho-Slovakia [*sic*] is the white man's business.

It is precisely the minority group organizations and their leadership which portray minority chauvinism in boldest relief. Organizations and leaders seek only escape for their group. They flounder about, desperately and often blindly, in their ghettoes of thought, seeking a break in the dams of oppression through which they may lead their flock to a more dignified and secure existence. The tiniest crevice in the barriers is magnified into a brilliant ray of hope. So great is the desperation that daily disillusionments are angrily shaken off; they pound away at impregnable walls, dash triumphantly down blind alleys, yet dare not stop to calculate lest it is learned that ultimate escape is generations, even centuries, removed.

American Negro organizations and leaders run true to minority type. Color is their phobia, race their creed. The Negro has problems, and they are all racial ones; ergo, their solution must be in terms of race. In general, whites must be regarded with suspicion, if not as enemies. White allies are recruited, it is true, but only from those who think of Negro problems as Negroes think of them. There is little appetite for social theories and limited ability to digest social forces. There is but one social force for the Negro, and that is color. As long as the Negro is black and the white man harbors prejudice, what has the Negro to do with class or caste, with capitalism, imperialism, fascism, communism, or any other "ism"? Race is the black man's burden.

Generally speaking, it may be stated that the weakness of organizations devoted to the salvation of the Negro is implicit in their structure and philosophy. In the course of the Negro's post-Emancipation history, numerous organizations, black, white, and mixed, have directed their efforts toward lifting him out of the muck of subjection. These organizations, in varying degree and with minor exceptions, have had the following fundamental characteristics:

1. adherence to policies of escape, based upon racialism and nationalism;
2. lack of mass support among Negroes, and mass appeal;
3. dependence upon white benefactors for finance;
4. reluctance to encourage the development of working-class psychology among Negroes and avoidance of class interpretations;
5. tendency, directly or indirectly, to take their main ideological cues from white sympathizers;
6. lack of a coherent, constructive program;
7. lack of broad social perspective and the ability to relate problems of the Negro to the main social currents and forces of the American society; and
8. pursuit of policies of immediate relief and petty opportunism.

The two principal historical schools of Negro thought had as their ideological leaders Booker T. Washington and W. E. B. Du Bois. Washington, who founded Tuskegee Institute in 1881, was the great exponent of what has come to be known as the policy of conciliation.[1] In this policy of appeasement Negroes were advised to cast down their buckets where they were; to avoid conflict with the white man; to accept racial separation and its implication of inferiority as inescapable; to rely upon the good-will of the white upper classes; to work hard, develop thrifty habits, and strive for economic independence. Washington discouraged the Negro worker from the identification of his interests and organized efforts with the white working class, whose objectives he mistrusted. That he should advocate the dignity of labor but not the importance of its organized unity in an industrial society did not appear inconsistent to him. In short, his was a policy of cautious expediency, designed to win the approbation of Southern whites and Northern philanthropists. This was a very racial sort of "realism," and its immediate objectives were realized. It has left an indelible impression on the South and landmarks in the form of industrial schools for Negroes. But the great problems of Negro-white relationships remain unaffected.

Du Bois early began a vigorous assault on the teachings of Booker T. Washington.[2] He instituted an insistent campaign for full social and political equality for the Negro. Where Washington advised the Negro to eschew politics, Du Bois made the attainment of the franchise a cardinal objective in his program of Negro betterment. Du Bois went back beyond Washington to Frederick Douglass in thus exalting the indispensable virtue of the ballot.

Though Washington and Du Bois differed sharply on the issue of political and social equality for the Negro, and industrial versus cultural education, they were never very far apart in their basic philosophies. Both confined their thinking within the periphery of race. Though Du Bois emphasized the helplessness of a disfranchised working class, the direction of his effort was toward

Negro enfranchisement rather than toward working-class unity. In recent years he has expressed strongly the view that union between white and black workers is a futile hope and has advocated the full exploitation of Negro segregation as a means of increasing group strength, especially in economic matters. Both Washington and Du Bois strove for: (1) improved living conditions for Negro city-dwellers; (2) greatly increased educational facilities; (3) equality of economic opportunity; (4) equal justice in the courts; (5) emphasis on racial consciousness and dignity.

Two of the more important Negro betterment organizations sprung up under the aegis of these two influential Negro leaders: the National Negro Business League, established by Washington in 1900, and the National Association for the Advancement of Colored People, which Du Bois helped to form in 1910. Du Bois had organized the Niagara Movement in 1905, which protested against racial discrimination in all of its forms.

In the decade prior to Emancipation, Martin Delaney and McCune Smith had advocated the principles of thrift, industry, and exploitation of economic separatism as a means of economic escape for free black men. Some 50 years later Washington made these principles foundation stones for his National Negro Business League. In terms of its influence on economic betterment of the Negro the National Business League has been inconsequential. As a factor in shaping the psychology and thinking of Negroes, however, it has been vastly important, especially in the period following the migrations under the leadership of Dr. Washington's successor, Major Robert R. Molton. It has fed the Negro on the traditional American illusion that even the man or group in the very lowest rung of the economic ladder can, by industry, thrift, efficiency, and perseverance, attain the top rung. It has pursued the narrowest type of racial chauvinism, for it has organized not business, but "Negro" business, and has employed the racial situation as its main stock in trade in bidding for the support of Negro patronage. The League is the ideological parent to the traditionally reactionary philosophy of Negro business advocates. This is cogently stated in the resolution formulated by the Business section of the first meeting of the National Negro Congress in Chicago, in February 1936:

> The development of sound and thriving Negro business is most indispensable to the general elevation of the Negro's social and economic security . . . all Negroes consider it their inescapable duty to support Negro business by their patronage.[3]

This hope for the salvation of the Negro masses by the erection of black business within the walls of white capitalism is clearly futile. It is obvious that the advocates of the Negro business attempt to labor a policy of "expediency" through exploitation of the segregation incident to the racial dualism of America. Negro business suckles at the breast of the poverty-stricken Negro ghettos and is inevitably undernourished. And must remain so. It exists only on the sufferance of that dominant white business world which controls credit, basic industry, and the state. The appeal which Negro business makes for the support of Negroes is a racial one, viz.: that the race can advance only through economic unity. Yet the small, individually owned Negro businesses cannot meet the price competition of the large-capitalized, more efficient white businesses. The very poverty of the Negro consumer dictates that he must buy where he can find cheapest prices. Negroes in the United States spend approximately $4,150,000,000 per year for the three essential items of food, clothing, and shoes,[4] but only some $83,000,000 of this sum is spent with Negro retailers.

In 1929 the National Negro Business League organized the Colored Merchants' Association (CMA) stores. These were individually owned stores which attempted to reduce overhead by cooperative buying and group advertising, and by consequent lower prices to attract Negro trade. The membership fees were modest, but only a few Negro businesses were attracted to the scheme. The Negro consuming public did not take to the untested brands sold by the CMA stores, preferring the nationally advertised standard brands offered by the white chain stores. In 1934, in the midst of the Depression, the CMA experiment met a quiet demise.

At best, Negro business becomes a parasitical growth on the Negro society. It must eke out a meager existence from the segregated Negro community, as a middleman between large white business and the Negro market, through exploitation of the "race problem." Negro business, recognizing its inability to compete with white business on equal terms, demands for itself special privilege and marches under the chauvinistic banner of "race loyalty," thus further exploiting an already sorely harrassed group. It represents the interests only of the pitifully small Negro middle-class group, though receiving support for its ideology from the race-conscious masses.

The development of Negro capitalism in America, even granting its possibility, would offer no hope for the betterment of the Negro masses. There is no evidence that the 12,561 employees of the Negro retail stores[5] reported in 1937 worked under better conditions for their Negro employers than did Negroes working for white employers. There is no reason to believe that the Negro employer is any less profit-minded than the white, or that he is any less reluctant to exploit his fellow blacks as employees than any other employer. The Negro population is a working-class population. Negro business may offer an uncertain escape from economic oppression for a handful of the more able or more fortunate members of the group. But the overwhelming majority of Negroes in America will continue to till the soil and toil in the industries of the white employer.[6]

A logical corollary of the Negro business philosophy has recently come to the fore in the guise of the don't "buy where you can't work" or "buy where you can work" credo. This movement began about 1931 in Chicago and rapidly spread to the East. It has been sponsored by organizations such as the League for Fair Play, the Afro-American Federation of Labor, and the New Negro Alliance. These organizations occasionally have employed the labor weapons of boycott and picketing against white stores in Negro districts which refuse to employ Negro white-collar workers. This has been of educational value to the Negro in that it has given him some inkling of his latent economic power and an acquaintance with the recognized weapons of labor. The most violent manifestation of this movement was in the Harlem riot of 1935, when thousands of Harlem Negroes vented their fury, born of poverty, against the small white shop-owners on Lennox and Seventh Avenues.

The philosophy of this movement is narrowly racial. If successful, it could only result in a vicious cycle of job displacement, since it creates no new jobs but only struggles to displace white workers, and since Negro communities do not offer sufficient economic activity to absorb even a small number of the Negroes now employed in white industries. Its appeal has been primarily in the interest of the Negro white-collar worker, and its support has come chiefly from Negro middle-class professional and intellectual groups. It appears unable to realize that there is an economic system as well as a race problem in America and that, when a Negro is unemployed, it is not just because he is a Negro but, more seriously, because of the defective operation of the economy under which we live—an economy that finds it impossible to provide an adequate number of jobs and economic security for the population. More seriously still, this movement tends to widen the menacing gap between white and black workers, by insisting that jobs be distributed on a racial basis. It is a philosophy which, like that of Negro business, offers only racialism, with no significant hope for the mass Negro population.

In 1910 the National League on Urban Conditions among Negroes was founded, as a social-service agency devoted to the task of aiding rural Negroes in their adjustment to urban life and securing positions for them in industry. The work of this organization, subsequently named the National Urban League, assumed increasing importance with the great migration of Negroes to Northern cities after 1916. The chief financial support of the Urban League is from white philanthropy. Its headquarters are in New York, and it has some 40 local offices in the large industrial centers. Negroes hold all responsible executive offices, but the local directing boards are interracial. Its slogan is "not alms but opportunity," i.e., economic opportunity.

This organization advocates a policy of racial expediency and conciliation, which is characterized by extreme opportunism. It tries to make the most out of the condition of racial separatism and appeals to the conscience and good-will of the white community, especially the employing class. It maintains

an industrial department, which attempts to place city Negroes in white industry. It runs "Negro-in-industry-weeks"; it sends its secretaries to white employers in an effort to sell them the idea of employing more Negroes; some of
the local offices run employment bureaus and send welfare agents into the
plants to aid in the adjustment of Negro employees. Feeble attempts have been
made toward lifting trade-union bars against Negro workers, but there has been
no real effort to advance the doctrine of solidarity between white and black
workers. In fact there have been instances in which Urban League locals have
encouraged scabbing and strike-breaking by Negro workers.[7]

That the Urban League has rendered valuable services for urban Negro
populations throughout the country can scarcely be disputed. But it is equally
true that its policy operates within the genteel framework of conciliation and
interracial good-will. Moreover its efforts have been directed at winning the
sympathies of white employers, professional and intellectual groups, and the
top ranks of the hierarchy of organized labor.

There is no single element of economic realism in this policy. It barters
away the economic future of the Negro worker for an immediate but transitory
"gain" in the form of a temporary job. It is severely race-conscious but socially
blind. It encourages the development of a racial caste within the American
working class, and it lacks the independence and courage necessary to give
honest direction to the Negro working population.

The programs of organizations like the YMCA, the YWCA, the interracial groups, such as the Atlanta Interracial Commission and the Department
of Race Relations of the Federal Council of the Churches of Christ in America,
are similarly committed to the rather dubious task of developing interracial
fellow feeling. Their appeal is to the enlightened groups in the dominant
population. They divorce race and economics. They operate on the assumption
that, when the two races know and understand each other better, the principal
incidents of the race problem will disappear. They almost invariably shy away
from the harsher aspects of the problem, such as the Negro's relation to organized labor and, therefore, even when sincere, tend to confuse and obscure the
vital issues. They are exclusively middle class and have but slight contact with
the working masses of either race. For these they offer no effective program.

The most extreme example of black chauvinism is found in Marcus
Garvey's UNIA.[8] Garvey came to the United States from Jamaica in 1916 and
began the gospel of a return to Africa and international pan-Africanism. His
movement developed into a sort of black Zionism. But in its immediate objectives and its influence on the thought of American Negroes, it conformed to the
typical pattern of Negro betterment organizations. It was intensely nationalistic; it sought to arouse race consciousness and pride among Negroes. It boasted
a realism of sorts, in that it adopted a fatalistic attitude toward the Negro dream
of attaining equality in a white man's country. Garveyism was opposed to the

policy unity of black and white labor regarding all white labor unions with suspicion and counseling the Negro worker to ally himself with the white employer until such time as the Negro could become economically independent and his own employer.

The movement received amazing support from Negro masses of both North and South. No other organization has ever been able to reach and stir the masses of Negroes to the same degree, or to receive from them such generous financial support.

Garveyism collapsed when its leader was convicted of fraud. It had made but feeble gestures toward Africa, but it did afford a psychological escape for black masses. It provided an emotional release, through its highly charged "race" meetings, its fiery, race-conscious orators, its emphasis on pride in things black, its elaborate parades, ceremonials, brilliant uniforms, and the pomp and circumstance of its meetings. When the curtain dropped on the Garvey theatricals, the black man of America was exactly where Garvey had found him, though a little bit sadder, if not wiser.

Dr. Du Bois had organized the Niagara Movement in 1905, as a broadside of protest against racial discrimination of every kind. This beginning sounded the tocsin of Negro civil libertarianism, and it was designed as a militant departure from the Booker T. Washington philosophy. Out of the Niagara Movement there emerged, in 1910, in New York City, the National Association for the Advancement of Colored People, with a bold program of complete political and cultural assimilation.

The NAACP accepted struggle on the political front as the most promised means of attaining equality for Negroes. Through the use of the ballot and the courts strenuous efforts were exerted to gain social justice for the group. Full faith was placed in the ability of these instruments of democratic government to free the minority from social proscription and civic inequality. Under this banner the NAACP has fought for full equality for the Negro, involving the eradication of all social, legal, and political disabilities tending to draw a line of distinction between the black citizen and the white. The Negro, like the white American, is to quaff the full draught of eighteenth-century democratic liberalism. The Negro citizen must have the franchise, freedom of economic opportunity (consisting of the right to employment without discrimination), the right to accommodations in public places and on common carriers, the right to voluntary choice of place of residence, the right to jury service, equal expenditures of public funds for education and other public services, and protection against lynch violence.

In the pursuit of this great struggle, the Negro has been seriously handicapped, in that he has never yet been able to win any large measure of suffrage. Thus, his political pressure power is limited to those relatively few sectors in which the Negro votes and holds or threatens to hold the political balance of power. Perhaps 90 percent of the potential black voting strength of the South is eliminated by the devices of disfranchisement employed by the states of the solid South.

The NAACP has carried on its struggle valiantly and has won many notable local victories, in both the political and judicial arenas. Its collaboration with labor in the Senate's rejection of Judge Parker's nomination to the Supreme Court; its recent fight on the educational front, culminating in the celebrated Gaines case triumph; and its unceasing demand for an anti-lynching law, deserve prominent mention. Yet it has never succeeded in developing a program which has that bread-and-butter appeal necessary to command the support of the mass section of the Negro population. Its court success have often proved to be Pyrrhic victories, even as the Gaines case promises to be, in that they merely reassert rights that the Constitution clearly promises to all citizens, but which the white population stubbornly refuses to recognize as exercisable by Negroes. Nor has the NAACP broadened its interests to include a constructive, clearly defined, and practical program for the economic betterment of the race.

The inherent fallacy in this type of political militancy is found in the failure to recognize that the instrumentalities of the state, Constitution, government, and laws can do no more than reflect the political, social, and economic ideology of the dominant population and that the political arm of the state cannot be divorced from the prevailing economic structure.

Thus, the NAACP policy of civil libertarianism is circumscribed by the dominant mores of the society. In the final analysis, whatever success it may have must depend upon its ability to elicit a sympathetic response to its appeals from among influential elements in the advantaged population. In the long run, therefore, its militancy must be toned down, and the inevitable result is that the programs of organizations such as the NAACP tend gradually to conform to the general pattern of the genteel programs of interracial conciliation, which strive to cultivate the good-will of the white "better classes." They are forced to cajole, bargain, compromise, and even capitulate in order to win petty gains or hollow victories. The NAACP has elected to fight for civil liberties rather than for labor unity; it has never reached the masses of Negroes and remains strictly Negro middle-class, Negro-*intellegentsia,* in its leadership and appeal. It has received increasing financial support from Negroes but has often had to lean heavily upon its white benefactors for monetary aid and advice and it has cautiously maintained its respectability.

The first meeting of the National Negro Congress was held in Chicago in February 1936. This organization, taking its cue from India, was an attempt to develop a Negro united front and to work out a minimun program of action which could win wide acceptance among Negro as well as sympathetic white organizations. The Congress has held two national meetings and has many regional and local branches. These undertake to unify the local protest movements against injustices on the united front principle. That is to say the Congress has proceeded on the assumption that the common denominator of race is enough to weld together, in thought and action, such divergent segments of the Negro society as preachers and labor organizers, lodge officials and black workers, Negro businessmen, Negro radicals, professional politicians, professional men, domestic servants, black butchers, bakers, and candlestick makers. The Congress mountain has twice labored and has brought forth many contradictions,[9] but no program of action in advance of that already formulated by previously established Negro organizations.

A Negro Congress with a strong labor bias and with its representation less diffuse and more homogeneous in its thinking could conceivably work out a clearer, more consistent and realistic program than has yet come from the National Negro Congress.

The Negro churches and schools reach more deeply into the Negro masses than do any of the deliberate and formal Negro protest organizations. But it cannot be said that either church or school is a tower of strength in its influence on the social thinking of Negroes and in its contribution toward the improvement of the status of the group. Negro schools, even more than white schools, are controlled by the dominant group and have never been characterized by their courage in leading any frontal attack upon the problems of the group.[10] The schools are responsive to the interests of those who provide the money for their support, and they are not free. The churches have more independence, but they are controlled by reactionary and often ambitious, self-seeking gentlemen of the frock, and they too lack courage, as well as intelligent leadership.

It is a sad but true commentary that, despite the universal grievances endured by the harshly buffeted Negro, there is no single organization, save the church, the school, and, in lesser degree, the fraternal order, which can boast any intimate contact with and support from the common man who represents the mass Negro population. The Negro church has consecrated itself to the spiritual salvation of its charges and has leaned heavily on the side of social reaction and racialism whenever it has concerned itself with the black man's worldly life. The Negro lodges and fraternal orders have contributed little of a constructive nature to the social thought of their Negro membership, though they indulge in ritual and social activity. The Negro schools are socially vacuous and have shown no disposition to meet the challenge offered by the problems of the group whose interests they are designed to serve. The Negro school, its principal or president and its teachers, are content to seek refuge in the tranquil atmosphere of the academic cloister and to look down upon the problems of the group and its neglected masses, in "scholarly" detachment. The students are infected by this false isolation and are not equipped to understand nor to attack the social problems with which they are confronted in their post-school life.

It is not surprising that the narrowly racial conceptions of the Negro have caused him to be seduced by anti-Semitism. He thinks only in terms of jobs for Negroes, business for Negroes, Negro landlords, bankers, and employers, and vents his emotional spleen on the Jewish shopkeeper in the Negro neighborhood, who exploits the black trade quite as enthusiastically as would the black shopkeeper. The Negro anti-Semite does not reason, nor does it matter, that all Jews are neither shopkeepers nor prejudiced. It is sufficient that the Jew makes profit from a store in a Negro section that Negroes ought to own and work in or that a Jewish professor holds a position at a Negro university that a Negro, if even a less competent one, should occupy. Such bigoted attitudes are deliberately nurtured by the self-seeking, sensitive Negro middle class—the business and professional groups, who seek an economic base for their middle-class aspirations.

In view of the obvious social implications for the Negro of this sort of blind, suicidal emotionalism, and the certain truth that racial generalizations and prejudices are luxuries which the Negro can ill afford, it is a bitter indictment of Negro organizations that none has been rational or bold enough to wage a vigorous campaign against Negro anti-Semitism.

Again, in a world in which the major issues affecting the future of humanity are increasingly defined in terms of fascism, with its fundamental racial and totalitarian dogmas, versus democracy, imperfect as it has been for minority groups, no Negro organization makes any serious attempt to define these issues in terms of Negro interest, or to align the full power of Negroes with those forces which are struggling heroically to preserve the last vestiges of human liberty in a world gravely threatened with enslavement. Negro organizations herald the Gaines case and the anti-lyching bill while the eyes of the rest of the world are turned on Munich, Prague, and Memel, Albania, Spain, and China.

It is typical of Negro organizations that they concern themselves not with the broad social and political implications of such policies as government relief, housing, socialized medicine, unemployment and old-age insurance, wages and hours laws, etc., but only with the purely racial aspects of such policies. They are content to let the white citizen determine the expediency of major policies, and the form and direction they will assume, while they set themselves up as watch dogs over relatively petty issues, as whether the laws, once made, will be fairly administered. They thus demark for the Negro a residual function in society.

There is no coordination of thought or serious collaboration in action among these several important Negro organizations and their numerous satellites. Each has marked off its little sphere of action and guards it with professional jealousy. No effective use has ever been made of the numerical strength of the Negro population, nor of its economic importance in labor and consuming power. Race pride does not permit most Negro organizations to make intelligent and practical overtures to the white working population, since a rebuff would result in loss of dignity.

The Negro is sorely in need of organization and leadership which is sufficiently independent and intelligent to give courageous orientation to the group and to guide it rationally through the bewildering maze of social forces which characterize the modern world. This organization and leadership would presumably adhere to some such policies as the following: (1) it would place less emphasis on race and more on economics forces; (2) it would understand that the major problems of Negroes are not entirely attributable to race but are intimately linked up with the operation of the economy; (3) it would attempt to gain a mass basis among Negroes by a simple program designed to raise the economic level of the Negro worker; (4) it would devote its full energy toward the incorporation of Negro workers in labor unions and would carry on incessant educational propaganda among both black and white workers toward this end; (5) it would attempt to throw the full support of Negro workers behind the movement to organize labor on an industrial basis, since the vast majority of Negroes are unskilled workers; (6) it would not cease to fight on the political and judicial fronts but would subordinate this to the fight on the economic and union fronts; (7) it would recognize that the future interests of Negroes are closely related to every general effort to improve the lot and increase the security of the working man of whatever color, and it would back every such measure to the limit; (8) it would include Negro labor leaders in its leadership and among its most influential advisors and avoid dependence on professional Negro leaders and professional white interracialists; (9) it would interpret for Negroes, and relate their interests to, every world event and every foreign policy of importance; (10) its interpretations would be less in terms of race and more in terms of group economic interest; (11) it would recognize that the problems of the Negro cannot be solved in the courts, nor yet by the ballot, even under American democracy; (12) it would take its cue from the sharecroppers' and tenant-farmers' unions formed in the South in recent years and realize that, above all, these successful efforts have broken down once and for all the stubborn legend that prejudice between white and black in the South is invested with a mystical quality and is insurmountable; (13) it would recognize that under oppressive conditions identity of economic interests can overcome racial prejudices and that black and white unity is possible.

Existing Negro organizations are philosophical and programmatic paupers. They think and act entirely in a black groove. In a world in which events move rapidly and in which the very future of themselves and their group is at stake, they are unable to see the social forests for the racial saplings. They, like Hitler, even though for different reasons, think that "all that is not race in this world is trash."[11]

Because of the extreme provincialism of its organizations and leadership, the Negro population of America suffers from stagnation in its social thought. The traditional stereotypes and clichés of Negro thought have become outmoded and a new set of values, tooled to fit the political and economic conditions of the modern world, are indicated. Negro organizations should take close inventory of their policies and discard shop-worn doctrines and should realize that freedom in the modern world is not to be bought at bargain-basement prices. Unless the Negro can develop, and quickly, organization and leadership endowed with broad social perspective and fore-sighted, analytical intelligence, the black citizen of America may soon face the dismal prospect of reflecting upon the tactical errors of the past from the gutters of the black ghettos and concentration camps of the future.

CHAPTER 8

Introduction to a Confidential Report to the Republican Party
1939

Despite the New Deal, many of the most visible Democrats were Southern segregationists, and the party platform refused to embrace civil or human rights until 1948. That the Republicans had not conceded the black vote to the Democrats is demonstrated in the commission they gave to Bunche to set forth the current problems of the Negro population, examine what the federal government was doing and was not doing, and make recommendations to improve conditions for Negro citizens. Both Bunche and the Republican officials agreed in writing that either the whole report be published or nothing be published. Soon after its completion the Republicans wanted to publish only those sections critical of the New Deal, which Bunche vetoed. Later Bunche was asked to reveal those sections critical of the Republican Party, which he regretfully was forced to decline. In the 1950s Bunche would be approached by both parties to seek public office. The report itself runs 140 pages and is remarkable today for its call for a national health care system and federal job quotas.

Introductory

The primary objectives of this report are three:

1. To present a general picture of those needs and problems of the Negro throughout the country (or in that particular area where the need or problem is most acute) that can be served by a practical, constructive political program;
2. To indicate, wherever possible, what the Federal Government is doing or failing to do at present to ameliorate those needs and problems;
3. To present general, suggestive recommendations which look toward broad improvement of the condition of the Negro citizenry.

In order to keep within reasonable bounds and to present a national rather than a local picture of the plight of the Negro, a minimum of data on local conditions has been employed. It was not deemed desirable to clutter up the report with the great mass of material available on the condition of Negroes in specific localities. In so far as the information at hand permitted, broad principles and conclusions have been deduced. It was not always found easy to obtain figures which are susceptible to racial break-down; this is especially true with respect to relief. Deliberately greater emphasis has been placed on those subjects considered to be of most vital interest to Negroes, viz., agriculture, housing, the wage-earner (including relief and relief work), social insurance, and education.

The great pity is that in a vast, rich, powerful nation, founded upon principles of democracy and nourished on the traditional ideals of liberty and equality, a report such as this should have to be written at all. If democracy is to survive the severe trials and buffetings to which it is being subjected in the modern world, it will do so only because it can demonstrate to the world that it is a practical, living philosophy under which all people can live the good life most abundantly. It must prove itself in practice or be discredited as a theory. Democratic nations such as our own have an obligation to all mankind to prove that democracy, as a form of government, as a practical means of human relationships, as a way of life, is a working and workable concept. This America can do only by making democracy work; by abandoning the shallow, vulgar pretense of limited democracy—under which some are free and privileged and others are permanently fettered. The Negro, and especially the Negro in the South, already has had too vivid an experience with embryonic fascism in the very shadow of democracy. Within our own gates are found intense racial hatreds, racial differentials which saturate the political, economic, and social life of the nation, racial ghettos—all the racial raw materials for a virulent American fascism. Clear-thinking, liberty-loving Americans, however, will readily appreciate that a fascist cancer on the body politic ultimately respects neither race nor color nor creed.

Of necessity, considerable emphasis is placed on the needs and problems of the Negro population of the South. It is in this section of the nation that the great majority of Negroes reside. These Southern Negroes are not permitted to exert much direct political influence, but they are American citizens and entitled to full protection of the laws and government. Their plight finds reflection in the status of Negroes in every section of the country, and no honest political program can evade coming to grips with this serious problem of the nation.

This report is not a polemic, and no effort has been made to build up a case. It is a sober attempt to summarize, though somewhat hurriedly and incompletely, those needs of the Negro that can be served by a political program. Within the time limit, and with the facilities available, it has been impossible to compile a comprehensive and detailed account of the status of the American Negro. But the broad outlines are here sketched. Actually the Negro needs more of everything except taxes, prejudice, and religion, and I have tried to state this need in rather casually scientific terms. It has been my purpose to remain as impartial and objective as possible and to keep free of political partisanship. There should be enough material in the rough here presented, however, to permit any party, seriously interested in the welfare of America's black citizenry, to formulate a constructive program for the economic and political betterment of this neglected tenth of our population.

What the report really boils down to is that the Negro is in need of everything that a constructive, humane, American political program can give him—employment, land, housing, relief, health protection, unemployment and old-age insurance, enjoyment of civil rights—all that a twentieth-century American citizen is entitled to. The New Deal has done much to help, unquestionably, but it has fallen far short of meeting adequately the minimal needs of the Negro. It has gotten off on the wrong foot in some instances, gone up blind alleys in others, and has often run afoul of race prejudice. No indictment is contained herein, but only an effort to mirror the present plight and needs of America's Negro citizens.

General

Negroes constitute roughly one-tenth of the total American population. This black section of the citizenry tends to diffuse itself increasingly throughout the nation, though its great concentration is still found in the Deep South. Some 3,500,000 Negroes migrated from the South to the North in the decade 1920–30, most of whom settled in the industrial centers. Today approximately 32 percent of the total Negro population of the North is found in New York (327,706), Philadelphia (219,599), and Chicago (233,903). At least 10 southern cities boast Negro populations in excess of 50,000.

The regional distribution of the Negro population is indicated in the following table:[1]

Southeast	7,778,475
Southwest	7,040,761
Northeast	1,570,459
Middle states	1,181,115
Northwest	97,229
Far West	90,658

The diffusion of the Negro population throughout the country has converted the "Negro problem" into a distinctly national rather than sectional one.

The future of the American Negro is a problem of the American society. It is to be solved only in terms of opportunity for development and assimilation in the political and economic life of the nation.

The Negro in America has but one fundamental objective: to attain the full stature of American citizenship. The Negro, for centuries now, has contributed his labor, his intelligence, his blood, and even his life to the development of the country. He asks nothing from the society except that it consider him as a full-fledged citizen, vested with all of the rights and privileges granted to every citizen; that the charter of liberties of the Constitution apply to the black as to all other men. The Negro desires no "special" consideration as a group but only an equal opportunity with all others, under the Constitution. The Negro citizen has long since learned that "special" treatment for him implies differentiation and that differentiation on a racial basis inevitably connotes inferior status and treatment. In a world in which democracy is gravely besieged and its very foundations shaken, the United States must consider seriously the implications of its own failure to extend the democratic process in full to some 13 million of its citizens whose present status tends to make a mockery of the Constitution. The Negro appreciates fully the difficulties inherent in the American society system. It is recognized that deep-seated social attitudes are not quickly changed. Yet it can be readily understood that in a world in which dogmas of racial superiority and racial persecution assume an increasingly dominant role, the Negro views with great alarm the stubborn persistence of racial bigotry in America. The Negro knows too well that whatever progress he has made in his relatively short period of freedom has been made over the barriers of racial prejudice. There is obvious contradiction between democracy and racial intol- ·erance. This contradiction is especially marked today in view of the known practice of the undemocratic Fascist countries in translating racial dogmas into fundamental law.

The Negro asks only his constitutional right when he demands that the laws of the country be designed so as to extend their benefits to black as well as to white citizens and that political parties pledge themselves to extend the full measure of law and Constitution to all men, regardless of race, color, or creed. Never since the Civil War has the Constitution assumed such vital importance in the ordering of the country. The Negro seeks shelter under its protective wing against the menacing forces of a world bullied by nations to whom Constitutional guarantees appear as weakness, if not democratic madness. The future of the Negro rests with the future of democracy, and Negroes in great numbers now know that every blow struck on behalf of democracy is a blow for the black man's future.

It is to be noted too that there is a virtual identity of fundamental interest between the Negro and white citizens. Not only are all citizens of the country, but the Negro is learning rapidly that whatever relief is extended to the white working man is reflected in improved conditions for the Negro laborer; that whatever is done for the white tenant-farmer beneficially affects the Negro tenant-farmer; that whatever housing provision is made for low-income whites will also ameliorate the wretched housing conditions of millions of Negroes, even though seldom in proportionate degree.

The great masses of Negroes remain disfranchised. But those Negroes of North, East, and West who do vote have a much keener sense than formerly of the uses to which the ballot can be put. They know that the ballot is negotiable and can be exchanged for definite social improvements for themselves. There is no longer blind loyalty to one party, based upon traditional attachment. The Negro regards the vote as a new bargaining power.

The white voter ballots according to his individual, sectional, and group interests. The Negro votes on identical interests, but the social system of America dictates that the Negro must give prior consideration to his racial group interests in his polling. So long as the dual social system persists in America, just so long must the Negro justifiably expect that political parties desiring his political support will devote specific attention to ways and means of Negro betterment in framing their platforms. The Negro finds himself in the uncomfortable position of decrying racial differentiation, while being compelled to demand it when important political policies are in formulation in order to hold his ground in an uncongenial social system.

Defection of the Negro Vote

The Negro has always been the forgotten "forgotten man" in this country. So long as the Negro remained socially backward and lacked an understanding of the operation of the political system, it was relatively easy for a small group of self-picked Negro "leaders" to deliver the Negro vote, lock, stock, and barrel, to the Republican Party. Only the leaders received reward for this vote. But city life breeds sophistication in all phases of life, and the only recently urbanized Negro soon came to realize that he is due something more than periodic lip-service for his vote. The Depression quickened this attitude, and it is unquestionable that Roosevelt's appeals on behalf of the "common man" sold him to the Negro vote. Relief work on government projects, better housing projects, employment of white-collar workers, etc., are tangible programs, the significance of which the Negro quickly caught.

The Negro is kept on the ragged edge of the society even in good times, but in a period of depression, when the Negro worker is first to be laid off, it is either government aid or starvation for the black citizens, the vast majority of whom have never received a wage from which any reserve for periods of stress could be saved. Roosevelt in 1932 and 1936, therefore, spoke the only language the Negro could understand.

It should be noted, too, that many Negroes were seriously disturbed by the lily-white gestures of the Republican Party in the South. The Negro had too long believed that his best interests were irreconcilable with the interests of the white South. In the main, Negro Republican leadership of today is of the old school. It is incapable of representing the interests of the group because it cannot understand the issues of present-day society in their relationship to the Negro. It is conservative to a fault and lacks courage. The Negro knows that this leadership has never been willing to risk its own precarious position in favor of the higher councils of the party in order boldly to represent the interests of the Negro. Throughout the country it is regarded as pussy-footing, cowardly, and stupid. It is for a new Negro Republican leadership to arise, assert itself vigorously, and pitch its appeal to the Negro voter on an entirely different level than the past has known.

Again, thinking Negroes are bound to reflect the opinion that, despite the long loyalty of the Negro to the Republican Party, and the extended periods of power enjoyed by that party, no significant progress has been made toward realizing the fundamental political objectives of the Negro, viz.:

1. the enfranchisement of the Negro in the South;
2. the protection of the civil rights of the Negro;
3. the enactment of an anti-lynching bill;
4. the appointment of Negroes to responsible policy-forming positions in the government.

The plain truth is that neither major party has exerted any significant effort toward moving the mass of this black minority from its precarious perch on the banks of the society into the mainstream of American political and economic life. Considering the return received, the great numbers of Negro votes have been the most cheaply purchased and purchasable in the nation. Thanks to increasing urbanization, this Negro electorate is becoming, if not more intelligent politically, at least more shrewd. It must be certain that the old slogans, the shop-worn dogmas, and appeals used so effectively in the past by the Republican Party in courting the Negro vote will no longer work. The Republican Party must be aware of two important factors effecting change in the reaction of the Negro vote: (1) the greater education of Negroes on matters affecting their interests, and the growth of a younger, more group-conscious, and less politically loyal leadership; and (2) the keen competition for the Negro vote offered by the Democratic Party. To attract the Negro vote the Republican Party will need to offer more than the Democratic Party and will be asked to give concrete evidence in its program of a determination to fully integrate the Negro in American life. It must be clear that in politics one cannot successfully run with both hare and hound, and the Republican Party will need to decide whether it prefers to court the dissident white vote of the Democratic South, through continuance of its lily-white program and an obscure Negro policy, or really desires the Negro vote. It cannot seduce both.*

---

*I gather that there is a rather widespread conviction among Negro Republicans that the party gives neither equal nor adequate representation to Negroes in its local, state, and national councils. There are many suggestions as to ways and means of affording a stronger voice to Negroes in the party. I propose no specific recommendations in this respect, as I feel that these should more properly come from prominent Negroes within the ranks of the party, as an internal party matter.

CHAPTER 9

The Negro in the Political Life of the U.S.
1941

*Bunche's 1,500-page memorandum on "The Political Status of the Negro"
prepared for the Carnegie-Myrdal study represents the most sophisticated and
detailed analysis of black politics then existing. Even then the focus of the
memo is on the disenfranchisement of the black voter in the South, with relatively little attention devoted to Northern politics. In the brief summary of this
work, reprinted here from the* Journal of Negro Education *(1941), we see a
marked moderation of Bunche's view as compared to his article in the same
journal two years earlier. For example, Bunche praises the NAACP in its
effective use of the Negro vote in lobbying as well as the New Deal for giving
broad recognition to the "Negro problem" for the first time. This change in the
critical stance of a black scholar now working in what later became the Office
of Strategic Services in the U.S. Department of State may be attributed to two
basic factors. First, in his travels with Myrdal in the South, Bunche had
witnessed the positive effect such New Deal programs as the Agricultural
Adjustment Act (AAA) Cotton Referenda were having on black political consciousness. These more progressive New Deal programs had been the result in
part of pressure brought on the administration by young black activists such as
Bunche, Robert Weaver, John P. Davis, and William Hastie as well as older
leaders such as A. Philip Randolph, Mary McLeod Bethune, and Walter White.
The second factor was the rise of fascism. Bunche argued that the fight must be
on two fronts and that if Hitler won all hope of domestic equality would be lost.*

American political philosophy and institutions are rooted in the fertile soil of
eighteenth-century liberalism. The dominant influence in American thinking at
the time of the Revolution was civil libertarianism. This promised much for the
status of the individual in the society. The American Revolution, admittedly
bourgeois in character, and more a secession than a revolution, revealed a high
regard for the rights of property as well as for the rights of the individual. Of
greatest significance to the Negro, however, is the fact that this revolt handed
down to the American society a constitutional framework that has become a
sacred tradition, which embraces fundamental concepts of human equality and

human rights. It is within this conceptual milieu, inherited from the American Revolution, that the Negro has carried on his struggles for social, political, and economic emancipation. These concepts have given a measure of realism to the Negro's persistent assumption that he is entitled to equal status in the society, that he too has rights that he must fight for, that an individual black citizen is due as full a measure of human dignity as a white one. The Constitution itself, of course, represents a compromise solution between those conflicting groups in the Convention which actually feared democracy as a "hydra-headed monster," on the one hand, and those which sincerely subscribed to the principles of fundamental equalitarianism, on the other. The entire constitutional history of the nation has reflected this compromise in the quixotic tendency to sanctify its democratic creeds while stubbornly retaining its racial bigotries. Paradoxical as it may seem in the light of the historical record, however, the fact remains that the Constitution did lay the basis for the most broad ideological pattern of individual human equality, human liberty, and human rights that the modern world has known.

The goal set for this nation by the Founding Fathers is the attainment of political democracy. It is the people who are to count in this society. Government is to be theirs—of, by, and for them—all of them. Perhaps the most serious obstacle to the realization of this ideal goal has been the frailty of those who make up the society: the apathy, prejudices, intolerance, greed, and ignorance of the citizenry. Yet it is, in a sense, of the essence of democracy that this should be so. This is at once the promise and the hazard of the democratic way. As one author aptly puts it:

> . . . Democracy asks for reason, tolerance and sympathy, but paradoxically enough it takes full account of the fallibility of human nature.[1]

Dictatorships on the modern model are certainly less indifferent to the frailties of people; they are more selective and demand a far larger measure of conformance to the patterns of good conduct, proper attitudes, and strength of character—patterns which the dictators cut according to their own arbitrary standards and whims. They attempt to drive the devils out of the human soul by heroic measures, by brute force, by threat and intimidation, by the lash, the concentration camp, and the firing squad. But in the process they inspire and legalize devils far more vicious than any that the democracies have yet known. Thomas Jefferson wrote with great sagacity in 1784:

> In every government on earth is some trace of human weakness, some germ of corruption and degeneracy, which cunning will discover, and wickedness insensibly open, cultivate and improve. Every government degenerates when trusted to the rulers of the people alone. The people

themselves, therefore, are its only safe depositories. And to render even them safe, their minds must be improved to a certain degree. . . . The influence over government must be shared among all the people. If every individual which composes their mass participates in the ultimate authority, the government will be saved.[2] The totalitarian states of today graphically document the soundless of this dictum. The omnipotent dictator or the ruling bureaucracy subjects the many to the brutal will of the degenerate and corrupt few. Nations, such as Britain and the United States, which are now engaged in a desperate struggle to preserve the democratic way of life in the world, must never lose sight of the sobering fact that the people themselves, with all their demonstrated weakness, can alone be safely entrusted with political power, if freedom is to be preserved. The exclusion of any substantial number of the nation's citizens from participation in the political processes of the state is, therefore, a serious breach in the democratic armour.

The study of the political status of the Negro in America is itself a record of glaring imperfections in American democracy. Due to the sectional vagaries of the nation with regard to its racial mores, which find reflection in the nature and extent of Negro political activity, the political status of the Negro in the South and North will be considered separately.

The Political Status of the Negro in the South

Throughout American history, the South has been distinguishable as a separate region boasting peculiar social, political, and economic institutions and ideologies. Reference is commonly made to the "solid South," yet the South has really never been "solid" except in its traditional adherence to the doctrine of white supremacy, on the one hand, and the political derivative of that doctrine—blind allegiance to the one-party system—on the other. There have always been severe class distinctions in the South. Negroes and "poor whites" have consistently occupied the two bottom rungs on the Southern social and economic ladders, and the white landholders, bankers, and industrialists—the Southern "Bourbons"—have always perched at the top. In between the white and black masses at the bottom and the numerically small aristocracy at the top, there has developed an intermediate class of small farmers who today are in serious danger of being pushed out into the ranks of the agricultural and industrial wage-workers. Between these upper and lower white classes in the South there has been a traditional and deep-seated hostility. Only the clever manipulation of the threat of black dominance has kept the underprivileged white masses and the privileged upper classes of the South from coming to a parting of the political ways.

The Civil War, by striking the shackles from the black slaves, put a temporary brake on the rapidly developing antagonism between these white classes. This overt interjection of the racial issue on the new basis of free blacks checked what promised to become a vigorous upsurge of the lower-class Southern whites and what may have happily developed into a process of more extensive democratization of that region. Class differences and class antagonisms smoldered in the South and, in the Populist revolt of the postwar South, threatened to become a conflagration. For reasons of alleged self-preservation, however, the South convinced itself that it was necessary to call a truce on political division and to present a solid Democratic or "white" front.

The South is confronted with a number of problems of concern to government which are peculiar to that section and which are symptomatic of the lack of democracy there. These include the low standard of living of the mass population of the South, both black and white; land tenancy; lower wage standards; the poll tax as a heavy burden on voting; the Negro as a social, political, and economic "untouchable"; a below-average standard of education; the one-party system; an inferior quality of political representation and crude demagoguery; loose, inefficient, and often corrupt state and local administrations.

Though the Democratic party has in recent years given evidence of some progressiveness in national politics, the Democratic machines of the South are patently reactionary. The common white man of the South is in a worse plight than his Northern brother, for the former has only the alternative of supporting an illiberal Democratic machine or dispensing with his political privilege altogether—that is, assuming that the common white man in the South is able to surmount the poll tax hurdle. The South consistently reelects its officers of government, especially those in the national government, and this might not be an evil in itself, since it could lead to more experienced and wiser representation, were it not for the fact that it is, in the South, primarily an expression of machine control over a very limited electorate. The three most salient features of the internal Southern political scene are: the looseness and casual corruption in Southern politics; the disfranchisement of virtually all black and large numbers of "poor white" citizens; and the employment of the Negro issue as a political red herring.

The political status of the Negro in the South is intimately related to the registration systems in vogue in the Southern states.[3] The problem is presented in bold relief when the contrast is bared between the registration procedure as it applies to whites, on the one hand, and to Negroes, on the other. A mere analysis of Southern registration laws is not enough; it is only when the administration of these laws by the local officials is probed that the real story of Negro disbarment is revealed. There is scarcely ever any serious check on residence or age. Where character witnesses are required by state law, as in

Alabama, the provision is ignored, or openly scoffed at, since the registration official can "vouch" for the character of every white person in the county.

The entire procedure, especially in the rural areas, is characterized by its extreme informality, its laxness, and its brazen disregard for the application of the law. The registrars employ their own interpretations of the laws. Yet this laxness, this indifference to statutes, this easygoing and often gullible attitude toward white registrants, is usually transformed into a harsh, hostile, and rigid application of the law (and often something more than the law), when Negro applicants appear. As one Southern registrar puts it: "We register almost anybody. And . . . people in this county are so ignorant. So many of them can hardly write their names."[4] This same official recalled four white property owners for whom she "had to hold their hand while they made the cross" on the registration blank. Another Alabama registration official spoke quite frankly about Negro registrants and the methods for disposing of them:

> We never use any of those things [referring to such devices as Constitution interpretation tests] against a white man. I'll just be honest with you. . . . We have had a good little bit of trouble with niggers. . . . Way back in 1920 when I was on the board before, we had a world of nigger women coming in to register. There was a dozen of them, I reckon, come in one registration period. We registered a few and then we stopped. Oh, we put them off . . . tell them they had to bring in white witnesses. . . . Tell them how much poll tax it was going to cost them. . . . We got that pretty well weeded out now. Not many come around. I don't think more than one come in the last two years.[5]

It cannot be said how many of the approximately nine million Negroes in the South are registered for voting, and there seems to be no reasonable means of making an estimate other than by counting Negro names on the registration books in each Southern county. Even this would involve inaccuracies, however. For example, it was found that some names opposite which the tell-tale "col" appeared on the registration books of an Alabama county were the names of respectable white residents of the community. The number of Negro registrants, while still comparatively negligible, is more than it was two or five years ago, but the increase has been painfully slow. In some recent instances a sudden surge of Negro voting or the mere expression of Negro determination to vote has inspired violent resistance by Southern whites.

Negro efforts at registration are usually described by Southern registration officials as "trouble." Most of the registration officials simply take it for granted that the Negro registrants sought to be rejected. All sorts of handy rationalizations are available to support this view. The registrars frequently make fine distinctions between the "types" of Negroes presenting themselves and often admit that certain of the "better class" of favored Negroes ought to be put on the books. Responsible whites in the Southern communities are often willing to permit a token registration of the upper-class Negroes. This is not considered "dangerous."

The basis for the decision of the registrars with regard to Negro registration is often explained in terms of how "the white people in the county feel about it." Often it is enough to justify rejection in the minds of the registration officials to explain that "the people," meaning the white people in the county, "just wouldn't stand for it." Some of the Southern registrars are very boastful about the discretionary power vested in their office, and one went so far in an interview as to boast that he had it within his power to keep the president of the United States from registering, should he choose to do so.

The general social situation and mores of the South create an atmosphere of intimidation for the Negro registrant, who must present himself to officials who are usually certain to be hostile—not to mention the fact that the applicant must often run the horrible gauntlet of the leering hangers-on who habitually loaf about the courthouse offices in the Southern county seats. Southern registration officials (and also textbook writers on American government) commonly explain the amazing absence of Negro names from the registration rolls by stating that Negroes "just don't care to register." In some respects this is true. Negroes are intimidated, afraid to step out of their "place," and reluctant to encounter the hostility and insult associated with the registration office. Moreover, they realize that registration which permits voting only in the general elections is an empty gesture. Finally, even were it not for these barriers, Negroes can ill afford to pay the poll tax, and when they can afford it they are not eager to pay out money for the meaningless privilege of voting in the general elections, since participation in the only elections that count, the Democratic or "white" primaries, is denied to them.

There are not a few Negroes in the South, however, who agree that the election officials are right in permitting only a few Negroes with property to vote. Their position is that relations with the "white folks" will be better if only the "highest type of Negro" votes. There is a great deal of class feeling among Negroes in the South, and it is not unusual for "upper-class" Negroes— business and professional men—to take the attitude that the great mass of Negroes, being uneducated and illiterate, are "not yet ready" to exercise the franchise. Not a few reflect the view that this black mass of uneducated people is a definite liability to the advanced members of the race, in that all Negroes are lumped together in the prevailing racial situation. A good many of these "talented tenth" Negroes, far from expressing concern over the disfranchisement of their less fortunate black brothers, are proud of the fact that they are found among the chosen few in the community who are permitted to exercise the privilege of voting.

Despite the hardships often imposed by the registrars, there are increasing numbers of Negroes in the South who are demonstrating an amazing amount of patience, perseverance, and determination and who keep returning after rejections until they get their names on the registration books.

Negroes have discovered that Southern white men with whom they have business relations are often inclined to be quite sympathetic toward the registration efforts of their Negro customers and are willing to act as vouchers and character witnesses for them.

There is a strong difference of opinion among Negroes in the South as to the proper method to be employed in gaining increased registration for Negroes. Some Southern Negroes of prominence are content to go along with the customary method of getting a few Negroes on the books through personal contacts with friendly and sympathetic whites. Others vigorously oppose this tactic as an uncertain "back door" practice which holds no promise for the Negro's political future in the South. These latter desire to make an issue, at every possible opportunity, of the Negro's denial and demand that Negroes be accorded the same treatment in the registration office as given to whites.

The efforts being made by some Negro organizations throughout the South to give free coaching to prospective Negro registrants in order to aid them in answering the questions put by the white registrars is good civic education. Undoubtedly, many of the Negro applicants have a better knowledge of the functioning of the state and federal governments than the registrars who put the questions to them and, for that matter, than most white citizens in their localities.

The Poll Tax

The poll tax, employed as a qualification for voting, is a development of twentieth-century America and is peculiar to eight states in the South. The most significant result of the poll tax provisions in the South has been the disfranchisement of great numbers of poor whites. The new constitutions of the Southern states in which the poll tax provisions were incorporated were not popular constitutions and, in some instances at least, were actually "put over" on the population. In Mississippi and Virginia, for example, the new constitutions were adopted by proclamation and were never submitted to the people for ratification. In recent years vigorous efforts to do away with the poll tax restrictions on the franchise have developed in the Southern states, often in the face of almost insuperable obstacles. The disfranchisement of Negroes by registration devices and the white primary, and the restraint upon the franchise imposed by the poll tax, are mutually complementary. In most of the remaining poll tax states of the South, the Negro is disfranchised by means other than the poll tax. Significantly, one of the strong arguments advanced by those striving for the elimination of the tax as a requirement for voting is that, in those states which have abolished it, no great increase in the black vote has ensued. It is, in fact, true that the repeal of the poll tax in Louisiana, North Carolina, and Florida has resulted in no very great increase in the Negro vote. The introduction of the "threat" of Negro domination as an issue in the poll tax fight is sheer sophistry. Dishonest Southern politicians utilize the Negro issue as a means of maintaining themselves and their machines in power. The poll tax does effectively disfranchise thousands of white voters, however, and apparently was, in some instances, at least, deliberately designed for that purpose. Many thousands more of the white voters are corrupted by it.

The Democratic or White Primaries

The Democratic or white primary, operating under the rule of the state Democratic parties in the Southern states to the effect that none but whites can vote in the party nominating contests, is enforced strictly in all of the Southern states except Kentucky, Tennessee, and a number of counties in Virginia and North Carolina. Thus, in the Southern states, the Democratic Party is, to all intents and purposes, the *only* political party insofar as state and local politics are concerned. In those states the "nominations" of the Democratic Party for public offices are virtually elections to office. The general elections are mere gestures. It is in these "white primary" states that the political rights of Negroes are sacrificed on the altar of "white supremacy." The white primary has now become the most effective device for the exclusion of Negroes from the polls in the South and, therefore, the most effective political instrument for the preservation of white supremacy. The disbarment of the Negro from these party nominating elections usually takes the form of a declaration by the authorities of the Democratic Party in each state that only white persons are eligible to membership and permitted to aid, through the primary elections, in the nomination of the party candidates. For example, the Louisiana Democratic primary rule reads: "That no one shall be permitted to vote at said primary except electors of the white race."

In the celebrated case of *Grovey* v. *Townsend* the Supreme Court of the United States upheld the right of the Texas State Democratic Convention to establish rules governing membership in the Democratic Party and participation in the party primary,[6] even though such rules were based solely on race, and despite the fact that the Negro citizen of Texas was thus deprived of any possibility of an effective vote. The primary was held to be a party primary and thus the discrimination involved was not an act of the state. However, in the very recent case of *U.S.* v. *Patrick B. Classic et al.*,[7] involving alleged fraudulent conduct in a Democratic Party primary in the Second Congressional District of Louisiana, where the Democratic nomination is and always has been equivalent to election, the court took a view which may hold much promise for future attacks upon the validity of the exclusion of Negroes from Democratic primaries—at least when Congressional seats are at stake. Mr. Justice Stone, in his majority opinion in the Classic case stated:

> Interference with the right to vote in the Congressional primary in the Second Congressional District for the choice of Democratic Candidate for Congress is thus a matter of law and in fact an interference with the effective choice of the voters at the only stage of the election procedure when their choice is of significance, since it is at the only stage when such interference could have any practical effect on the ultimate result, the choice of the Congressman to represent the district. The primary in Louisiana is an integral part of the procedure for the popular choice of Congressman. The right of qualified voters to vote at the Congressional primary in Louisiana and to have their ballots counted is thus the right to participate in that choice.

It was the unwillingness of the court to recognize this fact now clearly stated, that inability to vote in the Democratic primary is tantamount to disfranchisement in the Southern states, that was so damaging to the Negro in Mr. Justice Roberts' opinion in *Grovey* v. *Townsend.*

Though Negroes are almost universally barred from the Democratic primaries in the South, even though they may be ardent supporters of the Democratic Party, white Republicans very commonly vote in those primaries. Republican Party primaries are comparatively rare in the Southern states and, with few exceptions, are virtually meaningless. Negroes have traditionally participated in and in numerous instances have controlled Republican organizations in the South. Since the advent of "lily-whiteism" in the Southern Republican organizations, however (a movement that began to develop as far back as the Taft administration), Negro power in the Southern Republican ranks has rapidly diminished. It never meant much more than significant votes of Negro delegates for the aspiring nominees at Republican National Conventions, a few Negro Republican committeemen, and a meager dole of party patronage for Negro political wheelhorses.

Negro Voting in the South

Rather ludicrously, some Southern officials claim that "clean government" in the South dates from the disfranchisement of the Negro, and that disbarment of the Negro from the polls remains essential to the continuance of pure politics in the South. Some Southerners are honest enough to admit, however, that the way in which Negro votes were "bought up" in the days of Reconstruction is not a bit worse than the way in which white votes are bought up by poll tax payment and cash gifts today.

The number and power of Negro voters in the South is commonly exaggerated fantastically, and stories of the "hundreds" or "thousands" of Negroes who are voting in one place or another go the rounds and are recounted daily among the ranks of the courthouse fence-sitters and tobacco-juice-spitters.

In the 8 most hard-bitten, anti–Negro vote states of Alabama, Georgia, Mississippi, Louisiana, Florida, Texas, South Carolina, and Arkansas, there are certainly never more than 80,000 to 90,000 Negro votes cast, at a liberal estimate, and scarcely any of these are cast in the Democratic primaries—the elections that count in the one-party states. If the mildly "border" states of North Carolina, Virginia, and Tennessee are included, another 100,000 to 115,000 black votes would be added. But the sum total of the Negro vote would be but a drop in the political bucket even for these 11 small-voting states, 8 of which are still poll-tax ridden, and therefore bar droves of whites as well as blacks from the polls. There has been a steady if not sensational decline in the percentage of Negroes in the populations of all the Southern states since 1901. The 1930 Census returns indicated that only Mississippi retained a majority of Negroes in its population and the 1940 Census will probably show that this ratio has changed. Throughout the South, of course, there remain counties and districts in which Negroes constitute a majority of the population, but on the whole there is no longer any physical basis for the South's hysterical outcry against the threat of "black domination." Actually this insistently uttered "fear" of the white South at the consequences of Negro voting is a fear not of Negro political domination through Negro exercise of the ballot, but a fear of the "in" groups that the Negro—that is, the Negro tenants on the plantations and the Negro workers in the mills and factories—will be voted by the "outs" to bring about a shift in political power and control. The view is commonly expressed throughout the South that the white South is now in position to "take care of" the Negro handily enough. The fear, then, is not of black domination, but of white domination in a political game in which the Negro voter is only a pawn. Some Southern politicians are quite pragmatic about the problem of Negro voting. Their sole objection to the enfranchisement of the Negro, they frankly admit, is that it would increase the size of the electorate, and thus make it more expensive for a candidate to get elected or for a machine to perpetuate itself in power, since there would be a black as well as white votes to be bought.

Many whites in the South quite frankly explain that, where there is resentment at Negro registration and voting, Negroes do not attempt it for fear they will stir up racial animosity in the community, and that this will affect them injuriously in other ways. This is undoubtedly true, and follows a well-established pattern used as a guide by many members of minority groups. The pattern is that rights and principles should never be demanded, and may even be tactfully refused by minority groups when there is danger of intensifying racial feeling. Thus, at the time of Professor Frankfurter's appointment to the Supreme Court of the United States many Jews felt that this was an unwise move in that it might serve to feed the fires of anti-Semitism already rampant in the country.

There is an ever-increasing political activity among Negroes in the municipal elections of the South. As many as several thousands of Negroes have voted in the city elections of Atlanta. Negroes in the few thousands have similarly voted in the municipal contests in Durham, Raleigh, and Richmond. Apparently the white populations of these Southern centers were not unduly alarmed by this new activity on the part of Negroes, for there is no record of any serious protest against it. On the other side of the ledger, however, is the attempt of the Ku Klux Klan in 1939 to alarm and stir up the white population of Miami against the threat of Negro voting. A similar episode occurred in Greenville, South Carolina, when only a few hundred Negroes got on the registration rolls in 1939, and some excitement surrounded the registration of some three score Negroes, mostly women, in Spartanburg, South Carolina, in the same year, when the warning was issued that "the Klan will ride again." Negroes vote, or rather, are voted, in Memphis also. The Crump machine sees to that—provides them with poll tax receipts, marked ballots and bad liquor, and herds them into the polling booths.

There are an increasing number in the South, and among these are some very influential people and some keen observers, who believe it inevitable that within the reasonably near future a two-party system will develop in the South. They see a second or opposition party springing up, due to the movement of population, the development of industry, the increasing class-consciousness of the workers of the South, and the tendency of the established parties to break up on ideological grounds. Such a development would have a very wholesome effect upon the political status of the Negro in the South. It probably provides the main source of hope for the political future of the Southern Negro.

Negro Voting in the AAA Cotton Referenda

One very large and very significant group of Negroes in the South has been having, in recent years, an unparalleled and unrestricted opportunity to express its will through the ballot. Not since Reconstruction days has any numerous group of Negroes had the opportunity to cast the independent ballot that is cast by the Negro cotton farmer in the cotton marketing quota referenda. Most significantly, many thousands of Negro cotton farmers each year now go to the polls, stand in line with their white neighbors, and mark their ballots independently, without protest or intimidation, in order to determine government policy toward cotton production control. These elections revolve about issues which affect directly the economic welfare of the producers and they are much more clear to the voters than are the often obscure issues confronting them in the regular political elections. The cotton referenda are run off as regular elections, with regulations governing the eligibility of voters, voting booths, and the Australian ballot—features that are often signally lacking in the political elections of those Southern states in which the cotton referenda are held.

The participation of Negroes in those elections, and on an equal basis with whites, is of the utmost significance in the South. That such activities will tend to bring about a recognition by both white and Negro producers of parallel economic interests would seem clear. Participation in these referenda has given to a great many Negroes in the South the first opportunity to cast a ballot of any kind they have ever had. Moreover, it tends to accustom a great many whites to the practice of Negro voting.

The Negro Influence on Southern Politics

While the Negro may exercise a very limited franchise in the South, the very presence of the Negro is a dominating influence upon Southern politics. It is the Negro bogey which has frightened the South into its traditional devotion to a one-party system that is essentially the negation of democracy. The South— the white South—enjoys only partial democracy. Its range of democratic freedom in the realm of politics is always circumscribed by the self-imposed limitations of party choice. Only by blind loyalty to the Democratic Party can the "Southern way" be preserved. Republicanism is still hereticism in the South, and the parties of the left are regarded as dire, revolutionary threats. In no other section of the country can such intense, self-imposed political provincialism be found. The net result is a political naiveté and backwardness which leaves its indelible imprint upon Southern life. No section of the country produces such virile and vituperative demogoguery; none is so unprogressive and politically bigoted. The South pays a high price for its white supremacy. The Negro remains the greatest single influence in the Southern scene. The South's representation in the Congress remains illegally based upon a total population that includes more than 9,000,000 Negroes who are unconstitutionally denied any voice in the selection of these representatives.

The Negro is often the essential vehicle of Southern politics. Though the "Negro issue" today, in any given campaign, is usually more imagined than real, it is a convenient handle for the campaign activities of many professional politicians in the South. It is a ready-made smear that can be effectively employed by the unscrupulous politician. It is still sure-fire in many sections of the South, and candidates make good use of it. The Southern mentality is receptive to "nigger-baiting" and so it is a legitimate instrument of political warfare.

There are many in the South today, however, who have grown weary of the Negro diversion. They feel that the South is paying too high a price for its past and that the Southern politician is playing the South cheap by holding office on the strength of nigger-baiting rather than by devoting constructive effort toward the solution of the more pressing economic problems of that section. The South is slowly awakening to the fact that it has many problems which are immediately more pressing than its black one, and is beginning to demand that its political representatives put all of their cards on the table at election time. In most places in the South today, the candidate must be "right" on more things than the Negro problem.

Implications of Negro Political Status in the South

There is certainly something ironical in the fact that this South which thus grossly denies an elemental democratic right to a vast population within its midst is more enthusiastic than any other section of the country over the fight to defeat Hitler and preserve democracy in the world. It may well be that the South is interested in the preservation only of that special Southern brand of democracy defined by a Southern newspaper in defending the poll tax. It observed with boastful candor:

> This newspaper believes in white supremacy. . . . It does not believe in a Democracy with a small "d," because it knows this country never has had such a Democracy and never will have such a Democracy as long as white supremacy is preserved. . . . If it is "undemocratic" to argue for white supremacy—as it certainly is—then we plead guilty to the charge.[8]

The Negro is disfranchised in the South, but certainly the direct implications for a democratic society of such denials of democratic rights are shamefully clear. Long tolerated abuses of this kind cannot but have a deleterious effect upon the democratic fabric of the entire nation. The continuing cultivation of a large corps of public officials who have no respect for laws, who tend to become a law unto themselves, who wink and connive at habitual violation of the laws they are sworn to uphold, will inevitably reap bitter harvests for all Americans who regard the democratic way as essential to decent living. Already the efforts toward erasing the Negro as an active political factor have had their repercussions in the mass disfranchisement of white persons, now typical of this section of the country whose voting record is surely a travesty on democracy.

The real strength of a democratic society is to be found in the full and hearty participation of all members of the society in its processes. Democracy's power is in the support it wins and merits from those masses whose servant it must be. A democracy in which vast numbers of citizens are denied democratic privileges is a fatal mockery. The political and psychological frustration of those citizens who are shunted into an inferior caste, the lack of morale among them, their inability to contribute to the common weal, the inevitable reaction upon the members of the dominant group who become accustomed to a dual set of moral values, must be seriously threatening to the ultimate survival of the democratic ideal. In the final analysis, a democracy that ignores and neglects many of its citizens, or is merely paternalistic toward them, is hollow. Democracy's vitality is in the liberation, the uplift, the inspiration, and self-confidence of the individual, who will willingly shoulder his burden of responsibility in the society in the full knowledge that he walks with freedom and dignity.

The Political Status of the Northern Negro

Within the limited scope of this paper it has been necessary to make some choice as to emphasis. The political status of the Negro in the South has been stressed for the obvious reasons that it is in the South that the overwhelming majority of Negroes reside, and, within the framework of democratic analysis, enforced non-voting is far more meaningful than voting. The Negro in the North votes; the Negro in the South does not and cannot.

Negro political activity in the North ties up importantly with the Negro migrations during and after World War I. It was these migrations which brought on the concentrations of Negro population in the Northern urban centers. An outstanding characteristic of these new Negro populations, which found themselves in a strange environment in the North, was their political innocence. Inevitably, they fell prey to the machine politics of the well-oiled political rings typical of America's great urban centers. An essential corollary of the Negro's exploitation by political machines is the frequent tie-up between Negro politics and politicians and the underworld. For the most part this underworld association reduces itself to the numbers and policy rackets and their numerous barons, to prostitution, and to petty vice.

The Negro population of the North has adjusted itself rapidly to the political customs of its new environment. Negro voting behavior in the North today approximates the average. Negro participation at first was timid and meager; today it approaches the average. Negro party affiliation, which was once inflexibly Republican, today is no longer so; nor is the Negro's behavior longer atypical with regard to third party support. Negro voting behavior in the North can no longer be described as generally atypical. The fact is that the Negro voter in the North is much more thoroughly assimilated politically than he is socially or economically. The Negro voter, like the white, is preyed upon by the political machines. The Negro voter, through his political leaders, who are professional politicians and therefore largely self-seeking, expects a direct return for his vote in the form of jobs, social and municipal services. Whereas in Chicago, New York, Cleveland, Philadelphia, St. Louis, and Detroit his vote is an important factor in determining election results, he does get improved facilities and services, though seldom in proportion to the real importance of his vote. Yet his vote, especially when political lieutenants can control it, is a voice that can command attention and gives to the Negro of the North an effective lever that is almost entirely foreign to his black brother in the South.

The concentration of the Northern Negro in segregated residential areas has made for a more effective Negro vote. The Negro vote thus often controls the selection of local and state officials. Dividends in the form of local, state, and federal patronage are now paid to the Negro as a matter-of-course. In numerous local elections the Negro vote has constituted the balance of power. In close national elections such as the last one, when the independent vote is considered a serious factor, the major parties carefully woo the Negro voters. The Negro vote is a constant threat, and Negro organizations such as the NAACP have made effective use of this threat in their lobbying activities on behalf of the Negro, notably in the successful fight against the confirmation of Judge Parker and in the less-successful efforts on behalf of the anti-lynching bills.

There is really no accurate estimate of Negro voting in the North. The figure usually cited during the last presidential campaign exceeded 2,000,000. The claim is frequently made that the Negro controls the political balance of power in some 17 of the Northern states. For the most part such "estimates" are mere guesses, based only upon the ratio of adult Negroes to the total adult population of the particular city or state. The Negro vote, moreover, is no longer a merely black vote, responsive only to racial appeals. Since 1928, when President Hoover pressed the Republican lily-white campaign in the South too overtly, and because the New Deal launched the relief and "forgotten man" appeals during the Depression, there has been a decided shift in the political allegiance of the Northern Negro. The spell of the Lincoln legend over the Negro has been broken. It may well be, as some contend, that among well-to-do Negroes it is still fashionable to be Republican, but it is also true that the working class, the unionized, and the underprivileged Negro gives enthusiastic support to the Democratic Party.

It is difficult to assess the real benefits accruing to the Northern Negro from his growing political activity. Prior to 1932, the great concentration on presidential campaigns paid only small dividends to the Negro masses, though Negro political leaders often plucked juicy patronage plums for themselves.

But the New Deal for the first time gave broad recognition to the existence of the Negro as a national problem and undertook to give specific consideration to this fact in many ways, though the basic evils remain untouched.

The more immediate gains from political activity have resulted from the strategic role played by the Negro electorate in municipal campaigns. Here the Negro of the Northern cities has been able to trade his vote for tangible results—better schools, playground facilities, sanitation improvements, hospital accommodations, police and fire protection, transportation services, improved lighting and paving, municipal employment and office holding, and direct representation. Though it can never be said that the Negro sections in general receive an equitable share of such benefits, it is undoubted that the conditions in the Negro residential areas of every Northern city in which the Negro wields a significant vote would be much more neglected were it not for the power of that vote. The Negro is rapidly learning that he can trade and make demands upon the strength of his ballot.

The question is often raised as to whether the Negro vote is or should be a solid bloc vote. It is not so now, and, even assuming that it were possible to make it so, this would be undesirable. The Negro population is properly subject to the same variations in interest as the white—there are sectional, class, religious, and ideological differences dividing the Negro vote as they divide the white. There is, for example, neither more nor less unanimity among Negroes with regards to the nation's foreign policy today than among whites. It is important to the proper functioning of democracy that this independence of attitude be preserved for all groups, granted the vital importance of national unity in this period of desperate crisis. While it is true that the Negro voter must always be a "race conscious" voter so long as racial division remains typical of American life, it is also true that there are many issues of even more fundamental importance than race to the welfare of the Negro voter here—not the least of which are those of broad governmental policy in the present crisis.

The Negro in the North experiences something of the real nature of political democracy. He has a political voice, a medium whereby he can express his views on and influence the direction of governmental policy. He has a hand in the selection of those who represent him in government. He is enabled, thereby, to develop a sense of responsibility and a feeling of dignity in a society in which he is permitted active participation. As an individual and as a group the Negro has a new, albeit proper, importance.

It is not enough, however, that the Negro in the North has attained political emancipation, that he is learning the value of the ballot, and that his voting behavior approaches the norm. In the broader sense, all voting in the North is still too much under the shadow of machine control to permit of maximum expression of the individual will. Ballots are still too frequently bought, corrupt politicians are still too influential, and the voter in the large, black or white, is still too easily duped in the campaigns.

Conclusion

The future of the American Negro is a grave problem of the American society. This problem can be solved only in terms of full opportunity for development and complete assimilation in the political and economic life of the nation. The Negro in America has but one fundamental objective: to attain the full stature of American citizenship. The Negro, for centuries now, has contributed his labor, his intelligence, his blood, and even his life to the development and protection of the nation. He asks nothing from the society except that it consider him at long last as a full-fledged citizen, vested with all of the rights and privileges granted to every citizen; that the charter of constitutional liberties apply to the black as to all other men. The Negro citizen has long since learned that "special" treatment for him implies differentiation on a racial basis and inevitably connotes inferior status.

In a world in which democracy is gravely besieged the United States must consider seriously the implications of its own failure to extend the democratic process in full to some 13 million of its citizens whose present status tends to make a mockery of the Constitution. The thinking Negro appreciates fully the difficulties inherent in the American society system. It is recognized that deep-seated social attitudes are not quickly changed. Yet it can be readily understood that in a world in which dogmas of racial superiority and racial persecution assume an increasingly dominant role, the Negro views with great alarm the stubborn persistence of racial bigotry in America. The Negro knows too well that whatever progress he has made in his relatively short period of freedom has been made over the barriers of racial prejudice.

The Negro asks only his constitutional right when he demands that the laws of the country be so designed as to extend their benefits to black as well as to white citizens and that political parties, governmental agencies, and officials pledge themselves to extend the full measure of law and constitution to all men, regardless of race, color, or creed. Never since the Civil War has the Constitution and its democratic tenets loomed so importantly in the ordering of the country. The Negro, as all other Americans, seeks shelter under their protective wing against the menacing forces of a world bullied by nations to whom constitutional guarantees appear as weakness, if not democratic madness. The future of the Negro rests with the future of democracy. Negroes in great numbers, despite the disillusioning imperfections of American democracy and its racial contradictions, now must know that every blow struck on behalf of democracy is a blow for the black man's future.

So long as this society professes to be a democracy, however, the Negro and other minority racial groups can deny that this is by right exclusively a white man's country, and that all others exercise rights and privileges here only on sufferance. For what is it that the Negro struggles? He makes no plea for special privilege. He asks only that democracy live up to its promise: that black citizens be permitted to join with all other citizens in making of America's democratic faith a vital, living force, whose preservation will be assured by the unlimited sacrifices both its white and black citizens will cheerfully make in order to continue to share its blessings. What the Negro seeks, finally, is a recognition of rights. There is no place in a democracy for the slave tradition that some people have rights by natural endowment, while others exercise only privileges as favors condescendingly handed down to them from a superior and dominant group, and subject to the will of that group. The Negro has also learned well the lesson that political freedom without economic opportunity is meaningless.

The Negro in America struggles to attain that dignity of the individual man, that decent respect for and recognition of the integrity of the individual, which is the first premise of our civilization. Although it has admittedly received but half-hearted application here, the conclusion is inescapable that the totalitarian systems, if victorious, would black it out permanently as an ideal and as a moral precept of future conduct.

The entire nation has a vital stake in the world conflict. But the ability of this nation to protect its interests is now seriously affected by the traditional imperfections in the democratic process. In an hour of great need the nation reaps the harvest of the racial disunity it has sown and cultivated. The Negro is grossly discriminated against in both the civil and military phases of the defense program. There can be no maximum unity in a military establishment that fosters a white army and a black army; in an economy that recognizes employment and wage differentials as between white and black workers; in a political system that extends political privilege to some and withholds it from others. It is tragically ironical that in a nation which has been guilty of so many injustices toward them, black citizens must now make a clement plea to the government to permit them to throw in their brain, toil, and sweat, and even their blood in the mighty effort for the defense of the nation and its cherished democratic ideals.

It is a fight on two fronts in which the Negro and all democracy-loving Americans must now engage. The unrelenting struggle to erect a true democracy upon our constitutional foundations must go on. The economic insecurity of vast millions of our population, the political and educational disabilities suffered by many, the slum areas, child labor, the migratory workers, sharecroppers, the disgracefully inadequate protection of the nation's health—these and many other evils must be eradicated. There can be no let-up in the crusade to make a reality of American democracy.

But full recognition must be given also to the external threat. The fight to make democracy work can only go on if the democratic concepts and traditions are preserved. The fight today is to reserve that capacity which Western civilization alone makes possible—the effort to achieve in practice the ideals of human equality and the essential dignity of man—the fundamental postulates of democracy. This fight will be lost the moment the United States finds itself marooned in a totalitarian world. This nation cannot exist as a democratic island in a Nazi-fascist sea.

There should be no illusions about the nature of this struggle, however, The fight now is not to save democracy, for that which does not exist cannot be saved. But the fight is to maintain those conditions under which people may continue to strive for realization of the democratic ideals. This is the inexorable logic of the nation's position as dictated by the world anti-democratic revolution and Hitler's projected new world order.

There are those who profess to agree with all of this, but caution that in these crucial times disadvantaged groups such as the Negro—or labor—should, for the sake of national unity and national defense, call a truce and suspend their struggle. But it is defeatist in a democratic society to counsel unquestioning acceptance of the status quo. A democratic society can never become static and remain democratic. The practical essence of a democratic society is in the mechanisms it affords for the solution of its problems. This is precisely why democracy is worth fighting for. This is precisely why democracy inspires hope among oppressed peoples. There are those also who say that it is of little consequences to the Negro whether this country maintains its present pseudo-democratic institutions or becomes nationalistic and totalitarian. This is dangerous advice for the Negro; it is an insidious type of defeatism. It suggests to the Negro that he adopt an attitude of resignation toward his future and, having no voice in the society, prepare to adapt himself to whatever ideology the future may bring. But the Negro as an American has a vital stake in this future and must struggle tooth and nail to have a hand in determining what course it shall take.

For all thinking people, the American Negro should be a shining symbol of the deeper significance of democracy. The Negro has demonstrated what can be achieved with democratic liberties even when grudgingly and incompletely bestowed. But the most profound significance of the Negro to the American society is found in the cold fact that democracy which is not extended to all of the nation's citizens is diseased. It is a dangerous pattern of caste and discrimination that is here cut for the Negro, and European experience now reveals how easily this pattern may be applied to non-Negro groups. It is a relatively simple step from a glib rationalization of the exclusion of the Negro from the fruits of democracy to the exclusion of Jews, of aliens, of Catholics, of labor unions, and ultimately of all those who do not belong to the chosen political sect. The treatment of its minority problems will prove to be the ultimate test of the ability of American democracy to function and to survive.

Part 3
Africa

CHAPTER 10

French Educational Policy in Togoland and Dahomey
1934

The award-winning dissertation "French Administration in Togoland and Dahomey," which Bunche produced at Harvard, was never published despite the urging of his committee, which consisted of Professors Arthur Holcombe, Rupert Emerson, and George Benson. This essay, originally published in the Journal of Negro Education, *is drawn directly from his dissertation work. Bunche's strong inclination toward social engineering so evident in the Myrdal memoranda are even more pronounced here. Indeed, here is a new political laboratory in which, says Bunche, previous mistakes may be corrected and a new and better civilization cultivated through the deliberate application of human intelligence and understanding. As in his dissertation, Bunche finds that French administration in the mandated territory of Togo is slightly superior to that of its colony Dahomey. In regard to educational policies in both areas, however, he expresses three basic concerns: (1) that the European education provided to Africans allow for the teaching of native customs, history, and languages; (2) that such an "adapted" education not be based on a stereotyped view of the African, e.g., Booker T. Washington's Tuskegee; and (3) that the knowledge gained be used to advance the independence of the Africans rather than the interests of the colonial power. While Bunche's African studies did not gain the academic recognition they deserved, they set the stage for his governmental service in the United States and later at the United Nations.*

The General Problem of Native Education

In its vastness and richness Africa rivals its sister continents. Because of its wealth it has long commanded the attention of the Western world. But perhaps the greatest significance of Africa is to be found in its possibilities as a proving ground in human relationships—social, economic, and political. Here is one place in a troubled world where mistakes previously committed may be corrected; where, indeed, a new and better civilization may be cultivated through the deliberate application of human intelligence and understanding. In this process education should play the leading role.

To the African, education is as significant as magic. In large measure the education which is permitted him by the Western world dominating him holds the key to his economic, political, and social future. In increasing degree the African himself is made aware of this fact. It may be interpreted as a sign of progress, therefore, that it is no longer an issue in responsible quarters that the African shall be afforded an education of some kind. True, there are many who still cling steadfastly to the belief that the African should remain as uneducated as possible. Some of these latter attempt to hide behind the romantic sentimentalism that the African must be left entirely to his own devices, in a foolish and not always honest glorification of the noble savage. This view, of course, ignores completely the present irresistible influences at work in Africa. Others, more candid, see the native only as a potential labor-supply to be drawn upon at will by white men, and with which his education would seriously interfere.

Such views, however, are rapidly becoming outmoded. In the words of one prominent colonial observer, "the cause of generalisation of native education has been won."[1] Most colonial powers now realize that both duty and interest demand that education be disseminated generally and that the desire of natives for it neither brooks denial nor too great restraint.

The fact is that "education" of the African goes on apace with or without schools and schooling. It is as true as it is commonplace to say that the native's education begins when he makes his first contact with the European. The resounding crash of the modern industrial system against the profoundly more primitive native life—the motor lorries, electric cranes, steam-boats, railroads, commerce, and all the other complex paraphernalia of modern industrial life in the Western world, which are paraded before the startled eyes of the African with such kaleidoscopic rapidity—makes it astonishing that he has not been left completely dazed by it all. If the African is not educated by this process then he requires a sophistication which will make true education vastly more difficult. The problem posed for the colonial powers is not whether the African shall be educated, but how may the inevitable education which the African will acquire be controlled and toward what objective shall it be directed?

It is true, as Mr. J. H. Oldham has pointed out, that the fundamental business of government in Africa is education. But that is not enough. Of far more significance to the native is the form which this education, as it becomes increasingly the direct concern of the state, shall take and the goals toward which it shall be directed. It may aim to train a few leaders, to create an intellectual elite and ignore the masses; or it may aim to teach the masses enough to make them more useful workmen and at the same time instruct them "to know their place" and to be content with their lot; or it may boast a more "liberal" viewpoint and advocate that the African be trained as a more or less expert artisan, which would make him still more valuable to his European masters; or again, his education may take on a political significance, and he may be trained to be a "good citizen" and a "collaborator" in the colonial administration, with a possible view toward eventual self-rule. Whatever the educational objective may be, however, it is conditioned by the attitude of the white man in his relations with the African. His influence is the dominating one in the present-day Africa, and the African's future is in his hands. As one English writer has put it in his admirable work, "What we think his future will be determines his present. If it is true that Africa of today conditions Africa of tomorrow, it is no less true that our hopes or fears for Africa of tomorrow condition Africa of today."[2]

Thus it may be readily assumed that from a consideration of a nature, extent, and policy of education in any given section of Africa a fairly clear reflection of the hopes for the African's future may be observed. A peek at this reflection affords little cause for optimism. If present-day native education in Africa is measured only by the test of preparation of the native for ultimate self-rule, there is much reason to agree with Mr. Woolf that no European government is yet guilty of serious efforts toward preparing the native to take his rightful place as a free man in the new economic and political society which European influences are shaping in Africa.[3]

In the early days of occupation of the African territories the colonizing powers usually left education to private initiative, i.e., to missionaries, sometimes aided by government subsidy. But the governments have gradually taken over this function in the colonies, and today the state is in virtually complete control of education in most of Africa. This has been brought to pass by a growing realization of the significance of educational policies (on the part of the colonial governments), since it is now generally recognized that the future success of colonial efforts is largely dependent upon the nature of the moral and intellectual development of the native subjects.[4] This tendency toward direct control of education by the state has made possible the formation of more definite educational policies, which could not be formulated under the more or less disorganized and varied efforts of the many separate missionary activities.

These governmental policies leave much to be desired, however. In the first place they provide for an education which is very narrow in scope. Except in a few places, as Dutch India, French Indo-China, and the French possessions in North Africa, organized native education rarely goes beyond the stage corresponding to our primary instruction.[5] In the second place the policy of education is too generally conditioned by subjective and selfish interest. As a former director of the French Colonial School observes, the primary result to be sought after in colonial education ought to be one of practical utility, for the French first and for the native later.[6]

One of the chief criticisms to be directed at African educational policies is one which is so often pertinent to our own systems. This is the practice of working out what appears to be a logical policy and then attempting to fit the people to it, without due consideration of the social, economic, and political conditions of the people. Common sense would seem to indicate that the policy should be cut to the measure of the people and these conditions, rather than that the people be cut down to fit the policy. For example, it is fundamental in the British West African educational policy that the objective is to preserve, so far as possible, all of the desirable elements of African culture and to train the Africans themselves to nurture its development. This has given rise to the policy that the native should be educated "along his own lines," the assumption being that the educated African will return to his own people and carry on the process.

In its essence this policy may be entirely good and in its application honest. Yet the indiscriminate application of it characteristic of the British in West Africa ignores many factors which demand consideration. At the very outset it should be kept in mind that the education which the European gives to the African must in the very nature of things be European education. A system of education controlled and directed and often taught by Europeans can do nothing more. All that can be given the native through such a system, therefore, is European, not native culture, for that is all the European has to give. In fact the very presence in Africa, on an ever-increasing scale, of the implements and customs of Western civilization would permit no other result.

Moreover, it is to be noted that African culture when presented to the African in this manner is something which perhaps the majority of educated Africans not only reject but resent, and on which the great mass of inarticulate Africans have had no expression. It is not surprising that the educated African looks with suspicion upon a so-called policy of "education along African lines," for he sees in it the germs of the hated segregation practice and a tendency to foist an inferior product upon his race. His ambition is to obtain the best that the world has to offer and every action of his European master not too subtly suggests to him that that which is European is best.

The difficulty is just at this point. The British policy fails utterly to take cognizance of the social and political conditions of the people whom it is destined to serve. The neglect may well prove fatal to any educational policy. Where the African and the Englishman are present in the same community, in whatever ratio, the African has an inferior status. The African, therefore, need not be as sensitive as he is, in order to conclude that a policy of differentiation in education and culture for the native and the European is one whose primary purpose is to further emphasize this inferiority. To him differentiation without prior equality simply means relegation of the black man to a permanent status of inferiority. Some English writers have sounded this note of warning. One writes:

> But we are not prepared to accept even the Englishman socially; we draw a color bar strongly, where, in the long run, a Frenchman does not. . . . We thus tend to build a wall right across the African's vista, to say to him: "Thus far and no further." Now, do what we will we cannot abolish contacts with the African, so he is bound to realize that wall more and more clearly; and we, . . . in helping him to educate himself have somehow or another to get that wall knocked down, even if we cannot adopt the French attitude. The native must have his vista and it must be a worthy one.[7]

The same approach would seem to be that so aptly suggested by another English author:

> the first and natural impulse of the African in his contact with the European is to have what the European has; that is to say, the native aspires to equality. This latter he must have before any fair and just differentiation can be brought about. Given this equality first, however, the African will soon come to modify the European culture and education and to adapt them to his own best interests.[8]

This is what education of the African "along his own lines" should properly signify.

Another fault characteristic of the policies of African education is that involving a too great willingness to reduce this education to formulae and to mechanize the process of its application. "Education of the African along his own lines" is one such formula; "industrial training," "agricultural training," "education by adaptation," are others. They too often appear to be unworthy substitutes for sound thinking. Certain it is that they are guilty of over-simplification of the problem. Rarely are they based on any understanding analysis of the different elements and interests in the races to which they are applied. For the successful operation of the formula the whole group must be identified. Like the American Negro, the African has often labored under the abuses of generalization and stereotyping.

For instance, the two reports of the Phelps-Stokes Fund on education in Africa under the direction of Dr. Thomas Jesse Jones have exerted considerable influence on the course of education for the native African, in the English, and to a lesser extent in the French colonies. They are regarded as authoritative because they boast a background of valuable experience with the black American population in the South. They start off with a formula—that industrial and agricultural training as exemplified by such institutions as Hampton and Tuskegee is the type of education most suitable for the American Negro. Upon this formula another is erected which concludes that since this type of education is good for the American Negro it must likewise be good for all Negroes, including the African, in itself a non sequitur, and based, moreover, on the dubious assumption that Negro life in America and Africa can be identified.[9]

In the first place it is now a commonplace that the educational ideals of the late Booker T. Washington were not embraced by a great many American Negroes. As the urbanization of the Negro has intensified along with his struggle for political and economic equality, these views have progressively lost support among the intelligent Negro population. The American Negro has also learned that differentiation because of race, without equality, too often perpetuates inferiority. In the second place there is no rational basis for assuming that what is good for the American Negro is good for the African.

The proposed "adaptation" for the rural African of the ideals of a rural education which has undergone a prior process of adaptation to the life of the rural Southern Negro, as outlined in the first Phelps-Stokes report, is too cut-and-dried and too indifferent to the facts of African life.[10] It fails to take into consideration the lack of unity in the African population, the many languages, the tribal organization, and the long-established customs and institutions of native life which place it in extreme contrast with Negro life of this country.[11] Moreover, it fails to consider that there are many Africans, and these the educated ones, who do not desire this type of education at all, if for no other reason than that is not typical of the kind of education prevalent in countries of the Western world for the dominant populations and that these natives may be justified in this attitude even for this reason alone. The social and political conditions of life of either the American Negro or the African would scarcely support the suggestion that adaptation of education to his needs would largely consist of covering him as a group with a thin blanket of instruction in gardening, handwork and hygiene.[12]

Education for the African thus appears to be as complex a problem as that confronted by the Western world in the education of its own populations. One thing is certain: the African will not long be content with a policy of education which offers him a specious and inferior product. The more enlightened elements of the African population demand the best that the European world can afford in education, as in all else, and rightfully regard formal education whose net result is to ensure the subserviency of the African peoples as worse than no education at all. African evolution has now advanced too far for the native to be deluded by the prospects of an education "truly colonial, racial, and local in character," which one writer cautiously suggests as a means of avoiding the impending danger of the development of an intellectual proletariat in Africa.[13]

This latter phenomenon is already in process of formation in French and British West Africa, and the discontent which it manifests in some sections is in no small measure the product of the short-sightedness of the educational policy imposed upon the native populations. The French, no less than the English, are guilty of this error of educating the African by broad formulae and "adapting" the education to the "needs" of the native as the French, not the natives, view these needs. The discussion of native education in the French mandate Togo and the colony Dahomey in the pages following will amply indicate the nature of the French educational policy.[14]

Native Education in Togo and Dahomey

There is a saying that when the Germans first arrive in a new colony they build a garrison, when the English arrive they build a custom house, and when the French arrive they build a school. The French, more than any colonizing power, have employed native education as an instrument of administrative policy. In consequence, education in French West Africa is predominately under rigid governmental control. This control extends itself not only to matters pertaining to educational organization, but equally to the more vital concern of curriculum and language.

The French attitude toward the education of the native in the African colonies is a combination of sense of duty and mutual benefit. In the words of the twice former colonial minister M. Sarraut:

> Instruire les indigenes est assurément notre devoir: c'est une obligation morale impérieuse que nous créent les responsabilités de la souveraineté vis-à-vis des populations indigénes dont nous avons assumé la tutelle. Mais ce devoir fondamental s'accorde par surcrolt avec nos intéréts économiques, administratifs, militaires et politiques les plus évidents.[15]

In the first place the dissemination of education will have, in M. Sarraut's opinion, a significant effect on the increase of the productivity of the colony in that it will provide better-trained and more efficient workmen. Furthermore, it will make possible a more extensive recruitment of native collaborators who can render valuable aid to the administration in the construction of public works and in the subordinate administrative offices. This will mean a less heavy burden upon the colonial budgets as native employees and agents are far less costly than European.

Early Educational Efforts

The French early concerned themselves with the problem of education in West Africa. In 1816, coincident with the repossession of Senegal after the

Napoleonic Wars, the French Government put at the disposal of Colonel Schmaltz, governor of the colony, an instructor whose mission it was to give the young Senegaelse an "elementary instruction."[16] A lay school was opened at Saint Louis under the direction of Jean Dard, who "thought competent, was misunderstood" and returned to France. Consequently, in 1829, the educational system at Saint Louis was reorganized by M. Ballin with emphasis upon the teaching of the French language. M. Balin was soon stricken, however, and was compelled to return home. Finally the government appealed to the Catholic brothers of Ploermel, who took charge of the schools of Saint Louis and Gorée in 1841 and enjoyed immediate success. The Catholic brothers turned the nature of the instruction given toward a more "practical education," involving chiefly agricultural and industrial apprenticeship.[17]

The Catholic teachers encountered difficulties with the Mohammedan populations, however, and when Faiddherbe took command of Senegal in 1854 he immediately perceived the necessity of pacifying the Moslems and proceeded to create a lay school by an *arrêté* of March 31, 1857.[18] Later other such schools were established in French West Africa whose chief purpose it was to familiarize the natives with the French language. No truly systematic efforts were put forth until the turn of the century, however.[19] The first such effort was embraced in the *arrêtés* of November 1, 1918, and May 1, 1924, and, with the governor-general's circular of the latter date, constitute the foundation of the French educational system in West Africa today.[20]

In Dahomey, mission schools had been established well in advance of French occupation in 1887, though their instruction was given in Portuguese and English. However, upon the conquest by the French, Governor Ballot decreed that the teaching should be in the French language and began the establishment of official lay schools directed by French teachers. By the end of the century there were approximately twenty schools in Dahomey, though it was only annexed to France in 1894.

Under the German administration prior to the Anglo-French conquest, native education in Togo was left almost entirely to the missions, which were lightly subsidized by the government.

Present Educational Organization

The organization of education in Dahomey conforms to the general set-up established for the Federation of French West Africa as a whole.[21] With some few exceptions the same system prevails in the mandate Togo, as provided in the arrêté of June 28, 1928.[22] The foundation of the system of primary education is the village or elementary school which embraces two types of instruction: (1) the *cours préparatoire* and (2) the *cours élémentaire*. The principal objective of the village school is the diffusion of the French language among the masses of the native population.[23] As stated by the Togo administration in its *arrêté* of 1928 organizing education in the mandate territory: "L'enseignement primaire élémentaire a pour objet essentiel de familiariser les indigenes avec notre langue et de les prépare a devenirdans leur propre milieu de bons travailleurs."[24] The *cours préparatoire* of the elementary schools performs the same function as the preparatory schools[25] and is offered wherever 30 pupils below the age of 11 are found.[26] The *cours élémentaire* is open to the best students from the preparatory schools and the *cours préparatoire*. The elementary schools are generally under the direction of a native *instituteur* assisted by a native monitor.

An *école régionale* is established at each important center, usually at the capital of the administrative district, or *cercle*. In Dahomey the *école régionale* comprises three different classes under separate instructors. These are the preparatory, the elementary, and the intermediate, or middle (*moyen*). In Togo, however, the regional schools include only the intermediate instruction.[27] The pupils attending the regional schools are recruited from the best students in the neighboring elementary schools. The work done in the first two classes of the regional schools is the same as that of the elementary village schools. But the intermediate class provides more advanced work and the students completing this course, which is generally of two years' duration, are awarded a *certificat d'études primaires* which entitles them to continue their education at the *école primaire supérieure* located at the capital of each colony. The *écoles urbaines* located in the urban centers are similar to the regional schools. These schools are generally directed by a European *instituteur* of superior rank who has the *brevet supérieur* and the *certificat d'aptitude pédagogique,* which would entitle him to teach in France.[28]

In order to train natives for administrative and commercial employment an *école primaire supérieure* (*école complémentaire* at Lome, in Togo) is established in the capital of each colony. These schools receive the best pupils from the regional and urban schools, who are admitted either by examination or by presentation of the *certificat d'études primaires*. The students preparing for jobs in the administration, such as messengers, stenographers, and clerks, together with the sons of chiefs and notables, may complete their instruction at this school after a period usually not in excess of three years. However, those who desire to become teachers and auxiliary doctors are sent to the William-Ponty Normal School at Gorée or the Dakar Medical School, after they have been awarded certificates at the *école supérieure.*

In addition there are special classes for adults, boarding schools and orphanages for mulattoes, domestic schools for girls, and grade and agricultural schools for the boys. In recent years scholarships have been granted which permit the recipients to pursue secondary education in certain designated institutions in France.

Perhaps the most distinctive feature of the French system, which distinguishes it in principle from the English, is that of gratuitous education. Of course the colony bears the burden ultimately, but it is a factor in making education more accessible to the native population. On the other hand, the added expense of a system of free education requires a more careful weeding-out of students, particularly in the classes beyond the elementary village schools. As will be seen, the French have adopted a rather unfortunate policy of limiting the number of students received in some of the schools in Togo and Dahomey.

The French educational organization also includes a system of inspection. There is an inspector-general of education, who resides at Dakar and who is directly responsible to the government-general of French West Africa,[29] whose duty it is to study all educational questions involving the colonies of the federation and to prepare the orders directed to the lieutenant-governors of the colonies. In each colony the lieutenant-governor is given an inspector of schools, who is assisted by several agents of control. Dahomey, like Senegal, engages an *inspecteur primaire métropolitain*. In Togo, education is supervised by a director of education assisted by a European teacher detached for that purpose. In addition, a consultative Committee of Education was created by an *arrêté* of 1929, which is presided over by the *commissaire* of the Republic for Togo and whose membership embraces the principal administrative officers of the territory together with the directors of the private educational institutions.[30] Its first session was held December 3, 1929, at which time the three following principal questions on education in Togo were discussed: (1) the education of girls; (2) the role of native language in education; (3) physical education.

The Language of Instruction

"Parler en français, c'est penser en français," stated one noted French colonial administrator. This may or may not be true, and there are many Frenchmen who, having heard some of their African protegés solemnly but elaborately abuse the language, think that it is not. But it hits upon one of the most debated problems in the field of colonial administration. What should be the vehicular language for the subject people? In Africa the French have not hesitated to decree that French shall be the universal medium of expression, though this is not their decision in Madagascar. The English have taken a contrary attitude in Africa though not so in India. Circumstances seem to justify the opinion that expediency and not native interest have quite generally dictated the language policy pursued in the colony. Certain it is, at any rate, that the French have adopted an extreme attitude in their West African possessions. From the stand-point of native interest the subject is fraught with vital concern.

The issue of principal controversy revolves about the language to be employed as a vehicle of instruction in the early school years. It seems generally agreed that the European language must be taught at some time and that it will virtually displace the native vernacular in the more advanced education by means of which the native leaders are trained. In the advanced courses where great emphasis is placed upon "moral" education the native language is generally found inadequate to express the delicate nuances necessary in the development of upright, loyal character on the Western plan. It is held essential that the native leaders know one European language "as a means of access to the great accomplishments and inspirations of civilisation."[31]

Assuming this widespread conviction to be true it is a matter of no great surprise that the French should adopt a policy of educating the native exclusively in the French. For the early policy of the French government in West Africa was that of assimilation and the educational process was pointed toward the dissemination of French culture among the native populations, who would eventually become black Frenchmen after the fashion of native populations of the Antilles. The natives, once having learned the French language, would think like Frenchmen and would be culturally bound to France. So far as many of the present-day native elite are concerned the French attitude was fully justified, for men like MM. Diagne and Candace, who have risen to high estate in the French political world, are as "French" in every respect but color as any living being.

Even today, under the modified version of the old assimilation policy which M. Sarraut likes to call association or collaboration, one of the most pressing aims is the development of an elite class of natives, who have become *assimilés* through absorption of French culture and education, and who are to be the valued collaborators in the *mise en valeur* of the human and natural resources of the colonies.[32] So far as the masses are concerned they are to become the *serviteurs utiles,* and it is much easier to train and command them when they understand the language of the Métropole.

Moreover, the French consistently point out that the large number of tribes inhabiting their territories, the localization and relative isolation of these tribal groups, and the varying degrees of evolution found among them have given birth to numerous dialects each differing from the other. Thus, they conclude, a European language must be taught as a lingua franca to link these peoples together.[33] It is this situation which many French colonial educators point to as the principal justification for the teaching of the French language.[34] The French also contend that their language must be widely taught in order that the administrators may make themselves and their orders understood by the natives[35] and feel that this is a means of avoiding the admitted abuses incident to the employment of native interpreters.

The justifications which the French advance for this policy are thus political or nationalistic on the one hand and utilitarian on the other. The validity of these explanations is subject to no little doubt.

In the French African colonies and in Togo and Cameroon the French language is introduced not as a course in the school curriculum, but is used as the sole medium of instruction from beginning to end of the educational process, in which process the vernacular has no role whatsoever. "La leçon de français parlé est done la base de tout enseignement" declares the official book of instructions for the teaching personnel in French West Africa.[36] In the mandate Togo, as in the neighboring French colony Dahomey, "Le français est seul en usage dans les écoles."[37]

In the book of instructions for the teaching personnel in AOF [Afrique-Occidentale française] the teacher is told that the French child entering school for the first time at the age of six is able to speak and understand the French language.[38] He is endowed with a limited elementary vocabulary consisting of the parts of the body, clothing, food, and domestic animals—not exceeding 500 or 600 words in all. The native child entering the French colonial village school, however, though possessing a similar vocabulary in his maternal idiom, knows nothing of the French and is therefore that much retarded in pursuing his education in French. Thus, the first problem of the teacher is to furnish the native beginner with this essential rudimentary vocabulary. This the French propose to do by the direct method of pointing to an object and pronouncing its name in French. It is calculated that on the basis of a school year of 9 months, 20 days to the month, 180 days are available for the purpose of equipping the young African with the necessary vocabulary of 500 or 600 words.[39] The French cautiously admit that, while by this method they may not succeed in giving to the young native the mind of the French child brought up in a different milieu, yet he is given in this short period the necessary word equipment by means of which he may increase his knowledge and understanding of things in terms of the French language.[40] Moreover, they contend, the direct method of instruction dissipates the necessity of translation which involves mere memory, and likewise renders it unnecessary for the teacher to know the native tongue.[41] M. Hardy describes the results obtained through this method as "astonishing."[42]

Sound pedagogy would seem to demand that at least the early instruction of the child should be given in his maternal tongue. As one writer indicates, the child in the village school knows his native language and in it every word has a meaning, whereas words in the European metier may have only an equivalent. "The distance," he writes, "by which an equivalent may be removed from a meaning is the wide basis of many language jokes against missionaries,"[43] a truism which is quickly apparent to the African tourist. It is doubtful if even by the direct method the French can readily break the native child of the habit of speaking the French word but thinking in Ewe or Hausa, or whatever his native tongue may be. The French teachers themselves readily admit that their task is made much more difficult by the fact that as soon as the child leaves the school room he resumes his native idiom, in which he continues to converse until his return to the school. In other words, the teaching of French does not wipe out the vernacular, though it no doubt restrains the expansion of the native tongue through the substitution of French words to describe the new phenomena incident to the infiltration of Western civilization, instead of the formation of native words for this purpose. For example, the writer engaged in conversation with a native youth in the employ of a French administrator in the interior of Togo and inquired of him the word in his language to describe a portable victrola owned by his employer. The quick reply was "phonograph." Similarly, it was amusing to hear natives in the south of Togo, along the Gold Coast border, passing along the roads engaged in conversation in the Ewe tongue, cordially greet passers-by with a polite "good-evening."

The Belgian and English governments have found it possible to employ a widely spoken native language as the lingua franca for their subjects and use it for purposes of instruction in the schools. Some French writers feel that this could be done in most of the French West African possessions by the encouragement of the use of such languages as the Ouloff, Mandingo, Hausa, and Bambara tongues, from which most of the other dialects are derived.[44] It would certainly be a more simple task then for the administrator and teacher to learn the universal native medium of expression in the particular colony than to attempt to teach the language of the administrator to all the natives. This would not alter the necessity of a knowledge of the European language by the elite class.

In the south of Togo the Ewe language is almost universal, though the languages are much more diverse in the central and northern regions. In Dahomey a greater diversity of languages is found. In these territories as in all the French West African possessions, the missions have not done as much toward unification of the native languages as in the colonies of other nations. This is perhaps explained by the official attitude of the French government toward the mission schools, which have received little encouragement.

However, English teachers in the Gold Coast schools, where the primary education is given in the native languages, informed the writer that the problem was not a simple one, though the theory seemed sound enough. In the first place they pointed out that when a school is taught in a particular native vernacular it means that a good many young natives must receive their instruction in a native tongue entirely alien to their experience and that therefore the instructor must teach them the new native language, which is quite as difficult as teaching them English. Moreover, the lack of a native literature constitutes a great handicap. The native teachers often attempt to make their own books in the vernacular in the English colonies—a practice with varying results. The absence of a vernacular literature undoubtedly weakens the policy of teaching in the vernacular. Without such a literature it would seem that the European language must increasingly assume the role of the native tongue, for it rapidly becomes the only language which can fix and transmit the ideas of the native in this new world which Europeans are creating for him.

The French policy purports to be based on the political grounds of nationalism (which many interpret as an innate sense of the superiority of a French culture which the natives should be happy to have crammed down their throats) and administrative expediency and convenience. Yet it is somewhat difficult to explain the official attitude toward the missions. The mission schools have vigorously defended bilingualism in native education.[45] But both in Togo and Dahomey the government has put the mission schools under direct governmental supervision and has applied to them the same rules under which the government schools are controlled. Thus, the teaching of the vernacular is interdicted.[46] However, two recent decrees in Togo have permitted slight relaxation of this strict policy on behalf of the private schools.[47] Under this dispensation the mission schools are permitted to give instruction in the native language during one hour each school day, and certain unofficial schools may be conducted as catechumenats in which rudimentary exercises in the vernacular may be taught, but nothing else. In the native language schools of the missions, books in the vernacular have been commonly employed.

The native, particularly of the educated class, looks with mixed emotions upon the question. While he may have a sentimental attachment to his native tongue, he regards the European language as an expression of what is best in the world outside and as an instrument by means of which he may obtain the best which Western civilization has to offer. Where the native language is forced upon the natives it is often regarded as an attempt to retard their progress and to perpetuate European dominance. The pride and ability with which the natives in Dahomey, Nigeria, and the Gold Coast publish their daily and weekly papers, all in the European language, and the fact that there are no papers in these colonies attempting to publish in the vernacular are something of an indication of how the native feels on the question. There is, as Mr. Huxley writes, "one overwhelming answer" to those who would withhold the European language from the African, and that is in the inescapable fact that "the African wants to know . . . [it]; as education spread, he will want it more intensely. . . . Any attempt to keep the progressive African from European languages is doomed from the outset to create friction and to end in failure.[48]

As a result of the French language policy the French native speaks much better French than the horribly distorted "pidgin" English of the natives in the English colonies. French is widely spoken in both Togo and Dahomey.

It appears that the French language policy is subject to criticism on political grounds in its application to Togo, because of the mandate status of this territory. The spirit of the mandate seems to demand that the natives be given an opportunity for instruction in their own language if they so desire. The arbitrary action of the French government in decreeing that the French language and no other shall be taught in schools supported by the funds of the territory may justly be interpreted as a disregard of the true nature of the trust conferred upon it. This policy has often been questioned by members of the Permanent Mandates Commission during consideration of the French reports on Togo.[49] To these questions the replies of the accredited French representatives at Geneva have been notably weak.

In the 1925 annual report to the League of Nations on the administration of Togo, the French government noted that the policy of teaching only the European language was a precedent set by the German administration which preceded the French in control of the territory.[50] An ordinance of February 2, 1906, decreed that German was to be the only European language admitted in the schools and that it was to be taught 6, 8, or 10 hours per week in both government and mission schools, according to the class. The French administration observes also that, if the French language policy was displeasing to the natives, the schools would be deserted instead of overcrowded, since school attendance in Togo is not obligatory.[51]

The French would do well to consider the possibility of modifying the present language policy to permit instruction in a common vernacular in the first two or three years of education. The French language might then be introduced in the advanced primary classes. This would enable the native to adjust himself more naturally to the new civilization in process of formation all about him and at the same time aid in the preservation of the best features of the African culture. At all odds the native himself should have some voice in the matter and an opportunity to make a choice. This could be achieved by permitting the private schools to resume their former policy of teaching in the vernacular.

The Nature of the Curriculum

As a preliminary to the consideration of the rationale of the French instruction and its adaptation to the native a brief summary of its content will be undertaken. Since, say the French, the object of education is to produce strong, honest, and intelligent individuals, the system of instruction must cultivate the physical, moral, and intellectual faculties of the child.[52] Thus, it is indispensable that the educational efforts embrace programs directed toward the physical, moral, and intellectual development of the child.

In the French program of primary instruction in West Africa the subject of morale is generally placed first in the curriculum and runs through the preparatory, elementary, and intermediate (*moyen*) courses as well as the domestic schools (*écoles ménagères*) for the girls.[53] It is not taught formally through class lessons but is aimed primarily at developing good habits in the children, such as cleanliness, exactitude and regularity, politeness, truthfulness, honesty, respect, and obedience.

The second subject in the curriculum is the French language, which is the basis of the entire educational process. In the elementary course the French grammar is taught and composition is essayed in the *cours moyen*. One of the most impressive lessons it has ever been the writer's privilege to witness was that of an elementary class reciting in French under a native Dahomean teacher in a regional school at Porto Novo, Dahomey. This native was said by the director of education for the colony to be the most efficient and inspiring teacher on his staff. In an elementary class in Togo it was interesting to observe that the subjects for the exercise in dictation were: "Nous chantons en travaillant," and "Yenoussi a payé son impot"; this may or may not have been a bit of subtle governmental propaganda. Again, in a second-year intermediate class in Togo, during an exercise in letter-writing, the pupils were required to write a letter to a hypothetical relative living in the interior who had difficulty in understanding the French taxation system. He was to be advised to pay his tax because it was used to pay the salaries of the administrative functionaries and to build roads and railroads. In another instance the subject for dictation was "My grandfather is a cultivator and I will be a cultivator also." This latter took on an added significance when the writer learned that the larger boys in this school were being encouraged to leave the school and return home to cultivate the crops.

Reading and writing (in the French, of course) are third and fourth on the program, followed by arithmetic in the metric system. The first two years are devoted to the first hundred numbers. In the domestic schools for girls arithmetical instruction is limited to simple addition and subtraction.[54]

Drawing and singing are also included. It was observed that the singing often was significantly pointed. Many of the songs lustily sung by the native youngsters were highly patriotic, one of which included the line "toujours la France, notre paie." In justice, however, it must be told that native songs are also sung under the direction of the native teachers, particularly in Togo.

Physical education is comparatively recent in the curriculum. This training receives a great deal more emphasis in Togo than in Dahomey. It was given official sanction and organization in the mandate under an *arrêté* of July 25, 1927, and, after a period of training, 15 natives were qualified and appointed as monitors in physical education.[55] The government's special interest in this subject is explained as due to the fact that in southern Togo, especially, the native children were found to have a retarded physical development.[56] This is of some significance since the development of an adequate labor supply is one of the pressing problems of the administration in Togo. It is an impressive sight to see the large squads of boys, dressed in shirts and khaki shorts, march out in military formation to the recreation grounds twice each week to take calisthenics and to play outdoor games.

Manual and agricultural training are also included. Most of the schools have a garden where agriculture is practiced as well as taught. In the preparatory, elementary, and intermediate schools the manual training, which includes lessons in the handling of tools, modeling of pottery, carpentry, etc., the teaching is chiefly academic. In the industrial schools (*écoles professionnelles*) the work done is much more practical. These often assume the aspect of small factories and the students and apprentices turn out articles which are sold to buyers in the colony. In the fine new industrial school at Cotonou in Dahomey the students are given three-fourths of the price paid for the articles which they construct. In these schools training is given in designing, carpentry, machine shop, cabinet construction, masonry, and, in the case of the school at Cotonou, elementary instruction in electricity, wireless, and radio. They also receive some instruction in academic subjects and must have completed the course at a regional school before admission. In Togo a government industrial school is located at Sokode, in the interior, but is not well developed.

An excellent example of the abuse of the practice of industrial education is to be found in the École Professionelle de la Mission Catholique at Lome.[57] This school was founded in 1914 by German fathers who were subsidized by the German government. In 1918 it was taken over by Les Pères Blancs de Lyons. It is an establishment of surprising extent for a territory of Togo's size and has modern facilities for machine-shop work, forges, carpentry, bookbinding, printing, lino-typing, tailoring, shoe-repairing, and the manufacture of rubber stamps. It has a contract with the Togo administration for all government printing, and it is noted for the excellency of the inlaid furniture which it sells at fancy prices. In 1932 it had at work some 40 native apprentices and 30 workers, who received a very small stipend from the "school." The apprentices serve four years and the best of them are kept on as "workers." By no stretch of the imagination can it be considered a school. There is no formal instruction and there is no program. The products are all sold in the public market and the apprentices and workers are sent out into the territory on repair and construction jobs. The tailoring department was recently closed because there was too much competition from the native tailors outside. The shoe department was also closed because of too great fluctuation in the price of leather. By masquerading as a school it employs native help for little or nothing to do the work of factory and workshop. This is a greater abuse than the practice common to the government industrial schools of requiring their students to serve a year of "apprenticeship" at the railroad shops after completion of their formal training at the industrial schools.

Under the *sciences usuelles* and *leçons des choses* the natives are taught bodily hygiene and learn about the human body and the nature of animal and plant life, minerals, food, clothing, varied diseases, and their prevention. They are likewise taught the elementary geography of their country and of France in the intermediate courses, together with history. The history includes the past and present conditions of life of the black men, the comparisons being made on the basis of such things as housing, clothing, lighting, and instruction, together with some attention to local history and legend. The director of native education in Togo informed the writer that there were no Togolese legends, however, through the director of the Protestant school at Lome compiled a book of them, and the official literary publication for the French African mandates has published a number of others.[58] The history of the French in Africa and their leading colonial adventurers is also taught. The natives are told the great debt owed to France and the duty of loyalty to the French flag. For instance, they are taught that Togo is indebted to the French for its administration, security, justice, education, commerce, and prosperity.[59]

The highest schools in Togo and Dahomey, the École Supérieur (Cours Complémentaire), of Lome, and the École Victor-Ballot, of Porto Novo), follow much the same program on a higher level, the limited number of students admitted receiving training for governmental and commercial positions. It was the writer's privilege to read a copy of the syllabus used in the history course in the École Supérieur of Lome, which was prepared by the wife of the director of education for the territory, who was the head of the school and the teacher of the course. This syllabus began with establishment of the post of the French West Indian Company at Ouidah in 1626 for the purpose of carrying on the slave trade. From the date it gave a complete sketch of the French activities in Togo, commercial and political, and the rivalry with Germany, up to the present day, including the details of the French occupation of the territory during the last war. It ignored completely the history of native tribes and chieftains, though there is much interesting material available.

Separate schools are maintained for girls, though they are occasionally found in the *cours moyen* of the regional schools. In the domestic training schools for the girls the policy is to afford them a little education along the lines of that given in the primary schools with the chief emphasis placed upon such "more practical" things as sewing, washing and ironing, and personal hygiene, which will "les préparer a leur tâche de ménagere."[60] In schools for girls which were visited in Dahomey, however, the writer found that most of the time was devoted to the three R's with but slight attention to elementary sewing and with even less results.

The courses for adults confine themselves exclusively to the teaching of the French language.

The content of the education given in Togo has been subjected to question in some respects by members of the Permanent Mandate Commission. The failure to include the teaching of native customs, at least in the first two years of instruction, has been questioned,[61] as well as the status of the domestic schools for girls.[62] Lord Lugard has called it to the attention of the French representative at Geneva that the charge has been made that the French classbooks used in the Togo schools deliberately ignore the existence of the mandates system and that the French mandates are treated merely as colonies.[63] Though the writer has visited a good many schools in Togo and has seen practically all of the books employed in the various courses of instruction, he has neither seen nor heard any mention of the status of the territory of Togo as a mandate. Some native leaders in Togo are of the opinion that the great majority of the natives know nothing about it.

Adaptation of Education to Native Needs

In a consideration of the problem of native education one is struck by the weighty importance which so many officials and writers recently place upon the necessity of "adapting" education to the native. It is now quite generally agreed that the Western systems of education must be "adapted" to native life before they can successfully educate these backward populations. "Education," it has been written, "should be adapted to the mentality, aptitudes, occupation, and traditions of the various peoples and races."[64] Adaptation of education for the African has carried with it too much mumble-jumble, however—the principle has been grossly overplayed. For all successful teaching everywhere is a process of adaptation. If it is meant by adaptation of education for the African that the teacher is to draw upon the wealth of local color for illustration and example, then the term is too profound for its use, which becomes a mere matter of mechanics. But it is when it is employed in a sense involving the deep-set principles of human thought and knowledge that it becomes weighted with fateful consequences for the native.

It may be assumed that education is at once a problem and a process of human development. The subject matter of this education therefore is not framed *in vacuo* but must be fitted to the lives and experiences of the people it is destined to serve. This is where the rub occurs in African education. The educational policy is too often one which is shaped by preconceived notions of what the native is to be, of what his status in the changing world shall be. Education is too closely bound to the political and economic policies of the colonial power. Thus, the political role of the school becomes as important as its educative function.[65] In this scheme of things the native is the mere tool to be fashioned rather than a partner in the process of increasing the number of those who share in the world's store of knowledge.

Many Africans find numerous grounds for criticism of the programs of adapted education mapped out for their people by the European. In the first place, they are usually based on a stereotyped view of the African—all Africans look and are like; therefore they must all be educated alike. They do not consider the natural differences among the African peoples which are identical in terms of class, wealth, and aspiration with those of Western peoples. These differences must enter into the educational equation, and in the words of one authority: "grave errors would be committed in seeking to melt the young of these different classes together by means of a uniform education."[66]

In the second place, education adapted to the African is too utilitarian, too patronizing, and too mean. It regards the subject African not in the light of his potentialities as a developed and maturely intelligent individual, but as a cog in an economic and political wheel which the Western nations are grinding primarily for their own and not his benefit. "The Dahomean," writes an official French publication, "is sufficiently intelligent to become an excellent worker."[67] Ergo, the educational system must place greater emphasis upon industrial training in order to get the most possible out of him. Furthermore, the African is told that he is fortunate in having a strong foreign government to interest itself in him to this extent, even though he must bear the cost out of his country's riches and his tax receipts, for otherwise he would remain a hopeless savage.

The African also sees many contradictions in the education adapted to his needs. There is one policy pursued alike in French and British colonies which purports to train native leaders. But when these leaders have been trained and are initiated into the privileged ranks of the elite, they are often confounded to discover that they have no longer the desire to "return to their people" nor anything to take back to them. If they do retain their interest in their people and consider native problems with an eye of critical intelligence, they are suspect, and will be subjected to banishment and vitriolic attack. This has been the fate of the gifted French Negro René Maran, a Pleiades of whom is not worth one good native workman, in the estimation of one fervent Frenchman.[68]

Again the education adapted to the African is often contradictory in its application. Sometimes it attempts to Westernize the African as regards religion and ethics, while withholding Western science, literature, and liberalism from him. The government policies often attempt to inculcate him with Western skill in the applied sciences, while discouraging the development of Western ideas and customs in other respects. Also, it may be difficult for the Africans to understand how they are to be made, through the education policy of Togo, for instance, "not mediocre Europeans but excellent Africans"[69] by being taught French exclusively in the schools and by being primed for "collaborators" in a French system of government and law.

Adaptation of education for the natives of Dahomey and Togo increasingly stresses the importance of industrial and agricultural training. The Dahomean administration frankly declares that "le but de l'école tend-il de plus en plus a la formation professionnelle, toute idée de rendement immediat devenant accessoire et étant toujours subordonnée a cette formation profession-nelle."[70] The administration feels it necessary to justify this policy by stating its belief that the Dahomean is sufficiently intelligent to become an "excellent worker" and rebukes itself for its previous policy, which trained the native only to be a robot and not a skilled workman.[71] The Togo administration is likewise converted to this policy of accentuating the "practical character" of native education[72] and perceives the necessity of inoculating the young natives with the idea that manual as well as intellectual labor is the "fundamental law of all organised society."[73] Toward this end the weekly programs of the schools have been altered to permit more time for manual and agricultural training.[74] The problem is made more pressing as the government agencies and commercial companies cannot longer absorb the number of pupils trained in the schools and it becomes necessary to divert them to other fields.[75] Moreover, this type of training is regarded as one of the essential factors in the *mise en valeur* of the colony.[76] The future progress of France in West Africa depends on an increase in population and the development of skilled native workers.[77]

Similarly, in the schools for girls the tendency is to give the work a more practical turn and, with the exception of a few girls who will be trained as teachers and mid-wives, "l'école ne doit chercher qu'a préparer les filles a leur tâche prochaine de ménagere."[78] Thus, the native girl will be taught to wash and iron, cook and sew, and little else, though it is but recently that the governments have interested themselves in the training of girls at all.

Teachers in the *écoles ménageres* recognize the fact that the proper train-ing for the girls must play a key role in the evolution of the native populations. Yet not the most ardent apologist for the French educational policy would venture to suggest that the "practical" training given the girls in the domestic schools will equip them to contribute very much to the intellectual and spiritual development of their people.

Thus, the present trend of educational policy in Togo and Dahomey sug-gests that the education of the natives has capitulated to the economic and political ends of the French administration in these territories. The French interpret the educational needs in terms of their own interest, and this program is reinterpreted by the French and native teachers in whose hands it is placed. In this manner, adaptation quite often becomes inadaptation.[79] For example, the commandant of one of the important *cercles* in Togo informed the writer that he ignored the gradation of schools and their courses because that "meant nothing." He believed in "teaching them all the same thing"—a little reading, writing, and arithmetic and how to work with their hands. A teacher in a regional school in Dahomey vigorously affirmed the necessity of keeping the native in his place and under authority.

Irrespective of these faults in French policy, the French have made sincere efforts to adapt the courses of instruction to the life and interests of the African.

In view of the surviving evidences of the old policy of assimilation and the French language policy, this is surprising. It is Dr. Buell's opinion, however, that the French educational system has made more progress in this respect than has been made in any other territory in Africa.[80]

While some of the books employed in the native schools are still identical with those used in the schools of the Métropole, a number of textbooks have been written by French colonial teachers which are designed particularly for the African student. Among these are the following: A. Davesne: *Mamadou et Bineta apprennent à parler français, Mamadou et Bineta apprennent à lire et écrire, Mamadou et Bineta lisent et écrivent couramment;* A. Davesne and J. Gouin: *Contes de la brousse et de la forét;* R. Imbert: *Mon ami Koffi;* L. Sonolet and A. Péres: *Moussa et gi-gla, Histoire de deux petits noirs;* and a *Manuel d'agriculture.* Most of these are illustrated with drawings familiar to natives.

In his introduction to M. Davesne's *Mamadou et Bineta,*[81] M. Georges Hardy indicates that adaptation of education must consider the capacity of minds, the needs of the country, the traditions of the social milieu, as well as the colonial policy. Moreover, it does not suffice merely to substitute in the reading exercises the native boy Mamadou for the French boy Gaston, nor the making of palm-oil for vine-cutting. Rather, the process of learning shall take the native child down familiar paths, in order that the impress shall be striking and permanent.

In contrast to the earlier *Moussa et Gi-gla, Histoire de deux petits noirs,*[82] the recent reader by M. Imbert, *Mon ami Koffi,*[83] is surprisingly free from administrative propaganda. The former, telling the story of two little native boys on a trip through West Africa with a European merchant, while interestingly written, injects a not inconsiderable amount of propaganda. The blessings of French occupation are shown, the duty of loyalty and obedience are emphasized, and the glory of military service under the French is vividly portrayed, so much so, in fact, that little Moussa ends up by expressing a desire to be a soldier when he grows up. In the book written by M. Imbert, who was the director of education in Togo at the time of publication, there are no such innuendos, though the book is written in terms and setting familiar to the everyday life of the African. In *Mamadou et Bineta lisent et écrivent couramment,*[84] the child is again told of his duty to France and is impressed with the solid virtues of work and cultivation and the acquisition of property and riches. Thus, even though the instruction is in French, the native child is taught a great deal about his own environment which he is able to better appreciate. At the same time, however, the French seize the opportunity to acquaint the natives with the nature of the French administration and impress them with its beneficence. In *Moussa et Gi-gla* the native boys are informed that there is little difference between races and that the black men are merely retarded. This difference in development between the white and black men is to be made up by the simple process of the black man toiling for his friendly and paternal white associates.[85]

If education in Togo and Dahomey is to make anything of the native other than a robot and rubber-stamp, it must be adapted not only to the local conditions of native life but must afford an opportunity for transcending those conditions as well. It is well and proper for educational training to prepare men and women to earn their living and contribute manual energy to the productive activities of the world, but it must be recognized also that the native is entitled to an introduction to that realm of literary, historical, religious, and scientific ideas which, having no immediate practical value, will nevertheless enable him to raise himself above the drudgery of his hum-drum life of daily toil. Only in this way can the African be expected to cultivate that spirit and articulateness necessary to the development of a national and racial soul, which alone will justify his ultimate right of self-control in his own country.

In short, there should be greater emphasis upon the cultivation of knowledge. If knowledge is of a universal character and knows neither race nor national boundaries, then there is little excuse for that type of adaptation of education which for the African is synonymous with differentiation and inferiority.

Extent and Results of Educational Policy

The problem of educating the native is attacked more seriously and vigorously in Togo than in Dahomey. Though Dahomey is a richer country than Togo the educational facilities of the mandate are much superior to those in the neighboring colony. This is no doubt due to the mandate status of Togo and the fact that the Permanent Mandates Commission has shown a keen interest in the French educational policy. Education in both Togo and Cameroon has made more rapid progress than in the French colonies of West and Equatorial Africa.[86] The attitude of the directors of education in the mandates is more sympathetic to the native and the programs of instruction somewhat more liberal.

It is noteworthy that, though school attendance is obligatory in Togo and Dahomey only for sons of chiefs and notables, the eagerness of the young natives to take advantage of this gratuitous privilege exceeds the available facilities. Some of the pupils in Togo are said to make daily trips on foot of as much as 15 kilometers, in good weather and bad, to attend school.[87]

In consequence, the schools have often been crowded, and both the Togo and Dahomey administrations have recently adopted a policy of limiting the number of children admitted to the schools. This is accomplished by fixing an age limit for the several grades.[88] The Togo administration justifies this action by explaining that experience has demonstrated that the older students receive but slight benefit from the instruction given.[89] In answer to a query put by a member of the Mandates Commission concerning the decrease in the number of students in the Togo schools, M. Bonnecarrere, former *commissaire* for Togo, explained that a large number of students between the ages of 17 and 20 had been put out of the schools, as it was better to "concentrate on quality than quantity."[90]

The natives have deeply resented this policy, however, and see in it a grave injustice and a ruse to rush the older boys into productive labor on the farms. The native journals in Dahomey have made vigorous protest against the restriction and affirm that the native child is entitled to a minimum of 9 years of instruction irrespective of his age.[91] The native editors point out the injustice of applying the age rule of France to a young colony like Dahomey which has had but 40 years of French occupation. So eager are the natives for education, declares Le Phare du Dahomey, that "tous les parents au Dahomey sont prêts a payer l'éducation de leurs enfants et demandent avec insistance au Gouverne-ment la création des écoles payantes. Ceci est le voeu ardent de la population dahoméenne."[92] If pay schools are not established, then the natives demand that the government subsidize the Catholic mission schools, in order that they may have full opportunity to educate their children.

In Togo the mission schools are given subventions by the government equal to two-thirds of the salaries of the official mission teachers, the mission providing the remaining third.[93] In Dahomey, and the other colonies of French West Africa, however, no such financial assistance is accorded the private schools.

While it is admitted that mere budgetary expenditures are no true criterion of the worth and effectiveness of an educational system, it is nevertheless significant to note that until the effects of the *crise mondiale* began to be felt in Togo and Dahomey the credits for education showed consistent increase from year to year. The first appropriation for public education in Dahomey was 20,000 francs in 1900, while the indicated figure for general and industrial education for 1932 was 2,885,939 francs.[94] In Togo, in 1922, a total of 204,050 francs was expended for public and industrial education, which had mounted to a total of 2,034,200 francs a decade later.[95] In addition to this the Togo admin-istration granted 218,300 francs to the private mission schools in 1932.

According to the calculations of the Togo administration 7.73 percent of the total receipts of the territory were devoted to education in 1930 and 34.77 percent of the receipts which were collected directly from the natives. This is compared with the percentages of 2.46 and 12.7, respectively, under the Ger-man administration in 1914.[96]

Despite the increase in the funds devoted to education the facilities remain quite inadequate in proportion to the population of the two territories. In

Dahomey, during the year 1930, there were in operation only 42 government schools, which enrolled 5,887 students, though the population of Dahomey is 1,076,829.[97] Of these institutions, only 1 offered advanced primary or industrial instruction; 11 were regional and urban schools; 29 were preparatory or elementary, i.e., village schools, and 1 was the orphanage for the *métis,* or mulattoes. Though the number of schools had increased to 46 by 1932 through the opening of three new village schools and the new industrial school at Cotonou, the total number of students enrolled had dropped to 5,585.[98]

The village schools were attended by 732 girls and 4,540 boys; 60 girls and 375 boys were enrolled in the intermediate course of the regional schools, while only 70 boys were enrolled in the *cours superieur* and 110 apprentices received industrial training.

To supplement the government schools there were some 22 mission schools which gave instruction to 3,218 native children.[99] The head of the administrative services in Dahomey estimated that in 1932 there were 101,700 boys and girls of school age in the colony.

As early as 1921 the Togo administration had recognized the inadequacy of the educational facilities in this mandated territory.[100] By 1930 a total of 44 government schools had been established which instructed 3,530 young natives in a total native population of approximately 750,000.[101] Of these, 34 were the elementary village schools, 6 gave the intermediate instruction of the regional schools, 2 were domestic training schools for girls, 1 was the industrial school at Sokode, and only 1 gave advanced primary instruction for the purpose of training auxiliaries for the administration. Of the 3,530 pupils in attendance over 345, or less than 10 percent, were girls. There were 2,847 boys and 92 girls enrolled in the village schools, chiefly along the coast—235 boys and 12 girls in the regional schools, 241 in the domestic schools, 49 boys in the industrial institution, and 54 enrolled in the highest course, the *cours complémentaire,* at Lome.

In addition, there were 30 mission schools operated by the Catholic, Evangelical, and Wesleyan societies, which instructed more than 3,000 boys and about 500 girls, thus raising the figure of the total number of Togo children in school during this year to 7,160.[102] By 1931 this figure had dropped to 5,586, largely due to the administration's policy of retrenchment.

In 1927 a special class designed for European children was created by *arrêté* of M. Bonnecarrere, which is taught by a European mistress and now enrolls about 30 children.[103] Courses for native teachers have also been instituted in Togo as a means of improving the caliber of instruction offered by native monitors in the village schools, both public and private.[104]

While the administration in Dahomey has not indicated any great interest in a scientific analysis of its population, the Togo administration presents each year in its annual reports to the Permanent Mandates Commission some interesting, if not always complete and accurate, demographic statistics. One such study reports that, in the total native population in Togo of 749,152, there are some 140,993 boys and 151,410 girls.[105] Further investigations in several of the *cercles* have shown the age group below 14 years to embrace between 35 and 40 percent of the population. In reply to a question put by the Mandates Commission concerning the ratio between the number of children of school age and the number of children attending school in Togo, the French administration arrived at an estimate of 7.48 percent.[106]

Those children who are fortunate enough to attend the schools do so with great regularity, for the French report in Togo that the percentage of absences rarely exceeds 7 percent.[107]

The school buildings are often very poorly constructed, ill-kept, and unnecessarily hot. In Togo several of the old buildings constructed by the Germans are still in use. The new construction now undertaken is usually devoted to the creation and enlargement of industrial schools, in keeping with the new emphasis in the educational policy. Two fine new buildings have recently been erected for the École Professionnelle at Cotonou, a classroom and dormitory building, costing 600,000 francs, and a shop building, which the students themselves constructed, costing 200,000 francs. The 70 boys who are in attendance there are given 75 francs per month by the administration over a three-year period.

Because of the French policy the mission schools are prevented from effectively carrying on their work. Even in Togo, where, unlike the French colonies, the missions are subsidized, the directors of the private schools complain of discrimination and point out that many parents prefer to send their children to the public schools because they will then be preferred for positions with the administration. In the opinion of the Togo administration the mission schools show signs of decadence.[108] However, in some official quarters it is admitted that the private schools carry instruction to natives in remote sections untouched by the official schools.[109] In general, the native in the bush must rely upon the missions for his education. In the bush the missions are permitted in Togo alone to establish the native-language, or "unofficial," schools, for which no government support is given. In these institutions, however, the native language is the vehicle of instruction, and textbooks and Bible history have been translated to the Ewe language.

In Togo the Catholic mission supports, with the government grants-in-aid, a staff of 12 European directors, 20 teaching sisters, and 31 "official" native teachers. In addition there are 70 other native teachers in the native-language schools of the bush. The entire staff, native and European, is required to learn the Ewe language. In many of the mission schools the children are better dressed and appear to receive better training than in the government schools.

In Lome, the Catholic mission also maintains a convent school for girls, with an enrollment of 466 in 1932. They are given the general program of instruction laid down by the French administration for the elementary and regional schools and devote but little time to domestic training. Since the Togo administration has not established an internat for the *métis,* this convent school has accepted 33 young mulatto girls, for each of whom the administration pays 60 francs per month to the mission. The *internat des métis* in Dahomey is not a school but an orphanage, and the young mulattoes take their instruction at one of the regular government schools. The government allows them two francs per day for upkeep. Their quarters are not clean, they are given hard boards for beds, meager diet, three clothing outfits per year, and little sympathy. On the whole they were a rather weak and pitiful looking group. It is very doubtful that the segregated treatment which they receive does them any good.

In addition to the scholarships granted to promising students by both the Togo and Dahomey administrations, *mutuelles scolaires* have been organized with some success, particularly in Togo.[110] These are student cooperative productive enterprises through which the garden products cultivated or the articles fabricated are sold to the public, the proceeds going into a general treasury for the benefit of the students. The Togo administration has also authorized the payment of traveling expenses for the selected students attending the *cours complémentaire,* the industrial school, and the school for the sons of chiefs maintained at Mango in the north.[111]

The fact that Togo is a mandate and, therefore, technically at least, held only in trust by the French should dictate a more liberal educational policy than the administration of the colony Dahomey might be expected to pursue. With one or two minor exceptions, however, the policies of the two territories are parallel. In both instances these policies are too severely governmental and too narrow. It is difficult to reconcile the French attitude toward the mission schools with a sincere interest in the intellectual development of their native wards. Since the French educational facilities are inadequate, better policy as well as sound economy would seem to dictate that the mission schools be encouraged. Moreover, private educational institutions should be given more latitude in respect to curriculum. However honest the French motives may be, the existing policy justifies the suspicion that the objective is the suppression of native culture in favor of French culture. But, since it has been quite generally agreed among the French writers and high colonial officials that the natives cannot be readily assimilated to the French culture, this attitude in respect to language and curriculum seems to present a paradox. Nor is the diversity of languages an ample excuse for the prohibition of native languages in the private schools. The missionaries have shown that this difficulty can be largely surmounted, and if they have the desire to do so there would seem to be no valid excuse for refusing them permission.

There should be a rapid expansion of the educational facilities and the institution of secondary work as early as possible. A greater percentage of the revenue of the territory might well be devoted to educational purposes. There should be an extension of the principle of compulsory school attendance also, which could be readily applied even now in the urban centers, and to all classes of the population, rather than to the select circles of the sons of the elite. If more widespread extension of gratuitous education is not possible for economic reasons the administrations might do well to experiment with a few pay schools in order that the native populations may have every possible opportunity to educate their young.

Finally, it would seem to be just and reasonable that the natives themselves should have more opportunity to indicate the type and content of the education which is afforded them. If the populations of Togo and Dahomey are as progressive as the French themselves profess them to be, and if the administrations are animated by a desire to further the development of these peoples, greater consideration should be given to the wishes of at least the articulate groups among the natives.

CHAPTER 11

Africa and the Current World Conflict
1940

Just as Bunche moderated his domestic views of the New Deal and American democracy in the face of European fascism, so too does he soften his criticism of European colonialism. This essay, reprinted from the Negro History Bulletin, *states that the "slow but steady" progress in Africa under European imperialism would be totally crushed if Germany and Italy were to replace France and England as colonial masters. This position is in sharp contrast to the view of French and English colonialism in Bunche's dissertation and a remarkable change in tone from the polemics of* A World View of Race. *Of course, the threat of fascism led Bunche and several of his friends and colleagues to enter government service for the duration of the war.*

The black men of Africa never have a chance to put their knees under the council tables of international politics. But the African continent and its population of 150,000,000 or more play a vital role in the game of international politics. They are the innocent pawns in the disgusting spectacle of the so-called civilized nations and their rulers fighting each other to the death, destroying their manhood and property in the periodic struggles to determine which nation will be dominant, which nation will receive the lion's share of African and other spoils.

In peace or war Africa and the Africans are never spared this turmoil. In times of peace the African continent and its people are subjected to brutal commercial exploitation. In times of war the continent is converted into a bloody battlefield on which the great "civilized" nations of Europe fight each other like mad dogs over a bone. It is never a struggle of the African's making; the black man has no desire for it, and no voice about it. Nor is he permitted to stay out of it. He is given a gun and a uniform and ordered to fight on one side or the other—and he is usually fighting against other Africans who are similarly controlled. It is just as though two ruffians engaged in a street brawl should break into your parlor, decide to have their fight out there, and force you to take sides and engage in the fight. Then, when it is all over, you discover that the burly victor has decided to stay on in your house and, at the point of a gun, will thereafter require you to be his hand servant. The Africans, lacking guns for his own protection, is quite as helpless as most of us would be should our homes be thus invaded by gunmen. The African suffers because he has not cared to adopt one of the most important customs of our Western civilization— the art of destroying fellow humans with guns; and because he prefers peace to war. Thus he is a constant and easy victim of European conflicts.

The past quarter of a century has witnessed two great wars—World Wars I and II—and numerous minor ones. In both of the world wars Africa has figured prominently, while in one of the lesser wars—the Italian conquest of Ethiopia—African loot was the sole objective. World wars and African imperialism are closely linked. Much of the first World War was fought in Africa and by Africans—a great many of whom fought and died on the battlefields of Europe as well. Africa, with its markets, its raw materials, and its labor supply, was a major cause of conflict and the chief prize of the victors in the war of 1914–18. Since 1918, when this first World War ended, another invasion of Africa has taken place, and the last but one of the independent African nations was conquered when Italy cruelly overran Ethiopia. Now Africa is once more the object of antagonists in a world-shattering European conflict, and at this very moment the main theater of the war threatens to shift from Europe and England to Africa, where Britain and Egypt are arrayed against Italy and her African colonies. As winter approaches and fighting on a large scale becomes impossible in already war-torn Europe, Africa obliges by offering a milder climate in which the white men of Europe may continue to murder each other at will under the full glare of the African sun. The pity is that a great many innocent Africans will also be slain in the process.

In addition to its valuable resources and its great manpower, Africa also has strategic geographical location. It controls the Suez Canal, the Red Sea, and Gibraltar; it dominates the South Atlantic, the Indian Ocean, and the Mediterranean; it guards the main route to the Orient; it affords the closest jumping off places for air traffic between Europe and South America.

During modern times, and especially since the last quarter of the nineteenth century, Africans have been under the heel of European imperialism— British, French, German, Italian, Spanish, Belgian, Portuguese, and Boer. There have been variations in the methods of control, differences in the nationality of the rulers, but all in all there has been little to choose with regard to native interest. The white imperialist has been top dog in the African's own backyard, and the African has been forced to obey the orders of the European masters. And always the objects of imperialism in Africa have been the same, by whomever pursued. The European nations have sought in Africa markets, raw materials, cheap labor, and military manpower. They have used Africa as a source of quick riches. They have built up their empires through the acquisition of possessions there, and thus have gained international power and prestige.

The welfare of the African, his interests and aspirations, however, have seldom been consulted. There have always been attempts to present rational-izations, false explanations of the white man's mission in Africa, of course. They have claimed that they only desired to bring civilization and Christianity to the African native; that they have had only the native's interests at heart when they forced their way into his country, took away his land, destroyed his customary institutions and ways of life, and compelled him to work at the beck and call of the white master. The same sort of rationalization was often em-ployed to justify the enslavement of the Negro in America. It was claimed that he was so child-like and irresponsible that he could be happy and secure only when under the care of a white master. In Africa, as in slavery, it is the white master who reaps the profits from the relationship.

Thus the picture of the plight of the African under European imperialism is not a happy one. Despite such conditions, however, the African has been making steady progress. The African has suffered from certain inherent handi-caps in resisting European oppression, and in looking forward to progress. Unfortunately for their ability to resist European encroachment, the people of Africa are not united. They suffer from many kinds of division. They are divided into an amazing number of tribes. Each tribe speaks a different lan-guage, has different customs and its own chief or ruler. There has not been, until recent times, very much inter-association between the Africans of one tribe and those of another. There has been a consequent lack of national, or "African," consciousness among African peoples. They have thought of them-selves more as members of this or that tribe than as Africans. There has been a lack of national, inter-tribal organizations among Africans, and of leadership to guide them in this direction. The African people have had excellent tribal systems of education, but these have not been of a nature to fit them for competition with the material and industrial way of life of the Western world. Only in recent years have they begun to get and profit by the type of education which we of the Western world know. Only recently have Africans themselves had the opportunity to visit the outside world, and to learn how to meet the European on his own ground.

As a result of such education and contacts Africans in many places have been rapidly taking steps to overcome the handicaps of the past in their rela-tions with the white intruders. A new leadership, especially among the edu-cated African youth, has begun to emerge, a new group and racial conscious-ness is developing, and strong organizations are formed with the object of uniting Africans in protest against and resistance to European abuses. There are now strong youth organizations in West Africa, particularly in such colonies as the Gold Coast, Sierra Leone, and Nigeria. In South Africa there are national organizations among the Bantu people, such as the All African Congress, which hold annual conventions just as the National Association for the Ad-vancement of Colored People does on our behalf here. In East Africa are found organizations such as the Kikuyu Central Association, which has for years maintained a competent African lobbyist in London. African schools on the Western model have steadily improved; advanced educational institutions have been established in many places. There is a growing racial consciousness, especially among educated Africans. Numerous publications owned and edited by Africans—newspapers and periodicals—are published and tend to impress upon the consciousness of their African readers an awareness of their problems and a realization of the need for unity in thought and action. The protest and civic organizations sponsor meetings, often of a mass character, in which the grievances of the people are aired, in which vigorous protests are made and criticisms fired against the injustices for which European administrators are responsible. Recourse is often had to the courts to uphold rights. In many parts of West and South Africa there is continuous protest and agitation on the part of aggrieved Africans, and a great many concessions have been wrung from the colonial administrations. For, after all, the African has the power of numbers; he is in the overwhelming majority everywhere on the continent; he is the indispensable labor supply; his country cannot be exploited without him; and, while concessions are made only grudgingly, they are nevertheless made.

The ability of the African to make this sort of slow but steady progress under the harsh rule of European imperialism has been in large measure due to the fact that the imperialist governments represented in Africa from the end of World War I until the present, excepting only Italy in North Africa and Ethiopia, have been democratic governments. These imperialistic democracies have not, of course, extended the privileges and benefits of democratic government to their possessions in Africa. Yet, even while oppressing their African subjects, these "democracies" have paid lip-service to the ideals of freedom. They have striven, because of international public opinion, to maintain the appearance of regard for the form if not the substance of democracy in their colonies; they have had to extend some of the elemental attributes of democracy, such as freedom of assembly, freedom of the press, of speech and of religion, the right to protest, and the basic concept of the right of the individual as against the state, and his right of appeal to the courts against injustice, to their African populations. And many Africans have learned how to make effective use of these instruments of individual freedom. It is only because of this limited freedom that Africans have been able to develop effective organizations, to become articulate in the presentation of their grievances, and to begin to mold a united African opinion and movement. The democratic imperialisms, and of these England and France have been most important in Africa, have not permitted such liberties out of any high regard or sympathy for the African, but only because they have had to. As democracies they have had liberal-minded groups in their own countries which have protested vigorously against abuses in the control of the African peoples, which have demanded the extension of democratic prerogatives to the African colonials. They have also had to be accountable before international public opinion for their treatment of their subject peoples in Africa. Democracies are necessarily more concerned about how people elsewhere regard them and their acts than are non-democracies, which are under the control of one man or a small ruling clique of men. Democracies have, in this regard, an entirely different set of moral values than the autocratic governments, such as Hitler's Germany or Mussolini's Italy.

The African in Africa, therefore, is much like the Negro in this country with regard to democracy. We are not permitted to share in the full fruits of democracy, but we are given some of the peelings from the fruit; and the nation is often self-conscious and apologetic for this defect in its democratic process. We are permitted freedom of speech, press, assembly, and religion. We can organize, protest, and appeal to the courts for the protection of our rights. We can let the American and world public know of the abuses we suffer. It is through the exercise of such rights that we have progressed in the past, and they form the foundation upon which our hopes for the future are erected. So is it with the African. His future, as ours, depends upon the preservation and extension of the democratic concepts throughout the world.

Thus the future of the African, his hope for continued progress, development, and ultimate control of his continent, is inseparably tied to the outcome of the current war. The burning question for him as for us is—who will win it? This question involves much more than the mere substitution of German and Italian for English and French imperialism in Africa. It embraces the relative significance of totalitarian, fascist imperialism on the one hand as against the imperialism of the democratic nations on the other. What does this imply for the African? Fascism, especially the brand peddled by Herr Hitler, embraces boldly and fundamentally a racial theory more severe and more brazen than any the modern world has known—more formal, more deliberate even than that to be found in our own Deep South. This racial theory, which elevates the "Aryan," or pure white, peoples to positions of absolute superiority and rulership in the world, and relegates all the rest of us to the role of servants or slaves, is clearly and fully set forth in Hitler's *Mein Kampf,* in the *Nazi Primer,* and in the acts of the Nazis in Germany and in all of the European countries they have recently invaded. Peoples who are not accepted by them as Aryans are held to be something less than humans; on more than one occasion the official publications setting forth the racial doctrines of Nazism refer to Negroes as "animal-like." Africans, under fascist domination, therefore, would have no rights that any German or Italian would be expected to respect. Under fascism individual liberties are destroyed for even the white citizen. Fascism completely disavows the concepts of democracy, which it considers a weak and outworn system of government. Fascism believes in government by force and at the will of the dictator. Under it even conquered white people have been enslaved, as in

Poland. Now that the Germans have conquered France, French Negroes, who formerly were able to walk as men in France, who knew nothing of Jim Crow in Paris or elsewhere in the French nation, who were extended full social equality in France, even to the extent of intermarriage, if not in the colonies, find Nazi-dictated signs barring them from cafes, hotels, and even prohibiting them from buying railroad tickets.

While this shocking transformation is taking place in Nazi-controlled France, British Africans in the British colonies are still able to present their grievances even while Britain is sorely beset. They publish their newspapers and magazines, their organizations continue active, they find champions who continue to debate their cause in the British Parliament, they are still able to demand concessions from the British government. Their bargaining power is enhanced, in fact, for their ungrudging support is needed for the successful conduct of the war. Yet even an Aryan German worker would be sent to a concentration camp, or perhaps shot, if he dared utter a word of criticism of Hitler's policy in Germany today. Even during the war the native African in a British colony, as badly off and oppressed as he may be, has more liberty, more rights, more hope for a free future, than does an Aryan in Germany.

There can be no doubt that, if Hitler and Mussolini win this war, the future of the African will be one of abject, hopeless slavery. Hitler and Mussolini now speak of their intention to "liberate" the African from the tyranny of British rule and to create a "new order" for Africa as well as for Europe. But we must consider what sort of liberation and new order this would be. Is this the sort of "liberation" the citizens of Germany and Italy enjoy, under which every individual must jump to the crack of the master's whip; where no individual dares even to whisper a word of criticism of the government, for fear a dreaded secret agent will overhear and doom him to a concentration camp? Is this to be the sort of liberation the North Africans in Italian Libya have suffered, under which they are forced to fight the Italian's battles, even when they must slay their own kind, as they were compelled to do in the Ethiopian war? There is no indication of any German or Italian desire to inquire of Africans the sort of new order they desire.

There are some naive optimists who claim to foresee African liberation as a result of this war, due to the weakening of all white imperialist nations. This is merely wishful thinking. It must be remembered that the African too is fighting this war, on both sides, on behalf of his white masters. The Africans are not unified or organized enough yet to offer any effective, forceful resistance.

CHAPTER 12

The *Irua* Ceremony among the Kikuyu of Kiambu District, Kenya
1941

In this remarkable article, which first appeared in the Journal of Negro History, *Bunche demonstrates his recent training in anthropological fieldwork as well as his skill as a political scientist. Taking on the then and now controversial act of female circumcision, Bunche argues that insensitive European attempts to abolish it have made the rite the central symbol of tribal chauvinism and the rallying cry of their cultural loyalty. When placed in the context of governmental attempts to alienate Kikuyu lands and shift their settlements, the circumcision rites are elevated to the status of an emblem of national self-assertion and recompense for lost power. In short, the Kikuyu are trying to make up in cultural rights what they have lost in economic rights.*

The Kikuyu are one of the three most important tribes of Kenya, British East Africa, along with the Masai and Kavirondo. They are an industrious, sociable people, typical peasantry, and, in large measure, of Bantu stock. They have had relatively brief contact with the European and his ways—only about 40 years in all—but their advance and rate of cultural change have been rapid.

Indeed, the Kikuyu themselves, in their present districts, are quite recent immigrants. They began to filter into the Kiambu area something less than three centuries ago, coming in a succession of waves. When they first arrived, the country was densely forested and inhabited by a pygmy tribe of hunters known as Gumba, and the wa-Ndorobo people. The Gumba were too primitive to bargain with, and so they were soon squeezed out, but the Kikuyu were able to buy hunting rights from the wa-Ndorobo. These early hunting rights were known as *githakas* (*ithaka*); they have been handed down by inheritance to the descendants of the original owner and constitute the basis for the land tenure system adhered to by the Kikuyu of today.

The Kikuyu soon began clearing bush and planting crops, and the practice spread until the tribe became almost wholly agricultural. Though new conditions developed, the *githakas* remained the basis of land tenure. A *githaka* may vary in size from several acres to several square miles. It remains the property of a group-unit and is divided up among numerous individual "share-owners" who remain in personal possession of their individual holdings as long as they cultivate them. Part of each *githaka* constitutes common grazing ground for the owning group.

The first Kikuyu Reserve[1] was established in 1906, but this did not preclude further alienation of native lands to the white settlers. The Crown Lands Ordinance of 1915, declaring all native lands to be Crown Lands, still further increased the insecurity of the natives, and created much discontent, in that all natives on the land became "tenants at will." The first settlers had been given such tracts of land in the Kikuyu country as were not occupied by natives. Since these early settlers were scattered among the larger native population, no question of reserves arose at first. But by 1903–4 all the available unused land was taken up, and serious encroachments on native land began.

With the development of modern conditions in Kenya, land has become increasingly an object of value in itself, and in the Kikuyu country a strong movement has developed for the introduction of a system of individual tenure of land by natives, as a means of real security. This is due to the following factors: (1) establishment of Native Reserve boundaries, thus tending to prevent native migrations in quest of new land; (2) the natural increase in population; (3) improved cultivation; and (4) the introduction of currency, which encourages individualism in ownership and disposal of property, as against clan control and communal rights.

The new conditions have exerted greatest pressure in the Kiambu district, where the native population is most dense, and where the pinch of land-hunger is most severe, due to the alienation of land to white settlers in the highlands, leaving whole clan sections and family groups without any *githakas*. It was only in February of 1938 that the governor of Kenya announced to the assembled Kikuyu chiefs and headmen at a *baraza*[2] held at Githunguri Court that the highlands area would be permanently reserved for white settlers and that new lands elsewhere would be found for the natives. This decision, issued through Orders in Council, would be backed, he warned, by the full force of the Crown.

The Kikuyu have other grievances, of course. They resent the fact that their chiefs are appointed by and responsible to the British administration. They are piqued because they have no direct representation in the Legislative Council of the country and feel that the two Europeans appointed to the Legislative Council by the governor as "native representatives" do not safeguard their interests. They regard the taxes, especially the hut taxes imposed on their women, as oppressive. They are humiliated because they are required to carry the hated *"kipandi,"* the registration certificates issued under the Native Registration Ordinance of 1921. And they bitterly complain that they are prohibited from growing the favorite coffee crop in order to protect the white coffee grower.

Yet, for the Kikuyu, no problem is more pressing than that of land, and it is because of their land conflicts with the government and the European settlers that the Kikuyu are regarded as the most worrisome "native problem" in Kenya and are least liked by the whites. Land tenure is the most important single factor in the social, political, religious, and economic life of the tribe. For the chief occupations among the Kikuyu are agriculture and the rearing of livestock—cattle, sheep and goats. They depend upon the land for their material and spiritual needs. The soil is sacred to them because their ancestors lie buried there. They herd large flocks of sheep and goats, and, in lesser degree, cattle, since their social organization demands a constant supply of stock for such purposes as "bride-price" or marriage dowry, payments for land, sacrifices, ceremonial feasts, purification ceremonies, magical rites, and clothing (as many of them still wear skins).

There has been much unrest among the Kikuyu because of their mistreatment on the land, and some settlers have even feared their ultimate insurrection. Powerful protest movements, such as that led by the Kikuyu Central Association, have developed, and even now the Kikuyu maintain their official native lobbyist in London. They have become extremely suspicious of the intentions of the European and are turning, in self-defense, to an intense nationalism which finds reflection in an increasing devotion to many of their traditional customs, such as the initiation rite.

The social organization of the Kikuyu comprises three groupings: (1) the family group (*mbari*), which includes all those who are directly related by blood—a man, his wife or wives, and children, and his grand and great-grandchildren; (2) the clan (*moherega*), which brings together several family units having the same clan name and descended from one family group in the distant past, thus associating distant relatives; (3) the system of age-grading or age-groups (*riika*). This latter is the means whereby the entire tribe is united and solidified.

Each year, thousands of Kikuyu girls and boys undergo the circumcision ceremony and become members of one age-group (*riika rimwe*), without regard to the family or clan to which they may belong. These individuals consider themselves bound by a strong bond of brotherhood or sisterhood, thus giving stabilization to the tribal organization.

Many changes inevitably have crept over the life of the Kikuyu since their first contact with the European. Their tribal wars and feuds have been suppressed; they have been subjected to a gradual process of Western education and Christianization; they have adopted improved methods of agriculture and higher standards of comfort. The imposition of the hut-tax has enforced periodical migrations to white towns and farms upon all able-bodied males, where they must work for wages as house-boys or laborers.

Yet these changes have been relatively slow, and not the result of an abrupt cultural ultimatum. There are many pitfalls inherent in any effort to close quickly the gap between two disparate cultures. And there is grave danger involved in any radical interference with particular native customs, when they are deeply imbedded, no matter how necessary it may seem to change them. For these customs quite often turn out to be indispensable parts of the very warp and woof of the native social structure. So it is with the Kikuyu circumcision rite.

In Kenya, as in many parts of Africa, circumcision is practiced in connection with the initiation ceremony, a *rite de passage* from childhood to adulthood. All those initiated during the same year belong to the same age-group. In East Africa, circumcision of both boys and girls is a vital part of this initiatory rite, among not only the Kikuyu but also the wa-Gogo, the wa-Ikizu, the wa-Nyamwezi. These initiation ceremonies change continuously in their details, varying from clan to clan, and from tribe to tribe, though they retain profound traditional value throughout. Among such tribes, girls between the ages of 9 and 15 undergo clitoridectomy, and the belief is deep that the practice improves the process of childbirth. This ceremonial and physical preparation for matrimony and motherhood is deeply rooted and is tenaciously adhered to. For example, according to Mrs. Thurnwald,[3] even Christian boys of the wa-Gogo would not today marry a girl who is uncircumcised, and the missions working among the wa-Gogo are resigned to this stubborn native resistance to the abandonment of their tribal customs.

With the Kikuyu, after initiation, the boys and girls do not marry for several years but are permitted a modified form of sex play while still unmarried, though physical virginity is unimpaired and conception rendered impossible. It seems to be a rather advanced version of the quaint old New England custom of "bundling."

Among the Kikuyu, the circumcision of girls has been vigorously attacked by a number of influential European groups, missionary, government, educational, medical, and emotional pro-African. The missions especially, and notably the Church of Scotland Mission, have vigorously condemned the practice and have attempted to apply sanctions in order to compel its discontinuance. They have contended that female circumcision and Christianity are incompatible. They have emphasized also the unhygienic nature of the process, and the fact that it is potentially dangerous to the life of the girls, in that this mutilation of the female genitals, if not very skillfully done, forms considerable masses of scar tissue, which may subsequently endanger the life of the mother and new-born at the first child-birth. After numerous unsuccessful efforts to get the custom abolished, the Church of Scotland Mission in 1929 began to refuse Holy Communion to all Kikuyu Christians who would not declare open opposition to the rite and ordered all of their followers and all of those who desired their children to attend the mission schools, to pledge themselves not to support this custom in any form, and to refuse permission for their children to undergo the initiation rite. Children of those not obeying this order were to be debarred from the missionary schools.

This was clearly a serious challenge for the Kikuyu, who are extremely anxious that their children be educated. Yet in Kenya, as in most parts of British Africa, the schools have been left largely under the control of the missions, aided by government subsidy. The native people petitioned the government, and many of the schools remained deserted pending settlement of the dispute. Finally a compromise agreement was worked out between the missions and the government, under which the ban on children attending the schools was lifted, but the missions reserved the right to insist that all the native schoolmasters in the mission schools must sign a pledge to denounce and work against the custom. The Kikuyu continued indignant; there was a resultant great dearth of native communicants, and most of the mission out-schools were closed. The native people then demanded the right to establish their own schools, where their children could be taught without interference with tribal customs. Finally the natives founded two groups of native controlled schools—the Kikuyu Independent schools and the Karenga schools. These are completely free of missionary control, receive no governmental subsidies, and are supported by small pupil fees and local contributions. There were 62 of them in existence in 1938, and they are monuments to the initiative of the Kikuyu, their group patriotism, and their stubborn determination not to submit to the arbitrary decisions of the European concerning their culture.

The net results of this blind and intolerant attempt of the missions to abolish the female circumcision have been to increase the attitudes of resentment and suspicion of the natives toward all whites. They regard the whole effort as unwarrantable interference, and it crystallized in opposition all of the reactionary traditionalism of the tribe. They see a plot against their liberties and traditions. And the rite itself has become the central symbol of tribal chauvinism and the rallying cry of their cultural loyalty. It is certain that the vigor of this resistance is intimately associated with native reaction to the attempts of the government to alienate their lands and shift their settlements. They fear a broad effort on the part of the whites to break up their tribal institutions and customs, disintegrate their social organization, uproot them from the soil, and leave them completely at the mercy of their white masters. Thus the circumcision rites become accentuated as an emblem of their national self-assertion and a recompense for lost power. It is significant that on most other issues the younger generations of the Kikuyu are quite willing to accept modern ideas, yet take a strongly reactionary stand on circumcision. The experiences of the Kikuyu with the Kenya European tend to induce them to exaggerate their declamations of tribal individuality and nationalism to a greater extent than other East African tribes which apparently have less occasion for assuming a defensive role.

The Kikuyu term *irua* connotes female as well as male initiation. The initiation itself involves several procedures: (1) an extended though loosely organized and sporadic course of education with regard to the phenomena of nature; (2) practical instruction in matters of sex; (3) inculcation of numerous social and individual virtues, including respect for tribal elders, custom, and authority; (4) the surgical operation or mutilation of the genitals, which is the external evidence of the passage from childhood to adulthood, and which, if endured with fortitude, is symbolic of the end of childhood.

For the Kikuyu the *irua* signifies the commencement of the participation in the governing groups of the tribe, since the age-groups date from the day of the circumcision. In the tribal psychology of the Kikuyu, the operation is regarded as the vital core of a cultural institution which has tremendous educational, social, moral, and religious importance. The average Kikuyu of today simply cannot visualize the one without the other. One of the younger Kikuyu leaders informed me that "a circumcised person is like a man having a higher degree of education." In another group with which I was discussing Kikuyu customs, an oldish elder, barefoot, with feathered head-dress and great earrings, arose majestically and exclaimed: "Amongst the Kikuyu if a man who is circumcised marries an uncircumcised girl, their children will be under a curse and destroyed."

The remainder of this paper will be devoted to a rather summary description of an *irua* ceremony which I had the privilege to witness at Githiga Market, in the Kiambu District of Kenya, in February 1938. It was only with difficulty that I gained permission to take pictures of it, despite the fact that I had been inducted into the tribe and given the name of Karioki.[4] Since there were 12 girls and only 1 boy in this group, I will confine myself mainly to an account of the activities of the girls, while mentioning that the boy's activities follow the same general pattern. It is to be noted that the ceremonies vary in detail from one locality to another. In the Nyeri district, for example, I was told that the boys and girls are kept apart during the running off of the ceremony. At Githiga, however, the lone boy and the girls were together throughout.

My informants and interpreters were Josaphat Kamau, editor of a Kikuyu paper, and George Ndegwa, secretary of the Kikuyu Central Association.

The preparation for the circumcision begins some two weeks prior to the day of initiation. At this time the girls are put on a special diet (*njahi* and *ngima ya ogembe*), consisting of a particular Kikuyu bean (*njahe*) and a heavy porridge made from the mixture of the flour ground from the grain *ogembe* and water and oil. It is claimed that this diet serves the purposes of preventing undue loss of blood from the cutting, aids in the quick healing of the wounds, and ensures against blood poisoning.

Each girl has a sponsor (*motiiri*), who acts as an instructor and examiner. The girl must not yet be mature, and menstruation should not begin until at least one month after *irua*. She must not have had sexual intercourse nor have indulged in masturbation. If she has broken the tribal code in either of these respects, her sponsor is required to report this fact to the girl's parents. A special "purification" rite must then be gone through with in order to purify (*koruta mogiro*) the girl and qualify for her participation in the *irua*. A special "family purifier" (*motahekania*) is employed for this purpose.

About four days prior to the initiation, the girl is moved from her home compound to the compound where the ceremony is to take place, and she then meets her fellow initiates. The elder of the compound and his wife greet the initiates and "adopt" them as their "children of the *irua*."

The last day before the cutting was devoted to final preparation of the initiates, and there was much dancing, singing, blowing of whistles, and many rites performed very solemnly by the elders. There were a dozen little girls and one boy. The initiates came marching up to the market in small groups, two or three to a group, escorted by a throng of attendants. They were attired in short sweaters and dresses and wore many beads, bracelets, and other ornaments. They sang, danced, and blew their whistles lustily, the gist of the songs being that they were seeking the place where the circumcision would take place. In the meantime the elders informed my host that I was to take no pictures. This threw him into a frenzy—a rather easy accomplishment, since he was already under the influence of *njohi,* the potent sugarcane liquor the natives brew. My host finally got a reversal of the edict by threatening to withdraw his two daughters from the ceremony.

Finally the entire group broke away and madly dashed across the fields to the neighboring compound where the ceremony was to take place. I was informed that in the pre-European days none of the initiates would have been clothed in anything save the ornaments.

This compound in which the ceremony was being held had never entertained one before, and criticisms were very strident that the man was not adept in his role of host to such a solemn affair.

An arch of banana leaves and sugarcane was erected at the entrance to the compound and was decorated with sacred flowers. No unauthorized person could pass through this arch, which was to appease the ancestral spirits and assure good fortune for the ceremony. Sugarcane was piled up on the ground outside the arch, from which *ijohi* was later to be made.

Dancing of the *matuumo,* the ceremonial dance, continued outside the arch for some time, while the elders remained squatting inside the compound.

Then large girls hoisted the initiates onto their shoulders and triumphantly carried them under the arch into the compound. After more dancing—the dancing by the spectators was becoming quite abandoned, since they were continuously swigging *njohi* from calabashes that were freely passed around—all of the candidates of both sexes were lined up before the elders and their "treatment" began. A brownish powder (*rothuko*) was sprinkled on the ground by the elders to drive away evil spirits, and also *njohi,* to appease the ancestral spirits. Small bands were tied about the ankles of the initiates, twigs covered with a black-looking concoction (*mothaiga wa umu*), said to have medical qualities, were waved over each initiate's head, and they were each made to eat a spoonful of a forbidding-looking, grayish-black paste (*ngima*) containing castor oil that had been prepared for them by the elders. I noted that one boy spit his out with a grimace and threw it back over his shoulder after the elders passed.

More spirited dancing followed and then, suddenly, the entire group of young people, led by the boys, broke and ran pell-mell across the fields and down into a deep valley, up the opposite hill and down the other side, into another valley, in search of the sacred *mogumo* tree,[5] from which leaves were to be plucked for the ceremony of the following day. The boys climbed the rather small tree and broke off the top branches, while the girls assembled below, singing and gathering up the leaves and twigs.

I was informed that in former days the advance on the *mogumo* tree was in the form of a formal race by the boys, who would start off at a blast from a ceremonial horn. The girls would not run in the race but, escorted by a group of senior warriors and women singing ritual and heroic songs, would walk to the tree in advance of the race. The boys' race was considered as a struggle between the spirit of childhood and that of adulthood. The boys carried wooden spears as they ran, as if going to battle, and the one who reached the *mogumo* tree first and threw his spear over it was regarded as the permanent leader of that particular age-group.

But both boys and girls ran at Githiga and there was no racing formality about it. The girls tied the *mogumo* leaves into branches and carried them back to the compound to keep the sacred fire burning throughout the night, to make the beds of leaves on which the girl initiates were to sit the following day while being circumcised, and to make the initiates' beds. The breaking of the sacred tree is known as *kuuna mogumo.*

En route back from the *mogumo* tree, our group met a group of Christian boys, who were also to be circumcised the next day, but who were dancing quietly in a circle and singing songs of protest against "all this wild dancing and racing after the *mogumo* tree."

The songs sung by all members of the party at the foot of the *mogumo* tree were strongly flavored with sex. During the return, groups of young women formed private dancing parties and sang obscene songs with vigor and good humor. The little Kikuyu boy scout from the mission, Douglass, who had accompanied me, was properly shocked and tried vainly to keep me from learning what "these bad women are saying." But it was explained to me that on these occasions only all restraint is thrown aside.

On returning from the *kuuna mogumo,* the initiates were all lined up outside of the compound and each took a few turns at pounding the sugarcane in the hollow-log mortar, from which *njohi* was to be made.

Then they were ready to come inside the compound again. But a slight hitch developed—the elder daughter of the owner of the huts had raised a shrill protest. She was married and living in another compound; however, when she had been living at home she had been circumcised, but in a foreign compound. Now she demanded a fat ram as compensation for the humiliation that others were to be the first to be honored by circumcision in her home compound. After a long delay during which the elders conferred, she walked off happily with a fat ram, which her father had had to contribute for "appeasement."

On this same morning the initiates had had their heads closely shaved, except for one small, round tuft of short hair, about as large as a quarter, at the top-rear of the head.

Finally the initiates were marched back into the compound under the ceremonial arch. Many adult members of the party were quite strongly under the influence of the *njohi* they had consumed by this time, and the dancing grew frenzied. The men and boys whose duty it was to make room for the dancers became violent with their grass whips and reed sticks, and were actually hitting people now, whereas previously they had only threatened.

Now the initiates were lined up before the elders, with their heads bowed, and the elders stripped the decorations from the heads of the girls. Then followed the ceremony of blessing the children (*korathima ciana*). The faces of the initiates were powdered with a white, chalk-like substance called "snow" (*ira*), which, it is claimed, is obtained only from Mount Kenya (Kere-Nyaga), the abode of the gods. Then symbolic markings were made with the *ira* on the forehead, cheeks, nose, throat, and navel and around the eyes of the initiates. Long, broad marks were made down the forehead and nose of the boy; large white dots were placed on the ankles and buttocks of the girls. The elder holding the senior office in the ceremonial council (*athuri a kerera*) performed the markings. He placed the *ira* in the palm of his left hand, dipped his right thumb into it, and carefully branded each initiate.

Following this, an elderly woman, also a member of the ceremonial council, anointed the heads of each initiate with oil which she carried in a bottle-shaped calabash (*kinando*). Finally, the elders took into their mouths some fluid from horns and walked along spewing and spraying it over the bodies and into the faces of the initiates. This liquid was a mixture of honey, milk, and a special "medicine" called *oomo,* which is alleged to stimulate bravery and fortitude. Another fluid called *gethambio,* which is supposed to protect the initiates against fear and temptation, was similarly sprayed over them.

About dusk, after more dancing, the initiates were released and allowed to go to their homes until early the next morning. They were to be carefully protected during that night against wounds (since the shedding of blood would be regarded as an ill-omen), against witchcraft and any temptation to sexual intercourse.

The lone boy initiate went away singing a song to the effect that he would be ushered into manhood on the following day and would be able to wear a knife.

It poured rain all that night, and it was only after a dangerous ride that we slithered into Githiga on the next morning, February 13th, to witness the circumcision. It was about 6 o'clock when we arrived, but a great crowd was already on hand. The Christian boys had been circumcised at 5 o'clock and were gone. But the pagan boy and the girls were even then at the Kamiti River, a little winding mountain stream in the bottom of a deep valley, and when we reached it we found the initiates being prepared for immersion in the cold water. They were divided into two groups. They were all stripped naked and rushed into the water, where they sat squatting, while the women, dancing up and down and singing, threw water over them. The boy was off to one side alone. They squatted in the cold stream for half an hour, while their relatives and friends milled about the bank and waded in the water singing ritual songs of encouragement. The immersion serves a double purpose; it cleanses (*gwithambia*), and the cold water numbs the limbs (*Kugandia*) and deadens the pain from the operation. However, since it was at least 45 minutes later that the operation was performed, the effect of the cold water must have been lost.

Then they were led out of the water and lined up in single file, the lone boy in front. It was extremely chilly in the early mountain air, and knitted sweaters were slipped over the upper bodies of some of the girl initiates. The long march back up the high hill commenced. Guards dashed about to keep the path clear for them. Each of the girl initiates held a small whistle between her teeth and blew shrill notes on it as the march progressed. Midway, the procession was halted, and decorations were attached to the heads, breasts, and legs of the girls. The boy remained completely nude, as were the lower bodies of the girls except for beads and bells on the legs.

It appeared to me that they all began to look frightened now, since the actual cutting was imminent. When we reached the market place, a huge throng had assembled, and a human semi-circle was formed, inside of which the sponsors (*motiiri*) of the girl initiates sat on bundles of *mogumo* and *mathakwa* leaves.

The girls entered this human enclosure and danced around in a sort of follow-the-leader fashion, blowing their whistles incessantly. The boy was taken to one side of the enclosure and sat on a small bunch of *mogumo* leaves. Promptly the male operator (*moruithia wa ihii*) began the circumcision, with a knife resembling an ordinary Kikuyu hunting knife, called *kahinga kuruithia*. The operation took about five minutes and was rather crudely done. But the boy, with his legs spread and knees bent, sat immobile while the foreskin was slit and removed; the only indication of the pain he suffered was the rolling of his eyes. Not a sound did he utter. The operator stood back, surveyed his work, and then knelt down and performed some final trimmings. Once, I noticed, the sharp point of his knife stuck the boy in his inner thigh.

By this time the girls had all taken seats in front of their sponsors on the bundles of *mogumo* leaves—all in a row. The sponsors, sitting behind, held their legs interwoven with those of the initiates, so as to brace the initiates' legs and keep them separated. The initiates leaned back against their sponsors, who held them by the shoulders. The faces of the girls were turned to the sky, and their whistles were grimly held in their mouths.

Then the female operator, the *moruithia wa irigu,* an old haggish looking woman, with one tooth prominently showing, and armed with a small Kikuyu razor (*rwenji*), resembling somewhat in size and shape our safety razor blade, began her work. With a deft strike she hacked off the tip of the clitoris (*rong'otho*), and a bright patch of red immediately appeared, as the sponsors held the girls more tightly. The labia minora of each girl was also trimmed, though it is said that formerly the operation was confined to the amputation of the clitoris. Immediately after being cut, each girl began to blow lustily on the whistle shoved into her mouth by her *motiiri.*

All went well, and the bright red patches on the leaves grew, until the last girl was reached. Here a complication arose. The *moruithia* bent down, examined the girl carefully, muttered to herself, and shook her head. It seemed that there was some abnormality about the girl. The sponsor of the girl burst into tears, and after a short conference the *moruithia* proceeded with the operation. The usual fee charged by the *moruithia* is 3/- for girls and 4/- for boys; the boys and girls of the owner of the compound where the ceremony is held receive the service free. But the parents of the girl with the abnormality were required to pay 20/- or one fat ram.

As soon as the last girl was cut the crowd surged forward and wild dancing and shouting ensued. Then the girl initiates, still naked from the waist down, acquired long sticks, and joined by the lone boy, began running about recklessly, chasing the older, circumcised boys and girls who had earlier taunted the initiates about fear, and who had threatened to beat them if they showed cowardice. Now that the initiates had been through the ceremony, and had exhibited no weakness, they were entitled to run after and beat their tormentors with sticks. Blood poured down their legs as they ran, and some seemed quite vicious about it all, probably due to the excruciating pain they must have experienced.

This latter practice—the running and beating—was said not to conform with the traditional ceremony, in which the initiates were led by their sponsors to huts where they were immediately placed on special beds made of three kinds of leaves (*marerecwa, mataahi,* and *maturanguu*), which are supposed to keep away insects and purify the air. The running and beating has begun only since the coming of the Europeans, it was said.

No medicine of any kind was applied to the wounds of the initiates immediately after the cutting. However the initiates are not permitted to return home but must remain under the care of the elders at the compound in which the ceremony occurred for a period of eight days. During this period the wounds are washed and treated with leaves and herbs (*mahoithia, kagutwi*), which are said to have antiseptic and healing qualities. Special food is prepared for them, which the girl initiates must eat from banana leaves since they are not allowed to touch food with their bare hands during this period. The sponsors entertain with songs, and on the sixth day they make a report on the condition of the initiates to the ceremonial council. If all are well and can walk, the ceremony of *gotonyio* is arranged for the eighth day. On this day the parents come to the compound of the *irua,* and a sheep is killed. The skin of this sheep is cut into ribbons which are placed on the wrists of each initiate, and following further ceremonial, the initiates are said to be born again as children of the tribe.

For several months following the ceremony the initiates do no work, but wander around the districts in groups singing the *waine,* the special "stick" song of the initiates, which is sung while they stand in a circle holding sticks (*micee*) in their hands which are used to beat out the rhythm of the song.

The ways and attitudes of the Christian white man are often understandably puzzling to the Kikuyu. Sage old senior Chief Koinange once told me that he could not understand why the church would refuse him conversion because of his plural wives yet baptize his wives. Similarly, the Kikuyu word *irua* involves the circumcision of both sexes, and is used without qualification in the Kikuyu language version of the New Testament; the Kikuyu have noted the support given to the practice of circumcision in that document. Also, since *irua* means not merely the circumcision but the entire process of initiation and teaching, and is the basis of the important age-groups, the Kikuyu regard any effort to modify the custom as a vital attack upon the foundations of their society. It would be true that the abolition of the circumcision ceremony, without provision for an acceptable substitute, would bring about the collapse of the age-group structure and hence of the social stability of the tribe.

But it should be reiterated that the determination of the Kikuyu not to permit any modification of this sacred ritual is largely the product of their bitter reaction to the English land policy. The Kikuyu Central Association was organized to protect land rights, but it has become almost fanatical in its devotion to the symbolic ritual of circumcision, and especially female circumcision. This is the barricade over which they must battle the invading European.

The fact is that the white influences have made the operation more severe and dangerous than formerly. It has already been noted that the cutting is more severe than in earlier times. Initiations are no longer easily held at central places, because native squatters are now often found off the reserves on white men's estates; because girls move into the towns with their parents; and as a result of the increased mobility of the population due to cars, buses, and railroads. Thus, instead of the operations being performed by a select group of skilled operators, they are now frequently crudely done by bungling hands, with harmful results to the initiates.

Perhaps the final word in this discussion should be permitted the native himself, and I quote from my notes the views expressed by Senior Chief Koinange of the Kiambu Kikuyu, who remembers when the first white man visited Kikuyu country and who is one of the wisest philosophers I have ever met:

> I do not approve of the circumcision of girls, since I do not believe that it does the girl any good to be circumcised. On the other hand I dislike the methods employed by the Europeans in trying to force us to abolish the custom. Most of our people used to have very large holes in their ears into which large wooden rings were placed, as my fifth wife had. But when she joined the mission, she had, of her own accord, her ears cut and sewn up again to close the holes. The same would apply to the circumcision of girls if the girls are properly educated; the more education they will get the more they will find that circumcision has no bearing on their lives, and they will stop it voluntarily. The circumcision among us Kikuyu is our method of giving the individual the right to become a full member of the group. When a boy or girl is circumcised, he is considered as fully grown. Moreover, the moruithia told the people that the cutting will make child bearing easier for the woman, through enlargement of the opening. But this was deceit and there is no truth in it. The pride in their community which the men and women have, and the belief that a circumcised woman would have easier child-birth, strengthened the people's belief in circumcision.
>
> The circumcised girl was more careful about going around with men, because she knew that one day she would be subject to severe examination by a moruithia and by other women, and even the woman at whose hut the ceremony is being performed would drive away any uncircum-

cised girl who had been known to have had sexual relations—for fear that if such a girl were to be circumcised in her place, she might displease the spirits and die from it.

Yet the Jalou girls are not circumcised, and are very good girls. The Nandi girls are circumcised and are very licentious, as are the Masai girls. So I do not think that circumcision of girls makes any difference, one way or the other, in regard to sexual activities and morality. Most people accept circumcision blindly as an old custom. Three of my own daughters are circumcised, but the two younger ones are not. One who was not circumcised is already married and is bearing children.

I believe that it should be left to the girls themselves to decide. I do not want any of my daughters forced into either circumcision or marriage or forced to forgo them, against their desires.

Part 4
The United Nations

CHAPTER 13

Man, Democracy, and Peace—Foundations for Peace: Human Rights and Fundamental Freedoms 1950

Delivered as one of five Walgreen Lectures at the University of Chicago in 1950, this is one of Bunche's most comprehensive discussions of human rights. He naturally links the struggle for minority rights in the United States with the worldwide movement toward human rights. His view of human rights is much broader than that of most American policy makers. Bunche contends that economic rights are as necessary as political rights. Moreover, he believes that the traditional United States view of individual freedom as freedom from the authority of the state ignores the positive role the state can play in ensuring rights, especially minority rights. He also states that the women involved in drafting the Declaration of Human Rights, led by Eleanor Roosevelt, made sure that the language of the declaration was inclusive of female rights. Bunche suggests that his views on freedom of speech are more limited than those of many civil libertarians and that rights must be balanced with respon-sibilities. The themes of peace through democracy and human rights at home and abroad are the chief elements in the five speeches he delivers in Chicago and the hundreds of speeches Bunche would deliver over the next two decades.

Nothing can be more sacred to free peoples than the preservations of the rights and dignity of the individual. This is man's birthright. This is the essence of democracy in our thinking. Yet we have had ample evidence that to many peoples the rights and dignity of the individual appear to be of less importance than the full guarantee by the state of the individual's economic security, even at the expense of the complete subordination of the individual to the state. The concept of economic as well as political and civil rights has a very strong appeal to those in any society who experience the pains of economic insecurity. In this modern age, the virility of any democratic society may be measured by the extent to which it gives its citizenry a real stake in both its political and economic systems.

The United Nations seeks a world of free peoples. But among the members of the United Nations there are those who exalt the individual as against the state and those who would completely submerge the individual in an all-powerful state. It is not the purpose of the United Nations to insist that the world must be cut after a uniform political and economic pattern. The United Nations does not seek to achieve uniformity at the expense of diversity. It accepts, even welcomes, diversity. But it does seek to achieve unity out of diversity. To do so in a world of such very great diversity of thought, custom, and concept, it must always find reasonable paths of compromise. It is essential to its effort that states and peoples learn to accommodate themselves to this necessity in the interest of international amity. National concepts must be adjusted to international concepts in a process of give and take if vital international instruments such as the Declaration of Human Rights and the projected Covenant on Human Rights are to be made possible and are to have significant meaning.

There can be little doubt that the work of the United Nations with regard to human rights is of utmost importance to its persistent effort to build firm foundations for an enduring peace.

The United Nations is dedicated to the herculean task of ensuring a world at peace. The men and women who just five years ago at San Francisco, in the flush of imminent victory in the war, were engaged in drafting the United Nations Charter, like the men and women since then who in the Councils of the United Nations have debated the application of that Charter, labored under no illusions about the enormity and complexity of their task. But they have all been realists. They have recognized that to ensure peace the United Nations must do more than put down fires wherever unhappily they may start—a "fire fighting" function—indispensable as it may be. The United Nations must undertake effective preventive work. Through necessarily long-range activity, the United Nations must make progress toward eliminating the causes of war; toward digging up the deeply imbedded roots of war.

The causes and roots of war, direct and indirect, are numerous and varied. They include all the sources of political and economic conflict between peoples and nations; all the foci of restiveness of peoples; all the misunderstandings among peoples which are often dangerous irritants; all the deep-seated animosities, bigotries, prejudices, intolerances, ignorances, fears, and suspicions which afflict human relationships throughout so much of the world today; and most certainly they include suppressions of peoples, deprivations of human rights and freedoms, and maltreatment of minority groups. All of these must be uprooted in preparing fertile soil for the cultivation of peace.

That the protection of human rights and freedoms is an important feature of the design for peace is fully recognized.

The general direction which must be taken to achieve results is equally well-known. The problem of the United Nations, as the problem of national societies afflicted with critical minority problems such as our own, is how to translate high ideals, noble objectives, and good intentions into efficacious action. The United Nations, too, is groping for the answer.

The preamble of the Charter of the United Nations points the direction as clearly as could be desired, when it states that the "peoples of the United Nations" are "determined . . . to reaffirm faith in fundamental human rights, in the dignity and worth of the human person, in the equal rights of men and women and of nations large and small. . . ." These objectives, if only in their reiteration, are given striking emphasis throughout the charter. It is, unquestionably, in itself a matter of fundamental significance and an important step forward, that the charter of the United Nations, to which 60 nations have now pledged themselves, should put such pronounced stress on equal rights among peoples, on human dignity, on human rights and fundamental freedoms. This is an encouraging reflection of the trend of thought in the modern world, of the aspirations of common peoples everywhere. These principles and objectives are now firmly entrenched in international law and morality. The Rights of Man are formally, if belatedly, confirmed by international edict.

But, despite the unassailable principles and objectives of the United Nations Charter, scores of millions of people are oppressed and deprived of the most elemental human rights and freedoms, and minority problems flourish. Within the borders of many of the members of the United Nations, including our own, minority groups continue to suffer the indignities and deprivations of second-class citizenship, prejudice, discrimination, and economic underprivilege. For these many millions of peoples the promises of the Atlantic Charter, the Four Freedoms, and the United Nations Charter remain unrealized.

It admittedly cannot be argued that the United Nations has as yet achieved any striking results in the realm of human rights and minority problems. Clearly, it would be wishful thinking to hope that the United Nations, however sound its principles and perfect its machinery, in only five years, could achieve impressive results in attacking problems with regard to which vested interests are so stubbornly entrenched, the twisted mores of peoples are so deep-seated and traditional, and resistance to change is so dogged. Minority and disadvantaged peoples know only too well that the emotional fervor with which an ideal is embraced is no gauge of practical results. Moreover, it is a stark fact that the protection to the principle of domestic jurisdiction given by the charter, while not affecting the nobility of the principles proclaimed, does put a very decided crimp in their application. The jealous regard for the prerogatives of national sovereignty remains strong among the nations.

The United Nations, ever since its inception, has been beset with a host of major political problems—Greece, Indonesia, Iran, Korea, Pakistan, Palestine, and the control of atomic energy—to mention only a few. As a result, human rights have not received top priority on its agenda.

In any case, it must be stressed that the United Nations has no direct jurisdiction with regard to human rights in any particular country. There is no remedial action which the United Nations can prescribe for any under-privileged group. It can formulate and endorse basic principles and hold nations morally responsible for their observance. It would be a grievous error, however, to underestimate the force of the moral sanction of the United Nations. The members of the United Nations have pledged themselves to accept its principles and to carry out its purposes. The pressure of international public opinion becomes increasingly strong. In the short history of the United Nations, member states have already learned that being confronted publicly with a somber charge of violating the principles of the United Nations is neither a pleasant nor profitable experience. The exposure to the full glare of world opinion which accompanies the airing of such matters in that "Town Hall of the world," the General Assembly, is not to be lightly dismissed; there is, fortunately, a world sense of morality. No nation has yet discovered a means of hushing the awkward rattling of the skeletons in its national closet once it takes a seat in a United Nations organ.

In this early stage of its existence the work of the United Nations in the realm of human rights and minority problems has consisted primarily of the efforts to formulate and win acceptance for an international bill and covenant of human rights and a convention on genocide. Substantial progress has been made toward these goals.

In the broad field of human rights one of the most striking and difficult problems is that of minority groups within national societies. These minorities may be racial, religious, cultural, or political. Perhaps the most distinctive feature of the minorities problem in the modern world is the widespread tendency to deny equal rights and freedom to minority groups. Dominant groups, complacent in their position of self-appointed superiority, evidence irritation at the persistent efforts of minority peoples to scale the ladder of equal rights, and profess not to be able to understand why these less fortunate peoples are malcontent and dissatisfied with a controlled and graduated progress. But minority groups, as for example, the American Negro, have long since learned that there must be no compromise on the issue of human rights; that a right compromised is no right at all.

Since the earliest days of organized society, the question of the position and rights of the individual in society has engaged the minds of thinking men. Early philosophers and religious leaders, in China, in India, in Islamic and Christian societies alike, developed concepts of individual rights and the obligations of rulers. Herodotus pointed to equality before the law as a distinguishing mark of the Greek state. In modern times human rights came to be enacted into national laws, with primary emphasis on civil rights and privileges rather than economic needs and security. The area and scope of the concept of human rights has steadily expanded. There is, it seems to me, no necessary conflict between the notion of individual civil liberty on the one hand and the right to economic security on the other. The desired goal should be, in my view, a concept which envisages the expansion of individual rights, political *and* economic, as opportunities for man's development necessarily enlarge in proportion to his control over the forces of nature and his own behavior. The threats to the rights of the individual may come as well from organized groups within the society as from the exercise of excessive authority by the state.

Human rights and freedoms should never be regarded as a gratuity. They carry reciprocal obligations and should be enjoyed only with a deep sense of responsibility. The surest way to lose them in a democratic society is for people to abuse them, to misinterpret rights as license. Those who do so are dangerous to the society.

If it is an abuse of the freedom of utterance to falsely cry out "fire" in a crowded public place, thereby endangering the safety of many, it is also an abuse of the freedom of utterance wilfully to try to incite an uncalled for and dangerous national hysteria, to undermine and demoralize the government, to damage its international prestige, and to destroy the confidence of the people in the public service during a period of great crisis.

In February 1946, the Economic and Social Council approved the establishment of a Commission on Human Rights. The functions of this commission, which is directly responsible to the Economic and Social Council, have included the submission of proposals, recommendations, and reports regarding an international bill of rights, international declarations or conventions on civil liberties, the protection of minorities, and the prevention of discrimination on grounds of race, sex, language, or religion.

At its first session, early in 1947, the Commission on Human Rights decided to establish a Sub-Commission on the Prevention of Discrimination and Protection of Minorities. This sub-commission has 12 members from as many countries. Its members act as independent experts rather than as representatives of their countries.

An important stage in the effort of the United Nations to give effect to one of its basic purposes was reached on December 17, 1947, when the Commission on Human Rights published its conclusions on the proposed international Bill of Human Rights after two and one half years of intensive work. This bill, now known as the Universal Declaration of Human Rights, was passed and proclaimed by the General Assembly of the United Nations on December 10, 1948.

The difficulty of making an effective and constructive international approach to the problem of human rights in a world in which the concepts of rights are so diversified has often been emphasized by Mrs. Roosevelt, who serves as chairman of the 18-member United Nations Commission on Human

Rights which had been charged with the task of drafting an International Bill of Human Rights.

Mrs. Roosevelt has explained that her first surprise came at the outset of her work when a number of delegates came to her and asked, "What is a Bill of Human Rights?" To Mrs. Roosevelt, as an American, a bill of rights seemed very clear; she thought of our own Declaration, of the French Bill of Rights, and of the Magna Carta. But these historical instruments were either unknown or meaningless to many of the delegates who came from non-Western countries.

I have also heard Mrs. Roosevelt relate one of her difficulties with the women members of Committee Three of the General Assembly which considered the Declaration of Human Rights after the Commission on Human Rights had completed the draft. The American Declaration of Rights reads, "all men are created equal," and this phraseology had been incorporated in the original draft of the international declaration. But as it came from the General Assembly, it read, "all human beings are born free and equal in dignity and rights; they are endowed with reason and conscience and should act towards one another in the spirit of brotherhood." The change from "all men" to "all human beings" was no accident. We take it for granted that "all men" in our Declaration includes women. But the women from other countries in Committee Three were not willing to trust the men in their countries to take it for granted. They moved that the declaration read "all human beings," and that, wherever in the declaration men were mentioned, "everyone or no one" should be substituted. Because, they pointed out, if the declaration should read "all men," when they got back home, it would *be* all men.

The Declaration of Human Rights covers a broad span of human rights—civil, political, economic, and educational. Certain fundamental principles are stated unequivocally: "All human beings are born free and equal in dignity and rights." "Everyone is entitled to all the rights and freedoms set forth in this Declaration, without distinction of any kind, such as race, colour, sex, language, religion, political or other opinion, national or social origin, birth or other status."

This declaration fails to go as far as many had hoped, particularly as regards the right of aggrieved individuals to petition the United Nations. But there can be little doubt that it is a highly significant step in the right direction.

It must be emphasized, however, that the Declaration of Human Rights, while setting international standards and voicing the universal aspirations of peoples, has no legal or binding force on any state. The Covenant on Human Rights, which is now being formulated and which will require ratification by states, is intended to have the binding force which the declaration lacks. There is the danger, however, that the covenant may be so watered down in order to make it to the states which must accept it by ratification, that it may minimize the very great moral force which the declaration now exerts.

It has unique significance that in the Trusteeship Agreement for former Italian Somaliland, which was formulated by the Trusteeship Council, the Administering Authority, i.e. Italy, is required to accept "as a standard of achievement for the Territory the Universal Declaration of Human Rights. . . ."

Since the inception of the United Nations, those who have attended its meetings and have been close to its activities have unmistakably sensed one compelling urge, omnipresent and universal, an urge to safeguard human rights and fundamental freedoms. One may sense that a strong current is running in the world today, which is manifested in the proceedings of the United Nations. That is a current against any abridgment of human rights, human freedoms, and human dignity; a current which stimulates spontaneous protest against sanctions of discrimination, racial and religious persecution, on whatever grounds. It is a current which needs to be harnessed.

Against the aroused conscience of civilized mankind, the principle of national sovereignty affords a weak defense and an unacceptable alibi for the violation of human rights.

As might be expected, the United Nations has been deluged with communications protesting alleged violations of human rights and freedoms and appealing to the United Nations for corrective action (prisoners; wives). Neither the Human Rights Commission nor any other organ of the United Nations, however, has as yet any established competence to conduct inquiries or hold hearings on complaints submitted by individuals, groups, or even governments concerning violations of human rights in any territory other than a Trust Territory. But the Commission on Human Rights does have the right to recommend to the Economic and Social Council, and through it to the General Assembly, such measures as it may consider desirable looking toward the establishment of machinery for dealing with appeals of this sort.

The Economic and Social Council has recommended that members of the United Nations should be invited to consider ways and means of establishing local information groups or human rights committees as a means of giving effect to the principles and purposes of the charter.

This council has also sponsored the general principle that treaties involving basic human rights, including to the fullest practicable extent treaties for peace, should conform to the fundamental principles on human rights set forth in the charter. The peace treaties concluded since World War II all contain clauses by which the former enemy states have undertaken to secure to all persons under their jurisdiction, without distinction as to race, sex, language, or religion, the enjoyment of human rights and fundamental freedoms.

The Sub-Commission on the Prevention of Discrimination and the Protection of Minorities has emphasized the importance of the prevention of discrimination and protection of minorities as having fundamental relationship to two basic principles of human rights, namely, that every right accorded to one person shall be accorded to all and, secondly, that not only individuals but groups are entitled to those rights and freedoms which would make it possible for them to develop along the lines of their particular characteristics, abilities, and aspirations.

The United Nations has devoted serious attention to genocide. A resolution adopted by the General Assembly at its first session, on December 11, 1946, relating to the crime of genocide, defines that crime in the following terms:

> Genocide is a denial of the right of existence of entire human groups, as homicide is the denial of the right to live of individual human beings; such denial of the right of existence shocks the conscience of mankind, results in great loss to humanity in the form of cultural and other contributions represented by these human groups, and is contrary to moral law and to the spirit and aims of the United Nations.
> Many instances of such crimes of genocide have occurred when racial, political, and other groups have been destroyed entirely or in part.
> The punishment of the crime of genocide is a matter of international concern.

A convention on genocide was adopted by the General Assembly at its Paris Session in the fall of 1948. The definition of the crime of genocide as a matter of international concern writes a new chapter in international law.

Women, technically speaking, are not a minority group, but, in their treatment in a man's world, they are frequently assimilated to that status (club in D.C.).

The United Nations has taken note of their plight and of the discrimination against them on grounds of sex. The General Assembly has called upon member states to grant equal political rights to women. It has become one of the important concerns of the United Nations to inquire into and to find remedies for the removal of discrimination against women on grounds of sex (Alva Myrdal).

A secretariat survey involving replies from governments and other available information from 74 states has been designed to determine where women stand in the matter of civic rights, including the right to vote and to hold public office and to check their present status against the charter objective of freedom from discrimination based on sex. This survey disclosed that, of the 74 states, 47 now have legal provisions giving women equal rights with men in the franchise and eligibility for public office, 23 do not have any such provisions, and 2 grant limited rights.

One specific case involving the status of a minority group deserves special mention. At the second part of its First Session, the General Assembly, by a two-thirds majority, and over the protest of the Union of South Africa, took jurisdiction of the case involving the treatment of the Indian minority in South Africa. The protest of the Indian delegation on behalf of the Indian community in South Africa asserted that Indian settlers in South Africa had progressively suffered discrimination and deprivation of elementary rights since 1885, and that because of this fact a situation had arisen which was likely to impair friendly relations between India and South Africa.

In accepting this case, the assembly decided not to refer the question of jurisdiction to the International Court of Justice. This was an extremely important decision, since the assembly in this instance set a virtual precedent by taking a broad rather than narrow interpretation of the charter. In the field of international action this decision has a wide significance. In the same decision the assembly took the position that the treatment of Indians in the Union of South Africa should be in conformity with the principles of the charter and with the agreements which had been concluded between the governments of the Union of South Africa and India.

Throughout the past three years the United Nations has been seized with what is, perhaps, the most complex and difficult minority problem in history. The political ramifications of the Palestine question are so wide and so sensational that it is often overlooked that the crux of that question was the problem of the Jewish minority in a land small in area, poor in resources, and with a population in which just two years ago Arabs outnumbered Jews by almost two to one. The normal majority-minority group conflict was acutely sharpened in Palestine by the facts that both Arab and Jewish groups are intensely if not fanatically nationalistic, while in addition the Arab majority feared the economic power and the encroachment by immigration of the Jewish minority. In this situation, the United Nations adopted the only practical course possible— partition—whereby a separate and independent Jewish State would be established in Palestine. That state, Israel, is now firmly established.

The United Nations, by virtue of having set up its headquarters in this country, has felt the direct impact of at least one aspect of a minority and human rights problem. The United Nations secretariat at the outset encountered difficulties in obtaining housing for its Negro personnel, many of whom were not American.

In one instance involving a projected contractual arrangement for a substantial number of its staff in a major housing project, the United Nations was confronted with a stubborn residential exclusion policy insofar as its Negro members would be concerned. In such instances the international secretariat, under the leadership of Trygve Lie, has steadfastly stood by the principles and objectives of the charter and has held principle above expediency and personal convenience.

It is revealing no secret that many delegates from abroad, as well as members of the secretariat, have been genuinely surprised and not infrequently shocked at anti-Negro and anti-Semitic attitudes and racial discrimination practices observed in this country. They may be pardoned for finding it difficult to reconcile such attitudes and practices with the not always modest professions of American democracy. That such conditions are an embarrassment to American moral leadership goes without saying.

The constructive work of the United Nations in the vital and related fields of minority problems and human rights lies ahead. Thus far it has only begun to break ground. The mechanical tools for the job are available to it. The ultimate success of its effort, however, must depend upon the willing cooperation of governments and peoples. If governments take refuge behind their national sovereignties and invoke domestic jurisdiction to cover injustices to peoples within their borders and violations of charter principles, the task of the United Nations will be long and arduous. But the dark shadow of international censure will ceaselessly fall across guilty nations; the pressure of international opinion and the shocked reaction of the conscience of mankind will be unrelenting.

Whatever may be the self-interested policies of individual states, the United Nations has taken one irreversible step. The problems of human rights, minorities, and discrimination have been lifted to the level of international concern. Underprivileged groups throughout the world will not fail to grasp the full significance of that development for the struggle in which they are engaged. Their appeal, henceforth, is to a vastly wider and perhaps more sympathetic jury.

I have firm confidence that the United Nations will play a vital role in assisting all peoples to attain the rights, freedoms, dignity, and self-respect which are the inalienable birthright of every man and woman, of whatever race, color or creed.

CHAPTER 14

Review and Appraisal of Israeli-Arab Relations 1951

A year after receiving the first Nobel Prize to be given to a black, for negotiating an armistice in the Palestine conflict, Bunche gave a detailed account of the subject at the National War College. In typical fashion he objectively describes the conflict between the Arab states and the new Jewish state, saying that the real victims are the Arabs in Palestine. Bunche points out the influence of domestic U.S. politics on the Arab position and contends that their refusal to accept the UN partition decision was a grave error. The four armistice agreements, which brought an end to the fighting, constituted the first major victory of the new world body, giving it much needed credibility in the postwar period.

General Bull: Gentlemen, I am sure you have been looking forward with considerable keen anticipation to this discussion on Israeli-Arab relations and related problems of the Near East which we are having today by Dr. Bunche.

You know, I am sure, of his great accomplishments in this particular area of our interest here. You are familiar, I am sure, with his very fine record as a scholar, as an educator, author, as a public servant, both with the OSS [Office of Strategic Services] during the war and since the war with the State Department and the United Nations. Also, you recall that last year, as a culmination of his great service in the Near East, he received the award of the Nobel Peace Prize.

It is a very great pleasure to present Dr. Ralph Bunche.

Dr. Bunche: General Bull, gentlemen: I am taking the advice set forth in General Bull's letter to me a short while ago quite literally. He said I might talk very informally this morning and direct my attention to the general question of the Israeli-Arab relations and the role of the United Nations in this conflict. I understand the most interesting part of these meetings is the discussion period which follows the lecture, or what may be alleged to be a lecture.

I think that it is not necessary to go into any detail on the question of the background of the unfortunate dispute, the violent conflict between the Arab states and the new Jewish state in Palestine. I think it enough to say in a sense one could describe this as a legacy of Hitler in that, if there had not been the intense persecution of the Jews in Europe by Nazi Germany and the Hitler satellite countries, it would not have been possible, I think, for the Zionist organizations and for the Jewish Agency to convert what had been a sort of religious attachment to Palestine, a concept of a homeland in the sense of a religious haven, into what has become a most vibrant and virulent nationalist, a political nationalist, with a great desire on the part of a great many Jews of different cultural backgrounds—Eastern European Jews, Western European Jews, Jews from North Africa, Jews from Arab states—to migrate to Palestine, now Israel, to a Jewish state as permanent settlers.

I think back to the situation in the 1920s when Weizmann, now president of Israel, the grand old man of Zionism, tried to raise money among world Jewry, tried to induce substantial Jewish migration to Palestine, but with not very much success. It was the startling, spectacular, the tragic persecution of the Jews which made this possible. I know when we were in Europe with the United Nations Special Committee on Palestine, the committee that finally recommended partition to the United Nations—this was in the summer of 1947—we visited a number of the Jewish refugee camps in Germany and Austria. We talked with leaders in those camps, and we talked with some of the ordinary residents of the camps. The committee was tremendously impressed by the fact that there was such great unanimity, or appeared to be, on the part of these people that there was no hope for them anywhere in the world except in a Jewish state; that they had said it couldn't happen here when they were residents of Germany but they had seen things happen which they had assumed could never happen. They were imbued with the idea there would be safety for Jews only in their own state, and there was only one place for this: that was Palestine.

We found it difficult to talk realistically about the possibility of settling somewhere else—in the United States, in Australia or Canada, or in some of the Latin American states that seem to have plenty of room. They constantly pointed out they weren't wanted in these places, the immigration policies were against them; they had to have their own state if there was to be any future for them, and all signs pointed to Palestine.

The result was, of course, that an intense Jewish nationalism developed. It found itself opposed to what had developed since the end of the first World War. And an intense Arab nationalism developed. The clash was inevitable when it took this shape. The fact is that in Palestine during the period of the mandate, the more than 25 years of the mandate, the general relations between Palestinian Arabs and Jews were good. There were no day to day clashes. They carried on business relationships and, there was certainly sound basis for assuming that, given the other conditions, it would be possible for Arabs and Jews in Palestine to live amicably together. But with the conversion of the idea of the Jewish homeland into the idea of a formal Jewish state, with the tremendous emphasis on immigration to Palestine that became necessary perhaps after the persecutions by Hitler, this clash was greatly accentuated.

There was, of course, the factor of complication added to the situation by the Balfour Declaration, the promise made to the Jews of a homeland which has been interpreted in many ways by the British. There was the inevitable, inherent conflict in the mandate because the terms of the mandate incorporated the Balfour Declaration and created a certain future trouble for the mandatory power because the mandatory power was enjoined to protect the interests of the Arab population on the one hand and at the same time to encourage the development of the Jewish homeland on the other.

And British policy in carrying out this mandate was one certainly of considerable fluctuation. At one time or another the British in Palestine found themselves fighting Arabs and fighting Jews. They put forward a policy after the second World War which many of us in the United Nations felt was an utterly unrealistic and impossible policy, because, confronted with this increasingly dangerous conflict between Arab and Jewish nationalism, the British took the position that no solution would be acceptable to them unless it was a solution which would be acceptable to both the Arab and the Jewish community. In that situation there just wasn't any possibility that you could get advance agreement of both Arabs and Jews to a solution because both of them were demanding a national state, both of them were impelled by almost fanatical nationalist views, and neither was likely to be found in a conciliatory mood.

So finally the British, because of the pressure of this very situation and also because of the pressure of the United Nations (which at that time on this issue meant very considerably the pressure of the United States), decided to give up the mandate, so notified the United Nations, and on the 15th of May, 1948, abruptly terminated all of their authority in Palestine. That created a most difficult situation in Palestine because this left the territory in the hands of the United Nations. The British, after the 15th of May, said they were interested only in the protection of their troops and in the evacuation of their troops. There was a vacuum in the territory so far as authority was concerned, and this was particularly true with regard to the Arabs of Palestine. The Jews were much better prepared to look after themselves after the mandatory authority withdrew than the Arabs, because the Jews, under the mandate, had been permitted to develop a semi-governmental apparatus. They had had a nation which had political organization which functioned almost like a government. They had their own schools, their own hospitals. They had their own local authorities who were held together by a national authority, and they could pick up where the British left off. But there was no such organization on the part of the Palestinian Arabs. They were left in pretty bad shape when this abrupt termination of the mandate took place.

The situation was accentuated by the fact that the British had persistently refused to permit the United Nations commission, which had been set up to implement the partition decision of the United Nations, to come to Palestine. The United Nations Palestine Commission, which was created after the adoption by the General Assembly of the partition resolution, November 29, 1947, constantly made overtures to the British about coming to Palestine, but the British felt, because their opposition to the whole partition scheme was mounting, that the presence of the United Nations commission in Palestine would only aggravate matters, would create greater security risks, and therefore would not permit the commission to come to Palestine until just as the British were terminating the mandate. So the net result of it all was that, as soon as the British stepped out, a war began.

It was almost inevitable that this would be the case because of the way in which the whole thing had been done. The surrounding Arab states were very much concerned about what was happening in Palestine. From my relations with them, I think, while many of their statements were exaggerated, there was an element of genuine fear, concern on their part as to what was going to happen in Palestine. In part it was a fear of the Jews, of future Jewish expansion, of Jewish immigration, and of Jewish technological skill. The Arab societies are certainly not very advanced. The Jewish population of Palestine under the mandate was perhaps the most carefully selected population of any society in the world because the immigration policy was a controlled one. They had deliberately taken the cream of the crop—the scientists, the professional men, the technicians, the skilled workers of Western and Eastern Europe, and the young people, strong of body and spirit who would be useful to them in the event war should come. So there was, from the standpoint of the Arabs, a rather dangerous Jewish population in Palestine, one that they would find it difficult to compete with, one that they felt because of the immigration policy would most certainly look toward expansion.

They constantly pointed out to us they had another fear which had nothing directly to do with the Jews, and that was the fear that the creation of a Jewish state in Palestine would establish another imperialist bridgehead in the Near East. This was reiterated to Count Bernadotte and to me time after time—that this would mean that the unfortunate experiences which they had already had for quite some number of years with imperialist penetration would be aggravated by a new bridgehead. They didn't know in Palestine whether it would be a bridgehead for the West or a bridgehead for the East. They claimed they didn't care very much. But this meant a new outside inroad on an already exploited Near East. This is the way they put it. As I say, there was undoubtedly great exaggeration on their part with regard to these fears, but I am convinced that there was a very genuine element of fear and deep concern in their position.

And so they acted. They acted by sending their armies into Palestine. You know what happened. The United Nations had adopted a partition decision, a compromise decision, as they thought. The Arabs never considered it a compromise decision because it did create a Jewish state, did provide for a Jewish state. It provided for dividing this very small and poor territory, and it put no restraint upon Jewish immigration. So for the Arabs it was considered just about a complete defeat, and they were not inclined to take it.

I think it should be pointed out that the United Nations did not go into this question, did not get mixed up with Palestine on its own initiative. The British themselves, after more than 25 years of struggling with the problem, brought it to the United Nations and asked the United Nations to help find a solution— asked the United Nations for help. This partition decision which was reached after the commission had visited Palestine and had visited the refugees in Europe was certainly never regarded by anyone in the United Nations as an ideal decision but as possibly the only thing that could be done in the circumstances.

Then the Arab states made this move, a move which I have always thought was a very grave mistake on their part, of sending their armies into Palestine to prevent the implementation of the United Nations decision. I say I consider that to have been a very grave mistake not only because the principles of the United Nations are against the employment of force to settle issues of this kind, but also a mistake from the standpoint of the ultimate well-being of the Arab population of Palestine itself. The real victims of this whole conflict—and they have been successively at each stage more victimized— have been the Arabs of Palestine. They are the ones who have suffered. The Jews have not greatly suffered as a result of the conflict. In fact, they are better off today than they were before it began. The peoples of the surrounding Arab states have not suffered from the conflict. It has all been taken out of the hides of the Arabs of Palestine.

Each move the Arabs have made, whether it was a move for delay—they were constantly moving for delay always apparently in the hope that some miracle would happen. It was amazing always to see how their minds would work on these questions. I remember vividly in Paris in October 1948, just a couple of weeks actually after Count Bernadotte's assassination, there had been a very sympathetic support quite generally in the world for the plight of the Jews and for their aspirations in Palestine. Certainly the United States had been strongly supporting their cause and had been strongly backing partition in the General Assembly. When I say "strongly backing," in terms of relations with other states that may even be called an understatement. But the Jews had been receiving very good support.

Then for the first time there was a world setback for them. The assassination of Count Bernadotte was a tremendous shock to the world. Immediately in

Paris, particularly because Count Bernadotte's report had just been released, there were public statements made by Secretary of State Marshall, by Foreign Minister Bevin, by Foreign Minister Schuman, supporting Bernadotte's report which the Israelis strongly opposed, a report which would have meant a partition, to be sure, but a partition involving considerably less territory for the State of Israel than the state now has, a partition which was not far-removed from the original boundaries in the original partition resolution of the General Assembly of November 1947. And so this was apparently a propitious moment for the Arabs.

The General Assembly was just meeting. The first item on the agenda in the Political Committee was Count Bernadotte's report, the question of Palestine. I was called to Paris to present this report since Count Bernadotte was now dead. When I got there, I found to my amazement that the item on the agenda had been postponed. I immediately sought to find out how it happened that this item had been postponed, and I found it had been postponed with the combined support of the Arabs and the Israelis. Both of them had stood for the postponement of the item on the agenda.

Then I began to talk with some of my Arab friends and asked, "What was the basis for this? What was your reasoning? This seemed to be for you the very best time to take up this question while the memory of the world was still fresh on the assassination of Bernadotte." They said no, that they had thought more deeply than that; that while they realized that, they wanted postponement because the United States presidential election was to take place in November and since it was certain that Mr. Dewey would win, there would be a change in the American position on Palestine which would be much more sympathetic to the interests of the Arabs. This was their reasoning: the papers say that Mr. Dewey is close to Wall Street and Wall Street is interested in oil. When I explained to them that this was probably specious reasoning, that Mr. Dewey had developed his political career on the sidewalks of New York and that it wasn't likely that he was going to be insensitive to the Jewish vote, they wouldn't believe this until a couple of weeks before the election came off and Mr. Dewey broke the gentlemen's agreement that had been entered into by him and Mr. Truman that they were going to keep the Palestine issue out of the election. Mr. Dewey wrote a letter to somebody in which he came out strongly for the Jewish position. Then my Arab friends were greatly disillusioned and sorry they had acted to postpone the item on the agenda. But this sort of thing was happening constantly and always at the expense of the Arab population.

There are some other aspects of this that no doubt would be of interest to you. The war started in the middle of May 1948 with the armed forces of Egypt, the Arab Legion of Jordan, the Arabs of Iraq and Syria—I don't say Lebanon because they didn't move in—with these forces I have named moving into Palestine for the avowed purpose of protecting the Arabs of Palestine against the Jews but with the obvious purpose of preventing the establishment of a Jewish state. It was a vicious war from the very beginning, bitterly fought. It certainly wasn't a great war. Neither side had anything great to fight with. By modern standards, the weapons they had were pretty primitive. Despite the Arab claims, we know definitely that the Jews at the beginning of that fight had very little except great spirit. It was spirit made necessary by the fact this was life or death for 650,000 Jews in Palestine because the Arabs were bent on driving them into the Mediterranean. The Arabs, certainly on paper, had far greater military strength than the Jews. There was one real army in the field; that was the Egyptian army, which was a full army with all the necessary support that goes with an army. The best fighting force undoubtedly was the Arab Legion. It was really a task force in a sense; it wasn't a complete army. It was largely under British officers and as a mechanized force fought very well indeed, and actually, after the first few weeks, was never greatly challenged by the Jewish forces.

And, of course, this was the significance of the whole fight out there. The great weapon which the Jews had was Arab disunity. The Arabs did not work together, they did not fight together. There was jealousy among them, there were rivalries. Some of them quite obviously were tickled when others were meeting setbacks at the hands of the Jews. And the Jews, of course, had counted upon this Arab disunity.

But I say that merely to say this: within three weeks after that war began Count Bernadotte, who had been quickly sent out there by the United Nations, had succeeded in achieving a truce. It was the first truce which went into effect, I think, June 9, 1948. It was a four weeks' truce.

In that regard I want to destroy one of the myths that has so often been peddled in this country, and that is that the war in Palestine came to an end because of the overwhelming defeat of the Arab forces by the Israeli forces. Mind you, I would not take anything from the valiant, heroic effort of the Israeli forces. They fought with very little and fought extremely well. But there were never any decisive battles won or lost in Palestine. There were never any armies destroyed nor any substantial components of any armies destroyed by either side. At the end of the war all of the armies were intact except the guerrilla forces which had come down from Syria and Lebanon which were ragtags and never amounted to more than three or four thousand people in any event. But before there were any victories in the field of battle the first truce had gone into effect—three weeks after the war began, or less than a month after it began. Count Bernadotte was able to negotiate this truce and put it into effect at a time when the Jewish part of Jerusalem was beseiged and surrounded by the Arab Legion, when there was no basis for anyone suggesting that it was impossible for the Arab armies ever to achieve their goal. The parties to that conflict bowed to the authority of the United Nations, not to the authority of military events, and that was the significant feature of this conflict throughout.

When that truce went into effect, there was a very great responsibility resting upon the United Nations to enforce it, to supervise it, to see that the truce lines were demarcated and kept inviolate, to escort convoys from Tel-Aviv to Jerusalem every day through the Arab lines with the guns of the Arab Legion forces lining the road all the way. And this worked. This work was done by military observers, officers, and later enlisted men who were made available to the United Nations by Belgium, France, Sweden, and the United States. And I understand some of the few men who did tours of duty out there in Palestine, in the Near East in the truce supervision work, are enrolled here; and some of those men are now fighting with the United Nations forces in Korea. I have received letters from them quite often. This was their responsibility. The American military observers were under the command of then brigadier general, now Major General William Riley of the United States Marines, who is still out there as chairman of the armistice commission and as chief of staff.

They did a remarkable job. There had been no previous experience for this sort of job. We didn't know much about it and therefore we couldn't brief them very well. They had to improvise as they went along. What it amounted to was these men would be flown out there, and we would have a short talk with them. We would tell them our purpose is to keep the Arabs and Jews from fighting each other—"You go out to the sector to which you are sent and you do everything you can to see that the truce lines are observed, to bring the local commanders together and stop local fighting, to order them back if they cross the lines, and see what happens." More often than not the orders and the commands were observed.

I have often told the story of one of our American observers out there in the early days of the truce. He was a naval officer and spent a lot of time in the Pacific. He might have become a little beachhead conscious from Iwo Jima and Okinawa, etc., I don't know, but he was enthusiastic about his job. We had sent him down to a station just below Tel-Aviv to supervise the truce. He had a small international staff with him—some Belgians and French. Very soon at Haifa, the supervision headquarters, we began to get urgent cables calling for reinforcements. Finally the cables got very specific. (We had our own communication system and transportation system. We didn't depend on local facilities.) These requests began to get very specific and he began to call for United States Marines. Admiral Sherman was then sent out there with the Eastern Mediterranean fleet and there were marines on some of his ships. He asked specifically for marines. Finally Count Bernadotte said to me, "Out of curiosity—there doesn't seem to be trouble with the truce—why don't you jump in a jeep and go down and find out what he wants to do with these marines?"

I got down there and found everything quiet and he was entirely happy. He said he had things well in hand. He really didn't know much about the United Nations or how much authority it had or how much power but, he said, "It sure as hell has the Arabs and Jews fooled. We give them an order and they obey it." I said, "That is the whole idea. That is the reason we wonder why you want these marines." And in exactly these words he said, "It is very simple. If I could just have these marines, we could move right on in and go all the way to Jerusalem."

This wasn't the classic operation at all. We didn't want to go anywhere; we wanted to keep the Arabs and Jews from going anywhere. This was a concept of limited peace. Well, he caught on and gave very good service, but he was enthusiastic.

On another occasion we had one of the French officers who was quite daring escorting convoys from Tel-Aviv to Jerusalem. They would go every day without any trouble, but after several weeks the first trouble occurred one day when a bunch of Arab guerrillas ambushed the convoy. They ambushed the convoy near Latrun. The French officer leading the convoy was in the lead jeep. (These observers carried no arms, not even side arms out there. I must say the Americans, particularly, were not a little puzzled when they first arrived and we told them to dispose of the side arms, particularly in view of the fact there was some hazard in this work. In addition to Bernadotte, 10 men were killed and 23 were wounded in just about a year of operations—sniper fire, firing on jeeps, firing on planes, and mines in the roads.) The Frenchman without any hesitation stopped his jeep and ran directly into the line of fire right up to the Arabs, shouting and gesticulating as he ran, and so surprised them, struck such consternation in their ranks—there were about 25 of them—they broke and fled. The first volley they fired killed 4 of the civilians, one of them an American. But they fled in the face of this one-man charge, unarmed charge, by this French officer, and did not return to the attack. This enabled him to get the remaining civilians and the convoy together, to return to Tel-Aviv and thereby saved the lives of a good many people. We had many actions of that kind carried on by these fellows.

Then came the second truce which was ordered by the Security Council in July 1948 and which was observed by the parties. There was fighting but there was never any resumption of the general war in Palestine, in fact, after the first truce went into effect early in June 1948. The armistice agreements then came. They were the result of a Security Council resolution of the 16th of November 1948 calling on the parties to supplant the truce with armistice agreements.

To put it in a nutshell, what was most important in these negotiations once we got the Arabs and Jews to sit down together—first the Egyptians, then the Jordanians, and then the Lebanese and the Syrians—what was important on both sides, and particularly on the Arab side, was face saving. What we found was often the key to agreement was to so word things that they would be palatable to one side or the other. I may say it was not only the Arabs who were interested in face saving, but it was often the Jews, too.

The most significant feature of the four armistice agreements, beyond the fact that they did bring an end to the military phase of the Palestine conflict, was the fact they set up a machinery for a continued collaboration between the Arabs and Jews, a collaboration which goes on. Each one provided for a mixed armistice commission of Arabs and Jews with the United Nations to provide the chairman and with the United Nations also to put at their service military observers to help them implement the agreement. On the whole these mixed armistice commissions with their international flavor have worked very well. As I say, General Riley is still out there as chief of staff and as chairman of each of the mixed armistice commissions.

You know, there has been some trouble between the Syrians and the Israelis recently over the drainage project in the Huleh Valley. I am not being facetious when I say in my view this trouble would not have developed if it had not been for two hot water bottles. The explanation is this: unfortunately Riley had to have an emergency operation for a kidney stone. He decided, because it was an emergency operation, to have it done in Jerusalem. Some people thought in view of all the circumstances it was quite courageous anyhow. It was done in Hadassah Hospital in Jerusalem. It was a perfect operation. They took exceptional care of him. They have excellent surgeons. He recovered from the operation perfectly. It was successful in every way except that, because Riley was the top United Nations man out there and an international figure, they wanted to be sure in the hospital that nothing would happen to him. So they got overcareful and apparently to ease the shock of the operation—it was a spinal anesthetic—they wanted to keep his feet warm during the operation. So they applied hot water bottles to his feet.

When he came out of the anesthetic he noted that his feet hurt—not where they had cut him. The diagnosis later showed he had third-degree burns on both heels as a result of these hot water bottles—they had kept him too warm. He had to be flown over to St. Alban's Naval Hospital and had to have skin grafting. He was laid up for a total of four months.

While he was at St. Alban's Naval Hospital getting skin grafting this drainage project began. Unfortunately his second in command, his deputy, a Belgian, Colonel [left blank], at the same time had an appendectomy and he was laid up, which left only a French colonel who had not much experience in charge. Well, these things are all cumulative. There were some misunderstandings at first, as I get it from Riley. This French officer had made a promise or two to the Israelis in writing, and when he got the Arab reaction there was some reneging on the promise, which means out there the person to whom the promise is made is going to go right ahead as though there was no reneging, which the Israelis did. Some of the Arab residents in the demilitarized zone shot at them. Each day this developed. There was no prompt and firm action taken as would have been taken had Riley been on the spot. The situation deteriorated until finally the Security Council had to order a cease-fire. Since then there has been no shooting, but the problem is far from settled. I don't see it as a problem of major concern, but any time there is conflict along the borders out there, there is reason for anxiety.

Well, I must finish, and let me do so by just quickly pointing out two things: first of all, while the armistice agreements are still in effect out there and will apparently have to remain in effect for some time because there is no immediate prospect they will be supplanted by full peace, it is well to bear in mind there are really no great number of outstanding problems between the Arabs and the Jews. The political atmosphere is bad. The relations between them are bad. But the problems, the issues between them, are relatively few. In fact, in my view the critical one is the issue of the Arab refugees, the 750,000 and more Arabs who were displaced by the fighting, who are not permitted by the Israelis to return to their lands and who are being kept alive by the relief effort of the United Nations with some help from the Arab states themselves.

This is the big, outstanding issue which is urgent because it involves lives. It is a humanitarian issue, and it is also an issue that much can be made of propaganda wise. The Arabs can use it to whip up emotions, to show just how bad the Jews are. And not much progress has been made toward its settlement. The Palestine Conciliation Commission, which was set up to deal with the outstanding questions, has been able to do nothing. It has made no progress whatsoever toward a solution of this or any of the other problems outstanding.

The question of Jerusalem—I recall General Bull mentioned this in his letter as one of the issues—the internationalization is a dead issue. It is dead not only because the Jews oppose it but more so because Abdullah opposes it. And I think Abdullah has to oppose it in the sense of any international consideration of Jerusalem. Certainly the Jews could be brought to accept a partial internationalization of Jerusalem, a token internationalization; but for Jordan it would mean cutting off the rest of Arab Palestine, the central areas—Nablus and Ram Allah—and the Arab forces there from Jordan. In this sense in the eyes of Arabs it would be seen as leaving the Arabs in the Arab part of Palestine completely at the mercy of the Israelis. It seems to me it is practically impossible for Jordan to accept it. The population on neither side of the line wishes it. And there is no basis for assuming there is any way in which the United Nations could enforce an international regime upon Jerusalem.

As regards the other problems outstanding—boundaries, war claims, and the like—I don't see that there is much in it. One of the tough problems that Riley has on his hands now is the continued blockade of Jewish shipments destined for Israel and diverted by the Egyptians at Suez. They won't let any goods which are bound for Israel through Suez, and this is a terrific blow at the economy and the well-being of Israel. Of that there is no question.

As regards the prospects for the future, I am not pessimistic but neither am I greatly optimistic, and that is not entirely because of the prevailing relations between the Arabs and the Jews, but it is because of the present policy pursued by the United States, the United Kingdom, and France. Since the armistice agreements have gone into effect, these three powers met and issued a declaration in which they said they would guarantee the sanctity of the boundaries of the Arab states and of Israel; and since then the policy, as far as I can divine it, has been one of drift, of not doing very much at all until trouble develops and then they have to jump in and try to stop it. No real effort has been made in the sense of putting pressure, because the United Nations has to operate on the basis of pressures. It can't do very much in Palestine or in Indonesia or Kashmir just by appeal to sweet reason, by the overwhelming force of its persuasive powers. It doesn't reach settlements, it doesn't get very far this way. It has to operate on the basis of pressures, and these pressures have to be formulated by governments. If the governments take an apathetic position, if they are diffident or indifferent, if they are content with drift, then dangerous situations my well develop simply by default.

That certainly is my concern about the Near East now—my concern unofficially because officially I have no further connection with the problem. I think there is latent danger there. I do not see any immediate danger. On the Arab side there is great resentment against the United States, against the United Kingdom, as well as against the Jews—against the United States because they feel the United States has always favored the Jews. What will happen in the event of a showdown in that area—and I mean by that in the event of a World War involving the Soviet Union—it is difficult to say, but my feeling would be the West could not hope for very much in the way of strength and support from either Arabs or Israelis in that area in the event of a showdown. Certainly no matter how much goodwill they would have, there wouldn't be much military strength of significance, and I am not sure how much active support might be forthcoming. On the part of Israel there is great economic difficulty, great internal problems. It has internal divisions, religious issues. There is the issue between the two parties, Mapai and Mapam, with Mapam a strong party, not at all a Communist party but certainly with strong leanings toward an Eastern orientation, whereas Mapai, Ben-Gurion's party, tends more and more to look to the West and to support the West. The Arabs have indicated pretty much what their position would be on the Korean question. They do not come in with us, but even if they did, their governments are weak, insecure. Their economies are weak and in some instances semi-feudal. There is tremendous need for development in the whole area, for development projects involving considerable capital.

So the net result of it, it seems to me, is we could not hope for very effective support for military effort in that area from the local peoples unless some very significant changes occur. What military force we might have would have to be provided from outside. Most of all, it seems to me there is a very great need for a firm and clear United States and United Kingdom policy, jointly if possible, in this area. I think that such a policy could do very much toward avoiding certain dangers which are bound to arise in the future unless a strong stand is taken. I think the present policy of drift is not at all to our interests.

Well, I have already exceeded my time. I am sorry to have rambled on at great length in this way, but I am afraid I am the victim of a label. Because I had a mediation function, people have always said, "You must have great patience," and I am afraid I assume my audiences have great patience too, but I thank you very much.

CHAPTER 15

The UN Operation in the Congo
1964

Bunche believed the 1960 UN operation in the Congo was his most dangerous and controversial mission. He almost lost his life in a Leopoldville hotel when he was mistaken by Congolese forces for a white Belgian. Dag Hammarskjöld, Bunche's close friend and favorite secretary-general, did lose his life in an airplane crash over the Congo, and Bunche pays tribute to him in this lecture at Columbia University. As the initial leader of the UN peacekeeping forces in the Congo, Bunche was strongly criticized by the Soviets and radicals in the United States for not supporting Patrice Lumumba. As Bunche makes clear in this speech, Lumumba either failed to comprehend or chose to ignore the limitations placed on the use of UN forces by Security Council decisions. Given his lifelong opposition to colonialism, Bunche does not fail to condemn the long-term colonial policy of the Belgians or their decisions once independence became a reality.

I have chosen as my topic in the Dag Hammarskjöld Memorial Lecture Series "The United Nations Operation in the Congo" (called ONUC for short), primarily because that operation meant so very much to Dag Hammarskjöld, and he far more to it, and also because I have been directly associated with the operation from its inception. Dag Hammarskjöld initiated the Congo operation in midsummer of 1960, encouraged it to become the biggest of all United Nations operations to date, and gave his major attention to it through many tense and unpleasant months until, in September 1961, he gave his life while serving it.

It is especially appropriate, I think, to introduce this particular lecture with a few remarks about Dag Hammarskjöld himself. It is, of course, never easy to talk about one's chief or former chief, and Dag Hammarskjöld was my hardworking and demanding "boss" for eight years. It is even less easy to present a balanced judgment about a man as remarkable and as remarkably complex as Dag Hammarskjöld.

One need not elaborate here on the widely accepted fact that he was one of the truly great men of our times; on his widely known and deserved reputation for being uniquely gifted in intelligence, wisdom, statesmanship, and courage or on his literally total dedication to the causes of peace and human advancement and the United Nations efforts to promote them. We who worked with him came to know Dag Hammarskjöld also as bold, sometimes daring in his moves and approaches to problems, but not reckless. He was not given to acting without cool and thorough calculation, and was never one to act impulsively, although when an idea firmly commended itself to him he would pursue it doggedly. It is not suggested, however, that he was above anger, even fury, or other emotions. He could and at times did erupt. He had an uncanny and almost intuitive sense of political timing, and this may have been one of his greatest assets throughout his years of devoted service to the United Nations.

The course taken by Dag Hammarskjöld's career in the United Nations was something of a surprising revelation to many. At the time of his first selection as secretary-general his strength was considered to be very largely on the side of administration and conservatism in action. He was expected to be safe and sound. In the early period of his regime at the United Nations, in fact, he did give a good bit of attention to administration, bringing about some administrative improvements in the internal workings of that United Nations structure which he liked to refer to as "this house." These improvements made a very helpful impact on the morale and esprit de corps of the secretariat, at a time when Senator Joseph McCarthy's attacks had seriously impaired the spirit and hopes of much of the staff, particularly its American members. But his interest and immersion in political problems soon began to leave him less and less time for the administrative aspects of his responsibilities, and both his attention to and interest in them steadily diminished. It also soon became clear that he would not be lacking in political initiative backed by courage, as demonstrated by his audacious mission to Peking in the interest of the release of the American prisoners. It cannot be said that Dag Hammarskjöld displayed any reluctance about being carried in this direction, and he never seemed to be sorry about becoming more and more exclusively a "political man." Quite the contrary.

The former secretary-general was a man of great reserve in his personal relations, to the extent even of shyness; he was not easy to know, even for those who worked closely with him. It sometimes seemed as though he were reluctant to let anyone see his relaxed side, as though out of fear that it might be regarded as a weakness, just as he stubbornly sought to avoid ever admitting an illness or an ache. But there was a warm and attractive human side of him which in time was gradually revealed to those closely associated with him and who came to know him well, or rather whom he came to know well. This congenial side of the austere man would be revealed in many ways: in the form of personal gifts, usually carefully selected by himself, either through shopping expeditions in town or brought back from a trip; through an arresting narration of some personal reminiscence which unfailingly would be a gem from life;

some startling hops of elation on receiving unexpectedly good news, perhaps from one of his field operations or an effort in quiet diplomacy; his poignant affection for Greenback, the little monkey he was given during his trip to Somaliland in the winter of 1960—the lively little pet who was a monkey in every sense, wildly playful, an irrepressible show-off, a born "ham" whenever visitors were present; or in an animated discussion of some lately published novel or essay in almost any language.

Although Dag Hammarskjöld became increasingly consumed by his dedication to the United Nations—even to the extent of giving up his mountain climbing, his walks, his occasional exercise at squash rackets, and his browsing in bookstores and antique shops—he did maintain to the end some of his other interests, such as his devotion to literature, by late night and early morning reading at the expense of his sleep. His interest in the arts, music, poetry, and painting gave him continuing pleasure and relaxation.

Dag Hammarskjöld was himself a dynamic person and he strove with, I believe, no little success to make the United Nations a dynamic force for peace and human advancement. Wherever in the world there was a conflict situation, actual or threatening, he believed the United Nations should actively seek to contain or avert it: by quiet diplomacy, when the circumstances permitted, in the form of good offices if the parties themselves demonstrated an inability to deal with the situation; and, if necessary, by overt United Nations action. He saw more clearly than any man I have known that the United Nations must do more than hold meetings and talk and adopt resolutions. It was good for the General Assembly to be the forum of the world and to afford a unique opportunity for a meeting of statesmen from all over, and for those statesmen to exchange views. But this in itself, he knew, could never be enough to save the world. In his conception, the United Nations must play an ever more active role, must project itself into the very area of conflict.

It was in pursuance of this line of thought that under Dag Hammarskjöld came the numerous acts of quiet diplomacy and the establishment, for peace-making and peace-keeping purposes, of the United Nations "presence" in a number of places, whether by a representative of the secretary-general, by the stationing of United Nations military observers, or by a United Nations peace force. It was his firm conviction that it was not only possible to conceive of but that there actually had been built up at the United Nations—at the very heart of world events—a body of thoroughly objective, if not "neutral," international officers who, under his leadership, when given opportunity and resources and the confidence of enough governments, could play a vital and at times even decisive role in averting conflict.

Thus Dag Hammarskjöld strengthened the United Nations truce and cease-fire operations in the Near East and Kashmir, which had begun under Trygve Lie, his predecessor, giving increasing attention particularly to the

United Nations Truce Supervision Operation (UNTSO) in Jerusalem. At the time of the Suez crisis in 1956, even though it was an untried idea, without precedent and without any prior provision for its financing, Mr. Hammarskjöld helped to initiate and proceeded speedily to establish the United Nations Emergency Force (UNEF) in Gaza and Sinai, in pursuance of a resolution of the General Assembly. He made an enormous miscalculation in this instance, for he had anticipated that UNEF would be needed in the Near East for only a few months, and he could not have imagined how indispensable it would become. After almost six and a half years, at an annual cost to the United Nations of approximately $19,000,000, that peace force is still deployed along the Gaza Strip armistice line and the international frontier between Israel and the United Arab Republic, and there is little prospect that it can be withdrawn in the foreseeable future without risking a new war.

The United Nations Operation in the Congo was mainly Hammarskjöld's in conception and reflected Hammarskjöld's boldness. From the beginning, it was apparent that this would be by far the largest and most costly operation ever undertaken by the United Nations, and it also soon became distressingly clear that it would be the most difficult and trying of all United Nations efforts. It began in mid-July 1960, and still goes on, although, in accordance with General Assembly action, the United Nations Force is definitely scheduled to be withdrawn from the Congo at the end of June 1964, which will be just short of four years after its arrival in the Congo. In the three and a half years to date of the Congo operation, the United Nations has expended some $400,000,000 in its military and civilian assistance activities.

The Congo task posed the sort of stern challenge that brought out the imaginative and courageous best in Dag Hammarskjöld. He loved to rise to a challenge. He was never so stirred and inspired—or inspiring—as when entering the lists with a tough new issue.

Dag Hammarskjöld anticipated the possibility of trouble in the Congo after its independence, even before that independence was achieved on June 30, 1960. It was well-known even then, of course, that the Congolese had had very little preparation for independence. How totally unprepared they were was to become fully and tragically revealed soon after independence day. In late May of that year, Mr. Hammarskjöld called me into his office to inform me that he wished me to go to the then Belgian Congo toward the end of June to represent the United Nations at the Congo's independence ceremony. He also informed me I was to stay on in the Congo for some time after independence to be of such assistance as might be required of me by the new government, bearing in mind, he added, that there might well be trouble in that new country.

His anxiety was justified. There was to be trouble in the Congo, profound and shattering trouble, and it came only a week after independence, when the ANC (The Armée Nationale Congolaise, which had been the Force Publique under Belgian rule) mutinied in early July and arrested or chased away all of its Belgian officers, which at that time meant quite literally all of its officers.

Soon after the mutiny of his troops, Patrice Lumumba, the Congo's first prime minister, who only a few months later was to come to such a tragic end, called me into a meeting of his Cabinet members make the government's first request for assistance from the United Nations. At that time the government was thinking only of military technical assistance and not a military force. When, however, only a few days later, the Belgian troops, to protect Belgian nations, moved outside of their bases in the Congo without the consent of the Congolese government, Mr. Lumumba, on July 12, 1960, urgently called on the United Nations for military assistance in getting the Belgian troops to withdraw and in helping to protect the country's territorial integrity. There was not at this time very much understanding on the part of any Congolese official about the nature of the United Nations, or about what it could or could not do, its functioning and structure, and particularly about the meaning and status of the United Nations secretariat. Indeed, even today, one could wish for much more understanding along these lines. The feeling in Leopoldville in July 1960 seemed to be that the United Nations would quickly respond with everything that was wanted and needed and that the United Nations personnel, military and civilian alike, would be constantly at the bidding of Congolese government officials, even at times to serve the most petty personal aims. Mr. Lumumba bluntly stated in his bitter letter of August 14, 1960, to Mr. Hammarskjöld, that the Security Council, by its resolution of August 9, 1960, "is to place all its resources at the disposal of my government." Congolese officials holding such views have naturally suffered profound disillusionment.

The United Nations experience in the Congo has demonstrated, sometimes painfully, the serious difficulties that will inevitably be encountered by a United Nations peace force stationed in a country under a specific mandate to provide the government with military assistance in preserving its integrity and in maintaining internal law and order, without clear, precise, and full directives about its function and authority in relation to the government of the country in which it is to be deployed, and prior agreement about these with the government concerned.

In July and August of 1960, I was seeing Patrice Lumumba almost daily. He was an electric figure; his passionate oratory could entrance an audience and, as it sometimes appeared, even himself; he was indefatigable; he was quickly perceptive and shrewd; also he was deeply suspicious of almost everyone and everything. He may have been subject to leftist influence, but I did not regard him as anyone's stooge and felt that he was not greatly concerned with ideology. Mr. Lumumba, it must be said, was one of the few Congolese who seemed to grasp the vital necessity of national unity in a new nation, and he strove against all the divisive forces of tribalism and special interest to promote his unity. Unfortunately, however, he and most of his colleagues in his Cabinet had little knowledge of and apparently no deep interest in government and administration as distinct from crude politics and political maneuver. It was this, combined with the mutiny of the ANC, the inability, which was all too clear from the beginning, of Kasavubu and Lumumba to reconcile their differences, the extraordinary atmosphere of rumor, fear, suspicion, and violence which pervaded the Congo at that time, that soon brought the Congo to near chaos.

It must be said that the Belgian decision to move their troops out of their Congo bases against the will of the Congo government, or, at least, the manner in which it was done, was a disastrous step. Some in Leopoldville at that time, including myself, had advised Belgian authorities that it would likely be so, before the fateful move was undertaken. I had suggested that a wiser tactic than unilateral military action would have been an appeal to the Security Council for assistance in protecting the thousands of Belgian nationals remaining in the Congo. The move of the Belgian troops left Mr. Lumumba furious and desperate and led him to broadside appeals for outright military aid to the United States (President Eisenhower advised him to turn to the United Nations), to the USSR, and, only as a last resort, to the United Nations. In response to this second appeal, I assured Mr. Lumumba that the United Nations would most likely respond sympathetically, but even with my deep faith in the United Nations I could not have imagined at that time that the United Nations response to Mr. Lumumba's call would be as rapid and as immense as it turned out to be.

It developed that virtually the entire international community was sympathetic to the cries from this newly emerged country in the very heart of Africa, and wished to help. As mentioned earlier, the second appeal was received at the United Nations on July 12, 1960, and the first Security Council resolution in response to it, promising assistance, was adopted in the before-dawn hours of July 14, 1960. The follow-up action by the United Nations was unbelievably rapid, for the first United Nations troops—the Tunisians, quickly followed by Moroccans, Ethiopians, and Ghanaians—landed at Ndjili airport in Leopoldville on July 15, 1960. For this swift and effective response, my friend and former colleague in the secretariat Dean Andrew Cordier deserves major credit.

The United Nations had no reasonable alternative to its favorable response to the Congo's appeal—the appeal of a weak government in a new state. In so doing, the United Nations strengthened itself morally and won new prestige. And it also gave to itself, no doubt unknowingly at the time, a far wider role and meaning in world affairs than it had ever had, and made indispensable a much stronger position for the secretary-general as the executive arm. An unfettered executive with authority to act is imperative to the effective conduct of a peacekeeping field operation.

The Congo issue, when it came before the United Nations, was not in the context of the East-West conflict or of the Cold War. This accounted for the unanimity and spontaneity of the early support for the Congo's appeal, the Security Council resolutions, and ONUC. But it was not long before this changed and the United Nations Operation in the Congo came to be an issue between East and West, with Dag Hammarskjöld caught squarely in the cross-fire because of his responsibility, as secretary-general, for the conduct of the operation. In any case, the United Nations, by having ONUC on the spot without delay, was able to fill what otherwise, because of the collapse of government in the Congo, would have been an inviting and most dangerous vacuum of authority in the heart of Africa, with obvious implications for rival East-West interests.

As soon as the July 12 appeal was received from the Congolese government, Dag Hammarskjöld began intensive consultations, particularly with the representatives of a number of African governments. He had seen immediately, with his usual keen perception, that the solid support of the Africans would be a decisive factor in getting the Congo operation launched. It was from these discussions that the idea—and the necessity—of a United Nations force which should be basically although not exclusively African in composition emerged.

The African members, although they later became much less of one view on questions relating to the Congo operation than at first, have continued to exercise a decisive influence on matters affecting the operation. It was their unified voice, for instance, that led the General Assembly last fall to respond favorably to the appeal of Prime Minister Adoula to extend the stay of the United Nations Force in the Congo from the end of December 1963, when it was originally scheduled to be withdrawn, to the end of June 1964.

The near anarchy and chaos which occurred in the Congo so soon after independence and continued for so long led to a most unfortunate if unavoidable diversion to military assistance of the major part of the United Nations resources for the Congo from the hoped-for program of massive technical assistance, designed to help the country get on its feet after the departure of the Belgians, who had been doing just about everything in the government, in administration, and in the economy. This military assistance was provided to help induce, as it did, Belgian troops to return to their bases and ultimately to leave the country, and to assist the government in maintaining law and order and preserving its territorial integrity. For the United Nations, this really meant undertaking for some time virtually the entire responsibility of holding things together in the Congo, while not trespassing on the authority of the government, at a time when governmental machinery was just about nonexistent owing to lack of experienced officials and the incessant quarrels of the politicians, and when the ANC was not only weak but dangerous owing to lack of officers and discipline.

In a United Nations operation which, in both its military and its civilian aspects, must be in such close and daily contact with a government which has to lean so heavily on United Nations assistance, the problem of relations with that government is a most serious one. The operation, obviously, must meticulously avoid any interference in the internal political affairs of the country or any appearance of such interference, although many persons unconnected with the operation seem to take it for granted that there is such interference. The government, on its part, requests and is dependent upon the assistance the operation can afford, but many of its officials actually resent the need for it, or at least having to seek and ask for it. The government also, of course, would resent any United Nations political intervention unless it could be directed against the opposition, when it would, naturally, be entirely welcome.

Considering all the delicate circumstances, the relations between the Congolese government and the United Nations by and large have been tolerable, although they have seldom been really happy. They are, in truth, none too good at this very moment, although there has been no change in the policy of the United Nations or Secretary-General U Thant toward the Congo, which is to afford that country the maximum assistance possible with the resources available. The difficulties leading to strained relations usually arise when the United Nations, most likely for reasons of sound principle, finds it impossible to grant one or another request of the government. In this regard, I cannot help but recall my own experience with Mr. Lumumba, Mr. Gizenga, and other members of the Lumumba Cabinet back in August 1960, when I was rejecting almost daily demands from them that elements of the United Nations Force be put instantly at the disposal and under the command of the Congolese government, which would then dispatch them to Katanga to fight Mr. Tshombe, or to Kasai or to Kivu to fight someone else—the ANC itself being unable to do so for lack of officers, retraining, and discipline.

I suppose one cannot speak of the United Nations Operation in the Congo without some reference to the attempted secession of Katanga, which has, perhaps more than any other single factor, the ANC mutiny excepted, complicated and bedeviled the post-independence history of the Congo. I say "attempted" advisedly because Katanga's secession never actually took place, and, indeed Moise Tshombe, from his retreat in Spain, was recently avowing without a smile that, after all, the secession of Katanga was never his intention.

Although Mr. Tshombe had attended the Brussels conference before independence and had agreed with the other Congolese leaders on the arrangements for independence, including the provisional constitution, it seems certain that the idea of secession was actively on his mind, possibly for a combination of personal political and financial reasons. I first met Mr. Tshombe in my suite at the Stanley Hotel in Leopoldville a few days after Congo independence. He was peeved, rather justifiably I think, at having been ignored by Messrs.

Lumumba and Kasavubu. Mr. Tshombe at that time also expressed great dissatisfaction that the concept of a centralized government had been adopted and informed me, with a surprising knowledge of the United States Articles of Confederation, that he favored a loose (and weak) federation in the Congo along those lines. He seemed only to be encouraged when I protested strongly that the United States Articles of Confederation had failed woefully to work.

A few days later, Mr. Tshombe returned to Katanga and proclaimed secession. This declaration of July 11, 1960, was about the only basis Katangese secession ever had, and it would have had little or no meaning if Mr. Tshombe had not acquired disputed access to very large financial resources as well as the support of the European community in Katanga and of mining interests in and outside of that province. He was thus able to raise a Katangese army and employ non-African mercenary officers to lead it. Even so, Mr. Tshombe and Katanga and the mercenaries would not have been able to cause nearly as much trouble as they did had it not been for the utter incapacity of the central government and its army.

It deserves passing mention that Mr. Tshombe had at his bidding throughout the secession effort a quite formidable propaganda apparatus which was very active in the Western world and had especially strong impact in the United States. In this country, strangely, it succeeded in blinding a surprisingly large number of people, including some in public position, to the verities of the Katanga situation particularly and the Congo situation generally, and led them to oppose the policy of the United States government on the Congo.

The specter of Katanga and Mr. Tshombe always had highest priority in the thoughts of Congolese government officials, sometimes to an obsessive and paralyzing degree. Although this may be less the case today than it was three years ago, it could become so again very quickly should Mr. Tshombe emerge onto the active scene, as he may well do, once the United Nations troops are withdrawn from the Congo at the end of June. In fact, at this very time we are receiving a number of increasingly disturbing reports from reliable sources of a renewed concentration of the relics of Tshombe's army and of the mercenary officers' corps along the Angolan-Congolese border.

I recall an evening in Leopoldville in August 1960 at Patrice Lumumba's home when he was vigorously lodging a series of complaints against ONUC until, in sheer self-defense, I took out of my case a cable that I had just received from Dag Hammarskjöld, giving the text of the long message he had recently sent to Mr. Tshombe firmly rejecting the latter's claim for Katanga's membership in the United Nations. Mr. Lumumba's face lighted up with near ecstasy when he read the message. He immediately dropped the subject of his complaints and asked only that he be permitted to make a copy of that message.

It is a most difficult situation for any government, and particularly for a new and proudly sensitive one, to have a right to a certain line of action, and a desperate need to take it, as in the case of the Congo's opposition to the attempted secession of Katanga, but to lack completely the means to launch the action, while at the same time there is in their country an international agency which they think has the right, as well as the means, to undertake the action for them, but which refuses to do it except in its own way and time. The resulting emotions and frustrations lead to many unrealistic attitudes. For example, on one of his visits to the Congo, Mr. Hammarskjöld informed Mr. Gizenga, who was acting prime minister in the absence of Mr. Lumumba, and his colleagues, of his intention to send me to Katanga to prepare the way for the entry of the United Nations Force into Katanga. This was in early August 1960. Mr. Gizenga was insistent that several members of the Congolese government should accompany me on the flight, although he knew very well that the only possible result of this would be that all of us would be promptly arrested on landing in Elisabethville, if not shot down before landing there. Mr. Gizenga was furious when Mr. Hammarskjöld decided that only United Nations personnel would take this trip. We went alone and got into trouble anyway.

While it was apparent that Katanga had no military force of consequence at that time, Mr. Tshombe was appealing by every means to the people of Katanga to resist United Nations entry. It would clearly put the United Nations Force in an untenable position if it had to fight the people of Katanga to enter that province and to remain there, for this would give it the posture of an army of occupation. Therefore I advised Mr. Hammarskjöld not to send the force to Katanga for the time being. I greatly doubt that a United Nations peace force could be stationed for very long in any country if, even in self-defense, it would have to turn its guns on civilians rather than military forces. The political realities of the United Nations, I imagine, would not long permit a peace force to be in the posture of an army of occupation.

Subsequently, the secretary-general, with characteristic decisiveness and courage, decided to go himself to Katanga to talk with Mr. Tshombe, following a quick visit to New York to report to the Security Council. He went and succeeded in convincing Mr. Tshombe that the United Nations troops should be permitted to come into Katanga without resistance, and this they promptly did. Far from pleasing Mr. Lumumba, however, this accomplishment infuriated him, and on Mr. Hammarskjöld's return to Leopoldville from Katanga he received some incredibly angry and insulting letters from Mr. Lumumba about his trip to Katanga and his interpretation of Security Council resolutions. In fact, from that time on, Mr. Lumumba rejected all normal relations with the United Nations.

Before concluding this lecture I feel in duty bound to take advantage of the opportunity to try to clear up or dissipate certain misconceptions and myths about the Congo operation.

The United Nations Operation in the Congo at no time has had any executive authority there, or any share in executive authority. Its role has been exclusively that of assistance and advice. We do not participate in governing the country and have no responsibility for the actions of government. There are those, for example, who still say that the United Nations made a fatal mistake in the early days of the operation in that it did not disarm the mutinous ANC. It is quite possible that if the United Nations could have done this at that time— although to do it would almost certainly have involved considerable fighting— the course of events in the Congo might have been considerably different. But the United Nations had no authority to do this except at the request of the Congolese government, and that request never came, although it had been made clear to the government that the United Nations would also undertake this type of assistance upon request of the government.

There has been much talk also, and some still persists, about United Nations "offensives" in the Congo, about the United Nations thwarting secession, conquering Katanga and returning it to the Congo, and otherwise using force to achieve its ends. The United Nations Force in the Congo has always adhered strictly to the principle that it is a peace force and that its arms are for defensive purposes only, although they may be used for its protection when it is discharging responsibilities assigned to it by Security Council resolutions, such as the prevention of civil war or the removal of mercenaries. In its three and a half years in the Congo, the United Nations Force has had to use its arms on remarkably few occasions. It has not undertaken any offensive actions in Katanga. If it had, it could very easily have dealt with the problem of Katanga secession in 1960, or at any other time in the last three and a half years. It did, in pursuance of directives from United Nations Headquarters based upon Security Council action, undertake to round up Tshombe's mercenaries in Katanga. In September 1961, this led to fighting in Elisabethville, with the United Nations troops being on the defensive. The attempt of the mercenaries, now admitted in various memoirs, to liquidate the United Nations Force in Elisabethville in December 1961 led to heavier fighting, which stopped the moment the security and freedom of movement of the United Nations Force had been restored.

In the classic manner of propaganda, naturally, the Katangese Information Service asserted on both these occasions that Tshombe's troops were the victims of "an offensive," and this distortion received credence in quite a wide circle.

The decisive fighting in Katanga occurred in December–January 1962–63. Then, it may be said quite frankly, the Katangese troops, led by mercenaries, played into the hands of the United Nations Force by launching an attack on United Nations positions in Elisabethville and continuing that attack for several days with no reaction from the United Nations troops. Finally, however, when Mr. Tshombe's own cease-fire orders to his troops were disregarded by them, the United Nations Force was commanded to react firmly and it then proceeded to clean out all threatening pockets once and for all and also to assert and realize fully for the first time its undoubted right, under an agreement with the Congolese government, to freedom of movement throughout the Congo, including Katanga. Tshombe however, remained as president of Katanga Province and was even at times given physical protection by the United Nations when it seemed that his personal security might be in danger.

We speak of the Congo, but the unhappy fact is that at the time of its independence, and to a considerable degree still, there was not, and there is not, a true national spirit or wide sense of national statehood and government in the Congo. The divisive factors of tribalism and sectional, or even personal, interests are still very strong, and there are too few leaders who staunchly believe in and well understand the concepts of centralization, central government, and national loyalty.

While there are some who charge that the United Nations Operation in the Congo has not taken a strong enough line and has failed to exercise the necessary authority, there are others who have from the early days of the operation used the unkind expression of "neo-colonialism" to describe United Nations action in the Congo. In truth, the United Nations operation has bent over backwards to avoid most scrupulously the least basis for any such charge and has carefully refrained from any interference in Congolese internal affairs except upon the specific request of Congolese authorities. Thus, for example, the United Nations in 1961 at the request of such authorities as there were, in a situation in which there was no constitutional government, undertook to find, transport, and protect the members of Parliament throughout the country, many of whom were in fear of their lives and in hiding, in order that the Congolese Parliament might convene in Leopoldville and establish a new government. The successful search for its members and the protection of the reconvened Parliament prevented the country from falling into anarchy. In brief, the United Nations operation has been criticized most unjustly by groups who, in theory at least, are at the opposite poles of political thought, the one crying "Communist agent" and the other crying "neo-colonialist." This testifies to the genuine objectivity and impartiality of the United Nations in the Congo.

One still hears it said occasionally that Dag Hammarskjöld took an unnecessary risk in going to the Congo in 1961, on a trip that tragically proved to be his last. There was always a risk, of course, when he went to the Congo, as there was when he went to a number of other places, but to say that there was an unnecessary risk is to say that it was not necessary, or at least not important, for him to go to the Congo when he did, and even to imply that he was acting recklessly in doing so. In view of the situation and of what Dag Hammarskjöld had in mind, his trip to the Congo in September 1961, was of major importance. He went on the eve of the 16th session of the General Assembly, knowing that the issue of the Congo was likely to arouse a bitter and divisive debate in the assembly.

Dag Hammarskjöld did not go to the Congo in gracious response to a polite and not at all pressing invitation received from Prime Minister Adoula, but for more compelling reasons. He had it definitely in mind to try to induce Mr. Tshombe to enter into talks with Mr. Adoula, preferably in Leopoldville. He knew that if this could be achieved it might well relieve the assembly of the necessity of extensive and poisonous debate on the subject of the Congo, which would do neither the Congo nor the United Nations any good. In this regard, I wish to present a passage never before published from a message which Mr. Hammarskjöld addressed to me from Leopoldville on September 15, 1961, two days before his death. I had informed him of certain criticisms of the operation, and he replied:

> However, the key question is this one: What have our critics done in order to bring Mr. Tshombe to his senses? . . . It is better for the United Nations to lose . . . support . . . because it is faithful to law and principles than to survive as an agent whose activities are geared to political purposes never avowed or laid down by the major organs of the United Nations. It is nice to hear . . . parties urge . . . that we do everything in our power to bring Adoula and Tshombe together after having gone on our side, to the extreme point in that direction without any noticeable support at the crucial stages from those who now complain.

It was Mr. Hammarskjöld's misfortune that a totally unanticipated fighting situation should have developed in Elisabethville at the very time of his arrival in the Congo. While there were standing instructions to the United Nations people in Katanga to seek to round up and evacuate all mercenaries, Dag Hammarskjöld had not authorized any specific action involving fighting and was indeed surprised and shocked to learn about it. This is established beyond a doubt by another passage from the message just mentioned, one of the last he sent from Leopoldville before his fatal trip. He said the following with reference to the fighting that had broken out in Elisabethville on September 13, 1961: "It belongs to the history . . . that the first I knew about this development, I learnt by a tendentious Reuters report in Accra on my way to Leopoldville."

The "tendentious Reuters report," by the way, was a press story to the effect that Conor Cruise O'Brien, the United Nations representative in Elisabethville, had announced the end of Katangese secession, a statement which O'Brien subsequently denied to the United Nations that he had ever made. One can readily imagine Mr. Hammarskjöld's feelings at such a report in the light of his intention to try to bring Tshombe and Adoula together.

Because of the success that has attended the deployment of the United Nations peace forces in Gaza-Sinai and in the Congo, there has been a recent tendency to regard a United Nations peace force as a panacea for conflicts. It has happened increasingly, lately, that whenever a conflict situation is brought to the United Nations there will be some automatic suggestions that a United Nations force should be organized and dispatched. This is a misconception which overrates the true possibilities in the employment of a peace force, which are, in fact, limited.

First of all, a peace force is a very expensive device. The Congo force, for example, at its peak strength of 20,000 was costing over $10,000,000 a month; and the small UNEF force—just over 5,000 officers and men—has been costing approximately $19,000,000 per year.

The locus of responsibility for the cost is a controlling factor in determining the ability to obtain contingents for a force. If the United Nations is able to defray all extra expenses, the force can be recruited rather easily and quickly; otherwise not.

The composition of such a force has to be most carefully selected in the light of the particular conflict situation and the political considerations that apply to it. A basic determinant is the definition of acceptable contingents by the government of the country on whose territory the force is to be stationed. This is a serious and built-in limitation which has also vital implications for the extent to which the troops of a standing force could be used in a particular situation, as, for example, in Cyprus.

The nature of the conflict situation with which the force is to be involved also affects the ability to obtain contingents, for naturally the countries providing the contingents never fail to examine carefully the situation in which their troops will be placed before they agree to make them available to the United Nations. The states providing contingents also wish to know in advance the extent of danger for their troops, the likelihood that they would have to fight, and particularly the prospect that they might become embroiled in fighting with the civilian population or segments of it or be charged with intervening in the internal affairs of a country.

Such considerations have all come very much to the fore in establishing the United Nations Peace-Keeping Force in Cyprus in response to the decision of the Security Council in its resolution of March 4, 1964, not the least the financial restriction and the limitation on acceptable contingents. Here was to be found the reason for the delay in constituting the Cyprus force. All necessary preparations—transport, logistics, etc.—had been made; only the contingents were lacking.

The United Nations Operation in the Congo, in the light of its mandates, has certainly had great success; it may even be considered the most successful operation the United Nations has undertaken when measured in terms of what it was called upon to do and has in fact done. Striking evidence of the success of the operation is found in the almost complete cessation of organized attacks on it from whatever source, West or East. It is especially noteworthy that some governments that had been most critical of the military aspect of the operation became the strongest voices in urging the retention in the Congo of the United Nations Force.

There is very, very much still to be done in the Congo, of course, particularly in the realm of civilian assistance. The anxious question now is what will happen when the United Nations troops are withdrawn. Will much of what has been done over four years be then undone? Since the United Nations Force in the Congo could be extended beyond the end of June of this year only through action of the General Assembly called in special session for this purpose—and this seems next to impossible—we may only wait and see—and hope. Not much encouragement can be derived from the barbarous raids of the Jeunesse rebels in Kikwit Province in recent weeks, which have taken many lives. The raiders have encountered only feeble opposition by the ANC. It is good to be able to say that ONUC has succeeded in rescuing many of the victims or potential victims of these youthful terrorists. The Congo operation thus displays vividly the problem which we also have with UNEF in Gaza-Sinai: how can a successfully functioning United Nations peace force ever be withdrawn without disastrous consequences?

In concluding this talk with a look to the future, it may be said that there is clear need for a critical but honest appraisal of the United Nations and its present effectiveness in peace making, not only in the Congo but elsewhere. Improvements in existing practices, even new methods, may be found. On the one hand, we see that the interdependence of countries and situations in the modern world makes the United Nations essential as a last resort in critical emergencies when all other efforts at a solution have failed, as in Cyprus now. By the very nature of things, the tough problems come to the United Nations when they have been found insoluble by others, and this is especially true when these problems, as in the case of Cyprus, may be fraught with the gravest danger for the wider peace. At the same time, it is becoming a way of life for the United Nations, though by no means a happy way, that there is a vast and increasing discrepancy between the peace aims and responsibilities of the United Nations and, on the one hand, what it is called upon to do about them by the Security Council or the General Assembly and, on the other hand, its resources, its authority, and its support, both political and material. The "tin cup" approach to financing provides a most uncertain and insecure financial basis for a peace operation. Except for a rare and exceptional set of circumstances, such an arrangement cannot fail to affect adversely the efficiency, expedition, and effectiveness of the operation.

The United Nations is a young organization in the process of developing in response to challenges of all kinds. In its peace making it operates, notoriously, not only largely by improvisation but on a shoestring. This has been seen in the Congo, where a force, which is now less than 5,000 men and at its largest was only 20,000, was given the task of assisting a weak government to restore law and order out of chaos in a country the size of the subcontinent of India. This is being seen again with regard to Cyprus, where there have been great difficulties in establishing an international force on that island, although failure to do so could well mean war in the eastern Mediterranean.

Serious people everywhere should cogitate on this, the indispensability of the United Nations in our present world, in situations where it alone affords the chance to avoid war, measured against its present meager resources of money and authority. It bears emphasis that, while most governments in the end give the United Nations their warm and loyal support in critical situations, the organization (and the world) sometimes finds itself on the very brink of disaster of incalculable dimensions before the essential support is forthcoming.

Dag Hammarskjöld left a great legacy of high idealism wedded to great political and practical wisdom and imagination. The United Nations and the world have been fortunate in having a man with the devotion, wisdom, and courage of U Thant to inherit, carry on, and expand the aim of the United Nations in a strong and dynamic enough manner to meet its great challenges.

Part 5
Race, Education, and
Human Rights

CHAPTER 16

What Is Race?
1936

When Du Bois declared that the problem of the twentieth century was the problem of the color line, he reflected the then dominant racial thinking among both black and white scholars. While black scholars such as Du Bois, Carter G. Woodson, and Kelly Miller refused to accept the notion of black inferiority, they did embrace biological concepts of racial difference. By the 1930s a new generation of black and white scholars challenged the old views of biological difference. Bunche was a leader of this group, and this chapter, taken from his 1936 monograph A World View of Race, *sets forth his position most clearly. In emphasizing the role of environment and culture in establishing "racial" traits, Bunche also emphasizes the capacity of social intervention to change such characteristics. For two years following this 1936 work, Bunche would immerse himself in anthropological training and fieldwork.*

Our concept of race is a comparatively recent one. The term *race* is one employed, however, with a looseness and inaccuracy matched only by its frequency in our literature. Even the social scientists, the sociologists and anthropologists, have great difficulty in explaining what is meant by "race," and often disagree in their conclusions. The average man in the street, however, will demonstrate an ability to expound at length on the term at the slightest provocation. That is because race is so intimately related to the social and national doctrines with which the layman is familiar, superficially, and to which he gives unreasoning loyalty.

For dominant groups and powerful industrial nations the definition of race is usually cut to suit the pattern of their economic and political policy. The subtle fallacy and the power of emotional stimulation inherent in the idea of race serve to make it a perfect instrument of politics. People, blindly, and often contrary to their own interests, find it a compelling sort of social voodoo. In the passionate embrace of race they are led to bloody slaughters and barbaric orgies of human torture and lynching. Yet, as employed in the world today, it is a not very consistent myth.

Origin and Meaning of Race

The origin of the word *race* is uncertain. It is said to have first appeared in the English language in the sixteenth century. In usage, however, the term soon acquired a vague and confused meaning which has persisted to the present day. At present it is used in several very different ways. In our early geography lessons we were taught that there were five divisions of the human family according to color—white, black, yellow, brown, and red. These peoples were supposed to be distributed geographically with no direct relation to existing national lines. However, this classification is much too broad to permit race to be used as an effective instrument of national policy. The term often has been employed, therefore, to denote what is asserted to be the physically homogeneous population of a particular country, group, or nation, which, supposedly, is distinguishable by its hereditary characteristics—as the "British race" or the "French race." Again, it is used to indicate a non-existent "pure race," which is said to have existed historically, though subsequently it was contaminated by "foreign or alien blood." This is the basis of the current racial theory in Germany which pays tribute to and thrives on the doctrine of the "Germanic race." Sometimes, also, the concept is mistakenly used to identify peoples who happen to speak the same language, as in references to the "Latin races." Herbert Spencer adopted an explanation of race which tickled the ego-palates of many peoples. He explained races by evolution, on a sort of "step-ladder" basis, and the idea developed that races represented distinct levels of advancement which were determined by nature. Thus there were "superior" and "inferior," "advanced" and "backward," races—which became the basis for the moral justifications and the grand rationalizations of modern imperialistic tutelage of millions of peoples. Since color was the simplest means of identifying "races," race traits were usually definitely associated with color.

On one point in all these conceptions of race there seems to be general agreement: there must be certain physical characteristics which are determined by heredity and which are handed on from one generation to another. But even on this point there is great disagreement among those who advance theories of race as to what type of physical characteristics should be employed to detect and measure race.

Classification of Race

In the attempt to establish rigid racial classifications for particular groups, the scientist encounters the greatest difficulty. If two groups of peoples are said to be racially differentiated by distinct physical characteristics, then, strictly speaking, every member of one group should be different from every member of the other group in respect to these physical features. This would be more certain if there were any such things as "pure" racial groups. However, if short stature and tall stature are supposed to be characteristic of two different racial groups such as Japanese and Norwegians, not even the most ardent racial theorists would contend that all Norwegians would be taller than all Japanese. There is a great variety in the stature of the members of both groups and much overlapping. Thus there would be many Japanese who would be found to be taller than many Norwegians. The same condition prevails in respect to all other physical traits of human groups. That is, there is a great variability among the members of any particular group to which a racial label is given.

Since there is no homogeneity within any given race, it follows that there can be no clear line of distinction between one race and another. This variability makes it impossible to compare accurately one race with another. Because of the great overlapping in biological features among groups of peoples, it is clear also that general descriptions of so-called racial groups need have no application to individual members of a group. And often do not. It cannot be assumed that because a man is a Japanese he must be short or that a particular North European will be tall. It may be true that "all Negroes look alike" to some white men who are socially conditioned to regard Negroes in this light. But it is equally true that all Negroes are not alike, that the particular set of physical characteristics ascribed to the Negro "race" by the particular racial theorist are subject to great variability among the members of the group, that all Negroes do not behave similarly in the presence of similar conditions, and that these same physical traits, called "Negroid" traits, will be found in varying degree among many whites.

The plain fact is that the selection of any specific physical trait or set of traits as a basis for identifying racial groups is a purely arbitrary process. On the basis of anthropological studies now existent, it would be difficult to say whether there are a few races or several hundred. It may be admitted that physical differences exist among peoples and also that these differences can be discerned and are significant. Yet a brief survey of the classifications of races will demonstrate convincingly that no satisfactory method of classification has yet been devised and that, in all probability, none can be devised. In consequence, on the basis of any scientific standards, we are forced to conclude that existing racial divisions are *arbitrary, subjective, and devoid of scientific meaning.*

The earliest efforts toward a systematic arrangement of human groups were made in the eighteenth century. These early classifications took skin color, the most obvious physical trait, as their basis. The Dutch Linnaeus (Carol Linné), with little detailed information concerning the distribution of human types, listed four races, representing the types of human beings inhabiting the four large continents. The German J. F. Blumenbach later worked out a system of anthropological classification based on physical measurement. He distinguished five races of man based on distinctions of color, hair, and descriptive features of skull and face. They were Caucasian (European), Mongolian, Ethiopian, America, and Malayan. According to Blumenbach, however, these various types of men differ from each other in degree, and not in kind, and are connected by innumerable gradations. Later, F. Müller based his classification on hair texture and reached results quite different from the earlier systems. According to Müller, human groups could be divided into the Woolly-haired (including the Tuft-haired and Fleecy-haired) and the Straight-haired (including the Stiff-haired and Wavy-haired).

Thus, color, hair texture, form of nose, and shape of skull became in modern science the primary bases for distinguishing human races. The extreme diversity in methods and results of classification of human types is illustrated excellently in a comparison of the systems of J. Deniker and G. Sergi. Deniker adopted a combination of skin color, hair texture, eye color, and shape of nose as his test of race. As a result, he established 17 main races and 29 sub-races. Sergi, on the other hand, was interested in head and face shape and measure-ments and arrived at only two divisions or species, the long-headed (dolichocephalic) and round-headed (brachycephalic). In Sergi's system, the long-headed category included the African, Mediterranean, and Nordic peo-ples, who were held to be closely related. The differences in skin color among these races were explained by him as being due to differences in temperature, climate, and food. The round-headed species included the Slavs, Celts, Ger-mans, and Asiatics.

One of the classifications which receives qualified acceptance today among many anthropologists is that which postulates three main racial types: the Negroid, or black; the Mongoloid, or yellow-brown; and the Caucasian, or white. The Negroid race is characterized by dark pigmentation, frizzly hair, full lips, broad noise, long arms and legs, and comparatively little bodily hairiness. The Mongoloid race is described as yellow or brown in color, with straight hair, short arms and legs, thin lips, slight bodily hairiness, and slanting eyes. The Caucasian, or white race, divided into a number of sub-classifications such as the Nordic, Alpine, and Mediterranean, is held to be characterized by light pigmentation, blond, wavy hair, and narrower nose. Among these sub-varieties of the white race, there is admitted to be considerable differentiation, however. The Nordic or North European type is described as long-headed, with tall stature, blue eyes, blond hair, and light pigmentation. The Alpine or Central European is round-headed, shorter, and more swarthy. The Mediterranean or South European type is even more short and dark but is long-headed.

Such wide divergence in theories of racial classification inevitably leads to great confusion and contradiction. For example, if head shape is used as the distinguishing feature, the African and North European peoples, differing in respect to other physical characteristics such as skin color, hair texture, and nose form, are classified together. Again, if skin color is employed, the North and Central Europeans, who show marked difference in head shape, are lumped together. Such inconsistencies, particularly in the popular understanding of race classifications, can be multiplied endlessly. In fact, the more scientific we become in attempts to designate specific race categories for human groups, the more glaring and shocking are these discrepancies and contradictions. The mongrelization of *Homo sapiens* frustrates at some point every possible scheme of racial classification.

All this difficulty arises from the tendency to view races as clearly defined units. The problem has been oversimplified by picturing the race as an individual who embodies all of the most pronounced (or the most desirable) traits of the particular group considered. However, few individuals in the group can be found who possess all of these so-called typical traits.

There is, accordingly, much reason for contending that the term *race,* when applied in the biological sense to groups, has no scientific validity today. It is a convenient tool for the anthropologist, who employs it as a more or less artificial and arbitrary means of classifying peoples. On the other hand it is an increasingly vicious weapon in the hands of fanatical rulers and irresponsible demagogues who wield it ruthlessly to flatter national egos and to carry out sinister political and economic policies. The fallacies inherent in this use of race can be demonstrated, and will be dealt with later.

Race and Heredity

The concept of race revolves around the idea of heredity. The study of hereditary phenomena, or genetics, has made rapid strides in modern times and throws much light upon this human problem of race. Man's heritage is, of course, both biological and social; part of us is handed down from our physical ancestors—our hereditary constitution; but another part and an equally important one is the product of our social ancestry and our environmental experience. This biological heritage, the hereditary constitution, carried in the reproductive cells, is known to consist of a great number of separate kinds of units of matter called genes—so our best biologists tell us. Each gene is distinct from every other one and has a fixed location within the particular chromosome. These genes, which are self-perpetuating and self-multiplying, play an important role in the development process. In general it is thought that each gene is responsible for a particular kind of character or physical trait; i.e., one gene will control stature, another eye color, another hair texture. In respect to the make-up of each individual the influence of each gene will depend upon all of the other genes present, thus forming what may be called a "gene-system." The constitution of the individual will consequently be the result of the interaction between the total gene-system and the environmental conditions. Thus if two given individuals differ in their biological constitutions in respect to a particular gene, as, for example, the gene affecting eye color, these individuals will differ in respect to this particular physical characteristic. It is also known that one type of gene may have several sub-types and that a process of change also takes place in the genes themselves, this change producing not new genes but new sub-types of genes. It is known too that nature has provided a system of automatic favoring of such hereditary tendencies as best suit the environment, known as the process of Natural Selection. This process of Natural Selection constitutes the directing mechanism in the evolution of any particular species, and accounts for the great basic principle of variation in human and animal types.

Race and Environment

This sensitiveness of the hereditary constitution to environmental conditions is of prime importance to the problem of race in man. For the physical character of the individual man can be altered either by change in the gene in his biological constitution or by change in the conditions of his environment. Thus human stature can be altered either by feeding and other environmental influences or by internal change in the hereditary combination of genes. The significant fact is that both sets of causes, genetic and environmental, are constantly at work in shaping human characteristics and that with our present knowledge it is impossible to determine the degree to which each of these causes contribute to the resultant character of the human type. To quote one recent work on the subject:

> With the best will in the world it is, in the present state of knowledge, impossible to disentangle the genetic from the environmental factors in matters of "racial traits," "national character," and the like. . . . Such phrases are glibly used. In point of fact they are all but meaningless, since they are not properly definable. Further, in so far as they are capable of definition, the common presupposition that they are entirely or mainly of a permanent or genetic nature is unwarranted.[1]

In the latter part of the nineteenth century, a group of European writers developed a refined and qualified version of the narrow racial theories which had been advanced by earlier writers. The new system of thought on the subject of race is called "social selectionism." It was based on the older concepts of race, but it did recognize the importance of *social environment* in determining the status of human groups. The leaders of this movement were G. Vacher de Lapouge, Otto Ammon, and the Englishman Francis Galton. In fact these men were interested in studying the reciprocal action of race and environment. But their theories were still only a new phase of racial determinism, since they consisted in applying the fundamental doctrines of Darwinism to the problems of population and social life. The leader of this group, Lapouge, regarded all history and the fundamental processes of social life as a combination of a Darwinian struggle for existence, elimination and survival, heredity and race substitution. The process of social selection was held to operate through war, and political, legal, economic, moral, and religious institutions, whereby one or another racial trait was afforded some survival advantage. They felt, moreover, that though the process of natural selection tended to perfect racial types, the process of social selection was not always good, for often the weak and unfit might be protected. They saw the final outcome of the processes of social selection, due to constant race substitution, as the destruction of those very racial qualities which create and maintain a progressive and superior civilization upheld by superior peoples. Ammon and Lapouge considered the "Aryan race" to be superior—they too worshipped at the shrine of blond superiority. The Englishman, Galton, however, steered clear of these characteristic racial and nationalistic biases. He was chiefly interested in checking on differences among individuals within racial and social groups. But at least Lapouge did not believe that there was any such thing as a "pure" race, not to mention a Germanic, a Slavic, or a Latin race. He saw that all nations had long been racially composite, though he concluded that the rank in civilization which a nation held would be determined by the character and quantity of the original "superior" elements in its population.

One significant deduction that can be made from knowledge of these modified theories of race is the tremendous importance of environmental and social conditions for the individual or the group. The inherent ability of any individual or group is dependent for its realization and expression upon the presence of proper conditions for its cultivation. Thus social, economic, and political systems, by determining the financial resources, educational, and all other opportunities in the society, are intimately tied up with the physical and psychological character which the individual or group will develop. And *social race* becomes as important a factor as *physical race* or biological heredity.

Race and Human Migrations

Man is unique in many ways. He is unique in the extent of his biological variation. He is further unique in the extent to which his mentality and temperament have been and are subject to the influence of his environment. Again, unlike most other species, he possesses mutual fertility even in cases of crossing between extremely differentiated types, such as the African pigmy and the Nordic. By this fact, Nature says boldly and undeniably that man is a single species. Moreover, man has a stronger tendency toward migration than any other animal. This latter tendency has highly significant consequences for our discussion of race.

There is much historical evidence of constant human migration and the resultant intermingling of all human groups. Even in earliest prehistoric times, human migrations must have occurred. Consequently it would seem clear that any differentiations in the fundamental physical forms of man that are now said to exist must have developed during periods of complete isolation of small groups of men. But obviously such periods must be extremely remote; so remote, in fact, that they could have little significance to present classifications of racial groups. For, keeping in mind the unusual fertility of even extreme cases of physically differentiated types of man, and man's history of constant migration, it must be concluded that human groups have been cross-breeding for tens of thousands of years. For example, the invasions of Mongolian peoples from the East have left their physical marks upon the peoples of Eastern Europe. Even the great majority of the natives of Africa, who are popularly thought to have lived in comparative isolation and to be "racially pure," have inherited Caucasian genes as a result of historical crossing with Hamitic stocks. As a result, with rare exception, *all existing human groups are of definitely mixed origin.* In the vast majority of cases it is impossible to refer to the population of any region as belonging to any definite race, since every such group inevitably includes a great number of types and their various combinations, as a result of group migrations and cross-breeding. It is for this reason that some scientific writers now suggest that we drop the term *race* with reference to existing groups and substitute some more accurate description such as *ethnic groups* or *peoples.* Such designations are non-committal and realistic, taking into consideration the fact that present groupings of men are the product of migration and crossing, thus making clear-cut biological definition in terms of race impossible.

It must be concluded, then, that these modern racial classifications are based on *man-made distinctions;* the resultant groupings are thus *purely artificial and do not represent racially pure groupings.* Nature has a means of protecting the purity of her intended classifications and her basic species by making successful cross-breeding impossible, or at least difficult. But human types, even in instances of apparently extreme difference, interbreed freely and successfully.

Such conclusions knock into a cocked hat the frantic efforts now being made in many parts of the world to found national policies upon the concept of "pure races." It is thousands of years too late for modern peoples to hope for such purity, *for there no longer remain any pure races to be kept pure.* In fact there is no positive evidence that such "pure" races ever existed. Human variation is so great, in fact, that perhaps such homogeneous groups never existed at all. The most that can be said for these theories, then, is that they hark back to a hypothetical past. They more probably are prompted by wish fulfilment in looking toward a highly problematical future.

It remains vitally true, however, that though racial concepts may have no scientific meaning in their biological application to human groups, they are stubbornly fixed in popular usage. Racial classifications are not in themselves necessarily harmful or dangerous. But they lend themselves readily to the support of social and political doctrines that spell injustice, oppression, and exploitation for great numbers of people in many lands. Indeed, the exigencies of anthropological, political, and economic theories have often broadened the meaning of the term *race* beyond its narrower biological connotation, by relating it to cultural and psychological conditions. Thus *race* has been identified frequently with *nation*, with *culture*, or with *language*. On the basis of such broadened concepts of the connotation of race, elaborate theories of "racial difference" have been worked out, respecting the innate abilities, intelligence, emotions, and capacity for civilization of different races. We turn to some of them.

Race and Language

The extension of biological terms and principles to the realm of language and culture has given a false front of scientific respectability to many theories of the interrelation of human groups which are often much more the product of selfish interest, passion, and prejudice than scientific fact. In this sense it is completely wrong to identify race with language, though this is frequently done. Language, habits, religion, mannerisms, traditions, ideas, and all such things are products of the social environment of human beings. None of these "traits" are inborn; they are learned from social experience. They are transmitted from one group to another by culture contacts and have no necessary connection with ancestry or physical constitution. Thus there is no "Latin race" in any biological sense. Latin is a language which constitutes the origin of a number of other languages, such as French, Italian, Spanish, Portuguese, and Romanian. The peoples speaking such languages evidence great physical diversification, and there is clearly no race or type to which "Latins" belong, though many of them may have a common cultural background and a closely associated social history.

Language and culture are transmitted readily from one group to another. In some instances a conquering people force their language on the conquered; in others the conquering group adopts the language of the conquered. Thus the Normans who invaded England adopted much of the Anglo-Saxon language of the conquered people and actually were absorbed by them. American Negroes speak English, except in the French-speaking districts of Louisiana, where, by the same social process of culture contact, many speak French. The Arabic language spread by conquest. In the nineteenth century the Sanskrit term *Aryan* came to be used to denote a large group of languages. Soon, however, it was used to indicate not only a definite "Aryan" language and its philological descendants but also an analogous "Aryan race"—an idea which proved fertile soil for European and American romantic and nationalist writers. In fact the modern idea of the innate inferiority of certain races stems from this myth of the Aryan race. In the middle of the nineteenth century the French count Joseph de Gobineau advocated the inherent superiority of the Aryan races. The Aryans later came to be identified, ironically enough, with the "Nordic race," leading to the disparagement of the Latin-speaking peoples and to the popular doctrine of "Nordic superiority," more properly designated as the "Nordic myth." Under the spur of racial fervor, writers, especially German ones, dressed up this theory. Thus it was claimed that throughout the prehistoric ages advances in culture had been made exclusively by peoples who could be identified with the Nordic, Teutonic, or Aryan groups. It went to ridiculous extremes. In order to be consistent it claimed that all great men in history, including Jesus Christ, were identified as "Teutons." In the United States, it has been called upon to rationalize our pet theory of "white supremacy." This same mythical "Aryanism" is the basis of the ridiculous but cruel racial policies of Nazi Germany today. It is the idea behind the arbitrary system of selection found in our present American immigration laws with their unjust and discriminatory quotas.

The Nordic theory, so popular today, assumes a strictly hypothetical historic race in which were found many of man's most virtuous qualities. Thus, whenever these qualities, such as initiative and leadership, are discovered in mixed national groups, they are held to find root in the Nordic elements or Nordic "blood" in the population. It logically follows therefore that the ideal of national policy should be the cultivation and preservation of "pure" Nordic blood.

Such groups are in reality held together not by racial but by cultural forces. There is no Nordic race, though there is a Nordic "type." Where the group in which the physical characteristics of this type originated and when its great migration took place is a matter of great uncertainty. The type is found in moderate degree in parts of Northern Europe, but it is not the prevailing type in any known area of population.

It is entirely true that the Aryan languages have been of great historical and political importance. But the term *Aryan* has no meaning when applied to racial concepts. Indeed, it is not known to what physical type the original Aryan-speaking peoples belonged. In spite of its scholarly origin and defense, the idea of an Aryan race amounts to nothing more than an Aryan myth. Nothing can be more fanciful, therefore, than the frantic agitation in Germany for the preservation of the purity of the Aryan race and for purging it of "non-Aryan" influences. English and American scientific writers no longer employ the phrase "Aryan race," but it still plays a prominent role in the literature of political propaganda, where it appears as the holy concept of the white race, with its gospel of white supremacy and a white man's civilization.

Similarly there is no Semitic race. Though Arabs and Jews are given this racial designation, the term *Semitic,* like that of *Aryan,* can be employed only as a cultural and linguistic description. The Arabic and Hebrew languages both belong to a group of languages designated as Semitic. But among the peoples speaking the Semitic languages there is great physical differentiation. For instance, the majority of Jews have very little physical resemblance to the supposedly "pure" Semitic type inhabiting northern Arabia. Like most other peoples, the Jews have migrated for countless generations and have crossed with other peoples. They have retained a rather definite cultural unity. In physical type, however, they show great variability; in skin color they range from very light to very dark and in skull shape from extreme long-headedness to extreme round-headedness. Though the concept is often used as a scapegoat for political and economic policies, there is no such thing as a "Jewish race," with distinctive "Jewish" physical characteristics. The tendency is rather for the widely scattered Jewish peoples to approximate the physical characteristics of the dominant peoples among whom they live.

It follows therefore, that such terms as *Jewish, Arabic, Celtic, Indian, Irish, English,* and *American,* merely serve to describe peoples who are bound together by cultural or linguistic ties—by language, religion, tradition, political custom, or geographical propinquity. Such peoples will generally be found to be greatly diversified in origin and physical traits. Certainly they have no common biological or ancestral unity.

Race and Nation

Attempts to associate race with nation are equally untenable. Nation is a social and political concept. Race is a genetic concept referring to physical type. The two concepts should never be confused, though they often are. Without exception great nations are racial melting pots. This is nowhere better illustrated than in the case of our own nation. Though the United States, like other nations, in recent years has steadily become more nationalistic, i.e., more proud of its own culture, population, and traditions, we obviously cannot refer to an "American race." Virtually every physical type in existence will be found represented in our population, many in large numbers. The peoples who founded the country were themselves mixed types, and this condition has been accentuated by the great successive waves of European migration to the country. A nation is a culturally homogeneous social group which is conscious and tenacious of its cultural and psychic unity. It consists of such a group of people inhabiting a common territory, boasting a common history, traditions, and social organization. And though a common language is also often characteristic of a nation, it is not essential, since some nations, such as Belgium and Switzerland, do not have or need a common language. But nation and nationality are not inherent in human nature.

It follows that the idea of a German, Italian, French, or American race is a meaningless but dangerous political fiction. Similarly the idea that a particular race must be kept pure by protecting it against race-mixture becomes not a matter of race, but rather a matter of nationality, class, or social status. Thus when political leaders and their handy-men, the official propagandists, attempt to make a case for race purity and against a particular racial minority group in the population, it can be safely concluded that this is merely a ruse to promote group antagonisms as a smoke-screen for some ulterior and ill-conceived political or economic policy. The real root of such theories will always be found in some social condition such as economic fear, nationalist ambition, class hatred, religious conflict or misguided cultural pride.

Race Differences

Still more recently, efforts have been made to establish racial differences in respect to the properties of the blood by analysis of blood groupings; in respect to the endocrine glands which are thought to have an effect on personality; in relation to the constitution or totality of individual characteristics, physique, cranial capacity, and size of the brain, differences in growth, and even physiological functioning, such as respiration, blood pressure, basal metabolism, speed of nerve conduction, and body odors. But objective scientific investigation discloses either that such group differences as are found to exist have no known relation to heredity and race or that they can be explained without recourse to the hypothesis of race by factors of social and physical environment.

Somewhat dubious efforts to establish race difference and the inherent superiority of one race over another have also been made in the psychological as well as the biological field. For example, it is popularly believed that less advanced peoples are more acute in their sense perceptions; i.e., that physically they react more quickly, see further, hear more keenly, follow a scent better, and are less sensitive to pain. Such differences have been shown to depend upon the training of these particular faculties and to have no relation to race. The reason the primitive man responds better in this field is because his way of living makes life more dependent on such reactions.

The racial psychologist has been intrigued greatly by the problem of the inherent intellectual superiority of certain races over others. Elaborate methods of intelligence testing have been devised, but many of the results are so obviously biased and their results so distorted as to be scientifically worthless. The psychologist as well as the anthropologist and biologist has often played the role of panderer to national policy.

In the matter of intelligence tests the psychologists have run into a number of obstacles. In the first place they have discovered that groups within particular races, such as the Negro, showed marked differences. Moreover, they discovered that supposedly inferior racial groups do not always show up as inferior. For instance, the army intelligence tests made during the war found that Negro recruits from the North were far superior in intelligence to Negro recruits from the South. Moreover, it was discovered that Negro recruits born and reared in the North were superior to Southern whites. While these tests have been severely questioned, subsequent tests, conducted largely upon children, have tended to corroborate the army test findings. It is recognized, therefore, that superior environment is a determining factor in intellectual capacity. In other words, it now seems safe to say that, as the traditionally inferior environment of a group such as the American Negro approximates more and more closely the environment of the white groups, social traits interpreted as permanent race traits and related to a presumed hereditary basis of racial inferiority of the Negro tend to disappear. The inability of the psychologist to properly rate and control such factors as culture, social and economic status, language, and schooling makes it difficult to establish a racial psychology based on intelligence tests. It can be said with certainty that there is at present no scientific proof of racial difference in mental ability. Thus psychology finds itself as helpless as biology in its attempt to classify races.

It is also true that race cannot be considered as the origin of any particular culture. Nor can any validity be accorded to those claims now made so blatantly in some quarters that any particular race is responsible for the development of culture in general. There is no trustworthy evidence to support any such views.

So finally we may conclude that though racial antagonisms constitute a serious world problem, they have no scientific basis in biology, nor can they be accepted as the inevitable result of group differences. Such antagonisms must be analyzed and understood in their social and historical setting. *Group antagonisms are social, political, and economic conflicts, not racial,* though they are frequently given a racial label and seek a racial justification.

Discussion Questions

1. What is the meaning of the modern concept of race?
   a) When did the term *race* originate?
   b) What significance does color have to race? To heredity?

2. Why are existing racial classifications unsatisfactory?
    a) What traits are employed in the attempts at racial classification?
3. What relation is there between race and environment?
4. Why can it be said that there are no "pure" races?
    a) What has been the effect of human migrations on race?
    b) Is interbreeding possible between all human groups?
        —What bearing has this on race?
    c) Are the Africans a pure race?

CHAPTER 17

The Role of the University in the Political Orientation of Negro Youth
1940

In the same year that Bunche called for a less subjective, less propagandistic Negro history, he asks universities in general and black universities in particular to abandon their role as "an objective and disinterested clearinghouse for the scientific truth." The rise of Hitler and Mussolini, says Bunche, leaves only two choices: either we must actively teach and support an admittedly imperfect democratic politics, or we face the dangerous consequences of a totalitarian victory. Included among the totalitarians are the "no longer" radical Communists who have now sided with the fascists in a Soviet-Nazi pact. Negroes, contends Bunche, are no longer indispensable in this country. In fact, they are entirely dispensable everywhere, and the victory of an American fascism would seal their doom.

In discussing the role of the university in serving the needs of Negro youth, it appears to me that one glaring weakness of our universities protrudes like a sore thumb. I allude to the haphazard and uninspired efforts with regard to the political orientation of the students. It is notorious that the student which we run off of the production belts in our American universities is in general a disoriented, placid, and smug product; uninspired, unequipped with any ordered dynamics, philosophical or moral; lacking in political creed and drive.

I would wish to see us continue to cultivate scholars, but I would also like to see some crusaders—some crusaders for democracy—stride forth from our somber portals. Is it not clear that it is only through democracy that we can hope to continue to produce scholars? It is no secret to anyone now that the democratic principle is sorely beset throughout this world and is indeed threatened with total annihilation. If democracy as even an ideal is to be salvaged from the present world carnage, it will be only because the vast majority of citizens of all colors, classes, and creeds in the remaining few democracies of the world are imbued with an unquenchable love for it and are eager to make heroic sacrifices in its behalf. Democracy cannot be saved by people who merely take it for granted; who assume that its fires of freedom and liberty can never be extinguished.

The universities have a heavy responsibility in these times. We who toil within the severely insulated cloisters of the universities like to pride ourselves upon our intellectual integrity—a sort of puritanism of the mind. We transfix, with a stern and forbidding eye, all who would suggest that we deviate for a moment from our unceasing quest after that elusive concept "Truth." And to this there can be no objection. It is our proper duty to winnow out the truth of things. But we must recognize, however, that too often our search for Truth becomes an escape device—whereby we can divorce ourselves from the tough and dangerous controversies of the world. We may come to conceive of the quest after Truth as an end in itself and fall into the unconscious error of assuming that there is no connection between the Truth and the practical and that it is not academically respectable to tackle the practical.

We university folk have our code of academic morals. There must be no heretical mote in our pedagogical eye; no maverick purple in our professional shroud. We pure scholars, intellectual vestal virgins, are of the world but not in it. Rumor reaches us that the worldly world is sordid, vulgar, barbarous, lying, intriguing, ruthlessly lacking in moral fabric. But we dare not stray far from the path of Truth lest violence is done our intellectual chastity by the unacademic and unprincipled rogues who roam menacingly in the world outside our sanctuary.

And what is our function within this detached, unrealistic dream world in which we lead our ethereal existence? We are charged with the responsibility of herding our young and tender flocks—naive, intellectually innocent, gullible young creatures who thrill at the prospect of the "lift" they will get from smoking intellectual opium with us for four or five or six years. We expose them to the *verities* while they traipse irresponsibly through our corridors. We nurse them along in the pure sciences and the pseudo sciences; the classics, the humanities, the languages. We dose them with music, art, and literature. We inject them with culture with a capital *C*. We regale them with the beauties of life, with the enduring human ideals, with sagas of the great geniuses, the noble heroes, the immortal martyrs. We, or some of us, transport them high in the heavens, to a universe so rarefied, so beautiful—so unreal—that they can never again feel at ease in the mundane world of real life.

For years, then, we teach them just about everything except the true nature of the unsavory world they are going to have to live in and in which they are likely to meet disillusioning frustration. We decorate them in tinsel and glitter and turn them loose as B.A.'s—"babes in arms"—with our benign but vacuous blessing. We have thus kept the faith of our profession. We do not *indoctrinate*. We do not try to influence their beliefs, their points of view. We do not proselyte or convert. We are objective. We avoid "soap-boxing"—and anything not purely "objective" *is* "soap-boxing"—that is left to the "agitators."

Many of our wards are in fact far ahead of our educational process.

Discontented, feeling the pragmatic inadequacy of the educational curriculum, they seek a broader and more realistic base for understanding the world in which they live and struggle. Failing to obtain an understanding knowledge of things in the university, many of them satisfy their urge by turning to the radical and lunatic fringe organizations, which at least make a pretense at grappling with the harsh realities of an unpleasant world. That the so-called education gotten from the tracts, pamphlets, forums, and lectures of such groups is more often than not distorted and perverted miseducation is not the fault of the student. He has a gnawing at his intellectual innards for an understanding of things that the universities fail to give them. The universities cannot give it because they are so weighted down with the heavy, boring, formal requirements of their traditional educational curricula. The university curricula would indeed profit from an educational *blitzkrieg* which would destroy much that is now taught and thus make room for the development of a dynamic and rational educational process that would better serve the needs of our students on a functional and practical plane. Unfortunately, the faculties of our universities are products of this same hide-bound system and, involved in their narrow specialties, are themselves more frequently than not politically unsophisticated, confused, and inarticulate.

It would seem obvious that it is a prime responsibility of any university to equip its graduates with the tools necessary for an intelligent understanding of the world—its forces, institutions, ideologies, and conflicts—in which they must live. In times of stress and calamitous crisis such as the present this is a responsibility of the gravest moral and physical character. For Negro universities this is an even more solemn and imperative obligation—not only because the complexities of race make social comprehension more difficult, but because of the very precariousness of the minority racial group's existence in the modern world. Are we not guilty of gross and unpardonable neglect if we do not provide the Negro student, and more, the Negro community on our borders, with a sound and reasoned interpretation of the relation of present day conflicts, currents, and forces, to the welfare of the Negro people? This is assuredly no simple task. We may briefly sketch its broad configurations here within the framework of my own interpretation of attitudes and events.

There is an annoying indifference among Negroes of all classes—from day laborers to the highest ranks of the *intelligentsia*—about what is transpiring in the rest of the world, and where thought is given to the subject it is so often distorted and confused. We may mention, for "laboratory" purposes and in attenuated form, a half-dozen typical Negro reactions, often heard recently, toward the European conflagration and its threat to the Negro's future here:

1. Nazism or fascism is nothing new to the Negro since he has always experienced it in the South anyway.

2. The Negro couldn't be any worse off than he now is in the Deep South. Therefore an American fascism would make little difference to him.

3. American democracy is so imperfect, so hypocritical in its shabby treatment of the Negro, that unless it can quickly perfect itself and demonstrate its workability, it doesn't deserve to survive.

4. Even under fascism there would always be a need and a place for the Negro in America, since he is indispensable to the profit-economy of the great white American middle class.

5. The war abroad is an "imperialist" war, and the Negro and the United States should have nothing to do with it. Let us concentrate on achieving democracy at home; let us win freedom and equality for labor and the Negro first; "the Yanks are not coming." This is the "line" of the American Communist Party and is being parroted by many Negroes who unknowingly fall into its subtle trap.

6. The war is a white man's war and a good thing for the Negro. Let the white folks kill each other off and then the "black Aryans" will be the master race and rule the world.

What is the framework of thought within which we must appraise such attitudes? Any attempt at logical thinking must be controlled by the answer to the very practical question: "What are the alternatives confronting the Negro today?"

The Negro of today is not permitted the luxury of choosing between ideal systems. He is socially blind even if he permits himself to build his hopes in such a dream world. The Negro must make his immediate choices from imperfect, buffeted democracy on the one hand and totalitarianism on the other. And this may be a privilege which will not too long endure even in his thinking. We are all too familiar with the many and serious shortcomings of American democracy, and these should require no narration here. But do we not also know that democracy as a concept, as a way of life, has afforded us the sole basis for whatever progress we as a group have made since slavery; for the heroic struggle we have incessantly waged; for our aspirations in the future? Democracy, even imperfect democracy, has been the ideological foundation upon which our lives have been based. It has been our spiritual life-blood. Without it—if in this country it had not been superimposed upon a deeply rooted, social undertone of white racial supremacy—where would any of us Negroes be? Democracy has certainly failed to live up to its promise for us and for many whites in this society too. We fought to preserve it in the first World War, but as an ideal it has not progressed very rapidly in the world we know. But what else has the world to offer us? If I were perched in a window on the top floor of a burning building and below me were typical slit-mouthed, washboard neck specimens of the Southern "cracker," holding a net and yelling profanely, "Jump, you blankety-blank nigger, jump!" I would jump. I would resent the insult, resent the crackers, and feel not at all happy about the fire that created the unpleasant situation. But I would indeed jump, and then, having landed safely, proceed to "cuss" them out for calling me "nigger"—unless the fire happened to be in some parts of Mississippi. The Negro would indeed be fortunate if in the world today he were in position to translate his decisions into action even on any such basis as that.

The other alternative, we have said, is totalitarianism, the authoritarian state, dictatorship. In terms of the immediate menace this must be considered to be the brand of fascism peddled by Herr Hitler, for he alone now casts his swastika-decorated, blood-drenched shadow across the democratic world. Italy and blustering Il Duce are now clearly only Hitler's satellites. Russian totalitarianism—the other side of the fascist coin—is significant to us now only insofar as the purge-drunk dictator Joseph Stalin sees it to his interest to support or oppose Hitler and the Soviet-Nazi pact.

Hitler's Nazism—National Socialism—is a world revolutionary movement. It involves a revolution in the political, economic, and social spheres of modern life. This cannot be impressed too greatly. It is the martial state in which all values are the values of war.

First of all it considers constitutional democracy as an archaic, outworn political system, because of its inefficiency, its toleration of opposition within the state, its decentralization of power, its concept of individualism and the right of the individual as against the state, its devotion to concepts of individual freedom, liberty, will, and human equality. German fascism bitterly denounces all these ideals of democracy, proposes to scuttle the democratic ship, and substitute for it a system of rigid totalitarianism in which the individual is completely subjugated to the will and interest of the state. It jettisons the democratic institutions of government, the legislatures, parliaments, constitutions, the process of elective office holders, the exercise of a free franchise by the people, and replaces all of these with a dictator, a ruler whom all must worship, whose mere word is law, and who governs with the mailed fist—a Hitler or a Mussolini. Under this dictator there emerges a heavy-fisted, nihilistic, immoral, and ruthless bureaucracy, whose members constitute a new privileged class in the state, and for whose especial benefit the state is administered. The members of this ruling bureaucracy are revealed to be not the big business men of the state, not the aristocrats, nor yet the laboring masses—but the small middle-class men, the previously dispossessed and unstable group, the frustrated youth, the lumpen, or "slum," proletariat—the hoodlum elements in the society, who, never having before had power, know well how to abuse it. No opposition is tolerated, and dissenters are liquidated by means of the concentration camp and the firing squad.

In the economic sphere Nazi fascism substitutes for private capitalism or socialism a powerful "planned" state economy. It is not socialism that is found in fascist Germany and Italy, nor yet state capitalism. It is a corporative system which is really a bastard offspring of the syndicalist theory, and under it the society is organized into producing units, in which employers and employees are theoretically banded together into parallel and collaborating groups, which under the law control the economic life of the nation. But ever under the stern and watchful eye of the dictator.

As in the political, so in the economic sphere, all freedom is destroyed. The employer and the laborer are completely dominated and exploited by the state, and they live and operate only to serve the will and interests of the state— a will and interest determined by Il Duce or der Fuehrer, and administered through the power-crazed, sadistic bureaucracy. Labor unions as we know them are destroyed and likewise employers' associations. The sharecropper or day laborer in darkest Mississippi has more economic freedom and, even if a Negro, more civil liberty than the Aryan worker of Germany today.

In the social sphere racial tolerance is decried by the fascist states as a fatal weakness of democracy. For the concept of human equality there is substituted the concept of the superior race, of the German or Aryan master and ruling race, who are predestined to rule the world. Under the superior German master race all non-Aryan races must live permanently as inferior, whose role it is to serve the interests of the superior race. This is more than a tactic of the Nazi ideology; it is fundamental in the fascist ideological fabric. When Hitler in *Mein Kampf* writes that "all that is not race is trash," he means it. And he means that all but "Aryan" peoples must be permanently reduced to inferior and subordinate levels in the society of the world as a menace to the superior blood of the ruling race, as Hitler, the *Nazi Primer,* and the empirical evidence of Nazi tactics in Germany, Czechoslovakia, and Poland have amply demonstrated. And now France has joined the circle.

Thus politically, economically, and socially under German fascism there is created the essential slave state—a state to which obedience is assured through the frightfully efficient and ruthless operation of the gestapo, or secret police. And it is to embrace all the world, for the Germans boastfully sing: "Today we own Germany, tomorrow all the world." Abraham Lincoln once truthfully proclaimed that the American nation could not endure half-slave and half-free. It is equally true today that this world cannot endure half-Nazi and half-free. The sheer economic logic of National Socialism makes this axiomatic—80,000,000 Germans, dominating the European continent under a giant economic trust, controlled by and serving the political interests of an authoritarian government and backed by the mightiest war machine in the world's history. What private corporation or cartel could compete with or stand against it? National Socialism's economic war is as total and as ruthless as its military war.

And now, before this realistic backdrop, to comment briefly upon the specific Negro reactions previously mentioned.

First, the American South is not fascistic. The South is neither totalitarian nor highly centralized. It more nearly approaches the chaotic, to the contrary. It is prejudice-bitten and lacking in morality, but at the same time irrational in its treatment of the Negro. Life for the Negro in the South would be far more harsh, unbelievably harsh, under a highly centralized, highly rational, and brutally efficient fascism which would give total, authoritative expression to the Southern doctrine of white supremacy.

Second, the Negro in the South, and in the North can and would be in a hopelessly distressing plight once there occurred in this country a complete destruction of the concepts of human rights, liberty, and privilege, and the constitutional basis for our appeals to justice. That would create for us an entirely new world, devoid, for us, of either rights or hopes.

Third, to say that if democracy cannot perfect itself and accord us proper treatment we will have none of it is, in these times, sheer nonsense and racially suicidal. It is not intelligent to think of burning down the barn in order to destroy the rat. This "all or nothing" position employs the liberty afforded by democracy to aid and abet not its perfection, but its destruction in times of stress.

Fourth, we Negroes cannot rely for our future upon the great American middle class. We must reckon upon the possibility that a total Hitler victory in Europe will produce economic repercussions here that will throw our middle class into hysteria and economic collapse. The neutralization of our huge gold stores, the loss of trade in Europe, the necessity for astronomical sums for defense, will all hit the Negro, as a marginal population, first, last, and most severely—if not fatally.

Fifth, white people have no monopoly on fascist ideology nor on human exploitation. Black, brown, and yellow tyrants in a world in which white supremacy would be destroyed would be as ruthless as the present white ones. Changing the colors of the aspiring master races of the world is no solution to human suffering.

Sixth, the Communist position is sophistry of the cheapest variety. To say: ignore the imperialist war and bend all efforts to perfect democracy at home, in the world today, is to deliberately mislead the Negro and to set a cunning trap for him. The Communists know that the Negro can always be enthralled by appeals for his rights. The Communists, who are no longer radicals, want us to forget, however, that it was only a year or so ago that we were urged by them to support, in our own interest, the fight for democracy in Spain—and they were right then. That was when Hitler and fascism were regarded as the twin forces of darkest evil for the liberty-loving, working masses of the world. But then came the Communist shift from the popular front line, the Soviet-Nazi pact, and now Russia and the Communists are on the other side.

We are now told that this is an "imperialist" war, that imperialist, pluto-cratic England is now to be more feared, apparently, than the Nazi menace. This is sheer soap-box logic. Of course this is an imperialist war—between imperialist France and England and former imperialist, aspiring-to-be-imperialist-again Germany and empire-intoxicated Italy. But that is beside the fundamental point, and the Communists well know it. The vital war question for us is "who will win it?" England and France, before her collapse, have given recognition to the basic concepts of the democratic way of life, even though guilty of serious violation of the rights of subjects. But even during the war African natives in British colonies are able to publish criticisms of govern-ment policy that would put a fine Aryan German worker in a concentration camp if he merely listened to them over a radio in Hitler's domain. Moreover, it would seem that the Communists can now condemn imperialism with bad grace in view of the adventures of the Soviet Union in Poland, Finland, the Baltic States, and Bessarabia.

Thus Negro interest for the Communists is tied to the uncertain and constantly shifting foreign policy of the Soviet Union. This was the ridiculous position taken by the Negro Congress at its sessions in Washington last spring. The Communists know well enough that there can be no democratic islands in a fascist world, that American democracy cannot survive the triumph of total-itarianism in this world. This position only serves to achieve a psychological immobilization of our people in the fight against fascism. And, to use an apt phrase of my colleague Dr. Harris, when applied to the Negro it is a crude "trafficking in human misery."

The Negro faces grave danger from the repercussions of a Nazi victory in Europe—less from the possibility of direct military invasion than from the penetration of the Nazi ideology. Hitler also wages a total psychological war. To reassure ourselves on this point we need only refer to his long string of broken promises, his brazenly false "reassurances" to Austria, Czechoslovakia, Poland, and the Low Countries, and his, until now, successful reliance upon the complacency and gullibility of the democracies. The United States has all the necessary raw materials for a native American fascism. It will suffice to enu-merate them:

1. Racial intolerance.
2. A badly functioning economic system, with widespread and continu-ing unemployment.
3. A traditional admiration for things that work well and for spectacular successes.
4. A naive mass public, easily deceived, misled, and duped. Witness our large crop of successful demagogues, our Huey Longs, Fathers Coughlin and Divine, and the wide appeal of our slogans: "every man a

king," "two chickens in every pot" "$30 every Thursday," "Ham and eggs every Friday."

5. A huge mass of wandering, future-less, discontented, and frustrated youth.
6. A vast South in political, economic, and social chaos.
7. A property and profit-loving class that will grasp at any straw in a desperate crisis to salvage what it can of its vested interests.

And against these factors, to hold the dykes against fascism, we have only what we are told is a traditional and determined love of freedom, individualism, and democracy, for which we will fight to the death. Perhaps so. I hope so. We may be put to the test. But we have never had seriously to fight for democracy since we first won the right to it more than 150 years ago. I wonder if we would do so now. Or would we fight only as France fought?

And, given fascism here, what of us? In conclusion let me sketch briefly a picture of what could happen to us. Then, five years ago, or even last year, it might have been utterly fantastic to think in these terms. But is it so now?

The Negro is no longer indispensable in this country. He is entirely dispensable everywhere. He is increasingly a relief burden. There are no longer jobs that whites will not take and need. Fascism is a highly rational system. Its ends justify its means. And its ends are to organize the resources of the state for the benefit of the master race. The Negro is already virtually an alien race here. White supremacy under fascism, or a "100 percent Americanism" could seal our doom. Under a rational fascism there might well be:

1. No education for the Negro.
2. No government positions for the Negro.
3. No licenses for Negro professional men.
4. No business or automobile licenses for Negroes.
5. No home- or land-ownership for Negroes.
6. No legal rights for Negroes in the courts.
7. No political rights for Negroes at the polls.
8. Negro labor and concentration camps.
9. Registration of all Negroes.
10. Armband identification for Negroes of all shades.
11. Severe penalties for "passing."
12. Decrees for the sterilization of Negroes.
13. Expatriation or exile for Negroes, as per Senator Bilbo.
14. No Howard University for Negroes; no conference on the "Needs of Negro Youth."

But why go on? I have no desire to incite nightmares. American democracy is bad enough. But in the mad world of today I love it, and I will fight to preserve it.

Certainly Negro universities have a vital role to play in the definition of Negro interests in the world today. For the sake of all of us I hope they play it well. I think that the Negro university should today employ every means at its disposal to convert its charges to an ardent faith in the principles of democracy; to make a fetish of the worship of democracy; to activate them in every way possible to the defense of democracy. The classroom, the seminar table, the lecture platform, the university press, the chapel, should all be enrolled in this crusade.

Indeed, many of our universities themselves, Negro and white, need to get the spirit of democracy, need to be democratized from the top down. Most of them, in their administrations and their ideologies, are much closer to the authoritarian than to the democratic pole; most of their administrators pay only lip-service to the basic precepts of democracy, many of their heads undoubtedly have a personal admiration for the power and prestige of the modern dictator.

Perhaps in less crucial times it was enough for our universities to serve as an objective and disinterested clearing house for the scientific truth, though even objectivity must operate within some scheme of values. Perhaps in such times the universities could properly discharge their social obligations by striving to cultivate a discriminating and critical intelligence in their wards. But that is not enough today. Our universities must take a stand. They must marshal their resources into a vigorous force for the defense and perpetuation of the democratic ideal. Their own very existence depends on it.

CHAPTER 18

The Framework for a Course in Negro History
1940

This 1940 lecture, delivered to the Toussaint L'Ouverture Society at Hunter College, is remarkable for two reasons. First, given his preference for economic and political analysis, Bunche seldom addressed such concerns as Negro history. Yet, as we have seen in his criticism of colonial education for excluding African history and culture, he is consistent in his desire to see the omissions and stereotypes in American history addressed. Second, the two possible types of history courses he describes—subjective and propagandistic versus objective and scholarly—are currently reflected in much of the debate surrounding Afrocentric education and black studies. Bunche clearly favors a Negro history course that is integrative in intent.

Surely it would be easier to advise you on what *not* to do in a course on Negro history than to attempt to relate just what it should embrace. I will not be at all surprised if my emphasis in this discussion proves to be rather heavily on the negative side. But this requires no apology. Many errors of commission and omission have been and are being committed in the name of Negro history and in Negro history courses. I am sure that you, in your constructive purpose, would wish to avoid such mistakes and would expect to be made aware of them. When I responded to Miss Gowdy's kind invitation to meet with you here, I took pains to point out that the subject of Negro history is full of pitfalls: pitfalls of racial chauvinism, of stultifying provincialism in thought and concept, and self-imposed isolation. I suggested that it would be my prime purpose to emphasize the broad framework into which a course in Negro history should be fitted. This I propose briefly and quite humbly to undertake. But I must warn you in advance that my thesis derives from the sober conviction that the study of any aspect of American Negro life is essentially an anlaysis of the integration of the Negro into the main currents of American life and history; and more importantly still, that it is my belief that courses in Negro history as such in white or Negro institutions of learning can have no magical effect on the solution of the problems of race.

What is to be considered as the dynamics of a course in Negro history? It may well be true, as often contended, that all history has been written with an "other" purpose. Writers and teachers of history are not without their points of view, their motivations, and their biases. History is written and taught by men of the present who set down and relate, not merely the facts of the past, but their thoughts about it as well; and it may well be, as Beard suggests, that history is in this sense an act of faith.[1] The writer or the teacher of history, certainly, cannot write or teach in a vaccum. He must choose his frame of reference, some complex of ideas, some social values, some ideology, on the basis of which he makes his interpretations and draws his conclusions. History has become much more than an unadorned recital of facts. Moreover, the writer or the teacher of history exercises a broad power in the selection of historical facts and the emphasis and coloration to be given to them.

Thus Negro historians, if not the historians of Negro, would be inclined to accept Reddick's dictum that "Negro History has a purpose which is built upon a faith."[2] According to Reddick, and his view would be rather universal among the Negro historians, the essential purpose of Negro history would be three-fold:[3]

1. To discover and record the role of African peoples in world as well as in the more restricted histories;
2. To awaken and "educate" a majority population to the significance of this role;
3. To inculcate a dynamic pride in the Negroes themselves.

The Negro historians here respond to very clear motivations. They feel, and not unjustly, that white historians have been guilty of misrepresentation of the role of the Negro in history; that they accept without question the racial stereotypes and, indeed, create many of them; that they have ground the white edge of the ax too conscientiously and have relegated the Negro to an [unreadable] role. The Negro historian then proceeds to grind the black edge of the ax, and not infrequently to repeat the same sins with "reverse English." The Negro historians also see a need for bolstering up the Negro's own pride in his racial origins; the Negro is thus given an historical "needling" intended to perk him up and stimulate him to more active participation in the struggle for Negro progress. Finally, they regard Negro history as an effective offset to the stereotypes—"the pictures in our heads"—and the popular misconceptions of the Negro so prevalent among members of the dominant majority. They are struggling against the popular conceptions of Negroes as buffoons, or Uncle Toms, or grotesque caricatures of what a human is supposed to be.

Thus Negro history comes to be regarded as an instrument for the social progress of the group: a veritable weapon which can be turned against the forces which imprison the Negro in mental and physical ghettos. But it must be observed that the excessive laboring of such attitudes itself develops a ghetto mentality and tends to hobble the Negro ever more firmly with the shackles of race. The Negro is even encouraged to nurture a defiant pride in his ghetto existence.

Broadly speaking, there are two types of Negro history courses that might be given, or that have been given, viz.: (1) courses which are deliberately and overtly propagandistic, and which put these objectives above meticulous adherence to fact; (2) courses in which a serious effort is made to emphasize historical fact and rational interpretations rather than propagandistic objectives.

The overtly propagandistic courses are designed to inculcate respect among whites and pride among Negroes in the African background of Negroes, in their history, their achievements, their culture, their leadership, their heroes and geniuses. If insufficient glamor is discovered, then some is invented. This occasionally requires a [*sic*] deal of ingenuity.

Examples:

1. Touching up pictures of ancient Egyptian monarchs.
2. Tracing down Negro blood in monarchs of Europe.
3. Admitting no limitations to the greatness of Negro heroes—Garvey— "He's a young man yet."
4. Finding Negro blood in prominent historical figures. The list compiled by Negro psuedo-genealogists is long; some of the findings may be authentic; others are exceedingly dubious. But in either case it is of little significance. Among the names of such lists the following are included:

a) Alexander Hamilton

b) Beethoven

c) Warren Harding

d) Alonze Pietro Nino, pilot of one of the ships in the fleet of Columbus during his voyage to discover America.

The story of this Nino legend is rather humerous. Nino was the pilot of the ship *Niña*. His name was translated into Latin and became Nigno. Written in script it came to be misspelled as Nigro, and subsequently an *il* was added, making it "Alonzo Pietro il Nigro." A subsequent German translation produced "Pietro Alonze der Schwartz." This was perfect. The *Negro Year Book of 1921–22* took it over; so did Carter Woodson, and Senor Nino was now a full-fledged member of the race. Congressman Madden of Chicago, who relied heavily on the Negro Black Belt vote, found an inspiration in the story and proposed that a monument to the now black Mr. Nino be erected at government expense in the heart of the capital's northwest Negro section.

All this is a manifestation of racial introversion, e.g., "I don't care if he's B. T. Washington." Racial chauvinism is a product of faith and emotion, not knowledge. It provides no basis for understanding anything in the modern world.

This is the opposite side of the coin of unmitigated anti-Negro bias shown by some white historians, as, for example, with regard to the horrors of Reconstruction.

Examples:

1. gold spittoons
2. nicks in steps of capital building at Raleigh from beer kegs rolled down by Negro legislators.

The Negro history propaganda courses inevitably lead to a gross distortion of values and perspective. They become jingoistic and egoistic in their approach. They tend to magnify the incidental and trivial. They are at one with that narrowly racial and double-standard thinking which finds pride in the "first" Negro to do this or that, the "youngest" Negro to get something or other, the "only" Negro to have attained some position of little consequence.

The Negro teacher of Negro history often enters whole-heartedly into this little propagandistic conspiracy, designed to pull the historical wool over the eyes of both innocent whites and Negroes. In doing so he concocts rationalizations, which often read something like the following:

Many of us forget that the laws of racial preservation, like those of self-preservation, are much older and certainly far more vital to us than the so-called "scientific methods" of thought. For however scientific we may be, after all, we live in a world of feeling, of sentiment, and of emotion, and, however much we will it otherwise, the actions of most of the people around about us are motivated not by reason or a sense of fair play but rather by their hopes, faiths, and desires. For Negroes, then, to depend upon scientific processes of thought to any too great degree in such a world is suicidal.

Race is older than science.

We must at all cost present the Negro Case and Cause in the best possible light.

The Negro intellectual often succumbs to this weakness because of his wounded sensibilities, the humiliations he has to endure. He seeks escape, he wants to be proud and to be respected by his white fellow man.

The second or less subjective and licentious type of Negro history course may result from either or both of two stimuli, i.e.,

1. A purely cultural and academic interest, directed toward filling a yawning gap in the pages of legitimate history; or
2. An honest desire to do "missionary work," in other words, to undertake a form of interracial promotion.

There can be no criticism of the first motive, certainly. But in my estimation the second, i.e., the response to the interracial urge, would be a misguided effort. This would be ineluctably so for the simple reason that no significant advance toward the solution of the race problem can be made in this way.

Merely "understanding" the Negro and his history, his problems, his maltreatment, his culture, and his achievements under stress can make no serious impression on the fundamental conditions which nourish the problems. I mean to say that the belief of some well-meaning inter-racialists that race prejudice evaporates when the races "understand" each other better is wishful thinking. This is important to note because the motivations of a course will largely determine its tone and content.

An approach of this nature might have some effect on relations between a few white and Negro students, or between white and Negro professors—such groups are selective and meet in no continuing competition. But it wouldn't touch the problem where it is rife, nor affect those who hear it. Sympathy, fellow-feeling, inter-racial understanding, and brotherly love are all commendable traits, but they are futile gestures in the face of the harsh realities of the American Negro problem.

There is a more simple, yet more convincing argument for the presentation of a broad course in Negro history by American universities, however. It looks upon the Negro problem as one of the aggravating problems confronting American democracy. The very existence of this problem is evidence of an alarming weakness, a menacing fissure in the walls of the democratic dyke which alone holds back the fascist flood. All of the intelligence and applied energy of the American public is now necessary to the preservation of our democratic way of life. The university has a serious responsibility in preparing its students to be intelligent defenders of the democratic faith and effective trouble shooters against its break-downs. In order properly to discharge these obligations the student must be equipped with the essential tools—not the least of which is an understanding grasp of the background and elements of each of our pressing national problems, including the *Negro problem*. A course in Negro history with this sort of orientation could become a valuable addition to the curriculum of any school, and it could be taught with proper dignity.

The course in Negro history should be a course in the main currents, forces, and institutions of American life. It should be primarily a course in American history with directed emphasis on the role and status of the Negro. It would of necessity require a wide sociological, political, and economic base. It should deal less with personalities than with events and forces. With regard to any important aspect of Negro life, as, for example, Negro labor, it should attempt to demonstrate the interaction of forces and races. A useful course in Negro history is a symphony in black and white, not a dirge in black. It would obviously presuppose a sound knowledge of American history, political, economic, and social.

Negro colleges increasingly offer courses concerning the Negro in history and in several other subject fields, including English, education, French, sociology, anthropology, economics, and religion. Negro history is the most widespread and popular of such courses. Ordinarily, the scope of these courses in Negro history is broad, with considerable emphasis on African culture and civilization. One such three semester hour course is described as "designed to acquaint the student with African civilizations and with the contributions of the Negro to the civilization of the world. The history of the Negro in America and his present-day achievements are given consideration." Generally, however, these courses are resolved into a survey of the Negro in America, with selected treatment of slavery, abolition, colonization, the Civil War, Reconstruction, the struggle of the Negro for social and political justice, and the contributions of the Negro to American life.

It needs scarcely to be mentioned that quite frequently these courses become "contribution" or "self-admiration" sessions in which there is a rather self-conscious but monotonous recitation of the exploits of Crispus Attucks, Phillis Wheatley, Frederick Douglass, and Booker T. Washington.

Clearly, there is very little that can be gotten out of a highly specialized course such as Negro history (and Negro history can only be an advanced and specialized course), unless the student is acquainted with the fundamental facts of American history. Of what significance is the story of how Crispus Attucks was shot down by the red coats without prior comprehension of the basic causes of the American Revolution and the psychological reactions of Bostonians and other New Englanders to the presence of the king's troops?

The elemental danger in the Negro history course is always that, lacking the broad approach and the grasp on fundamentals, the presentation becomes one in which isolated facts stand out without meaning and where no attempt at integration is made (Myrdal's experiences). The Negro problem can be understood only if America is first understood.

The course in Negro history presented in the History Department at Howard University exerts some effort toward extensive integration. A conscious attempt to avoid the chauvinistic is made. Increasing attention is directed to American movements and forces and an analysis of how these have impinged on the Negro, and less to isolated examples of Negro achievement, heroism, and distinction. It is recognized that continued stress on personalities, detailing unrelated episodes of racial interest which do not lend themselves to any continuing and related historical interpretation, soon converts the Negro history course into a course on oddities, a sort of "believe it or not" entertainment.

The Howard course devotes itself to the following broad topics:

1. The African Background
2. The Rise of the African Slave Trade
3. The Negro in the Exploration of America
4. Servitude and Slavery in the Colonies
5. The Free Negro in the Colonial Era
6. The Negro in the War for American Independence
7. From the Revolution to the Constitution
8. Organization and Achievement
9. The Period of Reaction
10. The Negro in the Second War with Great Britain
11. The Negro and the Indian
12. Colonization and Compromise
13. The Rise of the Plantation
14. The Beginnings of the Abolition Movement
15. Slavery in Its National and International Aspects
16. The Free Negro Population
17. Abolition Reaches Its Climax
18. The Negro in the War for Southern Independence
19. Reconstructing the Nation
20. Social and Economic Ferment
21. Education and Religion
22. Political Striving and Economic Transition
23. Economic and Social Organization
24. The Negro in the World War
25. From the World War to the Depression
26. On the Threshold of a New Day

The latter topic would seem to be purely rhetorical.

Each of these broad topics is broken down into a number of sub-topics. In any event it is clearly an ambitious undertaking. The greatest problem is that of acquiring a teacher with a background sufficiently rich to make the subject vital. Not only must he be well informed on American history, he must be a specialist in his knowledge of the Negro and should also possess a working knowledge of the other social sciences. There is no text available for the sort of course here postulated. The works in the Woodson and Brawley tradition would be virtually useless in the course here suggested. They plug the racial angle for all it is worth and merely string together an unrelated series of racial facts to produce a "strange as it seems" melange. A history of America into which the Negro has been woven without strain, distortion, or bias remains to be written.

The truly valuable course in Negro history is the fearless course, presented without regard to feelings or sensibilities, black or white. It should have no ulterior motives other than a determination to cling to ascertainable historical fact and realistic interpretation. It should zealously avoid propagandistic, missionary, and inter-racial motivation. It should above all stress integration. It should recognize that the apparent physical separation of the races in this nation is a purely superficial observation: that to the contrary the Negro has been intimately related to every important political and economic movement in the nation's history. The Negro resents insult and disparaging interpretation in his history; but he should resent equally patronization and the invention of romantic myths in that history as soothing syrup for the violence done to his rights. The history of the Negro in this nation doesn't need to be padded.

The struggle of the Negro for rights to which a democratic society entitles him as a birthright, is one of the dramatic chapters in the history of the nation. Today, for all thinking people, the Negro is a shining symbol of the true significance of democracy. America's black citizens have demonstrated graphically what can be achieved with democratic liberties when even grudgingly and incompletely bestowed. The history of the Negro in America is the history of the struggle of the democratic ideal. It is within this framework of reference that the Negro history course should develop.

CHAPTER 19

NAACP Convention Address
1951

After 1950 the hundreds of public speeches Bunche delivered tended to focus on one of two themes—the necessity for granting blacks full equality or the necessity to support the United Nations in its peacekeeping efforts. Quite often the speeches combined both themes linking peace to the achievement of equality and justice here and in the countries struggling for independence. After his criticism of the NAACP in his Howard years, Bunche joined the board of directors and participated in a number of annual conventions. This speech, delivered in Martin Luther King Jr.'s hometown of Atlanta, reflects the themes of full integration and applied democracy combined with personal anecdotes of racial discrimination that Bunche repeated many times across the country. In fact, Bunche states that the "Negro problem" is a national problem, not a sectional problem, and that the pace of progress must be greatly accelerated. When it was greatly accelerated, by King among others, Bunche was one of the first to endorse their actions.

Bishop Gregg, fellow Americans:

I am happy to be able to participate in this, the 42d Annual Conference of the NAACP, and especially to have the opportunity to greet you this afternoon. Quite frankly, however, I would be much happier—and so would you, I am sure—if the occasion could be of a different nature; if the NAACP or any other organization no longer had to carry on an incessant struggle against great odds to win for the Negro citizen the simple rights to which the Constitution of his own country entitles him. This is the Negro's burden and the nation's shame.

You are here, and I am here, because we have this deeply vital problem very much on our minds, and because every one of us is directly and adversely affected by that problem. Indeed, every American, whatever his color or race, is directly and adversely affected by that problem, though far too many Americans have not yet awakened to this fact.

All of us could be doing many things this afternoon which would be far more pleasant than attending this meeting and listening to speeches, particularly this one. As for myself, for example, if there were no Negro problem in my country, I would probably be with my young son at Ebbets Field in

Brooklyn rooting for the Dodgers to win and cheering the brilliant playing of Jackie Robinson, Roy Campanella, and Don Newcombe. But do not misunderstand me. As a rabid Dodger fan, I would be cheering for such stellar white Dodgers as Pee Wee Reese, Gil Hodges, and Carl Furillo too, since I harbor no racial prejudice. But race relations being as they are, there is a difference, and somehow I cheer a little bit more enthusiastically for Jackie and Roy and Don than I do for the others. I know that is not quite fair, but neither was it fair that Jackie and the others had such a tough time getting up there. Most of you, no doubt, will understand what I mean.

To be quite frank, I can never be fully relaxed in Atlanta, fine city that it is and good friends that I have here, since I abhor racial prejudice and its evil end-products, discrimination and segregation.

I feel a sense of personal insult whenever I see a sign reading "For Colored" or "White Only." I believe strongly in human dignity. But how can any one have dignity if he must be constantly reminded that here he is not welcome; here he cannot sit; here he cannot sip a drink of water or enter a restroom? I can, to be sure, find more than enough of that sort of thing, if no so overt, far to the north of Atlanta. This leads me to say that the problem of race relations in this country is a national problem. No section of this nation is free of the problem. So long as it persists, it is the responsibility of every American citizen, North, South, East, and West. The fight against racial prejudice, therefore, must be nation-wide and must continue, and will continue, until the society is completely purged of this evil.

This is my fight as it is yours, as it is the fight of everyone who believes in democracy. The NAACP conference is here as the spearhead of that fight. It is good that this conference is held here. For racial bigotry must be boldly fought wherever its poison is found, and particularly where it is most virulent. Atlanta and the state of Georgia are in the Deep South and have more than their share of racial bigotry. I imagine that it would be helpful if an NAACP conference such as this could be held here every month. For we must all keep battering away at the undemocratic barriers of discrimination and segregation. They are not impregnable. Indeed, they are beginning to crumble everywhere, and if we continue courageous and never relax our effort they can be obliterated.

Because I feel and think this way is good enough reason for me to be here. Racial bigots could exclude me from hotels, refuse me every civilized courtesy, and do much worse, but that would not deter me from being here with you, for we are here to carry on a historic struggle for our rights, our dignity, and our self-respect. What could be more important? If Negro citizens were welcome in Atlanta's hotels and otherwise treated as equals here, there would be no good reason for holding this conference in Atlanta.

I hope to live to see the day when this will be the case in Atlanta. This is not at all beyond the realm of possibility. For I must say that there has been much progress in race relations in Atlanta since I first visited this city more than 20 years ago, and Atlanta is a better city for it.

The NAACP has been very well treated here during this conference, and the city authorities and the local press are due an expression of warm appreciation from us.

I must add that I received a most cordial welcome from Mayor Hartsfield immediately after my arrival yesterday, and I wish to state publicly my personal thanks for the courtesies extended to me by the mayor and the police force. Twenty years ago I would have been not a little worried to have those Atlanta police coming after me.

There can be no doubt that many things—good things—are happening in Atlanta today which would have been impossible, and even unthinkable, a quarter-century ago.

There are many things that I would like to talk to you about this afternoon. There are many things which in the long view are more vital than the problem of the Negro in America, although I know that it would be difficult to convince the average Negro who daily suffers the harsh disadvantages and indignities of racial prejudice that this is so. If our American democracy had reached maturity, if we Americans were a fully sensible people, I could talk to you as I have talked to many other audiences, about such fundamentally vital issues as the United Nations and the prospects for peace, about Korea, Palestine, and Iran, about the 200 million colonial peoples who aspire to self-government and independence. You are interested in these subjects, I know, and in a very true sense, in this atomic age, they directly relate to our future freedom and security, and perhaps to our very survival. In passing, I must say that all who earnestly wish peace, and who hope for the success of the UN, will be greatly encouraged by the recent developments with regard to peace in Korea.

It is through no choice of our own, however, that you and I must today devote our attention to an imperative problem which no longer has any justification for existence in a society that aspires and claims to be democratic. I am compelled to talk about the Negro problem because it is our number one domestic problem, because I am a Negro, and because it is the business of the NAACP. The NAACP, fortunately, has been tending to that business for 40-odd years with highly commendable results. If this were not so, we could not be holding this kind of meeting today in Atlanta. Every living Negro may thank God that the NAACP has been carrying on this heroic struggle for so long and so well. And every American, whatever his color, may be grateful that the American society is more democratic today than it was a half-century ago precisely because of the efforts of the NAACP and like-minded organizations.

I pose as no expert on race relations or on the Negro problem. But I have been a Negro in America for almost 47 years now, and I may assure you that even without much effort I have learned a great deal about the problem, and the lessons have been by no means pleasant. Nor do I have any claim to speak with authority on behalf of anyone but myself. I cannot even claim to speak for my wife, since being born and reared in Montgomery, Alabama, she knows more about the problem than I do, and, believing in the equality of the sexes, speaks for herself. Moreover, my three children already regard me as decidedly old-fashioned. Always one to avoid crowds, I shy away from the swollen ranks of the millions of self-appointed "Negro leaders." I am not a Negro leader, and I much prefer to be accepted simply as an American than to be called a "leading Negro."

Yesterday, I am told, when that caravan of black Cadillacs in which I was riding passed by, one Negro lady asked: "Who's that?" When she was told, she exclaimed: "Zat so? When he die?" So I speak to you strictly on my own, representing no one but myself. Even so, I speak no less earnestly.

There are many approaches which might be employed in any consideration of the Negro problem, but of all of them I prefer the common-sense approach. One may try to justify the differential treatment of white and Negro Americans by history, by emotion, by racial stereotypes, and by just plain prejudice. But it cannot stand the test of common sense.

In this nation, from its earliest history, we have been a society of diversified peoples—peoples diversified by race, color, religion, cultural background, and national origin. No nation in history has known such diversity, nor has any ever had such spectacular success in welding diversified peoples together in firm unity. That unity has derived from the compelling force of the great ideals upon which our nation has been erected—the equality and dignity of all men before God, the inalienable rights of every individual being, the concepts of individual freedom and government of, for, and by the people. This is the rich source of our unparallelled strength.

What utter nonsense it is, therefore, and how dangerous to the very foundations of our society, to contend that there must be two catagories of American citizens, first-class and second-class, and that in terms of status in the society the most able and valuable Negro citizen must be considered and treated as inferior in status to the most incompetent and useless white citizen, even the criminal. Americans are a proud people and are rightly proud of their heritage of ideals and freedom. But can anyone be proud to be a second-class American? Second-class citizenship contradicts democracy. In the name of democracy, second-class citizenship for the Negro must go.

In this attractive, bustling, and, in many respects, progressive city of Atlanta there are white and Negro citizens. Among them, both white and black, are the many who are good and valuable, and others, who are misfits and social liabilities. What ignorance and superstition, what demagoguery for selfish political and economic ends, is it that keeps the good citizens of Atlanta, who comprise the preponderance of both races, from living and working together with mutual respect and goodwill, as sensible human beings? What is it that a good white Atlantan sees and thinks when he sees a good black Atlantan; what is it that keeps his eyes from seeing through the superstitions and illogic which perpetuate these senseless and neo-primitive racial attitudes?

But I am quite convinced that this ignorance, these superstitions and prejudices, are by no means as deep-seated in the generality of the white citizens of the South as some would wish us to believe. I know this is so, because too often in my own experience have I seen white Southern citizens shake them off quickly and with apparent relief. I know very many white citizens, of the South as well as the North, and a good many of them are to be found in Atlanta, who are men and women of genuine goodwill. I know some others, of course, who are decidedly not. It is scarcely necessary, on this occasion, to call their names.

I have great faith in people. I believe that most people prefer to be human in their attitudes toward all of their fellow men. But I realize also that people can be rather easily intimidated into sublimating their better attitudes. In the South, and to only a lesser extent in the North, there is such intimidation. It comes primarily from those who would recklessly exploit the racial problem for selfish political and economic ends, with irresponsible disregard for the broad interests of the nation and its people.

Atlanta is a fine city. It could, no doubt, be a great and outstanding city. But no city which finds it impossible to solve the problem of the relations of its people can lay claim to greatness. I know, to be sure, that there are some in this city who would claim there is no problem of race relations in Atlanta, that the two races get along well enough so long as each keeps to its place, and that it is only when Northern "troublemakers" like the NAACP and myself interfere that trouble develops. I doubt if many Negroes could be found in Atlanta who would share that view. If there are any, they are more mice than men.

There are some people—bitter-enders, they are, and I hope there are not many of them in Atlanta—who are determined that the Negro shall never, under any circumstances, win his fight for equality in the American society.

They are like the tourist guide at the Gettysburg Memorial. This guide, a solid white son of a no longer solid South, drives tourists around the battlefields of Gettysburg in a bus, describing the historic scenes to the tourist passengers as he drives along. His routine runs something like this:

"Here the Confederate forces routed the Yankees."
"Here the sons of the South destroyed the Union Army."
"Here the heroic boys of Jeff Davis made the Northern blues turn tail and run."
One day, a lady, a Yankee lady, of course, had the temerity to ask:
"But didn't the Northern forces win any battles at Gettysburg?"

Replied the guide, with disgust:
"Lady, where you bin? Them Yankees win any battles? No ma'am, they didn't, and what's more, they ain't gonna win any so long as I'm drivin' this bus."

Americans traditionally have had a deep and sensitive conscience and a highly developed sense of justice and fair play. The white people of the South are Americans, and in every aspect of our life save human relations they have made invaluable contributions to the growth and defense of the nation. But it may well be questioned what kind of conscience, what kind of sense of justice and fair play, many of the white citizens of the South have.

Let us be specific for a moment. Josephine Baker and her company have been denied accommodations in the hotels of Atlanta, though hotels are clearly for the benefit of the public. Josephine Baker contributed far more than her share during the last war, a war strenuously fought to preserve democracy, freedom, and human dignity for all mankind. She worked tirelessly to entertain the Allied troops, including the GI's, and to keep up their morale. In this regard, she served many a southern white GI, not a few of whom, no doubt, were Georgia and Atlanta boys. But this celebrated, world renowned, and universally acclaimed artist cannot rent a hotel room in Atlanta. Any hotel in Atlanta, any hotel in the South, ought to feel honored to have Josephine Baker enter its doors. She is a personality of great charm and high culture. She knows what civilization means. Her rejection is an attitude not of an enlightened society; it is a crude and primitive expression of prejudice in the raw. And ironically, were Jo to appear here, white Atlantans would no doubt break down the doors to see and hear and applaud her.

The ability to sleep in a hotel has nothing to do with any individual's private opinions about races or individuals. When one sleeps in a hotel he takes his chances on who his neighbors may be. I have had some white neighbors in hotels whose conduct left much to be desired. But I could never be either arrogant or silly enough to demand that hotels give assurance that my neighbors will be to my liking. Moreover, hospitality to a weary traveler is one of the oldest and most elementary traits of human society. It marks one of the elemental differences between mankind and the animal world. The whitest and most racially prejudiced hotel owner in Atlanta would be welcomed without question in the huts of the most primitive tribes of darkest Africa. They would have an instinctive feeling for the fundamentals of civilization.

I am sorry to dwell so long on the comparatively insignificant question of hotel practices, but, if we carry this Atlanta hotel situation a step further, an even deeper significance is revealed. In Korea, for over a year, the military forces of now 16 nations, representing many races and creeds, have been fighting with brilliant heroism against communist aggression. When that international hero, Captain Jabara, the first jet "ace" in history, recently returned to this country, he stated that he knew very well what he had been fighting over there in Korea. He said simply, "We are fighting over there in Korea so later on we won't have to fight in Wichita, Kansas"—his home. Among those heroic men fighting for the freedom of all of us in Korea are many American Negroes. A great many of these Negro GI's have been listed among the casualties. But not one of these Negro heroes, even if he wore the Congressional Medal of Honor, could rent a hotel room in Atlanta. Yet any non-Negro, even if he were a deserter, a traitor, or a communist conspirator, could do so.

One may well imagine that many people in this community must sleep with an extremely heavy conscience, whether they are bedded in hotels or out of them.

We may take renewed courage from the fact that a rapidly increasing number of non-Negro Americans are awakening to their responsibility as citizens to convert the American ideal of democracy into fuller reality by removing the shackles of racial underprivilege from the Negro citizenry. And we may be encouraged also by the fact that the sympathy of a large part of the world is with us in this struggle.

Let there be no doubt about the ends we seek.

I know, of course, that there are some Negroes who advocate, whether from cowardice or avarice, that it is harmful and bad tactics to run the risk of shocking some white Americans by stating our objectives bluntly and revealing all at once where we aim to go. I vigorously disagree with such views and have no respect for those who hold them. We shall never achieve our full rights unless we are willing to struggle and sacrifice for them. Indeed, unless we are willing to do so we are not deserving of them.

We Negroes need to learn one lesson better than we have: fate helps only those who help themselves.

We are not helping ourselves as much as we should with our own resources of ability and wealth. We certainly do not give to the NAACP the full measure of our support, monetary and otherwise, which it deserves, which, in our interest, we should give.

There are Negroes of substantial wealth all over America—quite a few of them right here in Atlanta—professional and business men, who could do much more to support this struggle than they have done.

In my view, no Negro, however high he may think he has risen, no matter how much wealth he has amassed, is worth very much if he forgets his own people and holds himself aloof from the unrelenting struggle for full Negro emancipation.

The Negro should have no hesitation about stating in terms as clear as day what he demands, and should feel no self-consciousness in doing so. Why should any American feel timid about trying to make democracy work? If there are those who would be shocked at the demands of the American Negro, it is only because they do not believe in the democracy which our Constitution prescribes. They are an even greater liability to the nation in these critical days than to the Negro.

I think that what the Negro demands is as simple as it is incontrovertible. He demands complete integration as an American citizen. That means simply that he insists upon his constitutional heritage, without let or hindrance; equality, without qualification of race or color; an end to discrimination and segregation, for segregation itself, in any form, is discrimination. To speak of "segregated equality" among American citizens is to indulge in wanton sophistry.

Segregation by law, enforced segregation, in fact demeans the white Southerner as well as the Negro. It is a form of state paternalism as outmoded in this day and age as feudalism. Its very existence in the South and its nonexistence in the North, even in those communities where Negroes constitute a substantial element in the population, implies that the Southern white citizen is considered to be less mature, less to be trusted, more in need of protection by the state, than the citizens of any other section of the country. An underlying assumption behind the segregation laws has to be that in the absence of such laws many Southern whites would voluntarily associate with Negroes.

There is tyranny of law in the South, a tyranny over human relations which is all but unique in this twentieth century. The tyranny of the segregation laws of the South is designed to prohibit normal association between white and Negro Americans even in those instances where both may be willing if not eager to enjoy such association. This is a paternalistic tyranny of the law that is so arrogant as to defy description.

Equality is all the Negro citizen demands, and I am positive that the Negro will never give up this struggle until he achieves it. I am equally positive that he can and will achieve it, the hysterical antics of the racial bigots and demagogues notwithstanding. I am categorical about this because I have a deep faith in democracy. The force of democracy on the march is inexorable, and democracy is on the march in American society. It is the driving force of our society, and if it should ever be lost it will be not only the Negro citizen who will suffer the loss of his freedom and individual liberty.

I am aware that there are some white folks down here who will argue, as on occasion they have argued with me, that what I have been saying is "dam Yankee" talk, uttered by a "black dam Yankee" at that, which is much worse, and that this does not represent at all the thinking of the "good Nigras" of the South. I would advise my good white friends that they are likely to discover sooner than later that they are gravely mistaken. They often claim to "know the Negro," but they should know that even most of those Negroes who seem to agree with them, or who at least do not oppose them, employ what might aptly be described as a "survival language." This is a form of double talk carefully selected according to the color of the listener. One thing may be said to the white man, solely for reasons of self-preservation. But it would be both revealing and painful to him if the white man could hear what is later said within the protective walls of the Negro home.

I have said earlier that the Negro problem is a national, not a sectional, problem, and that it is a national responsibility. There have been in recent years not a few encouraging developments on the national level, as, for example, the progress being made toward full integration in the armed services. But in the field of national civil rights legislation the record is dismal.

Could there be any greater mockery of democracy than the performance of the national Senate with regard to civil rights legislation? Senators indulge themseves in breast-beating oratory about our democratic way of life; they embark upon rhetorical flights about the free world and free peoples; they threaten to use our growing military strength and our atomic weapons to protect the free world at large against any aggression; they declaim that our nation's God-given mission in the world is to protect and preserve freedom. But how transparent is this oratory, how blind, what a hollow ring it has, in the face of the fact that these same senators cannot embrace the simple and mild civil rights program proposed by the president—a program designed to give only a minimum guarantee of civil rights for 1 out of every 10 Americans, for one-tenth of the senator's own constituents. There is an aggression on their own threshold which urgently demands their attention—a long continued and shameful aggression against the constitutional rights of 15,000,000 hard-working, devoted, and loyal American citizens, who work, pay taxes, and shed their blood for their country exactly like all other American citizens, though their advantages from the society are arbitrarily restricted. Many of our senators, and not a few of them from sections of the country other than the South, need to be vigorously reminded that freedom and justice must begin at home. All fair-minded Americans should mark well those senators who are brave enough to have us risk a world war but who quail like chipmunks before our domestic racial prejudice. Does hypocrisy know no bounds? Can there be any greater devotion to flag and country than American Negroes fighting in Korea to protect rights and privileges for the Koreans which the Negroes who fight and die have never enjoyed at home?

We Negroes must suffer no illusions and expect no miracles. Grave social problems cannot be solved overnight, and the Negro problem will never be solved that way. But it can be solved, and the pace of progress toward its solution can be and must be greatly accelerated. It is not time that will solve the Negro problem; there is not time to wait, in any event.

That encouraging progress has been made and continues to be made is not to be denied. But time is much shorter than it has ever been before. It is shorter for the Negro, because as he becomes increasingly aware of the rights and privileges denied him, he also becomes increasingly aware that each day of his life he loses something that is irretrievable. It is shorter for the nation, precisely because the nation is confronted with its gravest international challenge and needs desperately its maximum strength, unity, moral position, and prestige.

Indeed, it might well be said that rapid progress toward the full integration of the Negro in the society is of even greater urgency for the nation today than for the Negro. Who can deny that bad racial relations are a serious divisive factor and therefore weaken us when we most need unity? Who can deny that racial prejudice prevents one-tenth of the nation's manpower from being utilized to its maximum potential when we most need all of our manpower? Can it be doubted by anyone that our position of leadership of the free and democratic peoples of the world is subject to doubt, suspicion, and even ridicule, because of our own inability to apply fully the democratic principles we so vigorously profess to one-tenth of our own citizenry? Can there be any question that our moral position and prestige in the world deeply suffer from these dangerous defects in the life of our society, defects which are known to all the world; and that this is so even among our friends? Can there be any question that undemocratic racial attitudes and practices are rich and fully exploited sources of effective propaganda for those who are opposed to us and all we stand for?

The costs to the nation of the Negro problem are incalculable. These costs are borne by every American, whatever his color or race.

In the struggle in which our nation is engaged it is the attitude of the peoples of the world which will be the decisive factor. We need many friends to win this struggle, and we seek friends. We would be shortsighted if we ignored the fact that the preponderance of the world's people are non-white, and that the vast millions of Asia, Africa, the Middle East, the Caribbean, and Latin America are extremely sensitive to our undemocratic racial practices. In our design for democratic living by a free people we have something of compelling appeal for all peoples. But we must first demonstrate that this design can be applied to peoples of all colors.

We perhaps never will have and we need not expect a perfect society here. But it is imperative that we go much further than we have gone thus far in applied democracy for all Americans.

Full equality is the answer. There is no other. In a democracy there can be no substitute for equality. The Negro can never be content with less. I am sure you agree with me that we shall carry on this fight until we achieve full equality; until, Americans all, we are all free and equal.

CHAPTER 20

Gandhian Seminar
1952

Integration was a basic goal of human life for Bunche, not only in domestic race relations but in international society as well. Nothing illustrates this better than his address to a group of Gandhi's associates in New Delhi, in which he rejects any fundamental difference between the "Western" mind and the "Eastern" mind. He therefore feels very much at home in India and offers two perspectives on Gandhi's accomplishments. First, Gandhi's call to the spiritual power of people to find truth and goodness rather than selfishness and greed was unsurpassed in human history. Second, Gandhi demonstrated that there were moral forces in the world far greater than armed forces. Bunche applied Gandhi's contributions to both the United Nations and the United States. That is, both the United Nations without the power of arms and black Americans without the power of numbers could effectively promote their respective goals.

Dr. Ralph Bunche: Mr. Chairman, if, with no little diffidence, I now make bold to offer these quite tentative remarks, it is only in obedience to the subtle tyranny of conformity; since all members of this unique seminar are apparently expected to do so and, no doubt, quite properly. For never have I experienced a deeper sense of inadequacy in confronting a challenge.

I hasten to say, however, that if there be anything wanting in my speech, this is exclusively a result of my own shortcomings, and in no sense a reflection on this seminar, which has been utterly serious in purpose, intensely devoted to its task, and, for me at least, extremely enlightening. I have learned and profited immensely from our discussions thus far, but the time has been short as measured against my own lack of knowledge, and I have by no means, as yet, learned enough to speak with any degree of authority about the rich heritage bequeathed to us all by one of the truly great personalities of human history. If, therefore, I cannot speak of Gandhiji with authority, I can and do speak of him with reverence and humble appreciation.

I realize, of course, that since I am an American, a product of "Western" culture, it will be assumed by many that I approach the subject of the Gandhian outlook with a Western mind and from a Western point of view. I discount any such suggestion very sharply. For though this is my first visit to India, and I am delighted at the privilege, it is not my first visit to the Orient. As a result of previous experience in the East and long association with colleagues and friends from Asia, reinforced by my experiences in Delhi during the week since my arrival, I feel that there is a tendency to exaggerate the differences between East and West. On the fundamental problems of human existence on this troubled planet, I have never perceived any significant difference between the thinking, the aspirations, the philosophy, or the spirituality of the common man, of people in the street and village, whether East or West, in India or America. Whatever their race or religion, their culture or geographical location, I am convinced that the hopes of people everywhere are for peace and freedom, for dignity and self-respect; for the elemental necessities of decent living; for food, clothing, housing, education, good health; for economic security; for equality with all other men. These find expression in a common language, universal in scope, and readily understood by all men of good sense and goodwill. I believe also that there is nothing regional about the essential goodness and oneness of human beings, faith in people, and reliance upon Truth as the sole acceptable basis for human relations.

I must say that, although a complete stranger to India, I have quickly felt very much at home here, my Western background notwithstanding. I find no mystifying differences in philosophy or approach. Indeed, I have often been more mystified by some of the mysticism, political and economic, of my own people in my own country than by anything I have encountered in India. I am not at all baffled by the Gandhian way because it is "Eastern"—a way, indeed, which is more unique in its methods and tactics than in its fundamental philosophy; I am only intensely eager to fill the wide gaps in my knowledge about it.

I am, in short, no little suspicious of concepts of the "Eastern mind" and the "Western mind." I see such concepts as often an expression of cultural provincialism, if not dangerous manifestations of nationalist chauvinism and arrogance. Such attitudes are serious obstructions to the effort to promote the Gandhian spirit of brotherhood among men, typical of all religions, and the concept in one world which, I note from Mr. Kalelkar's statement, Gandhiji himself embraced when advising against the formation of an Asian bloc.

This is not to suggest, of course, that cultures among the nations are not diversified or should not be, or to deny the cultural gifts and traits peculiar to specific societies and to particular groups within societies, gifts with which the society of India from ancient times has been richly endowed.

I find every facet of Gandhiji's outlook tremendously interesting. But in the brief span of this statement I am primarily concerned with two aspects of his contribution, namely,

1. the explanation of his extraordinary effectiveness as a leader of his people;
2. the implications and lessons available to a world in deep and persistent crisis.

Like all great leaders in mankind's history, and they have been all too few, Gandhiji stood with deep humility before God and people. But though he walked with humility he was not without pride, and his eyes [*sic*] courage was an indispensable virtue. Perhaps the real measure of his greatness as a leader is to be found in the striking effectiveness of his appeals to the people and the decisive support he commanded from them. Gandhiji reached and moved the oppressed people of India as he had earlier done among the oppressed Indian population of South Africa.

But it is not extraordinary that a leader should move people. Throughout history, in every society, demagogues have reached and moved people for their own and evil purposes, by false counsels, by appeals to man's base motives, by playing upon selfishness and greed. Nor is it at all unusual for people, at the behest of their leaders, to make great, and at times unjustified, sacrifices in pursuance of a goal.

The singularly rare quality in Gandhiji's leadership is that he provided for the people of India an inspiration and a guidance which enabled them to give expression to their greatest and noblest strength. His appeal was to truth and goodness, and he brought out all that was good in the people. His special genius was to plumb the depths of the latent, hidden genius of the people. He called upon them to express to the utmost their ability for self-sacrifice and self-discipline, and in large measure they responded. This was a call to the spiritual power of a people, unknown, I believe, to history.

It would be highly presumptuous of me, in the presence of tested disciples of Gandhiji, of men who stood the stern test of fire at his side, even to attempt to suggest how Gandhiji was able to perform this miracle in an age of disbelief in miracles. But it is clearly apparent that Gandhiji was identified always and completely with the people; that he walked with them; he was one of them and at one with them; that he considered himself with complete and simple sincerity as an ordinary man among ordinary men, and never an oracle or a demi-god. The cause of the people was his cause because he was of them. All of their problems and causes—the cause of the worker and of the untouchable, the overriding cause of liberation—were his causes.

That Gandhiji's leadership developed at a time when the people of India may have been ready for and in need of a new leadership, of a new approach; that the time of his advent on the Indian scene may have been fortuitous, all this is of secondary importance. It is always thus in the great episodes of history.

The time, the people, and the leader rendezvous. But in the leader, Gandhiji, were found congenially wedded qualities of deep spiritual dedication, devotion to truth, unflinching integrity in principle with flexibility in tactics, realism, and a masterful understanding of practical action which enabled him to inspire confidence in the people and to free them from long-endured shackles of fear.

I think it no detraction from Gandhiji to say, out of my unwavering belief in people, that no leader can ever achieve greatness unless the people led are also great. And history will certainly record the greatness of the people of India in their long and painful struggle. There were millions who accompanied the leader to the jails of the country and thus demonstrated qualities that ensure for the people and the state of India a future of outstanding contribution to the family of nations.

I must say also that in my view, leaders, however great, are to be revered but never idolized or defied. They provide guidance and inspiration. But leaders are men, and men die, while societies live on, in the present and into the undefinable future. Times change, needs change, and philosophies and tactics must accommodate always the needs, the hopes, and the will of people. Absolute truth is always difficult to define in human affairs; the well-being of the people, less so. Dogmatism becomes static; societies, to grow spiritually as in material well-being, must ever be dynamic.

The historic significance to the larger world of Gandhiji's role in India is that, through his guidance, India attained its freedom without resort to violence and war. This was a remarkable and highly encouraging departure from the classical pattern of emancipation of dependent peoples from imperialist rule. The United Nations, in its Trusteeship for Non-Self-Governing Territories, functions in the same way and seeks the same end—an assurance to colonial peoples that their aspirations for self-government or independence may and will certainly be achieved by non-violent means.

It seems to me that, although Gandhiji's efforts were concentrated on India and the Indian people, he was a true internationalist. Indeed the liberation of India was a signal service to the advancement of all mankind. He was a servant of humanity the world over in (1) his unyielding opposition to violence and war and his demonstration that intense conflict-situations could be resolved by non-violent means; (2) in his compassion for mankind; (3) in his devotion to the elimination of human suppression and misery; (4) in his disavowal of hatred as an instrument of policy even to attain a coveted goal, while practicing unparalleled tolerance and promoting understanding among peoples; (5) in his belief in freedom for the individual and for peoples and in the dignity and worth of individual man; and finally (6) in his implied if not explicit assumption that no problem of human relations is insoluble, and this by peaceful means, if there is the will and the moral force to do so.

The vital lesson which the peace-loving peoples of the world must learn from Gandhiji—and we all hope and pray that this lesson shall be learned in time—is that an irresistible force may be wielded by a people who are determined to achieve an honest goal, if they are willing and ready to endure self-sacrifice and self-discipline to that end. World differences may be settled without resort to force and peace may be preserved if the peoples of the world, all or some of them, are willing to make the effort. Peace cannot be won without cost and sacrifice. Gandhiji, the world may well recall, worked with peoples, never with arms and armies. The lesson is here for all to read: there are greater forces by far in the world than arms.

Gandhiji freed the people of India of fear and thereby they acquired a tremendous strength. Fear is the outstanding characteristic, as Paster Niemoller has pointed out, of the relations among nations—and particularly the Big Powers—today. The peoples of the world can never be strong nor peace ever be made secure until this fear is eliminated.

In this regard, Gandhiji also provides a highly pertinent lesson. It is the lesson of moral force and the confidence to be derived from its possession. As I read the Gandhian way, it counsels people to do always what is right and let the adversary beware of the new strength thus acquired by those who follow that path.

There are many, for example, who scoff at the United Nations because it has not at its disposal a vast international army or security force, and who assert that without such force it can never prove really effective. Except in the unfortunate instance of Korea, the United Nations has never had any sanction behind its actions other than moral force. In a number of situations, even situations involving actual fighting, this moral force has proved sufficient to stop the fighting and to make substantial progress toward peaceful resolution of the difficulty. This, despite the fact that nations and peoples throughout the world have paid little more than lip-service to the principles of the organization and have made few, if any, sacrifices on its behalf. Even so, United Nations' experience has adequately demonstrated that military force is not indispensable to the effectiveness of an international peace organization if peoples and nations will provide it with the moral force at their command.

Democracy also has much to learn from Gandhi. Gandhiji's foundation-stone was always Truth, his force was satyagraha, Truth force. What must this imply for democracy? I believe firmly in the democratic way of life. I believe that democracy is the only way of life worthy of the dignity of man, and when I speak of democracy, since words today often have different meanings in different places, I mean a political, social, and economic structure in which government and the state are the servants, and not the masters, of the people; in which the individual is free, endowed with inalienable rights, and can walk with dignity in his own right; in which all people irrespective of race, color, creed, culture, or national origin are equal, accepted, and treated as equal; in which men may worship according to their conscience, speak, write, and assemble freely; in which men are assured of a standard of living which will make for a decent life free from fear of want. This is the theory and profession of what some call "Western democracy."

Truth for democracy, if we take Truth in the Gandhian sense, obviously must be more than these beliefs and ideals of democracy, with which in themselves there can hardly be quarrel or quibble. Truth must be more than the profession of these great ideals, no matter how often and fervently reiterated, since professions are only words and Truth is not found in words alone. Truth, then, as Gandhiji would have it, must find expression in practice and actions. It is only in the application of democratic ideals that democracies can find Truth. True democracy must be lived by and for all the people.

It is precisely because an increasing number of the American people have come to a realization of this fact, of this acid test of the democratic way of life, that the struggle of my own group for full equality in the American society has met with much more success in recent years than ever before. The test has not been fully met, not by any means, but it is being met with increasing earnestness and determination to do the right, and I have confidence as to the ultimate outcome.

I have full confidence also that any society which is free and whose government is devoting its utmost effort to free its people from fear and from want, which eliminates its own internal tensions, need have no great anxiety that its people will be seduced by totalitarian or any other alien ideology.

In conclusion, I interpret non-violence as an instrument, as a means to an end. But even though the end is right, it will be dissipated if it is sought by means that are not right. Non-violence, the disavowal of resort to force, is the only right means to worthy ends whether within a society or in the relations among nations.

The fact is that there is no rational alternative to non-violence in international affairs today, since war solves nothing, achieves only death and devastation, and begets more war. Thanks to the combined efforts of science and the machine, against whose control over man Gandhiji warned, his message of non-violence has become truly prophetic for the world at large.

Thank you.

Concluding Session

Dr. Ralph Bunche: Mr. President, Ladies and Gentlemen. We have now come to the end of what has been for me a rich and stimulating educational adventure. I am deeply grateful to the Ministry of Education and the Government of India for the invitation which brought me here. What indeed could be more appropriate for a servant as I am of the great international peace organization, the United Nations, than the opportunity to examine at first hand how a subject people under the inspired leadership of Gandhiji successfully employed non-violent methods in a desperate struggle for freedom? We who came to the seminar from abroad have been privileged to learn and to exchange ideas with men who walked and who suffered with Gandhiji. Indeed, the president who honors us with his presence this morning has been a life-long associate and fellow-sufferer with Gandhiji. I assure you that I shall return to my duties at the United Nations richly inspired, Mr. President, with renewed faith in the ability of mankind to do what must be done to avert catastrophe, and with my original optimism about the prospects for peace in the world no little reinforced. Not the least of the benefits and pleasures deriving from participation in the seminar has been this first opportunity to visit India, a land in which unlimited promise and critical need are locked in titanic struggle.

In the few minutes appropriate to this occasion, I shall endeavor to present only a selected few out of the many impressions I have gained from the seminar's deliberations, with particular reference to international tensions. The Gandhian way is the way of non-violent action. Gandhiji was against the use of force and always kept himself outside the orbit of violence. But for him, as I read his life, non-violence did not necessarily imply a prohibition against striking back. It was not an advocacy of cowardice. Mahatma Gandhi recognized, if I understand him correctly, that if violence is discarded as both immoral and impractical there must be some effective substitute for it. In his own person and actions Gandhiji adhered strictly to the ideal and would accept no deviation from it. But he realized that it would be unrealistic to try to employ the method of non-violence if the moral strength indispensable to its use should be lacking. In that event, such strength as may be possessed may be used. Fortunately he found the people of India possessed of that moral strength in sufficient quantity.

Now this is the condition in which the world finds itself today. Nations and peoples have not as yet developed in themselves the moral strength to enable them to use exclusively the method of non-violence. This is why the United Nations at its inception could not, and I fear cannot now, rely exclusively on peaceful, non-violent methods of settling disputes, even though its fundamental purpose is to secure and maintain peace in the world. Although the only such instance as yet in its history, the United Nations thus has had to resort to armed force to repel aggression against the Republic of Korea. I deplore that necessity even while recognizing it, for, had the moral strength of a united international community been powerful enough and had it been exerted early enough, the tragedy of the devastation of Korea and the heavy casualties of that war might well have been averted.

But this was not the case, and that is regrettable. Still I cannot escape the conclusion with respect to the United Nations' armed intervention in Korea that, even though force has been employed there, this intervention, this show of a determination by the international community to resist aggression and to protect the unprotected may very well have spared us the anguish of other "Koreas" elsewhere in the world. May we hope that the United Nations can end the fighting in Korea soon and that efforts to re-establish peace, led by India's earnest conciliatory work, will meet with early success?

It is well to bear in mind that, though the Gandhian outlook is against violence, against the use of force, Gandhiji regarded meek submission to aggression or other injustice an even worse evil than the employment of force. Non-violence is an instrument solely for the courageous; cowardice is the mark of the doomed. As things stand today, I fear that the meek are not likely to inherit the earth or even keep what they have of it, through meekness alone.

It is said, if I understand it correctly, that the techniques employed by Gandhiji were somewhat relative, depending upon the exigencies of the prevailing situation. It is in the light of the dangerous, divided world, most of it rapidly and fearfully arming to the teeth, that the potentiality of a broader utility for the Gandhian way must be measured.

It is in this formidable world that governments, acutely conscious of their sobering responsibilities for the well-being and the security of their nations and peoples, must choose their courses of action and their tactics. What each government does in this regard relates quite directly to what other governments are doing, the motives of each being the subject of anxious, suspicious, and often excited speculation. And thus a vicious pyramid of arms and fear is erected which, if very long continued unchecked, can have only fatal consequences for most of us.

In this world complexity, it would be no cause for wonder if India itself, the mother of Gandhiji, might now find it difficult always to undertake an unqualified and unmodified application of the Gandhian way in its external relations.

Another highly significant aspect of Gandhiji's philosophy of human relations was his disavowal of hatred. The seeds of hatred are being widely sown among peoples today, and the ultimate harvest will be bitter beyond measure. I have been tremendously impressed by the many manifestations of tolerance in evidence in this country, despite the fact that your long struggle for freedom ended only a few years ago. This is a rich heritage which every society should envy. It would mean much for the world if peoples everywhere would emulate India's example in this regard.

I would now, Mr. President, like to conclude these remarks with a word about democracy. It is often said that the wonders of modern transportation and communication have made our world a very small one. In terms of distance, in bringing us all so much closer together, this is entirely true. But in another sense, thinking historically, the world today is very much larger than it was 50 and even 25 years ago; that is to say, in terms of people who count or who must be taken into account. In the past quarter-century, a vast revolution has been taking place among formerly forgotten peoples of the world—the people of Asia, the Middle East and Africa—where, indeed, the preponderance of the world's population is to be found. We no longer have a world in which only a few people counted and controlled the country, and the rest were ignored, subdued, and suppressed. Peoples the world over, of all races, colors, and cultures, have emerged and must now be reckoned with on a basis of complete equality. There is, for example, a new Asia, and in most of this Asia only the Asian's word is law. This is good for the world at large. This is the only kind of human progress worthy of the name.

The same development has occurred in the Middle East, and it cannot be doubted that it will not long be delayed in Africa.

We must have a world in which all men walk with full equality, with equal dignity and freedom, irrespective of race, religion, or language. There must be no more under-privileged peoples, no untouchables, racial or religious, anywhere in the world. People everywhere are entitled to and must have a decent standard of living in the broadest sense, in food, housing, clothing, health, and education. They must have freedom, but above all they must have the respect, not the tolerance, not the paternal condescension, but the man-to-man respect of all other peoples.

And, I say this from my heart, for I am identified with a group in my own country which knows a great deal about the struggle for equality and human dignity. I am happy to say that my people in America are winning that struggle day by day, and we are doing so, by and large, through non-violent means. In the history of racial conflict in America, there have been regrettable episodes of violence, for my people are not a cowardly people, and we have at times fought to protect our homes and our rights, as we have always fought willingly and patriotically for our country. But incidents of violence become increasingly less frequent, as out struggle for equality is conducted through the courts and by appeals to the very conscience and morality of the American people, within the framework of a constitutional structure that is at once free and democratic. You may be sure that our effort will be unrelenting until full equality is won. We gained much inspiration and encouragement from the glorious success of the determined effort to the people of India.

As a veteran in the ranks of the campaign for freedom, I know that words about the glories of democracy are a cheap commodity and often very hollow. Words never bring freedom or equality to anyone, and only politicians seem able to grow fat from mouthing them. For my part, I will always take an ounce of freedom and equality in practice for a pound of words and promises.

In short, the proof of democracy is in the practice of it, in deeds, not in words. I would rather have a poor man shake my hand with sincere respect than a millionaire put a fortune in it with smirking condescension. Now when these ultimate lessons are well and earnestly learned, a sound basis for mutually friendly and trustful relations between the new Asia and the rest of the world will exist and democracy will be secure. I doubt if there is any other way to make it secure.

Finally, may I be so bold as to express the hope that the great new democracy developing in this country, expressed so magnificently in your general elections of last year, will grow strong roots and flourish vigorously? The future of freedom in the world is likely to depend upon it more than any of us can now calculate.

I shall not leave India worshiping Gandhiji, for I do not believe that men must be gods to be great. But this opportunity to live for a fortnight with his thoughts and actions has opened to my mind, Mr. President, a new vista which I shall explore and utilize to the fullest. I shall leave both wiser and humbler, and with profound respect for the man, Gandhiji, and his historic work, and with a warm affection for the people of this country. Thank you.

CHAPTER 21

March on Montgomery Speech
1965

An Ebony *magazine photograph of the front line of the Selma to Montgomery March in 1965 identified all of the leaders except the man linked arm in arm with King—Ralph Bunche. That Bunche's 40 years of struggle for civil rights could so easily be forgotten is disturbing. Plagued with his lifelong problem of phlebitis as well as failing health in general, Bunche made every sacrifice to be present for the conclusion of the historic march. His brief speech calling for the protection of the human rights of all citizens is unremarkable. Still, due to the public nature of the event, Bunche received bags of hate mail.*

By God, we are here! Little more need be said.

No words could be as eloquent as the magnificent, historic march, which has been made possible by the superlative leadership of Dr. King and his associates.

This morning, as we walked together, I said to Dr. King that this must be your greatest triumph in the sense of all the obstacles that had to be overcome; and he agreed that it was.

Incidentally, I have discovered in the course of this march that, in addition to being a great leader, Dr. King is quite a walker. In fact he walked with such ease, in a gliding sneaky sort of stride, that I began to wonder whether he was not getting a little help from the Lord. The Lord was certainly not helping my aching legs.

Governor Wallace and some others denounce many of us who are not Alabamians of being "outsiders" and "meddlers," and that includes me.

I stoutly deny this.

I am here as an American; an American with a conscience, a sense of justice, and a deep concern for all the people and problems of our country. I came here to identify with the just cause of the right of Alabama Negroes to vote as our president himself has said every good American should.

I say to Governor Wallace that no American can ever be an outsider anywhere in this country. And, Governor, all these people out here, who have come in a great phalanx, are very great people Americans, black and white, the greatest, for they seek to bring unity and maximum strength to this county to the end that it may become, as it can become, white and black together, the greatest society not only of contemporary times but in the entire history of mankind. And, lest the Governor has forgotten it, Alabama lost its attempt to leave this union more than a century ago. Apparently, he has forgotten it, for I see the Confederate flag flying up there over the dome of the capitol. I have never spoken before under the shadow of that flag, and I must say that it makes me feel uneasy, even a bit treacherous to do so. That flag should have come down over a century ago.

If Governor Wallace or anyone else doubted that two Southern causes have been forever lost—the cause of the Confederacy and the inhuman, un-American attempt to keep Negro citizens suppressed and oppressed—all doubts had to be dissipated when *we* marched through Confederate Square, not long ago, singing "We Shall Overcome."

What we are doing here is an all-American attack on an all-American problem.

In the UN we have known from the beginning that secure foundations for peace in the world can be built only upon the principles and practices of equal rights and status for all peoples, respect and dignity for all men.

The world, I can assure you, is overwhelmingly with us.

I am sorry that it was necessary for protection to be given to the march by the federal government by federalizing the Alabama National Guard. But the fact that the government did so was an indication of the firm determination of our government to protect the human rights of all of its citizens.

But I have a word of advice to our government if there is a next time: be sure that the federalized troops are not wearing confederate flags on their jackets.

There is a great old song saying "there'll be some changes made." Well, our presence here today testifies that some changes have been made in Alabama, and a whole lot more are going to be made and very quickly.

I earnestly salute every one of you for expressing by your presence here the finest in the American tradition; you are in truth the modern day "Minute Men" of the American national conscience. You have written a great new chapter in the heroic history of American freedom.

Part 6
Iconography

CHAPTER 22

Nothing Is Impossible for the Negro
1949

This essay is a brief and clear delineation of Bunche's basic philosophy of life. His belief in the American creed and hard work as well as the influence of his grandmother are presented to the readers of this middle-class black magazine. Two memorable phrases include Negroes "are Negroes primarily in a negative sense" and "a community of people cannot adopt an alibi [racism], however credible, as its philosophy of life." While these statements may lend credence to the view that Bunche sought to escape black culture and black history, I believe this essay is an attempt by Bunche to redefine the term American *to include blacks.*

What, at this very moment, in this great nation, does it mean to be an American, a citizen, and a Negro? We are part of a vast and powerful and dynamic nation, a great power whose responsibilities and influence in the modern world are frightening in their scope. The origin, traditions, and creed of this nation are an inspiration to all freedom-loving peoples. Our country's history is brave. Americans fought and died for their freedom and liberty. Having won by their blood the right to maintain an independent existence, our founding fathers established the nation on the cardinal principles of individual liberty and equality of man. They spoke of inalienable rights, of the incontestable fact that all men are born free and equal, of the dignity of man. The American citizen is at once the benefactor and protector of this great American legacy. The privileges and rights of the American citizen—of all American citizens—are writ large in our Constitution, in our traditions, in what has been called the American creed. They guarantee to every citizen of this great nation all of the essential attributes of a free and dignified existence.

But today there is a certain irony in the situation with which Negroes are faced. They are better Americans than they are Negroes. They are Negroes primarily in a negative sense—they reject that sort of treatment that deprives them of their birthright as Americans. Remove that treatment and their identification as Negroes in the American society would become meaningless—at least as meaningless as it is to be of English, or French, or German, or Italian ancestry.

All American Negroes are one hundred percent Americans. Who, indeed, is a better American, a better protector of the American heritage, of the American way, than he who demands the fullest measure of respect for those cardinal principles which are the pillars of our society?

If we could probe deeply into the minds of Negroes, we would discover, I am sure, that the basic longing, the aspiration of every one of them, is to be an American in full. Not a semi-American. Not a Negro-American. Not an Afro-American. Not a "Colored Gentleman." Not "one of our Colored Brethren." Just an American—with no qualifications, no ifs or buts, no apologies, condescension, or patronization. Just Americans with a fair and equal opportunity as individuals to make or break their futures on the basis of their individual abilities, without the un-American handicap of race.

The American Negro suffers cruel disabilities because of race which are in most flagrant violation of the constitutional tenets and ideals of the American democracy. But the saving grace for the Negro is the democratic warp of the society which permits the Negro to carry on his incessant and heroic struggle to come into his own, to win those rights, that dignity and respect for the Negro, individually and collectively, which are his birthright as an American.

And, fortunately, the American white and black alike, has a conscience. The Negro American daily wins increasing support for his struggle from all those other Americans who aspire toward a democratic, not a semi-democratic, America; who wish a four-fourths, not a three-fourths, democracy. Moreover, the sympathy of the world is with him. The Charter of the United Nations endorses his aspirations.

It is true that on occasion, an individual Negro may, by tremendous effort, successfully negotiate the racial rapids and find himself in the mainstream. But that this is a rarity and his group is far behind is abundantly testified to by the fact that this very presence in the mainstream is front-page news. The status of the individual, in the long view, can be no more secure than the status of his group.

We Negroes must be great realists. The road over which we must travel is clear, though the prospect may not be pleasant. We suffer crippling disadvantages because of our origin. But we are Americans in a basically democratic American society. That society is a competitive society. The going is hard even for white Americans. It is harder for us.

To make his way, the Negro must have firm resolve, persistence, tenacity. He must gear himself to hard work all the way. He can never let up. He can never have too much preparation and training. He must be a strong competitor. He must adhere staunchly to the basic principle that anything less than full equality is not enough. If he ever compromises on that principle, his soul is dead.

He must realize that he and his group have not attained the goal until it is no longer necessary to make reference to the fact that "X" was the "first Negro" to do this or that, and until accomplishment by a Negro is taken by the public at large as a matter of fact.

This may have a harsh ring, but it is the gospel truth. The road of Negro progress is no road for weaklings. Those who cannot summon up the courage, the resolve, and the stamina to travel along it can find refuge in a handy alibi; the disadvantages of race. And they can find ample documentation to support their plea. But a community of people cannot adopt an alibi, however credible, as its philosophy of life.

My own philosophy on such matters is quite simple: whatever is worthwhile is worth working, striving, sacrificing, and struggling for.

There is no substitute for hard work as the key to success in the American society. This is true for white Americans. It is even more true for black Americans. Few Americans of any color or creed can ever find easy the climb up.

But, while nothing is easy for the Negro in America, neither is anything impossible. The barriers of race are formidable, but they can be surmounted. Indeed, the entire history of the Negro in this country has been a history of continuous, relentless progress over these barriers. Like "Old Man River," the Negro keeps "movin' along," and, if I know my people, the Negro will keep on moving resolutely along until his goal of complete and unequivocal equality is attained.

In my own struggle against the barriers of race, I have from early age been strongly fortified by the philosophy taught me by my maternal grandmother, and it may be of interest.

She was a tiny woman, but a personality of indomitable will and invincible moral and spiritual strength. "Nana" we all called her, and she was the ruler of our family "clan." She had come from Texas, married in Indian territory, and, on the premature death of my grandfather, was left with five young children.

Nana had traveled the troubled road. But she had never flinched or complained. Her indoctrination of the youngsters of the clan began at an early age. The philosophy she handed down to us was as simple as it has proved invaluable. Your color, she counseled, has nothing to do with your worth. You are potentially as good as anyone. How good you may prove to be will have no relation to your color but with what is in your heart and your head. That is something which each individual, by his own effort, can control.

The right to be treated as an equal by all other men, she said, is man's birthright. Never permit anyone to treat you otherwise. For nothing is as important as maintaining your dignity and self-respect. She told us that there would be many and great obstacles in our paths and that this was the way of life. But only weaklings give up in the face of obstacles. Set a goal for yourself and determine to reach it despite all obstacles. Be honest and frank with yourself and the world at all times. Never compromise what you know to be the right. Never pick a fight, but never run from one if your principles are at stake. Never be content with any effort you make until you are certain you have given it the best you have in you. Go out into the world with your head high and keep it high at all times.

Nana's advice and philosophy is as good today as it was when she gave it to me in my childhood. I certainly cannot improve upon it, nor would I try to do so. For me it has been a priceless heritage from a truly noble woman.

I have great faith that the kind of world we all long for can and will be achieved. It is the kind of world the United Nations is working incessantly to bring about: a world at peace; a world in which people practice tolerance and live together in peace with one another as good neighbors; a world in which there is full respect for human rights and fundamental freedoms for all without distinction as to race, sex, language, or religion; a world in which all men shall walk together as equals and with dignity.

CHAPTER 23

What America Means to Me
1950

Reflecting Bunche's increasing fame, the American Magazine *published an unusually detailed personal account of his life shortly before he won the Nobel Peace Prize. Once again the themes of hard work to overcome obstacles, the American creed, and Nana's influence shine through. Bunche even goes so far as to describe "a couple of those strokes of good fortune" as "rather typically American." He adds that being a Negro may have been an advantage in pursuing opportunity in that it gave him a stronger competitive instinct. In fact, in his personal correspondence Bunche directly states that the desire to succeed in competition with whites made him a workaholic. While Bunche would often deny being a role model or Negro leader, the fact that he chooses to tell his life story to a popular mainstream magazine suggests otherwise. In these brief autobiographies Bunche walks a fine line between glorification of "the broad opportunities that America offers" and the continued discrimination against African-Americans. Unfortunately, Bunche was not able to control which one of these messages was emphasized by the media, especially during the cold war.*

Dr. Bunche has many firsts to his credit. A brilliant scholar (summa cum laude at UCLA in 1927), he was the first Negro to receive a Ph.D. in political science, the first to be selected for a "desk job" at the State Department, the first to achieve an international reputation as a diplomat, resulting from his success as UN mediator for Palestine. Last year, President Truman offered Dr. Bunche an appointment as assistant secretary of state, the highest governmental post ever tendered an American Negro. He chose to remain with the United Nations, where he is a top-ranking director of the Department of Trusteeships.

* * *

I was a stowaway once—a youthful adventure, which turned out to be a stroke of good fortune.

I was coming home to Los Angeles from Camp Lewis in Washington, where, with other college students, I had taken an advanced ROTC course.

Short of funds, many of us decided to save the $125 train fare which the government had provided. Some of my friends hitchhiked, but I chose to return home by sea. I merely walked aboard the HF *Alexander* in Seattle and hid in a closet.

I had sadly underestimated my powers of endurance. By the time we passed Vancouver I emerged from my hiding place, ravenously hungry—and was promptly collared by a ship's officer. But, instead of being thrown into the brig, I was taken to the galley and put to work shelling peas and peeling potatoes. The atmosphere was leaden with the promise of grim reprisal; I was a badly frightened boy—and worked with great energy, hoping to mitigate my anticipated punishment.

By the time we reached San Francisco, I had become so diligent a pea-sheller that the ship's officer decided not to put me ashore just yet. I redoubled my efforts.

By the time we reached Los Angeles I was offered a job.

That job was a big help in meeting my college expenses. I spent three summers working on the ships—first as busboy, then as petty officers' mess-man, netting around $300 a season.

In a sense, that youthful escapade was typical of many subsequent experiences in my life. I have frequently found opportunity lurking in quite unexpected places. I have undoubtedly had more than an average measure of good luck. I have always been on the alert for opportunity and have realized that a Negro in America must often make and fight for his own opportunities.

I am asked by Mr. Ross what America means to me. A Negro American inevitably sees two Americas. There is, first, the land of the American democratic ideal, the America of the Constitution, in which all men, irrespective of race or color, would be equal and secure in their inalienable rights. But there is also the America of everyday life, which falls short in giving practical expression to the democratic ideals of the Founding Fathers, in so far as minority groups like the Negroes are concerned.

I like the American way of life, because I like the conceptions of equality and of the rights and dignity of the individual on which it is based. As every good American, I wish to see the country fulfill its promise to all its people. I dislike vigorously those practices which prevent this. American anti-racial and anti-religious practices make a mockery of both the Constitution and the Charter of the United Nations.

Yet, because of its basically democratic structure, the American society affords the opportunity, even for disadvantaged groups such as the Negro, to aspire for and make progress toward the good life. Every individual and group is entitled to put forth maximum effort to right wrongs, to obtain redress for grievances, to protest and struggle incessantly against disabilities such as discrimination, segregation, disenfranchisement, and denial of opportunity.

Within this democratic framework, the Negro, because of his persistent struggle, has made progress and will continue to make progress. But to date this progress has not yet brought most Negroes to the level of the minimum standard for first-class American citizenship.

My own career perhaps indicates that there is opportunity for the Negro here, even though more limited than for others, and that the barriers of race, which are very formidable, can nevertheless be surmounted.

I am a Negro, the son of an impoverished barber who never got beyond grade school. Born in Detroit in 1904, I remember vividly the old frame house, east of the railroad tracks, where I lived as a boy. Like most poor families, ours was a large one. My parents, maternal grandmother, and her four other grown children all lived together. It was a sort of tightly bound, matriarchal society, ruled by my grandmother Nana, a remarkable woman, tiny in stature, indomitable in spirit, who had been born in slavery in Texas. Widowed at an early age, she had single-handedly raised and educated her five youngsters.

I can never remember a time when we weren't very poor. In the summer my sister and I seldom wore shoes. We saved them for school in the fall. Later, when we moved to Albuquerque, my mother, who was afflicted with rheumatism, used to enjoy going to band concerts held in a park some distance from our adobe house. I would accompany her, but we couldn't afford carfare for both of us, so I used to put her aboard the trolley car and race alongside to our destination, a distance of some 20 blocks.

It was a happy boyhood, however impecunious. One early learned the value of money—and very little could bring endless delights. A pennyworth of candy could last a day; a nickel bought a movie show. Much of our fun cost nothing. We used to play baseball with a broomstick and a tobacco sac filled with grass and pebbles. Hockey was easy to arrange—sticks bent over a fire and a tin can. I was a pretty good swimmer by the time I was seven. I used to trail around with a group of older boys in Detroit; they taught us youngsters to swim by the simple expedient of tossing us into deep water.

There was never a time when I didn't have to work. In Detroit, when I was 7, I ran errands for a grocery store and hawked newspapers on a downtown street corner. In Albuquerque, my efforts were more ambitious. I was a helper in a neighborhood bakery; stripped to the waist, I used to work each evening until 11 or 12 P.M. I wasn't quite 12.

The following year I lost both my parents, and my grandmother Nana moved our clan to Los Angeles. While going to intermediate and high school, I held a variety of jobs. I peddled papers for the *Los Angeles Times,* spent summer vacations working as a house-boy in Hollywood or as a kitchen boy in beach hotels.

A little later I became a delivery boy on the *Times*—rather a pleasant assignment, bicycling around town every afternoon picking up advertising copy. Then I got a better-paying job—as composing-room "pig boy," the curious designation for the youngsters who carried lead bricks to the lino-type machines. It was hard work—from 5:30 in the afternoon until 1 A.M. I would get home close to 2, fall exhausted on my bed, get a bare six hours' sleep, and then dash out to school.

Saturday nights one of the pig boys could earn a little more money—if he won the wrestling tournament which we held, after work, for the amusement of the printers. All of them would chip in to make up a pot for the winner. It was a grim kind of sport, for we wrestled with great vigor on a bare concrete floor—but that bag of coins was an irresistible attraction.

One day, however, Nana read an article about "printer's consumption" and made me quit the job. It was no great loss, for soon thereafter I was employed by the City Dye Works as a carpet-layer. This paid well, up to 80 cents an hour.

But life was no idyll. I was learning what it meant to be a Negro—even in an enlightened Northern city. I once went on a newsboys' outing arranged by the Los Angeles newspaper publishers. The publishers bought out the concessions on the amusement pier at Venice, and we enjoyed ourselves hugely—riding the roller coaster, bouncing around in midget cars, stuffing ourselves with ice cream and spun sugar. Finally, the time came to take a dip in the Venice Plunge—and suddenly Charles Matthew and I, the only Negroes in the group, were told we couldn't come along. There was a color bar at the pool. That sort of thing made quite an impression on a lad of 14.

But I wasn't embittered by such experiences, for Nana had taught me to fight without rancor. She taught all of us to stand up for our rights, to suffer no indignity, but to harbor no bitterness toward anyone, as this would only warp our personalities. Deeply religious, she instilled in us a sense of personal pride strong enough to sustain all external shocks, but she also taught us understanding and tolerance.

As a youngster, I was soon to discover that, although a Negro is often treated unjustly, he may also meet with a good deal of decency and generosity. When I was on that newsboy outing I wasn't allowed to take a dip in the pool. But shortly thereafter, in the intermediate school that I attended, my classmates put on a minstrel show. I was cast in the role of interlocutor, the part normally taken by a white performer—and two white boys were done up in black face as end men!

When I came to graduate from Jefferson High School, I was kept out of the senior honor society, for there seemed to be an unwritten rule excluding Negroes. It was a clear case of discrimination, and I protested vigorously. On the other hand, I was selected as a commencement speaker as consolation.

In college I early learned that the strength of the American democracy lies in the individual citizens who believe firmly in its principles and have the courage of their convictions. Serious social evils obviously exist in America.

But the virtue of the system is that its defects can be attacked and eliminated. A revealing incident occurred in my freshman year at the University of California, Los Angeles. Leon Whittaker, a well-known Negro boxer in collegiate circles, was kept off the UCLA squad when it met Stanford, for Stanford at that time had an unwritten rule against Negroes and whites competing in individual sports involving contact. The UCLA coach withdrew Whittaker, despite the fact that he was collegiate lightweight champion. The upshot was that his white replacement lost the match to Stanford.

Next morning there was an uproar on the campus. Hundreds of students signed protest petitions to E. C. Moore, director of the college. Moore's response was immediate: he posted a notice on the bulletin board, stating that anyone who couldn't conform to the UCLA policy of complete equality had no place on the campus, and I believe the coach was released.

On one occasion I had a personal experience along the same lines. The color bar kept me out of a college debating society. My exclusion touched off a bitter fight, several of the members resigned, set up a new society, and elected me to an office.

Incidents of this kind were rare in my college life. Throughout the four years I had the same opportunity as the other students to gain an education and start preparing myself for a professional career. Like 70 percent of the students, I was completely self-supporting. I lived in a basement room across from the college, which I received in return for doing odd janitorial chores. I got a small stipend from the university for cleaning the women's gym. Somehow, the gym always got cleaned, but I never appeared there except on payday.

There were other jobs which I did do. For $25 a friend and I bought Model T Ford, stuffed it with mops, buckets, and brooms, and offered ourselves as a cleaning service to local stores and lunchrooms. At six each morning we set off on our route, gave a half-dozen establishments a thorough work-over, and were back in college for 9 o'clock class. Summer vacations, as I've already mentioned, I worked aboard the HF Emma Alexander.

I did well enough in my studies, winning scholarships for three years. Freshman year I played baseball, football, and basketball but for the last three years stuck to basketball. I worked on the college daily, was sports editor of the yearbook, president of the debating society, and was generally active in extra-curricular affairs.

I was graduated in 1927, having just received a fellowship for graduate work at Harvard, where I was planning to study political science. I felt wonderful on commencement day, but not so wonderful the day after. For my Harvard fellowship covered only tuition. Somehow, I had to raise train fare and living expenses. And then occurred, in quite succession, a couple of those strokes of good fortune which are rather typically American and which helped me over the rough spots.

What happened at this point was simple: a kindly Negro woman by the name of Mrs. Patton had taken an interest in me. When she heard of my financial plight she called a meeting of her social club. They decided to hold a benefit to send young Bunche to Harvard! I was somewhat taken aback by the proposal, but I had no alternative to accepting. To my amazement, they raised a purse of $1,000.

Shortly after I arrived in Cambridge, I walked into the Phillips bookstore on Massachusetts Avenue. I had a letter, from a friend who ran a bookshop in Los Angeles, asking Phillips to allow me a discount on my textbooks. But Mr. Phillips had poor eyesight. He glanced at the letter and promptly misunderstood its contents. "If you're looking for a job," he said, "I'll hire you."

I was at work the following day. (His poor eyesight had also prevented him from identifying my race, and he later told me that, had he known I was a Negro, he would probably not have hired me.)

I now had nearly $800 left in cash and a regular job; I was all set for a scholarship.

There have been many such occurrences in my career. I have found that, if I concentrated on doing a good job on the task in hand, the breaks would often follow. Good luck, I have often felt, is an abundant commodity in America, but it is usually a by-product of effort.

I worked hard my first year at Harvard, was awarded the Thayer Fellowship—and suddenly found myself with a job offer from Howard University. Professor Percy Julian, whom I had recently met, had sold the authorities at Howard on my qualifications. But he had neglected to tell me about the matter until the formal offer was tendered.

And so, quite unexpectedly, my teaching career was launched. My first year I met a young lady, a Washington schoolteacher named Ruth Harris, whom I later married. I remained at Howard—with interruptions for further graduate study and travel—from 1929 to 1942.

In 1934 I received my doctorate from Harvard University. In 1936 I took an extended leave from my teaching post at Howard to undertake two years of study and field research on a Social Science Research Council post-doctoral fellowship emphasizing the study of colonial policy throughout the world and an analysis of the status of non-European people in South Africa.

I prepared myself at length for the assignment—studying anthropology at Chicago, London, and Capetown—but one of my best breaks was completely unexpected. A major problem throughout my African junkets was to establish a close rapport with the Africans—not an easy thing to do, for I was lighter-skinned and dressed as a European. I had happened to make friends in the States with a student who hailed from the Kikuyu tribe in Kenya. He wrote his people that I would call on them, but I was hardly prepared for the reception that I received.

I arrived on safari one day and found the tribal elders assembled in a field to bid me welcome. Through an interpreter, I made a short speech. I told them about my African background, how my ancestors were carried across the water, enslaved in a strange land, how they had later been freed and begun to prosper. I ended with an expression of my happiness in being back in the land of my fathers.

When I finished, a grizzled elder clothed in little more than a loin cloth, stepped forward and began speaking very excitedly. He told me how happy he was to welcome me and said he truly believed my story, for when he was a young boy his mother had told him how their relatives in distant times had been taken down the long water and then across the big water, and how they had never returned. Now I had returned—the first to come back to the ancestral home. So he was welcoming me and giving me the name of Karioki, which means, "He who has returned from the dead." The name spread very quickly in East Africa, so that wherever I would go the children in the Kikuyu villages would run after me, shouting, "Karioki, Karioki!" This degree of acceptance greatly aided my research.

Unexpected opportunities kept punctuating my career. In September 1941 I was at my desk at Howard ready to start the fall term, after spending many months assisting Gunnar Myrdal on his monumental study of the Negro in America.

Suddenly the phone rang. A man named Conyers Reed, whom I didn't know, wanted to see me. Mr. Reed turned out to be a history professor at the University of Pennsylvania, who was now working for Col. William Donovan in the agency later to be called the Office of Strategic Services [OSS]. Reed needed a man to head up the colonial aspect of their intelligence work. He had asked his old friend Charles McIlwain, a former professor of mine at Harvard, for the names of qualified persons. McIlwain had suggested me.

I took the job. It was the beginning of my public career. It was also a good opportunity for wartime service in my specialized field. (The army had rejected me for physical disabilities.) Much of my work in OSS involved preparations for the North African invasion. In June 1942 I became chief of the Africa section and remained with OSS until I went to the State Department in January 1944.

This new appointment again came about unexpectedly—and in rather a curious fashion. In June of 1943 I was called over to State to have a talk with Phil Mosley, who was working on U.S. plans for the United Nations organization. His group needed specialized assistance on the dependent-territory phrase of the work. Would I be interested in such an assignment? I said I would, whereupon I returned to my desk in OSS and heard nothing more about it.

Six months passed. One day in December an OSS personnel office walked into my office and asked, with some irritation, why I hadn't told him that I was being transferred to the State Department. "It's news to me," I said, in all honesty. "Well, you're being transferred tomorrow," he informed me.

Later I heard an interesting story. In the months since my name had been proposed, two or three high-ranking officials in the State Department had tried to block the appointment because of my race. My sponsors finally brought the matter to Cordell Hull. He listened to the objections, received an account of my qualifications, and then his famed Tennessee temper flamed into invective. A man's color, he insisted, made no difference to him. He wanted qualified men in the department. That was the sole consideration that interested him. And so I was appointed—the first Negro ever to hold a "desk job" in the State Department.

I worked there for three years, being largely concerned with colonial questions. I got along fine and never had any kind of racial incident. I was an adviser at Dumbarton Oaks, at the first UN session in San Francisco, and at later meetings of the Council of Foreign Ministers and the UN Special Committee, which later recommended partition.

The following May, after fighting broke out in the Holy Land, Trygve Lie suddenly called me into his office. "I've just talked to Count Bernadotte," he said. "He's agreed to become mediator. I want you to take him to Palestine." This was on a Friday. Lie wanted me to fly to Paris on Sunday, meet Bernadotte, and accompany him to Israel on Tuesday. "You'll be away three or four weeks," Trygve Lie assured me.

I was away 11 months. The rest is history. In September of 1948 Count Bernadotte met his tragic death, and I became acting mediator. After months of effort, we managed to arrange armistice agreements that ended the fighting in the Holy Land.

I've often been asked the secret of our methods in mediating one of the most bitter and complicated disputes in modern times. The answer is difficult, but in terms of my personal approach one point may deserve emphasis.

Like every Negro in America, I've been buffeted about a great deal. I've suffered many disillusioning experiences. Inevitably, I've become allergic to prejudice. On the other hand, from my earliest years I was taught the virtues of tolerance; militancy in fighting for rights—but no bitterness. And as a social scientist I've always cultivated a coolness of temper, an attitude of objectivity when dealing with human sensitivities and irrationalities, which has always proved invaluable—never more so than in the Palestine negotiations. Success there was dependent upon maintaining complete objectivity.

Throughout the endless weeks of negotiations I was bolstered by an unfailing sense of optimism. Somehow, I knew we had to succeed. I am an incurable optimist, as a matter of fact. My own life, of course, has been fortunate. Through a combination of good luck and hard work I have experienced the opportunities of American life. In some ways, indeed, being a Negro may have been an advantage in making my way in the world. For the initial handicap put a keener edge on my competitive instinct; it has prodded me to exertions which I might otherwise not have undertaken.

I don't think my case is unique. In my lifetime I have seen a great improvement in the condition of the American Negro, and I expect to see much more. There has been a considerable increase in the educational opportunities available to Negroes. During the war, the bars against Negroes were let down in a number of fields of work; the severe manpower shortage caused the change. But much of the wartime improvement has remained; in the last four years laws against discrimination in employment have appeared on the statute books of a number of states—New York, New Jersey, Massachusetts, among them. We may not be able to legislate prejudice out of existence, but we can legislate against the effects of prejudice, and these state laws have been very helpful. Equally important has been the decisive change in the attitude of the armed services toward Negroes. All this deserves applause.

Many individual Negroes, despite the severe handicap of racial prejudice, can rise to an eminence which indicates the broad opportunities that America offers.

But, although the gains that have been made merit applause, Americans should not rest on their oars. The Negro citizen is still at a heavy economic disadvantage both as regards job opportunities and standard of living, as compared to the white. His educational standards are still much lower. In many states he is virtually disenfranchised. In the South he is by law a second-class citizen, segregated in his home, his school, his theater, his church. Conditions in our nation's capital are scandalous. If I visit Washington today I can't buy a meal, order a drink, see a movie, or, with very few exceptions, rent a hotel room—except in the Negro section of town.

Yet there is good reason to be hopeful. I look about me: my own children—Joan, Jane, and Ralph Jr.—are able to enjoy advantages which I never possessed. Yet they too have suffered those psychic blows which no Negro can escape. When we lived in Washington—in a "mixed' neighborhood—there was an excellent grade school right around the block. Yet my girls had to travel three miles each day—to a Jim Crow school. During the war I was a member of a car pool. On our way downtown we used to drop the children off at school. I was puzzled that they always wanted to be deposited on the corner, not in front of the school. Finally, Jane told me why— her playmates criticized her for having a father who drove white people in his car!

In rearing my children I have passed on the philosophy that Nana taught me as a youngster. Your color, she counseled, has nothing to do with your worth. You are potentially as good as anyone. How good you may prove to be will have no relation to your color, but with what is in your heart and head. The right to be treated as an equal by all other men, she said, is man's birthright. Never permit anyone to treat you otherwise. Who, indeed, is a better American, a better protector of the American heritage, than he who demands the fullest measure of respect for those cardinal principles on which our society is reared?

Nana told us that there would be many and great obstacles in our paths and that this was the way of life. But only weaklings give up in the face of obstacles. Be honest and frank with yourself and the world at all times, she said. Never compromise what you know to be the right. Never pick a fight, but never run from one if your principles are at stake. Go out into the world with your head high, and keep it high at all times. In America that is increasingly possible—for Negro and white alike. That, to me, is the true meaning of American democracy.

Part 7
Black Power and Blackism

CHAPTER 24

Upheavals in the Ghettos
1967

Following the violence in Watts in August 1965, Bunche issued a statement deploring the lawlessness and madness of those engaged in rioting. The statement ended with a warning for the country to disperse black ghettos across the country or suffer future Watts-like disturbances. For his statement Bunche was widely denounced by Black Power advocates. Two years later, after deadly violence in Detroit and Newark, Bunche wrote a much longer unpublished reflection on these uprisings. Having been born in Detroit, raised in south-central Los Angeles, and a resident of the New York area, he obviously felt deeply about these events. Having been an optimist all of his life, one detects a strong streak of pessimism in his post-Watts statements. Bunche's analysis reveals what many "riot" studies would report later, that, while the actual numbers active in the violence were relatively small, most ghetto residents and many African-Americans, including Bunche, shared the bitterness expressed by the rebels. Bunche attacks the argument that they are "outsiders" or that ghetto residents have no legitimate grievances. J. Edgar Hoover's intervention is anything but reassuring, says Bunche, and he compares U.S. ghettos to South African apartheid. Such sentiments would win him no militant friends, however, because he continues to attack the Black Power movement as racist and escapist. Curiously, he states that, "in seeking Negro unity, it has the same goal as the National Negro Congress" had in the 1930s. Of course, Bunche was a cofounder of the National Negro Congress.

Ghettos today spell trouble—increasing, violent trouble. That is the harsh axiom of this day and age in American urban life. When there are no more ghettos the specter of racial uprisings will loom far less ominously if at all. In Newark and Detroit, as elsewhere, the root-cause has been the black ghetto, that is, the solid concentration of substantial numbers of Negroes only in a particular area of a neighorhood, as in Newark's Central Ward. Detroit, with 30 percent of its population Negro, is rather different, since it has no single, great ghetto (New York City has four, one of which embraces a preponderantly Puerto Rican neighborhood), but rather a sort of checkerboard population pattern, with a number of concentrated Negro neighborhoods, in the nature of "sub" or "pocket" ghettos. That is why Detroit's recent outburst affected so much of the city, with the fire bombers roaming so widely over it.

The urban upheavals sweeping American cities, large and small, today, are the products, the bitter fruits, of the urban ghettos. The ghettos, in their turn, are the ugliest, meanest, and most dangerous manifestation of American racial bias.

The blow-up, in Newark and Detroit especially, in those black days of July, were sheer, raw catastrophe—for the Negro communities, for the cities, the states, and the nation. Indeed, they could be regarded as adversities for all mankind, because when some of the species so severely degrade themselves, the total image of man suffers. The savage lawlessness of those reckless and misguided Negroes who perpetrated the outrages in Newark and Detroit has caused a sense of burning shame in many Negro citizens throughout the nation. But make no mistake about that: this sense of shame is not shared by all Negroes by any means; that shame is felt mainly by those relatively few Negroes who have escaped from the ghetto and, I suspect, very little by the great majority who are trapped in them. Many may, and I believe do, disagree with and deplore the acts of violence, particularly because the Negro communities are so hard hit, but in the ghetto shame is counteracted by bitterness. After all, the ghetto itself is the constant, over-riding shame. The ghetto breeds cynicism, and the ghetto dweller becomes callous. There are many Negroes who will have mixed emotions over what happened in Newark and Detroit. There will be others who will applaud it in their resentment against the white community in the spirit of "they had it coming," and this is the only way to make "whitey"—white America—realize how costly it is going to be henceforth to keep the Negro deprived and apart. There are angry people in the ghettos these days; some, with good reason, are very, even desperately, angry.

The Newark and Detroit outbreaks, each in its own way, were a madness, murderous exercises in futility. They achieved nothing but death and destruction: in Newark, 28 lives, hundreds injured, at least $15 million in property loss; in Detroit, 41 lives lost and a billion dollars in property loss, the highest toll ever in the saddening history of American racial violence; with untold human suffering in both cities. Also, the psychological damage to the people in these communities, white and black, is incalculable, but certainly enormous. There can be only deepest sorrow for such senseless loss of life. As usual in riots in which there is extensive gunfire, most of the dead were Negroes.

Newark and Detroit, like Watts before them, were major disasters of racial ferment, but it must be borne in mind that Watts was not the first and Detroit will not be the last. Between Newark and Watts there had been violent outbreaks, only lesser in intensity, in a score or more of our urban communities, including Cleveland, Chicago, Cincinnati, Atlanta, Buffalo, and, simultaneously, with Newark, Hartford, Connecticut, and Plainfield, New Jersey. Between the Newark and Detroit upheavals came trouble in Englewood, New Jersey, and Birmingham. Since Detroit, racial strife in varying forms and degrees has hit Grand Rapids, Chicago, Saginaw, Toledo, East Harlem, Mount Vernon, Rochester, Cincinnati, South Bend, Phoenix, and Milwaukee, and numerous other places have had disturbances. There will be, I fear, others on the list and repeaters as well.

Newark's eruption, thus, was at the time only the latest in a series of sinister warnings to this nation. How many such warnings will it take to awaken the authorities and the people of the country to the colossal, nation-wide, and intolerable danger of increasingly widespread racial strife surely in store if truly heroic measures, actions of unprecedented magnitude, are not soon taken to change radically the present course of American racial relations and the prevailing conditions of life for Negroes in this society.

The chilling warning sent out of Newark and Detroit should put all Americans who wish this country well to sober thinking about the future and about what must be done and quickly. Because first Newark and then Detroit, which is my birthplace and where I spent my boyhood, struck me so hard, I have put down here some of my reactions to and thoughts about what happened in those cities and why. They are the thoughts of a layman and an American, who is also a Negro. I speak here only for myself. I lay no claim to speak for the Negro. The views expressed, of course, are entirely personal and my own and in no way involve the United Nations, which I am privileged to serve. I indulge here in assessing and analyzing, not reporting.

There is compelling reason to focus primary attention on the ghettos for they are the source of the riots, the majority of Negroes are ghetto dwellers, and the ghettos embody all of the worst and most intolerable injustices of racial discrimination.

These urban upheavals are not, I fear, a passing epidemic. They can be suppressed, but the underlying causes will remain and in one or another form they will recur. They are a sobering and unmistakable signal for the nation that white and black Americans must find the way to live together as one people in harmony, equality, and mutual respect or this land could become unfit to live in for anyone. Twenty-one million disillusioned and potentially disaffected citizens could become a mortal cancer in the body of this society.

The bloody rioting in Newark was one more episode of racially motivated, deadly skirmishing in a developing pattern, over many years, of violent racial conflict in our urban centers. If this trend is not checked, this nation one day could find itself engulfed in all-out racial warfare, in effect, a racial civil war. In the extensive sniper fire that characterized the turmoil in Newark and Detroit, we have had a frightening look at the ominous phenomenon of determined ghetto guerrilla fighting in the brick and concrete jungles of a modern metropolis.

The skirmishing thus far in riot-torn cities has been principally between the black inhabitants of the concentrated Negro population centers and the forces of law and order. But the danger is even present that the conflict would broaden into a Cyprus-type communal warfare, that is, war between substantial numbers of the white and black communities. The whites would be motivated by fear, by resentment against what Negro action is inflicting on their cities, by an inability to comprehend the causes of such action, and by racial animosity. On their part, the Negroes would be motivated by the inevitable complex of psychological reactions to ghetto existence—frustration, hopelessness, bitterness frequently bordering on hatred against those in control and on top, rebellion against the always all-white power structure, and plain desperation. There is perhaps something akin to a suicidal impulse amongst people forced to live permanently in ghetto conditions; a "what the hell" spirit is easily aroused. The most active rioters in every city, I think, are those who really have little or nothing to lose—property, comfort, status, pride, or dignity. There is also an element of conflict of the have nots against the haves, with regard to race. Young black rioters have been known to say that they would "get those fat black cats" (well-to-do Negroes in the ghetto), as well as "whitey." The active Negro participants in riots like Newark's and Detroit's are never more than a small fraction of the total Negro population. Most of the Negro inhabitants stay indoors or are innocent onlookers. But I have no doubt that very many, if not most of them, although I do not believe that they advocate or condone resorting to violence, share the deep resentment and bitterness which the riot reflects.

It was, I suppose, the intention to prevent the possibility of Newark's ghetto uprising escalating into warfare between the white and black communities that prompted Governor Richard Hughes of New Jersey to take a strong stand against a move toward activating white vigilantes in Newark. That was a wise stand, in my view, and averted possible worse trouble. Apparently, the reported action of the mayor of Saginaw in calling on white shop-owners to stand armed guard at their places of business did not backfire, but it was a risky step.

We already know too much about the tremendous pain and cost of guerrilla warfare in Vietnam, where, we may also reflect, large numbers of Negro citizens are fighting and many have died, in numbers in each instance considerably above the ratio of the Negro in the total population. The possibility of guerrillas, guerrilla tactics, and guerrilla fighting in our cities has to be averted at any cost.

When a riot catastrophe hits a city, it is a natural impulse of civic pride to place the blame elsewhere than in the city itself and on its good citizens, black as well as white. Consequently, the tendency is for city and state officials to point the finger of blame at "outsiders" and "agitators" who allegedly come in and stir things up. This is fallacious and misleading. The outbursts in Newark and Detroit, as those in Watts and a score of other American communities in recent years, were possible, whatever the specific incidents that sparked them and whoever may have spurred them on, only because the ghetto inmates of these cities were ripe for them in their frustration, despair, and growing hostility to the white man, who is so much better off and who wields all the power in a lily-white power structure and who, in general, shuns the black man as an untouchable and who has little or no association with him when the workday is over. In other words, even if outside agitators do come in, they are able to contribute to an outbreak only because all of the makings for it are already in waiting.

Wherever and whenever racial violence explodes, there is great shock and outrage, as there should be; there is much hue and cry by public authorities, the news media, and by the public itself about the tragic loss of life, the wanton plundering and destruction of property; and a shrill clamor arises for law and order to be restored and maintained by the use of as much force as may be necessary—there are many, moved by emotion, who say the more forces and the sterner it is applied the better.

In the midst of the high emotion generated by any riot with racial overtones, there are usually at least some few voices calling for a calm consideration of the basic causes of such a sudden visitation of violence and disgrace on a city, but they are rarely heard over the din of panicky outcry, bitterness, and recrimination. The concentration is on placing blame and establishing guilt rather than seeking out and attacking causes. That this is understandable in the dire circumstances of burgeoning riots does not make the attitude any the less shortsighted and against the interests of the suffering community.

Every city seems to be caught flat-footed and in a state of utter confusion and near hysteria when severe racial violence flares up. But the plain if brutal fact is that *any* American city anywhere in the country today, having a substantial Negro population, can have this traumatic experience at any moment, and any such city can consider itself quite lucky if it escapes it. Not many are escaping it. Nevertheless, very little is being done in any city to avert such a disaster by a realistic attack on the underlying causes, while still less attention is given to how to cope with such an emergency when it occurs other than by the police, their clubs and guns, and finally by calling in the troops. City officials never seem to realize that a sure means of incitement to violence is to send large numbers of police, usually predominantly white police, into the streets of the ghetto, brandishing their clubs and guns at black people, troublemakers and bystanders alike, ordering, threatening, and herding them. The black people invariably react angrily, with taunts, rocks, and bottles, the battle is then joined with Molotov cocktails and sniper fire to follow. It must be said for the police that in such situations their position is extremely difficult. White, or for that matter, black policemen, when emotions get heated, facing an angry black mob in a ghetto area may over-estimate their danger, but they are certainly in danger. Whatever they do is apt to be considered wrong by one group or another in the city. They will be charged with being too quick or too slow; with being tough and brutal or too restrained; with provoking the trouble by unnecessary action or with failing to prevent it. In my view, police brutality undoubtedly exists and anti-Negro bias among police as well, but these evils are not the cause of race riots.

In these critical emergencies in embattled cities, the responsible officials of the state and the municipality should be expected at the least, to try to get to the bottom of the trouble, to show understanding even while being firm in their necessary determination to restore law and order, and, above all, they should scrupulously avoid any utterances which could have the effect of inflaming the situation. On this score, Governor Hughes of New Jersey and Mayor Hugh J. Addonizio of Newark make a poor impression. I do not judge them otherwise, but as I saw them at the time of the riot they left very much to be desired in their handling of Newark's tribulation.

Here, solely by way of example, some statements may be cited which I heard Governor Hughes make, or which I read that he had made, during the heat of the Newark riot. Naturally, he is a white governor in a predominantly white state, which is the case in Michigan and every other state. He knows, much too obviously and all too typically, very little about Negroes in America or the Negro constituents in his state, their special problems, their underprivilege, and their thinking and motivations. The governor has been sitting on a smoldering volcano—as his predecessor did and only by luck got off of it in time—and he has not known it—just as his predecessor probably did not know it. When the top blew off, he was severely shocked but not beyond words, and, unhappily, some of the words left to him were decidedly the wrong ones. Some of his statements, in my view, could not possibly be helpful to the nasty situation and might well be harmful in an inflammatory sense of increasing Negro resentment and bitterness toward whites, thereby heightening community tension.

I heard Governor Hughes describe the Newark tragedy as a "criminal insurrection." He said bluntly and blandly that it was fomented and carried out by Negroes who say they "hate whites" but really "hate their country." On what he based this extreme indictment he did not say. In this context, he went on to say that everyone now would have to be on one side or the other, that is, with the rioters who hate their country or with the "good guys," those who uphold law and order, a gross oversimplification of the actual situation. Thus the crying need for social justice and decency apparently, in the governor's thinking, can be ignored, in times of crisis, at least. Governor Hughes dismissed allegations of brutality by Newark police made by responsible people as "platitudes," and he denounced bitterly those who made such charges as well as anyone who spoke critically of "white courts" in which the Negro citizen could not get equal justice. The governor ridiculed any such intimation, pointing out that there are two "colored judges" in Newark, one of whom he himself had appointed. The governor, who throughout appeared as an intemperate and angry man, at one point referred to Newark's largely Negro Central Ward as a "jungle," which conveyed racist implications, whether or not intended. But he did not say why the ghetto jungle was there and who bears responsibility for its existence or that it ought to be removed. The city and state police and the state troopers, with their heavy fire power, shooting at anything that showed in a window or on a rooftop and hitting innocent people as well as culprits, approached and treated the area as though they too regarded it as a jungle.

The governor not only rejected Negro grievances as a principal factor in the riot, he seemed to assume that there are no valid Negro grievances as such. The governor, obviously having no antenna which would provide him with any sensitivity about Negro reaction to such remarks, could never understand, I am sure, the unfortunate impact his remarks would and did have on Negro listeners, and, I imagine, on informed and fair-minded white listeners as well. When I heard them, I was listening with dismay and horror to news reports of the wild, insane lawlessness being committed by Negroes in the streets of Newark. I listened with mounting shame. I was asking myself, "Why this way? Why?" And then Governor Hughes was speaking and Mayor Addonizio. The latter's main contribution on that broadcast, incidentally, was that a New York City official who was reported to have said something uncomplimentary about Newark's treatment of its Negro citizens should "keep his nose" out of Newark's affairs. The implication was clear that the governor and mayor felt that anyone who brought up the question of the disabilities of the Negro was decidedly on the wrong side. It has to be assumed, I think, that the governor did know but chose to ignore that there is a black ghetto in Newark, that in it there is bad housing, much joblessness, especially among young Negroes, and many of the other customary injustices and indignities of ghetto existence. The governor, of course, has made many statements of which I am not aware, but my shame at Negro conduct in Newark at the time was quickly mixed with dismay and fear at the attitudes revealed in such public statements by highly responsible officials in the troubled areas.

Newark, of course, has never been known for forward-looking, progressive, or even good government. Detroit was much better off in this respect and had, I think, given much more attention to the problems and needs of its Negro citizens. In his statements, at least, Governor Romney showed a better grasp and understanding of what was happening and why than did Governor Hughes; at least he did not fall into any of the traps into which Hughes literally leaped.

It is perhaps relevant to say that the black uprisings which have occurred in so many of our cities are also political calamities for governors and mayors who may have aspirations for higher political office, for an elected office-holder can never win much in the way of laurels in dealing with extremely touchy situations of this kind. Whatever the official may do or not do, or say, is almost certain to displease one important group or another.

Governor Hughes was pointing to a much too simple explanation, in my opinion, by describing the Newark outbreak as an insurrection which was inspired by a "criminal element," mainly a few hundred Negroes with former criminal records.

In its defiance of authority, what happened in Newark, and in Detroit, was an insurrection in the limited sense that, while there was a rebellion against law and its enforcement agents, there was no intent or attempt to take over the reins of government or to overthrow it. The killing, breaking, and burning that occurred were certainly "criminal," but Governor Hughes was far off the mark in attributing its inspiration to a criminal element. I may repeat that Newark's ghetto, as Detroit's and all the others, was ready to explode. All the ingredients were there. Any spark, a relatively trivial incident, could set it off. It required no plan by criminals. In fact, there appears to be no "plan" in any of these outbursts. Governor Hughes should have known this. With as many Negroes as there are in New Jersey, he should have known also that Negro impatience with continuing underprivilege is everywhere growing rapidly. There is serious and dangerous disillusionment among Negroes from the inability of the traditional methods of struggle—appeal to the courts, to the administration, and to public opinion—to achieve new break-throughs at the racial barricades. There has been enough of a slow-down in progress toward full equality to warrant the conclusion that the old methods, embodying gradualism, have run their course. The Negro's traditional patience is giving way to an increasing impatience, which finds expression in militancy. There is increasing conviction among Negroes that only militant tactics can henceforth produce results. Militancy means demands and activism, applying pressure that hurts, and unrelenting clamor. This can readily lead to defiance of authority. The line between denunciation and defiance of authority and actual rebellion against it can be instantly erased by the heated emotions generated by a single incident. That is one way riots are born. Every ghetto today, therefore, can conceive them.

On the other side of the riot coin, city, state, and national governments can be charged with near criminal neglect of a substantial segment of the population when the neglect reaches such an extent that conditions are created in which criminal elements flourish, as they do in most, and probably all, ghettos.

No matter how deep the grievances, however, they cannot excuse or justify the disgracefully criminal orgies of killing, of arson and looting, which have been taking place across the nation.

A spirit of rebellion certainly pervades the Newark-type riots. But it is a blind, unplanned, and unorganized rebellion without any clear direction or objective other than to break loose, to hit back, to get even, and maybe pick up something for nothing along the way. As the pattern of the riots unfolds, they become orgies, black people's orgies, in which they roam the streets in wild abandon, throwing off all inhibitions and restraint. At the moment of participation, the riots are, to the participants and no doubt to the onlookers as well, triumphs of liberation, of throwing off shackles, of getting out from under white domination, of saying to the white bosses and the power structure and to white people generally: you do not want us or like us, and you mistreat us, but for once you are going to know who the hell we are, where we are, and what we are going to have—or else. The police, having worked some of them over with their night-sticks and by their very presence having worked most of them up, they set out on their orgy of destruction and looting, which many of the looters see, in any case, as only getting what is coming to them from white shop-owners who gouge them. The fire bombs appear and the fires intensify the excitement. The death casualties result from the guns of the police and the troops, and a relatively few snipers. But guns and deaths do not seem to restrain the revelry, not for a while, for fear has been overcome by emotional intoxication.

The atmosphere, characteristic of the riots, is both macabre and bizarre. The mobsters, particularly the young ones, are often festive, yelling and laughing as they race along, breaking every plate glass window in sight, hurling the fire bombs, and stealing anything they can tote. They are excited, out for "kicks," and, as they become intoxicated with their new-found license, bravado, and defiance, many who have never been criminals, become increasingly dangerous. They are exhilarated with even this fleeting moment of "liberation" which they know will soon be ended.

The spirit is that of rebellion, but what quickly results from the rebellion is anarchy, which reigns until police and troops restore order, which they cannot fail to do. Then, the rebellion over, what it was against, the ghetto, stark symbol of oppression, remains, charred, broken, uglier, meaner, and more brutish than ever.

The people of the ghettos, particularly outside of the South, can see little change in their political and economic status as a result of the civil rights activity and the civil rights legislation adopted in Congress, and no gains at all in other spheres. They are still just as black, segregated tightly in their housing, their schools, their hospitals, and churches. After working hours they generally see only black people, except for the white shop-owners and the police of the ghetto. About the only inter-racial association many of them have ever had off the job is at the precinct police station and in court. People constantly segregated and discriminated against ultimately come to believe they are outside the pale and despised. They do not belong, have no chance to join the "in" group. Being always treated as mavericks they react accordingly. So far as they can see they have little to lose whatever they do.

Resentment amongst Negroes in and out of the ghetto against the treatment accorded this one-fifth of the nation's population runs very deep, and it often borders on hostility if not actual hatred for whitey. There is resentment against government at whatever level and against the country which has so much and promises so much but gives to the Negro so much less than it does to its citizens of lighter hue.

In the background of these midsummer nightmares of our cities is the unpleasant fact that the United States, North as well as South, East as well as West, is still prejudice-ridden. That is the prevailing and governing attitude in the relations between white and black citizens in the country, and such attitudes are a two-way process. For Negroes, possibly increasingly, become anti-white or at least come to regard all whites with suspicion and skepticism. This tends to be a reflex reaction, if not almost instinctive. Anyway, it is built in. The majority of whites, if asked directly, will deny that they harbor any racial prejudice against Negroes, and they are being quite honest about it. But they do, often without really knowing it, nurture prejudice. There are many whites in this society who earnestly believe that the Negro citizen should receive equal treatment, who believe that he is entitled to equality with all other citizens, in rights, opportunity, and all the rest. They will *treat* the Negro as equal, but there are precious few who will *accept* him on their own plane as a person. This is the case throughout the country, including New York City, which, after dark, is little more integrated than Jackson, Mississippi, and whose economic and political power structure is entirely white dominated with only token Negro representation. There are only a handful of Negroes in the entire city of New York who experience real integration, that is, whose contacts with their white fellowmen are on a person to person basis without thought of race. There are many occasions, of course, when a Negro or two will be deliberately sought, because it is the thing to do these days to have a token "presence" from the black side of the community.

The pace of Negro advance, I feel, has, in very recent years, slowed almost to a standstill. I think this is because the hard core of the problem has now been reached in the U.S. All of the relatively easy steps have been taken—those that cause only a minimum of inconvenience and disruption to the mores of the white community. But little more progress can now be made without a violent invasion and dislocation of those racial mores; because any significant new advances require an all-out white *acceptance* of the Negro as a person—in residential areas, in the schools, the churches, in organizations, in the power structure, in every aspect of life.

Thus, ghettos exist because there is no acceptance of the Negro and therefore no equality of white and black in the society. Therefore, there is no equality in the ghetto. Indeed, equality and ghetto are mutually contradictory. The Negro cannot help but know this as a fact of life.

The orgies of breaking and burning are not only criminal, they are indescribably stupid as well, for those mainly deprived of homes and possessions, and even their lives, are Negroes. Community spirit is no bar to this for a ghetto provides slight stimulus for community pride.

During Detroit's disaster, I had a talk with a middle-aged Negro woman who has lived in Harlem for many years, since she migrated from the Deep South. She is a housekeeper who has had limited schooling. She is deeply religious, God-fearing, church-going, and entirely honest. But she has very little good to say about white folks. She said to me:

> I feel very sorry for those poor Negroes in Newark and Detroit who are now in the street because their homes were burned down. Negroes shouldn't do that to Negroes. But I don't care what the whites lose. My grandpa told us how they used to beat us and kick us around in slavery. The white people own everything in Harlem, the stores, the apartment houses and they charge us Negroes much more than people have to pay in other parts of the city. My apartment house is an old rat-trap and the white landlord won't do anything for us. I wouldn't give a damn if the Negroes burned it down. I'd get as many of my things out as I could and the insurance company would have to pay me for the rest.
>
> Negro cops? They're worse on us than the white ones.
>
> They just do what their white bosses tell them to do.

I am quite sure that these are typical views among Negroes in the ghettos today. I have heard such utterances many times.

The breakers and burners are a minority—a violent minority within a bitter minority. They go to excesses. They break the law. But even as they burn and rob they are over-expressing in their recklessness a dissatisfaction that is burning painfully inside every Negro in the country today, inside or outside of the ghettos. I am no exception.

When these lawless sprees come to their end, what can the ghetto dwellers contemplate other than debris and charred ruins? Where are the leaders of the defiance, if there were in fact any leaders other than spontaneous exhorters? And what have they to offer to the hapless people? What can the rebellions of Newark and Detroit show as gains to compensate and comfort those great many Negro families, most of whom had no participation in the mob violence, whose homes were destroyed, who lost all their personal possessions, who are homeless, penniless, and miserable with nowhere to go? They are the real victims of the orgies; they are paying the heaviest cost of them in their misery; and no doubt they will be having some bitter second thoughts directed against those whose mad and criminal irresponsibility have put them in the street.

A struggle such as the Negro is waging, which is, in fact, a revolution in the sense that it seeks a radical change in the attitudes of people and in the

communal relations of the nation, cannot be won without great cost in disturbances, disruptions, strife, even bloodshed. But to expend effort, property, and
lives needlessly, orgies of blind and purposeless emotion, is utter madness.
Those who do this are arch enemies not only of the law but of the people and
especially of the Negro people.

Where does "Black Power" fit into the pattern of racial violence? In my
view, this extreme and racist doctrine and its advocates are symptomatic of the
condition and not the cause, not even a contributing cause of it.

Black Power is a sloganized, grossly over-simplified exploitation of the
disillusionment of Negro Americans at the severe handicaps they are still
required to endure in this society more than a century after Emancipation. By
present indications this condition, in large measure, will still prevail a century
hence.

Black Power would have neither meaning nor impact without the ghettos.
Even with them it has not attained the proportions of a movement with the
backing of any substantial part of the Negro population. Its advocates are very
vocal and mobile, and they seek maximum exposure. In general, they are long
on exhortation and sensational slogans (such as "burn, baby, burn") but they,
like the civil rights organizations which are despised by Black Power leadership, are very short on tactics and tacticians.

If the riots do signify black uprisings—insurrection, rebellion, or
revolution—in the ghettos, where are the leaders in the thick of the fray, and
who are they? One hears nothing about the leading figures among the advocates of Black Power and resort to violence being in the front ranks of the
mobs, out in front in defying the police and the troops in Newark or Detroit.
There is no great risk in threatening from Havana, Cuba, to "burn America
down" or to "wage guerrilla war in American cities."

Some of the extremists among the prominent names in the Negro racist
and separatist organizations are more adept at getting publicity for themselves
than they are at leadership in the sense of building an organization and of
formulating a program for action beyond threats and slogans. They are not
leaders in any true sense. They are *ersatz,* owing their fleeting prominence not
to anything they have accomplished but to the perverse addiction of the American press to the sensational and to its readiness to publicize extreme, absurd,
and even inciting statements by persons of no real consequences, who by
responsible standards merit no such attention. Some of these persons currently
favored by press attention have this as their main prop and without it would
quickly fall into the limbo of insignificance and be soon forgotten.

I personally cannot accept the Black Power thesis or any separatist movement because I see them as racist and escapist. I abhor racism as a dangerous
virus, whether it is spread by white or black peoples. I seek total integration,
which to me means the Negro taking his place in the very mainstream of

American life on the same plane and with the same status as every other citizen. I see this as my right, indeed, my birthright as an American, and I hold my rights to be worth fighting for. I do not intend to abandon my rights by giving up and running away from the fight. My ancestors have contributed very much to the development of this country, and therefore I have a vested interest in it that I intend to realize and protect.

There is, incidentally, nothing very new about Black Power. It has no exact definition and means very different things to different people. It is black chauvinism, as was the Marcus Garvey movement (Universal Negro Improvement Association) of the 1920s and 1930s which had a considerable escapist appeal among Negroes. It was, in fact, more exclusively black and more separatist than Black Power. Being anti-white, Black Power is also racist. In seeking Negro unity, it has the same goal as the National Negro Congress had also in the 1930s. In its separatist doctrine, it follows a course similar to that of such earlier movements as Garvey's, the National Movement for the Establishment of the 49th State, the Peace Movement of Ethiopia, and the National Union for People of African Descent, before World War II. In the same period, W. E. B. Du Bois was urging Negroes to build a black economic, political, and social structure within the walls of segregation. This was the era also in which the Communist Party in the United States was following the misguided racialist and infantile line of "self-determination for the Negro in the Black Belt."

The promise of an all-black Elysium is, of course, an escapist dream.

In America today a black ghetto in effect is any area that is characterized by a substantial concentration of black people. The particular area may be largely slum tenements; or it may have cottages and houses, as Watts has, and it may even look attractive in spots. But everywhere barely beneath the surface it is ugly and restive because its black inhabitants are acutely aware of their second-class status and treatment and why they are confined.

The riots signify a dilemma in the American scene. As President Johnson has rightly said, the society cannot tolerate the violence and lawlessness which have been occurring in American cities recently. On the other hand, what the riots and their lawless acts are saying so shockingly is that the Negro is reaching the limit of his ability to tolerate any longer the searing injustice of racial discrimination.

Given the racial situation as it is in this country today, therefore, it can be said that there is only one true measure of racial progress: the extent to which these concentrations of Negro population, that is the ghettos, are diminishing, for this is the real measure of whether advance is being made toward an integrated society. As long as the ghettos remain there is, in fact, segregation for the Negro in virtually every facet of life; except for his work, the shops, and the police station the black man is confined to an all-black society today. By that standard, the American Negro has made and is now making very little progress.

Still, it is frequently pointed out, and it is true, that there have been significant advances made by the Negro in many specific directions in this society, particularly in the years since the last World War—in civil rights generally, in employment opportunities, in eliminating the barriers of segregation in public places and institutions, in the use of the ballot as an instrument of power. It can be said, therefore, that the Negro has made progress toward achieving equality and equality of status with other citizens in the society, but what is too little understood is that the fact of this progress itself creates an ever more insistent demand for more progress. It can be said to have the force of a social axiom or law that the more progress there is toward equality by a disadvantaged people, the more insistent they will be in demanding full equality without further delay. Because of this basic condition there are live volcanoes of racial unrest all over this country in its ghettos. They have been boiling and seething for many years. They can erupt at any time, on the slightest provocation, and have been doing so recently on an unprecedented scale.

The forces of law and order are bound to get the upper hand in the ravaged areas since, when necessary, as it was in Detroit, federal troops are called in and the Negro rioters find themselves facing tanks. Then the futility of their actions is at its peak.

The announcement that the FBI, under J. Edgar Hoover, is to have an active role (and has been having) will be anything but cheering or reassuring to the Negro community in the light of Hoover's well-known narrow views on the civil rights movement and his occasional intemperate and biased castigations of some Negro leaders.

Much attention is being directed now to new efforts toward riot control. That is understandable and necessary. But it is much more necessary and far-sighted to direct primary attention to the *prevention* of riots by eliminating their causes and their breeding grounds.

The riot over, while the ruins are still burning, responsible officials turn their attention to measures necessary to a return to normal life. When the Newark eruption subsided, Governor Hughes, for example, spoke of the big job of rebuilding and rehabilitating the shattered areas of the city. That is a natural and logical thought in the circumstances, as was President Johnson's remark during the Detroit holocaust about the need to "repair the damage." If these disasters are not to be repeated, however, a much broader, bolder, and more imaginative approach will be required. To what end should a ghetto be repaired or rehabilitated: to make it a little less poor, dirty, unhealthy, crime-ridden, jobless, ignorant, and generally neglected than before it was burned down? A more shiny ghetto will be no protection against it again being reduced to ruin. It will still be all black, and its inhabitants will become ever more bitter and demanding and defiant until the achievement of a true equality in the society forces them from the modern bondage of the ghetto.

In the Union of South Africa, under the overtly racist Apartheid policy of that country, Africans are compelled by law to live in separate areas apart from white citizens which are disarmingly described as "locations." They are South Africa's black ghettos, and Africans are confined to them by force of law. American Negroes are held in their ghettos by a more insidious force than law and one more difficult to attack: racial prejudices among whites, expressed in political, economic, and social barriers.

It would be a serious mistake, I believe, to assume that it is possible to remedy the injustice done to the Negro by pouring assistance of all kinds into the ghettos. It would be in truth a backward step if authorities were to become so solicitous about the conditions of the Negro in the ghetto that the Negro becomes so dependent upon this assistance that the ghetto, in effect, would become an urban reservation—for black men rather than red. In time, assistance efforts on behalf of the Negro in the ghetto, which elsewhere may be helpful, could reach a point where diminishing returns would set in and they actually become counter-productive precisely because being in the ghetto they obstruct what should be the prime objective of equality.

I do not argue against aid to the Negro, to the poor and disadvantaged of all races. Quite the contrary, I strongly endorse all programs of that kind. But I greatly fear that such programs are only palliatives and offer no cure for the ghettos. Anti-poverty projects, more employment, better teachers and better schools, slum clearance, Head-start, and all such efforts are immediate necessities, but everyone knows that the ghettos will still be there. The danger will be there as long as the ghettos are. I must repeat that people forced to live in these racial concentrations develop a characteristic ghetto psychology of feeling "different," unwanted and despised, and this makes for a volatile atmosphere. That is to say that the menace of the ghetto stems from a state of mind as well as body. Thus, expanded assistance may help to relieve some tensions but at best can only put off the evil day of ghetto reckoning. That is the rub.

Frankly speaking, I think there is much of wishful thinking in any expectations that the Negroes of the ghetto can be generally upstanding, self-respecting, law-abiding, love-your-country-citizens when they must view everything from behind a demeaning curtain reading "you do not really belong." To be a good citizen in the ghetto, the Negro has to do it himself, by himself, and with psychological magic mirrors.

I agree heartily with the goal stated by President Johnson in his television address on July 27 about the riots when he said that "We seek peace that's based on one man's respect for another man, and upon mutual respect for law." These are the obviously essential goals in our society. But the corrosive soil of the ghettos into which black citizens are herded is not at all congenial to the cultivation of any kind of respect among its inhabitants, including self-respect. What, for example, is the situation with regard to the national day of prayer on July 30 proclaimed by the president in that same address—in itself a highly commendable step. But on that day of prayer most of the Negro citizens who prayed were praying by themselves all over the nation in their all-black churches in their all-black neighborhoods within the society-inflicted walls of segregation. As they prayed, they could and no doubt did reflect that, in most churches over the land, Negro worshipers are not welcome and their entry is forcibly barred to many. They could reflect, in fact, that the American church is still the most segregated institution in the country and thereby proclaims to the Negro his unacceptability in the society even in worship. It is only the exception from the practice in this country when white and Negro citizens kneel together in prayer to a God that is supposed to be common to all.

The conclusion, therefore, in my view, is inescapable that the only solution to the intolerable outbreaks of the ghettos is to eliminate the ghettos— break them up, disperse their black populations, draw white peoples into the areas by deliberate attractions in housing, institutions, businesses, and other features. A radical social surgery is required to relieve our urban communities of the malignancy of the black ghettos. The prognosis calls for surgery, not slow treatment.

Money alone, in whatever amount, will not suffice to heal the affliction of the ghettos. Direction and goals are the decisive factors. Full equality is the clear goal, but it must be recognized that the ghettos are the most stubborn obstacles blocking further advance toward the goal. In my view, *ghetto* should become a hated word in our usage, and we should make it obsolete as quickly as humanly possible. I am sure that we will have to rue many a day if we do not.

Two years ago, at the time of the tragedy of Watts, I sounded a warning and reached a conclusion which subsequent events have confirmed and which, therefore, are even more valid today. At that time I said, *inter alia:*

> The ominous message of Watts, I fear, for all America, is that it has produced, raw and ugly, the bitterest fruit of the black ghetto. Every city in this country, if it has a substantial Negro population, can experience a similar tragedy at any time. . . . The root cause is already all too clear— had Watts not been a ghetto of unhappy, insecure and restive black folk there would have been no rioting there. There is but one remedy: city, state and national authorities must quickly show the vision, the determination and the courage to take those bold—and costly—steps necessary to begin the dispersal of every black ghetto in this land.

There are many valid questions about the roots, many "whys" that need to be answered, and the president expects his national commission to find the answers. There is one question, however, which is more pressing than any and which only high governmental authorities—the president, the governors and mayors—can answer and which need not await a commission's inquiry: "Why is there not the vision, courage and determination to meet the challenge of the ghettos head on, to take at least the initial steps necessary to set in motion the process leading to a co-ordinated decision, policy, and program jointly conducted and financed, to eliminate the black ghettos, to disperse their black populations, to resettle them, to achieve physical integration in this society?"

The elimination of black ghettos in the cities of the nation, naturally, could be accomplished only with tremendous effort and at staggering cost. It would require a concerted, determined, and imaginative program of action, with a pooling of resources for the task by city, state, and national governments. But, great as it might be, the cost in effort and dollars would be far less than the cost for even a short period of the war in Vietnam or the cost of placing a man on the Moon, and it would be small compared to the cost of some more billion dollar riots; moreover, lives would be saved rather than taken. I would like to hope that no cost will be regarded as too great to save American cities from becoming racial battlegrounds.

CHAPTER 25

The Black Revolution
1968

From the outright hostility to Black Power expressed by Bunche in the mid-1960s, he moves to a position of some ambiguity in his 1967 statement on Detroit and Newark. This unfinished 1968 statement fully embraces the Black Power movement and links the early National Negro Congress to it. Although Bunche finds many of the current Black Power leaders as having too much rhetoric and too little substance, he finds that "Blackism" promotes the newly developing pride in ethnic identity and that it is good for any people to look back with pride and gratitude on their origins and ancestry. What accounts for this remarkable turnaround in Bunche's thinking on race? In the first place, Bunche had instilled in him at a young age a race pride and confidence that he probably took for granted in others. As a young social scientist, he saw the artificiality of race as a scientific concept but neglected its emotional and organizing appeal. Relying on science and education to overcome the prejudice of white Americans, he (along with Myrdal) thought it best to downplay any type of Blackism in pursuit of the larger goal of integration. The failure of the civil rights movement to fully integrate blacks into the mainstream of American society led Bunche (along with King and others) to reassess the permanence of racism. When he confronted this institutional rather than individual form of racism, the only rational response was a form of Blackism.

[begun on August 20, 1968]

This is about the black man in the United States and the revolution he has mounted—the black revolution. It would be more accurate to say the revolution he has been forced to mount because of rampant racism in contemporary America. The American Negro is a familiar subject in the U.S. and much is known about this minority group of 22 million. But there is very little knowledge or understanding of the comparatively recent phenomena of the "black man," of "black people," and the black people's revolution. This is the country's greatest domestic problem. No other is so difficult, so stubborn, so challenging, or so fraught with danger. The primary concern here, therefore, is with black Americans, their actions, attitudes, aspirations, their disillusionment, and, above all, their increasing rejection of the established ways, the establishment, and the American system itself. In other words, the subject is Blackism, which is the darker side of the coin of Americanism. Unhappily, for the tranquillity of the country in the years ahead, these two *isms* are rapidly becoming antithetical.

Nowadays, in my "urban core," which is the latest terminology for the black ghetto, very many of the black young of all age groups and economic levels, non-militants as well as militants, and not a few of the older generation, will readily and frankly assert their loss, in varying degree, of faith in the ideals and promises of the American society and in the American system. There will be found much hesitation about acclaiming the country or even identifying with it. The emphasis in identification is on black, with black, and, unavoidably, with black against white.

Much more than a credibility gap, this disenchantment with America, which to the black man means a white-dominated America, is a widening chasm between the two major population masses in the society.

The only way to reverse prevailing fateful trend toward separatism and two sharply divided conflicting societies in this land is by a firm national commitment to move black Americans from the periphery of American economic and political and social life into its mainstream. That cannot be done by repeating old promises and slogans or by inventing new ones, but only actual fulfillment of promises, by action and immediate, concrete results.

This will require what would be, in effect, a plan of battle, the careful but determined and urgent preparation of action, nationwide in scope, and the marshaling and allocation of resources, human and fiscal, designed to eliminate completely the barriers which separate black from white in the society, which block black Americans from full participation in it, which divide the society racially and create disunity and racial conflict.

September 24, 1968

"Etiquette" in race relations is just about a thing of the past in these days. During slavery, the black man employed a protective code of expression—the humility, subservience, and flattery he purveyed at the "Big Gate" when talking to "Massa" and whites in general, was in sharp contrast to the ridicule, scorn, and bitterness spoken in the huts and cabins in his own circle. This was a survival technique. Following this and until quite recently, there were many Negroes who carefully avoided saying anything that might be offensive to whites when in their presence. Thus a frank discussion of the racial situation between blacks and whites was relatively rare. The "good" Negro, and there were many of these, would not speak out bluntly. There are not many "good" blacks today. Indeed, it has become fashionable for the black man to speak out, to be blunt, to shock, to "pour it on whitey." And whitey takes it, at times with understanding, at other times with resentment.

It is today tougher to be black in the American society than at any period since abolition. That may seem anachronistic in view of the long and persistent struggle that has been waged to achieve equality of treatment and status for black Americans in this society and the apparent fruits of that struggle in the progress that has been made in many directions. But now the Negro has reached the critical crossroad in the society, and he is forced to make the most fateful decision ever. He has to decide now whether there is still any real prospect, indeed, any possibility that, within the foreseeable future, the black minority which constitutes more than one-tenth of the nation's total population, can be accepted in full as an equal partner in all phases of the life of the society, can find a place in the society's mainstream. That is to say, is integration in the full sense a realizable goal, or is it only a dream that will always remain illusory, except in the realm of tokenism?

Even true believers of integration like myself, all of the firm advocates of it in the black segment, are assailed by unavoidable doubts these days.

Black Power is not a new concept. The need for unity of aim and effort by black Americans is as old as the black man's struggle. The National Negro Congress of the 1930s was, in this sense, a "Black Power" movement. Today's Black Power demand however, is stronger, more insistent, and more widely based, and therefore gives new strength to the development of black unity.

November 2, 1968

Revolutionary situations such as that in which the black American now finds himself provide a fertile field for leadership. Old leadership, in general, finds it difficult to keep up with the rapid changes of the times and becomes increasingly outdated and scorned by the new radicals, particularly of the new generation. There are opportunities for new leaders and a good many emerge, mainly of local stature and influence. Some are dedicated to the cause, others are self-seeking, whose ambitions far exceed their abilities. Many are only self-proclaimed. Few spring from the people. Their tactics, of course, vary according to their earnestness and intelligence. Demagoguery, of course, has a field day. The surest appeal, the unfailing grand stand play, of course, is to curse the white man and idolize the black.

With some, this will take the form of a shouting, belligerent, and vulgar imprecation. With others, more sophisticated, it will be more subtle. But in either case, it is sure fire with black listeners and with conscience-stricken elements in the white population as well.

A good many black Americans these days are giving expression to a newly found pride in race and ancestry by African type hairdos for men and women, by wearing African dress and jewelry, Mau Mau jackets, and paying lip-service to Africa. These manifestations would be more meaningful and impressive if they were accompanied by an active concern about the tragic plight of the millions of black people in the Union of South Africa under Apartheid and of many other millions in southern Rhodesia, Angola, and Mozambique. Why is there no Black Power pressure of any significance applied to the U.S. government to take a much stronger stand against racism and colonialism in these countries? Stokeley Carmichael, of course, has married Miriam Makeba, but this is a case of the oppressed leading the oppressed.

In this regard, it is to be noted that being a black man in the U.S. today is less a matter of actual skin color than of a state of mind. Being black is thinking black. But not for anyone. No white man can become a black man because, in fact, no white person can ever think black, lacking the indispensable racial background and experience to do so. But every Negro can become a black man if he begins to think black. By this definition, certainly, not all Negroes have as yet become black men, by any means.

   This, incidentally, is a quite different line from that taken by the Marcus Garvey movement here in the 1920s and 1930s. They were true color chauvinists—only black or near black skins were acceptable in their ranks.

   Is it sound to speak of a "black revolution"? I have no doubt about it. But there is little comprehension or realization among white Americans that in this restive and revolution-prone world, a revolution is under way in their own country—all over the country. It will become much more severe and quite possibly more violent.

   What has long been known as the struggle of the Negro, and in more recent times as the civil rights movement, has now gained the quality and dimension of a revolution. The nature of the demands of the black ghetto dweller, calling for radical and fundamental changes; the widening support for those demands among black people throughout the country; the insistency of those demands by supporters, many of whom are prepared to employ tactics of violence and some of whom have already done so, all signify revolution— black revolution.

   Blackism can be racist, of course, a counter black racism to white racism. But it is not by any means synonymous with racism. It embraces the newly developing pride in ethnic identity, which, inevitably may at times translate into exaggerated pride or color and racial chauvinism. But no one can deny that it is good for any people to look back with pride and gratitude on their origins and ancestry. As the Association for the Study of Negro Life and History began urging—years ago under the [sic] dedicated black Americans had no reason to be hesitant about looking back. Too many of them were reluctant to do so because of their misguided shame about the epoch of slavery and because school text books, history books, scholars, and fiction writers alike; press and periodicals; Hollywood; every medium of education and information rarely gave even a hint that black people had any past of achievement, culture, or civilization worthy of mention. The white man's well-springs were exalted and glorified. Those of the black man were ignored if not derided.

In a racist society, in which white men dominate, exercise all the control, while rejecting and discriminating against black men, Blackism—exalting blackness, thinking black—becomes an essential defensive reaction, it comes to be identified with survival.

The newly invigorated pride on one's background leads to many developments, including new vogues among black youth, such as African hairdos, African garb, distinctive costumes such as the Mau Mau jackets. Nowadays, if a black girl's hair is too "good" (in the pre-Blackism sense) to make up into a satisfactory fuzzy-wuzzy African do, a "hep" hairdresser can make her hair "bad" enough (in the pre-Blackism sense) for the purpose, or she can readily purchase an African wig made up of really bad hair.

Revolutions change styles and fashions as well as systems.

This is an exercise in thinking about "the" problem. My sole purpose in these pages is to try to put down some of my thoughts on the crisis of race in America, or, at least, some aspects of it and to iron out any kinks in that thinking. [Unreadable]

One can become frightened in the [unreadable]. That is to say, thinking seriously about the implications and potentialities about the [unreadable] present dangers in the racial situation. Frightened about the prospects for the black American. Frightened, indeed, about the future of this country. War frightened, in fact—not about war in Vietnam, but war here.

In my view, the United States can pull through this crisis and avert domestic disaster only by a huge amount of heavy thinking by a vast number of people, by good sense and goodwill in tremendous volume, by determination and resources on a war-scale. Indeed, it is a war, a domestic war, that must be waged—against racism, against rejection, against poverty, against slums, against the betrayal of the rich promise of America, inexcusably unfulfilled for black men.

I think it should be stated clearly here that I speak for no one but myself and that I make no claim to be an expert on the problem of race in America. I have no position of leadership in the black community. But I have had 64 years of living in this society as a Negro, and today I identify with my people, with black people. I have participated militantly over the years in the Struggle of the

Negro, in the civil rights movement, and today I am a partisan in the black revolution, as every black American must, unless he is blind or craven and unworthy of his birthright.

I identify, as I have said, with black people. I can think black, but not exclusively black. I eschew racial chauvinism and racism. I would prefer to live in a fully integrated society, if this is possible. I intend to devote some attention in these pages to whether it is or is not possible. Most definitely, I do not live in such a society now.

I am, admittedly, in a privileged position. At my age and in my line of work, I do not experience the discriminations, humiliations, and the degradations which are so intolerably a part of the daily life of most black people, and constitute so formidable a handicap. My dignity as a man is seldom assaulted. I harbor no ambitions which would be thwarted because of race. I do not live in the ghetto. I have free and wide contact with all people, white as well as black. In effect, I do not any longer *feel* the color bar, personally, in a tangible sense. But I feel it strongly, nonetheless, because I know it is there, because I daily see its brutalizing impact on most members of my group, because I have always had sense enough to know that, as long as black people anywhere in this country are discriminated against, deprived of opportunity, rights, and dignity solely because of race, there is no escape from the stigma of race for any member of the group, no matter how well off he may seem to be or think himself to be. When any black men are rejected by the dominant white society, all are rejected. No black man should have any illusions about that. There is a decisive difference between being accepted genuinely, as an equal, and being tolerated for some reason, such as recognition of ability and need for it, a minimal bow to a pricking conscience or a missionary-spirit compassion.

The demand and struggle of the black American has been and continues to be not only with liberation from racially motivated oppression and injustice but for human dignity and respect—respect by others and self-respect.

I am not bitter, nor am I angry. I rely only on reason, candor, and truth. They stand firmly enough without support from emotion. I am convinced that on the problem of race most Americans hide the truth or, more accurately, hide from it.

What can be said realistically about a complete separation of the races in this country? I do not know how many there are, but there are certainly black voices which seek a complete separation and mean it. That is, a separate all-black nation which would be the home (it might be more accurate to say a haven) of black Americans, owned, controlled, and run by them. That is to say, a state and government of, for, and by the black people.

That is the idea, born of a despair about the black American ever being accepted equally and treated decently in a predominantly white society in which all aspects of life are controlled by and for whites and which is going to remain that way in the foreseeable future. It is an expression of the complete loss of hope and faith in the American society, its promise and its dream of equality and integration, motivated also by animus against whites and a virulent black racism.

That is the idea. But the crucial practical question is: where is the land to be found on which to establish the black state, and how is it to be obtained? Some black separatist spokesmen have made some fanciful statements about this, moralizing about what this society owes to the black man, demanding that one or more states of the Union be ceded for this purpose. But I doubt if anyone has ever spoken in these terms with conviction that there was any real possibility that this could come to pass. There is, of course, no sensible or even plausible answer to the crucial question implicit in total separation.

What is left, then, is partial separation—black Americans, already largely separated by reason of the black ghetto communities, will demand an increasing degree of local autonomy through insistence on decentralization. But it is painfully obvious that the black communities can never be economically viable except on an intolerably low standard of living as compared with the white community. Bedford-Stuyvesant can never hope to come close to Manhattan in terms of wealth, employment, and other opportunities. Therefore, the black American, under partial separation, will continue to have his economic life in the white sector. The practical result of this in time will be an American version of Apartheid.

CHAPTER 26

Race and Alienation
1969

The newfound importance Bunche gives to race is reflected in this speech given at the Fifth East-West Philosophers' Conference in Honolulu, Hawaii. In many ways this speech represents the closing of a circle. He was back in the multicultural West again talking about philosophy—his first love. As he had as a young UCLA student, he sees race as a fundamental and all-pervasive problem. Race, not class, is the decisive element in the conflict between white and nonwhite peoples. Vietnam, says Bunche, "has very deep racial implications," and the unwillingness of the United States and United Kingdom to use force in liberating southern Africa is directly related to race. While he continues to see the core of the problem as the American dilemma separating theory and practice, his analysis of the practice is as radical as that of any Black Power advocate. Calls for "law" and "order" must be replaced with calls for "justice."

One might wonder a bit as to why the broad theme of alienation chosen for this Fifth East-West Conference should be limited to "modern" man only. It might well have involved man's alienation experience throughout his history. True as this is, however, justification for the concentration on contemporary times is readily found in the stark fact that acute alienation in an era of unlimited nuclear destructive power direly threatens the continued existence of man on earth.

It would seem that alienation in its various manifestations has been a prime trait of man as far back as knowledge about the species goes. In all of his thousands of years here man has lived in a constant state of alienation, in his relations with nature, with his fellow men, with younger generations, with himself, his gods, his beliefs, ideas, and values. Indeed, modern man himself is now responsible for an incredible alienation of his environment by polluting it to such an extent that something akin to global suicide is in prospect if heroic measures are not soon taken.

This, however, is not at all to endorse the Hobbesian view of the natural life of man as poor, nasty, and brutish, or to say that man is innately evil or warlike and that wars are therefore inevitable. I feel sure that man will still be here thousands of years hence. For I believe that, despite so much wickedness and evil design in the world, man is essentially good, that his capacity for fellowship, for compassion, and for self-sacrifice need have no limits, and that such a conclusion can be amply documented. It is not impossible for man to achieve a life on this planet of harmony and peace rather than discord and war. The United Nations has its being in this belief; it charts the way to peace.

But the road to such a state of human affairs is long and tortuous, and the grim and grisly evidences are all around us on a constant and, indeed, increasingly extensive alienation: man's inhumanity to man (so frequently cited as to have become a cliché); his penchant for ruthlessness and disregard for human life; deep-seated prejudices and bigotries, racial and religious; the widespread disenchantment with and alienation from the established order and the establishments. I may repeat that man will survive, but he has much to overcome in himself in order to do so. The best answer to dangerous alienation, I think, is change for the good, progress.

Man's propensity for dispute and conflict is a world-wide phenomenon. It has both international and national aspects and implications.

I have chosen tonight to consider race and color as a major, possibly a preponderant, factor in alienation.

First off, may I explain that I have made this choice not because of my own racial identity, but primarily because I come from mainland United States, where the growing alienation of the black American is the outstanding domestic problem and becomes ever more severe and dangerous. The implications of this, not only for my country, but for the world, are profound and far-reaching. In my view, the increasing estrangement of one-eleventh of the American people—the black citizen—and the divisiveness and corrosiveness of the American race problem, threaten the security of the United States far more than Vietnam.

Secondly, I come from the United Nations, where it is apparent that, on the international side, race is all-pervasive and often decisive and presents a formidable obstacle to that harmony amongst peoples that is essential to a world at peace, which is the main objective of the United Nations. To be accurate, I should say that it is not race as such that I shall talk about, but that perversion in social attitude called "racism," and the strains, hostilities, animus, and alienation which it generates.

There is, I fear, a steady tendency toward polarization of the white and non-white peoples of the world which can lead to ultimate catastrophe for all. I should explain that I use *white* and *non-white* entirely in their popular connotations. In my view, in the world today polarization of races and their alienation are virtually synonymous. The factors of race and color, directly or indirectly, figure prominently in almost all of the vital world issues and the dangerous confrontations.

There are, of course, alienations and conflicts among white people and among non-white people. The pages of history are replete with accounts of alienations between white peoples which had their most violent expressions in World Wars I and II. Among non-white peoples, conflict situations such as those in Nigeria, Malaysia, and between India and Pakistan over Kashmir have been inheritances from the colonial past. Mainland China has alienated many peoples, white and non-white alike.

Alienations of peoples, expressed in suspicions, fears, and conflicts, have led to the production of the monstrous nuclear devices. In this context, disarmament, the complete elimination of nuclear weapons and severe limitation of conventional arms, is indispensable to a secure future for mankind; "limited" nuclear disarmament is a delusion. Thus, the fateful alternative confronting mankind is alienate and perish or harmonize and survive.

Racism, certainly, is the foremost obstacle to harmonization of peoples; it is the antithesis of harmony, being alienation at its emotional worst.

The affluent peoples of the world, who are also the giants in development, trade, industry, technology, and military power, are mostly white. But the white peoples themselves are only a minority in world population, and each year they represent a smaller percentage of the whole. A 1967 United Nations estimate of the populations of the world gives a figure of 3,420,000,000 people. Of these, 1,068,000,000, or 31.2 percent, were white. A decade earlier, the white percentage had been 33 percent. The non-white percentage in 1967 thus was 68.8 percent.

Since Roman times at least, the leadership of the world, political and economic, has been controlled almost entirely by its white minority. The white nations tended to dominate the world and to have the only effective voices in its councils. But now that picture is changing markedly. The non-white nations, having for the most part only recently emerged from the suppression and subjection of colonialism, now have, numerically at least, the strongest position in world councils and their voices are ever more demanding. Wealth and military power, however, are still overwhelmingly on the white side. A majority of the member states of the United Nations, including the most populous member [*sic*], are non-white.

It is reliably estimated that on the basis of present growth rates, by the end of the twentieth century, that is within 30 years, the total population of the world will approximate 6,565,000,000 people. That explosive increase will be predominantly non-white, and the white minority, relatively, will then have become almost tiny; not to mention how diminutive it will be a century from now, in 2070, when projections foresee a world population total of 25,524,000,000 at current growth rates. One may already envisage with foreboding the prospect before long of a non-white backlash on a global scale.

Only those who have been the victims of racism can know the severity of the wounds it inflicts, and the depth of the resentment of the wounded. Such wounds—indignities, humiliations, insults, and deprivals [*sic*]—never fully heal.

I do not predict, nor do I like even to think about, the prospect of world-wide conflict between white and non-white peoples. But this cannot be excluded. In fact, there are not a few who regard war between the races as inevitable, some of whom, indeed, hold that it has already begun. Among militant black voices in my own country, for example, there are some who talk of a "third force" in the world which would be an alliance of all the non-white peoples, including the American blacks.

The threat of overpopulation is one of mankind's most critical problems. Efforts to control population growth, which is greatest among the developing peoples, mainly non-white, are handicapped to some extent by suspicions that such efforts are motivated and initiated by affluent white societies as one means of maintaining their dominance.

The world, unfortunately, is not yet nearly alert or responsive enough to the population crisis, its complexities and its dangers, nor to the prospect of increasing racial alienation implicit in that crisis.

The population explosion brings in its train a crisis of inadequate food supply. Predictions have been made in responsible quarters that, as early as 15 or 20 years from now, conditions of severe famine will develop in a number of areas of heavy population. The peoples who will suffer and die from starvation will be mainly non-white. The intolerable plight of great masses of these people, who have known for so long only misery as their way of life, may then reach the desperation stage and become unbearable to the point of violent reaction. This hostility almost inevitably would be directed in the end against the affluent white few.

There is no bigger obstacle to the building of solid foundations for secure peace than the great and dangerously widening gap between the haves and have-nots of the world. The affluent haves are few; the poverty-ridden have-nots are very many and are rapidly increasing. Here again the race factor looms prominently. The haves are very largely white; the have-nots are predominantly non-white.

Despite heroic international efforts to reverse the trend and narrow the gap by technical assistance to the developing states and by other means, the gap continues to widen ominously due to striking and continuous technological advances in the highly industrialized states.

In other words, a non-white society is a poor society, with a very few exceptions, of which Japan as a developed country is the most notable. The poor or developing countries do show advances in productivity, national and per capita income. But the developed countries enjoy higher rates of growth and income and thus become ever "richer" in relation to the developing lands.

During the period 1960–67, for example, the total product of the developed countries increased by 44 percent, for an average annual rate of growth of the total product of 5.5 percent. Population in the developed countries during this period increased by 9 percent, resulting in a seven-year growth of per capita product of 52 percent for an average annual per capita increase of 5 percent.

In the developing countries, total product during the same period increased by 36 percent, for an average annual rate of growth of the total product of 4.4 percent. However, the population increase during these years in the have-not countries was 17 percent, or almost double that of the have countries. This brought down the per capita product increase for the seven-year period to 17 percent, for an average annual per capita growth rate of only 2.2 percent, or less than half the 5 percent figure of the developed group.

Both the percentage increase and the rates of growth are lower for the developing countries than for the developed ones, both in absolute and in per capita terms. Thus, the economic gap has continued to widen between the white haves and the non-white have-nots, and the relative position of the latter has continued to deteriorate. It may be noted that there have been several instances of relatively underdeveloped economies which in recent years have achieved high rates of growth, actually reducing the gap as far as they are concerned. Among these have been Romania, Pakistan, Iran, Turkey, and Mexico.

In the 15 poorest countries of the world, all of which, to be sure, are non-white, the per capita national incomes, in U.S. dollars, for the year 1967, ranged from a low of $42 for the Maldive Islands and Upper Volta, to $75 for Haiti. In this list, the figure for Ethiopia was $60, for Nigeria $72, and for India $73.

In striking contrast, the per capita national income for 1967 in the United States was $3,303; in France $1,738; in the United Kingdom $1,560; in the Federal Republic of Germany, $1,512; and in the Union of Soviet Socialist Republics $1,069.

What counts most, naturally, is how this gap between have and have-not peoples affects human needs, how it relates to the conditions of life for the individual in the less developed societies. That is to say, what chance is there for the hundreds of millions of individuals in such lands to aspire to a life that is worthy of a human being—enough to eat, have decent housing, adequate education, and medical care, a normal life expectancy, and the opportunity to make the most of individual talent and ability.

Some of the basic statistics about conditions of life in the poor lands are sobering.

Over 60 percent of the people in the poor countries are chronically undernourished, with diets containing about one-third of the protein and two-thirds of the calories which are regarded as essential to the maintenance of health and productivity in a developed or industrial society. Children, especially, are victims of the conditions of life in these societies. In many of them, half of the children will die in infancy from malnutrition, while more than half of those who survive infancy will be physically and mentally stunted throughout the rest of their lives.

In a great many developing countries, average life expectancy is 40 years or less, due in large measure to malaria, tuberculosis, cholera, bilharziasis, and many other endemic diseases.

About half of the populations of the developing countries are functionally illiterate, that is, unable to read the simplest instructional material. The odds are 2 to 1 against a child receiving any education at all, and 10 to 1 against his going to college. A majority of the teachers have themselves had no schooling beyond the elementary level.

Even in the poorest lands, of course, there are some, usually a very few, who manage in one way or another to prosper and live well.

The unhappy but inevitable conclusion from all this is that the "civilization" which characterizes the planet earth is enjoyed mainly by a white minority of its inhabitants. How long can this endure?

In the international sphere, colonialism in its various manifestations has been the major cause of alienation and of estrangement between white and non-white peoples. The colonial system in its modern version, implicitly arrogant and self-serving, was instituted and perpetuated chiefly by self-righteous and superior-minded Europeans. Its positive achievements notwithstanding, colonialism's evil legacies will bedevil the world for years to come. It has been the cause of many wars since it was instituted and is the direct source of the major conflict situations, all of them having racial aspects, now confronting the world: Vietnam, the Middle East, Nigeria, Southern Rhodesia, and Kashmir.

Division along racial lines and alienation of races is the very essence of the institution of colonialism. I doubt if this ever has been more clearly and forcefully stated than by, surprisingly enough, John Foster Dulles in the course of a speech in October 1947 to the Fourth Committee of the United Nations General Assembly. Mr. Dulles said:

> . . . Now, Mr. Chairman, . . . I want to make my position perfectly clear. I believe, the United States Delegation believes, that the old colonial system should be done away with—it is obsolete, if indeed it ever had justification, but it certainly has no justification for the future. It has borne some very evil fruit primarily in that it has put people of one race to rule over peoples of another race and that has been very bad for both races. . . . I can't find words to express myself sufficiently strongly on my belief that that system must come to an end and it must be liquidated in a prompt and orderly way. . . .

There are no more abrasive issues in the United Nations than those involving racial injustice, and among those the colonial issue is foremost. After all, a majority of the 126 members of the United Nations—the members from Africa, Asia, and the Caribbean particularly—have had comparatively recent experience with colonial subjection.

There is a natural tendency among the member states of the United Nations to form regional blocs to represent common interests. Of these, the African and Asian blocs are numerically the largest. On racial and colonial questions, although not on others, they enjoy solidarity and unity and generally vote together. Debates at the United Nations on such issues as Southern Rhodesia, South West Africa, the Portuguese colonies, and Apartheid generate much heat and emotion. Very often, the voting on resolutions on such issues is near unanimity, the dissenting members being the Union of South Africa and Portugal.

With abundant reason, non-white peoples tend to be acutely sensitive about matters of race and color. It follows that the suspicions and resentments arising from racial consciousness and experience often complicate, obstruct, and frustrate efforts of the United Nations and other bodies in political, economic, social, and assistance fields.

It bears repeating that in all international affairs today the race factor is omnipresent. For example, the question would seem entirely valid, and now and then I hear it raised, whether the People's Republic of China would not long ago have been admitted to the family of nations and seated in the United Nations if the Chinese were not "yellow" people—and so many of them. It is not in the interest of the peace of the world to refuse membership in the international community to and thus to make a maverick of a nation of more than 700 million people.

All of the other communist states, including Albania, all having white populations, have long since been taken into the community of nations. The essence of the "yellow peril" bogey survives, even if the phrase itself is now unfashionable.

The Vietnam War has very deep racial implications. There, the United States is fighting yellow men who are also considered communists. This makes it rather easy for Americans to rationalize their involvement and to broadcast daily the number of those despised little yellow men that the American and South Vietnamese forces have killed. The derogatory name Americans give to their South Vietnamese opponents is "Viet Cong," which literally means, I understand, "yellow bandits." Would the United States be engaged in that war if the North Vietnamese and the National Liberation Front were white?

In this regard, it has racial significance, no doubt, that there is no disposition on the part of the United States (or the United Kingdom) to envisage the use of force, or even to apply strong measures short of force, to liberate the overwhelming majority black population of Southern Rhodesia from the ruth-

st tyranny of a small white minority led by an arrogant and shameless
ʒot, Ian Smith. The United Kingdom in recent years, however, has
_____ ... possible to send British troops to Kenya, Tanzania, and Anguilla.

The black Americans who have fought or are asked to fight in Vietnam
find themselves in a paradoxical position. They must employ every violent
means at hand to maim and kill the enemy—North Vietnamese and the South
Vietnamese enrolled in the National Liberation Front. This is to protect the
rights and freedom of 17 million South Vietnamese, a considerable number of
whom obviously resent and resist American presence in their country. On the
other hand, there are 22 million black Americans whose constitutional rights
are being violated flagrantly and persistently. But the black veteran from Vietnam, like all other blacks, is not permitted to do very much about that. He
cannot "disturb the peace" and must respect "law and order," although white
citizens are not compelled to respect the law of the Constitution where its
application to black citizens is concerned. The black veteran, along with all
others, may in some places even be denied permission to demonstrate or to
march peacefully in protestation against racism and racial injustice. The government requires black citizens to fight for the South Vietnamese but will not
even empower the issuance of a cease and desist order to white employers who
flagrantly deny employment to black men and women solely on grounds of
race. That, in the eyes of the senator from Abraham Lincoln's state, Everett
Dirksen, would be intolerable "harassment" of business.

The estrangement between white and black Americans intensifies and
becomes increasingly disruptive and dangerous. It could reach catastrophic
proportions.

The core of the problem is the glaring disparity between the theory and the
practice of American democracy. The attitudes and actions of white Americans
do not, and many begin to feel cannot, correspond to the ideals and promises of
the American Constitution and system. This is not merely because some Americans are hard-bitten racists who oppose bitterly and openly the very idea of
integration and equality in rights and opportunities for the black American. The
harsh fact is that most white Americans, many without realizing it, harbor in
themselves, as an inheritance from the society's history and mores, some
degree of racism or bigotry. This is reflex and sub-conscious bigotry, which
may become readily recognizable only in the face of some stern personal
challenge. One current symptom of this is the inclination of a good many "fair-
minded" Americans, including TV and radio media, to show much sympathetic
interest in separatism and pro-separatist voices. Many other whites, finding
their consciences whipping them, are gullible and susceptible to outlandish
black demands such as the claims for "reparations."

Thus, there has been all along in the American society a built-in and
comfortable complacency about the unequal status of and the injustices to the

black, second-class fellow citizens. It has been enough to be able to say that equality and integration will one day be achieved here and that progress is being made. That, until recently, could always be counted upon to avert acute trouble. That is no more the case. That is no longer enough for most black Americans. These black men, however involuntarily at first, have been on the mainland shores since the beginning of the country. With far less reward than has gone to their white fellow countrymen, the blacks have given their labor, their talent, their loyalty, blood, and lives in the building and protection of the American nation. They have made also distinct and distinctive cultural contributions to the American society.

In more than 300 years in the land, nearly 300 years since the adoption of the Constitution, and more than a century after the Emancipation Proclamation, the black American is still deprived of full citizenship, is still excluded from the mainstream of American life, is still the victim of gross social injustice by a white majority in which racism is widely prevalent.

Now, after a long-enduring faith and patience without parallel, I think, in human history, the black citizen has lost his patience—and his fear—and is, I am afraid, also losing his faith in the American establishment and system insofar as their promises to him are concerned. He is demanding, not appealing, nowadays, and his demands begin to take unexpected courses—courses which could only be born out of profound frustration and complete disillusionment.

It is said by some that there is already under way in the United States a black revolution. Others deny it. Certainly, such a development springing from the obvious inadequacy of the civil rights struggle, and a feeling of futility and desperation, cannot be excluded. In any case, the insistent demands of the black American today, the growing militancy behind those demands, the increasing involvement of ordinary black men and women in them, and the radical changes in attitudes and practices and even in the structure of the society required by them, are of the nature and dimension of a revolution. Nonviolence has been the traditional tactic of the black American in carrying on his struggle, but an increasing number of black people, especially in the ranks of the young, see violence as an essential weapon in desperate circumstances and scorn the non-violent, Gandhian counsel of leaders such as the late Martin Luther King. The majority of American blacks, however, still look upon integration and not separation as the desirable goal and believe in a non-violent struggle. However, last week's announcement of the national government's dismaying new policy of relaxing the deadline on school desegregation compliance by allowing "exceptions," is anything but reassuring to every black American.

Some of the leading voices in the "black revolution" seek to orient the goals and to build the future of black men on what has been the pattern of race in the United States all along—separate racial communities. The American society is, and has always been, a dualistic society—a white segment and a black segment of the population quite rigidly separated.

Ironically, despite the intensified civil rights struggle in the post–World War II years, the white and black communities are more separated—and alienated—than at any time since Emancipation. This is because of the increasing ghettoization of the black people in the urban centers, particularly of the North. Now, the majority of the 22 million Negroes live in the Northern cities, and most of them dwell in the black ghettoes of those cities. The increasing alienation of whites and blacks is reflected in Black Power on the one hand and "white backlash" on the other.

The black American in the ghetto is, by and large, confined there by the racial mores of the society, by the consequent economic and social forces, and because the ghetto understandably comes to be seen as something of a haven from an unfriendly white world. The ghettoite realizes soon enough that he is where he is because he is unwanted and rejected beyond the ghetto. He resents this as he resents his underprivilege in employment, education, health service, housing, and all other human needs. In such a situation, it is no big step to the conclusion that equality and integration are cruel mirages, to bitterness and animosity toward the white man, and to the determination that, if the white man rejects the blacks, he cannot expect also to continue to control them. The establishments are seen as white-dominated for white interests. It follows that black men begin to think of having their own establishments and controlling themselves. This readily translates into black separatism.

The depths of the despair experienced by the black American is best measured by the fact that white segregationists and black separatists now find, if for different reasons, some common ground: both reject integration and demand separation of the races; both are racist in their approaches.

Racism, white or black, is a sickness, and a society in which it is prevalent is an afflicted society.

The black American can attain no major goals in the American society except by his own determined, united, and unrelenting effort. He must believe in himself, he must know and have pride in himself, his background, and his culture. In these respects, Black Power serves a necessary purpose.

There are only two solutions: separation and integration (or, as some now prefer to say, an "open society"). Some black nationalists project a "black national community in co-existence with the white community." As I see it, separatism is based on a philosophy of defeat, of surrender to bigotry. It is unrealistic and impractical in the light of the unavoidable facts of a minority group in the world's most powerful society. It offers a false escape and is more emotional than workable.

It seems painfully clear to me that there is no possibility in the affluent, highly industrialized, and technological white-majority American society for anyone to be at once black, separate, and equal.

It follows that only the goal of integration makes practical sense. Whatever the outlook, integration and equality are worth struggling and fighting for. The black American has a huge investment, a vested interest, and a birthright in the American society.

The racial struggle will become increasingly harsh, with more frequent confrontations between whites and blacks. There will be more "hot summers" and likely hotter ones—and winters as well. There are signs of the direction the society may take which are disturbing, not alone for black Americans.

Racist backlash is widespread. The recent municipal elections in Los Angeles, Minneapolis, and New York marked triumphs for racism, reaction, and backlash. The order of the day was "law and order." President Nixon has said that the message of these election contests has come through "loud and clear": the American people are "fed up . . . with violence and lawlessness." There have been a good many warning signs that very many black Americans also are "fed up" with their inferior status. But the eruptions in the ghettos, disruptions on the campuses—unhappily, some of which recently involved clashes between white and black students—and crimes in the streets, though serious breaches of the law, are not the only serious manifestations of lawlessness. The ardent protagonists of law and order rarely refer to "justice" or to that intolerable form of lawlessness which denies social justice and constitutional rights to the black one-eleventh of the nation's citizenry.

As long as racism persists in the American society, alienation will characterize the relations between the white and black sectors of the population.

More ghetto eruptions are inevitable. These outbursts thus far have been confined principally to the ghetto areas. But there is no certainty that this will continue to be the case. Ghettoization of black citizens intensifies polarization of the races and nurtures conflict between them. This, in turn, will lead to more recourse to law and order. Racial conflict in the United States could intensify to such a degree as to approach a chronic state of guerrilla warfare in the jungles of glass, steel, and concrete which are the urban centers. If that conflict should ever extend beyond the confines of the ghettos and threaten the vital communications, transportation, and industrial facilities, the reaction of the white community would be severe, the hue and cry for more and more law and order could then transform the society into something in the nature of a police state. In fact, over-action by police in some places, the too obvious readiness of some high authorities to oppose dissent with force, the shocking wire-tapping by the Federal Bureau of Investigation of the private telephone of a highly respected citizen and leader, the late Martin Luther King, give cause already for alarm.

White men, whether in the majority, as in the United States and the United Kingdom, or in the minority, as in South Africa, Southern Rhodesia, and the

ge, must find a way, if such there is, to purge themselves completely
r face an ultimate fateful confrontation of the races which will shake
undations of civilization and, indeed, threaten its continued exis-
that of most of mankind as well.

The picture I have presented has been largely but unavoidably negative and gloomy. The theme of this conference requires the focus to be on alienation, which is a negative and disheartening subject. But alienation in its racial and many other forms is a bitter fact of life.

There is a brighter side of life, of course. A different topic and speech, however, would be required to elaborate on it. Suffice it now to say only that the system of colonialism, in its traditional form at least, is in its twilight. Since the United Nations came into existence in 1945, more than 800 million people have emerged from colonial rule to gain independence; 58 of the present member states of the United Nations were in colonial status at that time. The problems of overpopulation and hunger present unprecedented challenge, but they are not insoluble. The ever-widening gap between rich and poor is the most formidable of all problems. Still, astronomical sums are now being wasted in arms, nuclear and conventional, which the great military powers dare not use against each other; and for a war in Vietnam that no one can win, which makes it senseless and incomprehensible. A diversion of a substantial part of such sums and their intelligent use for and by the developing peoples to strengthen their economies and raise their living standards could at least reverse the present trend and narrow the gap. Racism is a matter of man's attitudes, and these can be changed, and, I believe, they will be changed when men come fully to realize the fatal alternative. Mankind is well-practiced at pulling back from the brink of self-extinction.

Mankind should be able to eliminate the causes of alienation, to work out reasonable and equitable solutions to all problems of human relations. The crucial question is, has man the will—the will to do what must be done to rescue the world? Can the will of man be summoned and mobilized in time, or shall the world continue to indulge in its tragically outmoded habit of futile warfare to the insane point of self-extermination?

The United Nations, I am confident, will persevere in its historic efforts to achieve secure and enduring peace in the world. It seeks always to induce the parties to disputes to rely upon reasoned discussion and negotiation rather than armed force in the resolution of differences. The UN, I believe, can succeed in this effort, but only if it receives resolute support from the peoples of the world.

I like to believe, and I do believe, that despite all of his frailties and follies man will not only survive on earth through reason, common sense, and the will to live but that, through the unlimited creative capacity of his genius, he will continue to advance.

Notes

Introduction

1. The *e* was added to the name in 1917. Many publications list Ralph's year of birth as 1904; however, school and UCLA records give the date as 1903. See Brian Urquhart *Ralph Bunche: An American Life* (New York: Norton, 1993), 25.

2. Urquhart, *Ralph Bunche,* 33.

3. Urquhart, *Ralph Bunche,* 39.

4. Personal interview with Kenneth Clark. New York, November, 1985.

5. This 1939 report commissioned by the Republican National Committee, which ignored its recommendations, is not the only indication of Bunche's new willingness to work with the political mainstream. In May 1940 Bunche requested and received permission to interview Mrs. Eleanor Roosevelt at the White House. As a result, Mrs. Roosevelt later asked Bunche to prepare a memorandum on the status of black workers. See Urquhart, *Ralph Bunche,* 95–96.

6. Robert R. Edgar has done a wonderful job in editing the field notes of Bunche in South Africa. See his book *An African American in South Africa: The Travel Notes of Ralph J. Bunche* (Athens: Ohio University Press, 1992).

7. Edgar, *African American in South Africa,* 11–12.

8. Urquhart, *Ralph Bunche,* 66; Edgar, *African American in South Africa,* 14.

9. Urquhart, *Ralph Bunche,* 101–2.

10. Chapters 11, 12, and 13 of the UN Charter deal with trusteeship and the non-self-governing territories.

11. Linda O. McMurry argues that Carver became famous largely as a substitute spokesman for Booker T. Washington's accommodationist views at Tuskegee and because of his religious rather than scientific approach to his work. See her book *George Washington Carver: Scientist and Symbol* (New York: Oxford University Press, 1981).

12. One casualty, however, of Bunche's success was his respectful friendship with Du Bois. In a speech to the American Jewish Congress at Madison Square Garden, Du Bois attacked Bunche for his "disgraceful betrayal" of Jews in conducting the Palestine negotiations. Du Bois implied that Bunche sold out for money and power, and Bunche never forgave Du Bois for the personal nature of the criticism. See Urquhart, *Ralph Bunche,* 198.

13. See, for example, King's commencement address at Lincoln University in 1961 entitled "The American Dream," in *A Testament of Hope,* ed. James M. Washington (San Francisco: Harper and Row, 1986), 212.

14. Bunche was not immune from attacks by McCarthyites. In February 1953 the FBI began an investigation under the United Nations Loyalty Program, mandated by Executive Order 10422 at the request of the Department of State. Bunche appeared before the Senate Committee on the Judiciary in March 1953 and before the International Organizations Employee Loyalty Board in May 1954. Bunche's was one of only thirty-two cases that were heard by the Loyalty Board out of the 1,700 Americans covered by Eisenhower's executive order. Shortly after the 12-hour hearing, for which Bunche prepared hundreds of pages of testimony to his loyalty, he was given a "favorable loyalty determination." See Charles P. Henry, "Civil Rights and National Security," in *Ralph Bunche: The Man and His Times,* ed. Benjamin Rivlin (New York: Holmes and Meier, 1990), 54–55.

15. Urquhart, *Ralph Bunche,* 435.

16. "A Conversation with Ralph Bunche," *Psychology Today* (April 1969), 49–58.

Chapter 5

1. Walter Lippman, *Public Opinion* (New York: Macmillan, 1992), chap. 1.

2. Arthur Raper, *The Tragedy of Lynching* (Chapel Hill: University North Carolina Press, 1933), 48.

3. Sterling D. Spero and Abram L. Harris, *The Black Worker* (New York: Columbia University Press, 1931), 466.

4. *Chiles* v. *Chesapeake and Ohio Ry.,* 218 U.S. 71 (1910).

5. *Corrigan* v. *Buckley,* 271 U.S. 323 (1926).

6. *Berea College* v. *Kentucky,* 211 U.S. 45 (1908).

7. *Gong Lum* v. *Rice,* 275 U.S. 78 (1927).

8. *Pace* v. *Alabama,* 106 U.S. 583 (1883).

9. 118 U.S. 356 (1886).

10. 163 U.S. 537 (1896).

11. *Grovey* v. *Townsend,* no. 563, October term (1934).

12. No. 532, October term (1934).

13. Italics mine.

Chapter 6

1. Hacker, *Short History on the New Deal,* 26.

2. "The Negro Worker and the NRA," *Crisis* S (1934).

Chapter 7

1. Booker T. Washington, *Up from Slavery; Future of the American Negro.*

2. W. E. B. Du Bois, *The Souls of Black Folk,* passim.

3. Cf. R. J. Bunche, "Triumph? Or Fiasco?" *Race* 1, no. 2 (Summer, 1936).

4. *Negro Year Book,* 1931–32, 132.

5. *Negro Year Book,* 1937–38, 92.

6. Abram L. Harris, *The Negro as Capitalist,* passim.

7. Spero and Harris, *The Black Worker,* 140.
8. Universal Negro Improvement Association.
9. Cf. Bunche, "Triumph? Or Fiasco?"
10. Cf. R. J. Bunche, "Education in Black and White," *Journal of Negro Education* 5 (January 1936).
11. Adolf Hitler, *Mein Kampf,* unexpurgated ed. (Reynal and Hitchcock, 1939), 406.

Chapter 8

1. Howard W. Odum, *Southern Regions of the United States* (1936), 479.

Chapter 9

1. Pendleton Herring, *The Politics of Democracy* (New York: Norton, 1940), viii.
2. Thomas Jefferson, *Notes on Virginia* (1784), 207.
3. There are many variations of the more or less subtle devices employed in the South to prohibit or discourage Negro voting. No uniformity of practice as between Southern states is found. Some of the more important measures in current usage are the following: exclusion from the Democratic, or "white," primary; requiring one or more (usually two) white character witnesses; strict enforcement of the literacy tests against Negro applicants; putting unreasonable questions to Negro applicants in constitutional understanding of interpretation tests; severe application of property qualifications and requiring only Negro applicants to show property tax receipts; basing rejection of Negro registrants on alleged technical mistakes in filling out registration blanks; evasion, by informing Negro applicants that registration cards have "run out," that all members of the registration board are not present, that it is "closing time," or that the applicant "will be notified in due course"; requiring Negro applicants to suffer long waits before the officials attend them; requiring Negro applicants to fill out their own blanks though those of white applicants are filled out for them; by officials' deliberate insults or threats by officials and/or hangers-on; discarding only Negro applications for conviction of misdemeanors; requiring enrollment in Democratic clubs, from which Negroes are barred; severe application of the cumulative poll tax to Negro voters only; loss of jobs or threat of loss of jobs; intimidation by physical violence or the threat of it. Only a selected few of these instruments can be discussed here.
4. Interview with a member of the Board of Registrars in an Alabama county, February 1940.
5. Interview with registrar in an Alabama county, April 1940.
6. 295 U.S. 45.
7. No. 618, October term (1940), *U.S. Reports,* May 26, 1941.
8. Tuscaloosa, Alabama, *News,* November 3, 1939.

Chapter 10

1. O. Louwer, quoted from report in Institut Colonial International, 21st session, Brussels, 1931, ("L'Enseignement aux Indigenes," *Minutes,* 14.

2. A. Victor Murray, *The School in the Bush* (New York: 1929), 5.

3. Leonard Woolf, *Imperialism and Civilization* (New York: 1928), 119.

4. Georges Hardy, *Une Conquête morale* (Paris: 1917), iii.

5. Institut Colonial International, "L'Enseignement aux Indigenes," 22.

6. Hardy, *Une Conquête morale,* iv.

7. Wyatt Rawson, *Education in a Changing Commonwealth* (report of British Commonwealth Education Conference); J. H. Fleure, "Problems of Interracial Understanding" (London: 1931), 124–25.

8. Murray, *School in the Bush,* 330 ff.

9. Thomas Jesse Jones, *Education in Africa* (New York: 1922), xvii, 12, 13.

10. Jones, *Education in Africa,* 28ff.

11. One writer asserts that the rural Negro communities of the United States are more akin to the detribalized Africans of the locations than to the African rural communities (Murray, *School in the Bush,* 307).

12. Jones, *Education in Africa,* 18ff.

13. Institut Colonial International, "L'Enseignement aux Indigenes," *Compte rendu,* cited in Report of M. Louwers, 135.

14. The French mandate Togo is a narrow corridor of territory lying beneath West Africa's "hump" and to the north of the Gulf of Guinea, between French Dahomey on the east and British Gold Coast on the west. What is now French Togo is about four-sevenths of the area of former German Togo. It reaches from the 6th to the 11th degree north latitude and immediately to the east of the Greenwich meridian, resting entirely in the African tropical zone. Its coastline on the Atlantic is only 50 kilometers, and in area it covers slightly more than 52,000 square kilometers. It is the most densely populated of all the French West African territory, with a total population of 749,152 natives and 588 Europeans, or an average of about 16 persons to the square kilometer. The Togolese have never boasted a homogeneous race or civilization similar to that of their neighbors in the Gold Coast and Dahomey. The principal tribal group is the Ewe.

Dahomey is better known through the exploits of Behanzin, its famous king, whose eventual conquest by the French led to the subjugation of the colony. It is situated between 0°41′ west longitude and 0°21′ east longitude and extends from 6°22′ to the 12th parallel. Its area of 122,120 square kilometers is equivalent to one-fifth that of France proper. As in the case of Togo, its western neighbor, its southern shores are on the Gulf of Guinea. Its population numbers 1,078,638, of which 1,809 are non-native, for an average density of 9 persons to the square kilometer. There are three important ethnic groups in Dahomey, which are divided into upward of 30 tribes. It is one of the most prosperous of the French possessions in West Africa and is important as a means of penetration and outlet for the French Sudanese empire.

15. P. Bourdaire, *Une Politique Coloniale Française et Rapport de M. Albert Sarraut,* (Paris: 1911), 22.

16. Institut Colonial International, "L'Enseignement aux Indigenes," *Minutes,* cited in Report of M. Georges Hardy on "Possessions of Francaises d'Afrique," 245ff.

17. Institut Colonial International, "L'Enseignement aux Indigenes," 265.

18. Institut Colonial International, "L'Enseignement aux Indigenes," 266.

19. Arthur Girault, *Principes de Colonisation et de Legislation Coloniale,* 5th ed. (Paris: 1927) 2:541.

20. Girault, *Principes.*

21. Gouvernement Général de l'Afrique Occidentale Francaise (hereafter cited as Gouv. Gen. de l'AOF), *Le Dahomey* (Paris: 1931), 121.

22. *Journal Officiel du Territoire du Togo,* 16 August 1928, 493ff.

23. Gouv. Gen. de l'AOF, *Le Dahomey,* 124. The village preparatory school, which teaches only the French language, is not existent in Togo, though it is found in Dahomey and elsewhere in French West Africa. The classes are usually taught by a native monitor and receive children under 11 years of age.

24. *Journal Officiel du Territoire du Togo,* August 16, 1928, 493.

25. Cf. note 23.

26. Fifteen years, in Togo.

27. *Journal Officiel du Territoire du Togo,* August 16, 1928, 493.

28. Gouv. Gen. de l'AOF, *Le Dahomey,* 124. In Togo he need have only the *brevet élémentaire* and, on occasion, none at all. Cf. *Journal Officiel du Togo,* August 16, 1928, 494.

29. Not including Togo.

30. Camille Guy, quoted in Girault, *Principes,* 2:544.

31. Jones, *Education in Africa,* 25.

32. P. Bourdaire, *Une Politique Coloniale Francaise et Rapport de M. Albert Sarraut,* 18, 26. See also *Rapport Annuel du Terrritoire di Togo,* 1925.

33. *Rapport Annuel du Territoire du Togo,* 1925, 20.

34. Hardy, *"L'Enseignement en Afrique Occidentale Française,"* Une Conquête morale, 187.

35. Permanent Mandates Commission, *Minutes,* 15th session, July 1–19, 1929, 35.

36. J. L. Monod, *Instructions au Personnel Enseignant* (Gorée, 1921), 41.

37. *Journal Officiel du Territoire du Togo,* 16 August 1928; art. 40 of the *arrêté* of June 28, 1928, 496.

38. Monod, *Instructions,* 41.

39. Monod, *Instructions,* 41.

40. Monod, *Instructions,* 41.

41. Monod, *Instructions,* 42.

42. Institut Colonial International, *Compte rendu,* Report of M. Hardy, 161–62.

43. Murray, *School in the Bush,* 135.

44. Henri Labouret, *A la Recherche d'une politique Indigene dans l'Ouest-African* (Paris: 1931), 114.

45. *Rapport Annuel du Territore du Togo,* 1929, 25.

46. *Journal Officiel de la République Français,* decree of February 14, 1922, 190.

47. *Rapport Annuel du Territoire du Togo,* 1930, 37.

48. Julian Huxley, *Africa View* (London: 1932), 313.

49. Permanent Mandates Commission, *Minutes,* 6th session, 1925, 34–35; 15th session, 1929, 35; 21st session, 1931, 167; 22d session, 1932, 191.

50. *Rapport Annuel du Territoire du Togo,* 1925, 20.

51. *Rapport Annuel du Territoire du Togo,* 1925.

52. Monod, *Instructions,* 38.

53. *Journal Officiel du Territoire du Togo,* August 16, 1928, 496 (annex 1 to *arrêté*).

54. *Rapport Annuel du Territoire du Togo,* 1927, 21.

55. *Rapport Annuel du Territoire du Togo,* 1927, 18.

56. *Rapport Annuel du Territoire du Togo,* 1927.

57. Mgr. A. Boucher, *A Travers les missions du Togo et du Dahomey* (Paris: 1926), 21.

58. L'Agence Economique des Territoires Africans sous Mandat, *Togo-Cameroun* (Paris: [January] 1932).

59. *Journal Officiel du Territoire du Togo,* August 16, 1928, 499. (annex 1 to *arrêté* of June 28, 1928).

60. *Rapport Annuel du Territoire du Togo,* 1929, 27.

61. Permanent Mandates Commission, *Minutes,* 21st session, 1931, 167.

62. Permanent Mandates Commission, *Minutes.*

63. Permanent Mandates Commission, *Minutes,* 15th session, 1929, 36.

64. Wyatt Rawson, *Education in a Changing Commonwealth* (report of British Commonwealth Education Conference, London, 1931), 79.

65. Monod, *Instructions,* 15.

66. Institut Colonial International, "L'Enseignement aux Indigenes," *Minutes,* Rapport preliminaires, 21st session, Paris, May 1931 (report of M. Louwers), 42.

67. Gouv. Gen. de l'AOF, *Le Dahomey,* 125.

68. Augustin Vallet, *Un Nouvel apercu du probleme colonial* (Paris, 1925), 173, 184.

69. *Rapport Annuel du Territoire du Togo,* 1929, 24.

70. *Budget Local de la Colonie du Dahomey* exercise 1932. Porto Novo, Dahomey, p. XI.

71. *Budget Local de la Colonie du Dahomey* exercise 1931, XX.

72. *Budget Local, Territoire du Togo,* exercise 1931, Lome, Togo, XIV.

73. *Rapport Annuel du Territoire du Togo,* 1929, 26.

74. *Rapport Annuel du Territoire du Togo,* 1931, 95.

75. Gouv. Gen. de l'AOF, *Le Dahomey,* 125.

76. Gouv. Gen. de l'AOF, *Le Dahomey.*

77. *Les Annales coloniales* "Les Bases du programme de l'enseignement technique en A.O.F.," (Paris) (July 1932): 1.

78. *Rapport Annuel du Territoire du Togo,* 1927, 21–22.

79. Institut Colonial International, "L'Enseignement aux Indigenes," *Compte rendu* (report of M. Hardy), 140.

80. Raymond L. Buell, *The Native Problem in Africa* 2:61.

81. Paris, 1931.

82. Paris, 1919.

83. Paris, 1932.

84. Paris, 1931.

85. The director of education in Dahomey in 1932 informed the writer that he was opposed to special texts for natives and believed that they should be made to read and understand the French books.

86. Girault, *Prinicpes,* 2:541ff.

87. *Rapport Annuel du Territoire du Togo,* 1925, 20.

88. *Rapport Annuel du Territoire du Togo,* 1925, 96. Cf. also Gouv. Gen. de L'AOF, *Le Dahomey,* 121. The age limits for the several courses in Togo are:

Preparatory course, 1st year: 7 to 10 yrs.
Preparatory course, 2d year: 8 to 11 yrs.
Elementary course, 1st year: 9 to 12 yrs.
Elementary course, 2d year: 10 to 13 yrs.
Intermediate course, 1st year: 11 to 14 yrs.
Intermediate course, 2d year: 13 to 14 yrs.
Advanced primary course: 14 to 17 yrs.

89. *Rapport Annuel du Territoire du Togo,* 1931, 96.
90. Permanent Mandates Commission, *Minutes,* 18th session, 1930, 97–98.
91. *La Voix du Dahomey* (Cotonou), October 1932.
92. Cotonou, Dahomey, October 1932.
93. *Arrêté* of 14 February 1932; *Journal Officiel du Togo,* 1930, 136.
94. *Budget Local de la Colonie du Dahomey,* exercise 1931, XXI.
95. *Budget Local du Territoire du Togo,* 1930, art. 3, chap. 12; art. 9, chap. 13.
96. *Rapport Annuel du Territore du Togo,* 1929, 34.
97. *Budget Local de la Colonie du Dahomey,* exercise 1931, XIX.
98. *Budget Local de la Colonie du Dahomey,* exercise 1932, VIII.
99. Gouv. Gen. de l'AOF, *Le Dahomey,* 126.
100. *Rapport au Ministre des Colonies sur l'administration des territoires occupés du Togo* (Paris: 1921), 7.
101. *Rapport Annuel du Territoire du Togo,* 1931, 96.
102. *Rapport Annuel du Territoire du Togo,* 98–99.
103. *Arrêté* of August 19, 1927, *Journal Officiel du Togo,* 1927, 506.
104. *Rapport Annuel du Territoire du Togo,* 1920, 24.
105. *Rapport Annuel du Territoire du Togo,* 1931, 83ff.
106. *Rapport Annuel du Territoire du Togo,* 1928, 114–15.
107. *Rapport Annuel du Territoire du Togo,* 1931, 96.
108. *Rapport Annuel du Territoire du Togo,* 1927, 23.
109. *Rapport Annuel, Cercle de Lome,* 1931.
110. *Rapport Annuel du Territoire du Togo,* 1929, 29.
111. *Arrêté* of October 29, 1940; *Journal Officiel du Territoire du Togo,* 1930, 551.

Chapter 12

Materials for this essay were gathered while Bunche was on a field trip in Africa as a postdoctoral fellow (1936–38) of the Social Science Research Council.
1. Land set aside by the government as exclusively for native use.
2. Conclave of chiefs.
3. Richard C. Turnwald, *Black and White in East Africa* (1935), 144.
4. Meaning "he who has returned from the dead."
5. A parasitic wild fig tree, under which sacrifices are traditionally offered to *Ngai,* the Kikuyu god, who is the creator and giver of all things.

Chapter 16

1. Julian S. Huxley and A. C. Haddon, *We Europeans* (New York: Harper and Brothers, 1936), 69.

Chapter 17

This essay was originally presented at the Howard University Summer School Conference on the "Needs of Negro Youth," July 16, 1940.

Chapter 18

1. C. A. Beard, "Written History as an Act of Faith," *American Historical Review,* 39, no. 2 (January 1934): 219ff.

2. I. D. Reddick, "A New Interpretation for Negro History," *Journal of Negro History,* 22, no. 1, (January 1937): 17.

3. Reddick, "New Interpretation."

Index